Christopher Wordsworth

Greece

Pictorial, Descriptive and Historical

Christopher Wordsworth

Greece
Pictorial, Descriptive and Historical

ISBN/EAN: 9783742808325

Manufactured in Europe, USA, Canada, Australia, Japa

Cover: Foto ©Thomas Meinert / pixelio.de

Manufactured and distributed by brebook publishing software
(www.brebook.com)

Christopher Wordsworth

Greece

GREECE:

PICTORIAL, DESCRIPTIVE, AND HISTORICAL.

BY CHRISTOPHER WORDSWORTH, D.D.,

ARCHDEACON AND CANON OF WESTMINSTER.

WITH NUMEROUS ENGRAVINGS ILLUSTRATIVE OF THE SCENERY, ARCHITECTURE,
COSTUME, AND FINE ARTS OF THAT COUNTRY.

AND

A HISTORY OF THE CHARACTERISTICS OF GREEK ART,

BY GEORGE SCHARF, F.S.A.

FIFTH EDITION.

LONDON:
JOHN MURRAY, ALBEMARLE STREET.
1868.

To the Right Honourable

GEORGE EARL OF ABERDEEN, K.T., M.A., F.R.S.,

ETC. ETC.

PRESIDENT OF THE SOCIETY OF ANTIQUARIES; CHANCELLOR OF KING'S COLLEGE, ABERDEEN,
ONE OF THE GOVERNORS OF HARROW SCHOOL;

TO WHOSE EXAMPLE AND ENCOURAGEMENT

THE PRESENT AGE IS INDEBTED FOR MUCH OF THE LIGHT WHICH HAS BEEN THROWN UPON

THE ARTS, ANTIQUITIES, AND GEOGRAPHY OF GREECE,

This Work,

WRITTEN WITH A HOPE OF CHERISHING THE LOVE FOR THEM IN THE SCHOOL,

OF WHICH HE IS A GOVERNOR,

IS,

WITH FEELINGS OF PRIVATE GRATITUDE AND PUBLIC RESPECT,

INSCRIBED.

GREEKS AND ROMAN SOLDIERS

THE PARTHENON FRIEZE (illegible caption)

PREFACE.

"The Emperor Hadrian possessed a magnificent Villa, at Tivoli, of which the ruins still remain. In it he endeavoured to perpetuate his own Recollections of Greece. He there erected buildings, to which he gave the names Pœcilè and Lycèum; by their side he planted the Grove of an Academy, and he carried the stream of an ideal Penèus through the pleasant Vale of an imitative Tempe.

"The Traveller in Greece constructs in his own mind such a villa as this. He furnishes it with the beautiful scenes which he once visited in that country; he refreshes it with the clear waters and cool shades of a Tempe; he decorates it with the fair porticoes of a Pœcilè, a Lycèum, and an Academy.

"But his recollections of Greece, like the buildings of Hadrian, are liable to fall into decay. The Author of the following pages has, therefore, attempted to give a permanence to his own reminiscences by constructing a humbler Tivoli, in which he hopes that others may perhaps enjoy some share of that pleasure which was felt of old by the Greek Traveller in the Villa of Hadrian."

Such was the Author's address, by way of Preface, to the original edition of his " GREECE " in the year 1830.

The Publisher has now the pleasure of stating, that in the period which has since elapsed, three large editions have been called for, and the work has been translated into the French and Italian languages. It may therefore be presumed to have taken its position as a classical authority. The present edition of the Work has been entirely revised by the Author; and the matter, as well as the engravings, in some respects rearranged, so as to bring the illustrations into more intimate connexion with their descriptions in the text.

In the present edition, Mr. George Scharf, the able illustrator of Dean Milman's Horace* and other classical works, has supplied notes and illustrations, in an Introductory Chapter, on the " Characteristics of Greek Art," which will be found explanatory of many allusions to the subject that occur in the course of the Work. The Publisher has to express his regret, that the number of pages to which this chapter was necessarily restricted has rendered it somewhat less complete than that gentleman desired to make it. He believes, however, that the varied information it contains will be a valuable addition to the Work; at the same time it will be understood that Dr. Wordsworth is in no way responsible for anything contained in that chapter.

---

* The Life and Works of Horace. Edited by Dean Milman. A new and beautifully printed edition of the text, illustrated by 300 Engravings of Coins, Gems, Statues, &c., from the Antique. Second Edition. 2 vols. 8vo. 30s.

" Not a page can be opened where the eye does not light upon some antique gem. Mythology, history, art, manners, topography, have all their fitting representatives. It is the highest praise to say, that the devotee throughout add to the pleasure with which Horace is read."—*Classical Museum.*

It may not be unbecoming in the Publisher here to express his belief, that, by the aid of the Author, Artists, and Engravers, and of the more humble but indispensable powers of the Press, he has been enabled to erect a Pœcile and Lyceum, in remembrance of Greece, such as Hadrian, with all the imperial power of Rome, would have attempted in vain.

London, *October* 1858.

WORKS ILLUSTRATIVE OF GREEK GEOGRAPHY.

... *It being inconsistent with the plan of the present Work that reference should be made to it in any extended authorities on the subjects mentioned in the text, the Author has deemed it expedient to prefix a general list of books which may be considered either as illustrative of its contents, or supplementary to them.*

SCYLAX, Periplus.—See Philological Museum, i. p. 215; Hudson's Geog. Grav. vol. I.

DICÆARCHUS, scholar of Aristotle, Status Græciæ.—Studium, Geog. Græc. vol. ii.

SCYMNUS, Chius, Orbis Descriptio.—Hudson, Geog. Gr. vol. ii.

DIONYSIUS PERIEGETES.—Bernhardy, Geog. Gr. vol. I.

STRABO of Amasia in Cappadocia, in the Augustan Age, books viii. ix. x.

POMPONIUS MELA, book ii. cap. 3.

CAIUS PLINIUS SECUNDUS, book iv. cap. 1 to 12.

PAUSANIAS of Cappadocia, Ten Books. Travelled in Greece in the time of the Antonines.

PTOLEMÆUS PELUSIOTA. About A.D. 165.

CYRIACUS of Ancona. Travelled in Greece about 1438, principally with a view to collect ancient inscriptions.

MARTIN KRAFT, or KRUSIUS, Professor at Tübingen. His Turco-Græcia. 1673.

SPONTO, Relation of a Journey in the Turkish Empire, 1678.

MEURSIUS, his geographical and antiquarian Treatises in Gronovii Antiquitates Græcæ.

BABIN, Relation de l'État Présent de la Ville d'Athènes, 1674.

CARREY's Drawings of the Parthenon, made about 1671, for the French Ambassador, the Marquis of Nointel, now in the Royal Library, Paris; copies in the British Museum.

JACOB SPON of Lyons, Voyage, &c., 1676. Lyon, 1678, 3 vols. 12mo.

GUILLET DE LA GUILLETIÈRE, Athènes ancienne et moderne. Paris, 1675. As Apocryphal work.—See Quarterly Review, No. 437.

PORMONT Græciæ Descriptio, 1673.

WHELER, Rev. Sir George, Journey into Greece. London, 1682, folio; with an excellent Map for those times.

CORONELLI, Description Géographique de la Morée. Venice, 1686.

MELETIUS, Bishop of Arta and Naupactus, 1662. His Geography, first published 1728. Venice, folio.

TOURNEFORT, Voyage du Levant, 1718, 2 vols. 8vo.

FOURMONT, travelled in 1729. His letters (of very doubtful faith).—Voyage, Mém. de l'Académie des Inscriptions, t. vii. p. 257.

GUY's Voyage Littéraire de la Grèce, 2 vols. 1771.

STUART and REVETT, travelled for the Society of Dilettanti, 1751.—The Antiquities of Athens, by Jas. Stuart and Nicholas Revett, Painters and Architects, vol. I. 1762, vol. ii. 1787, vol. iii. 1794, vol. iv. 1816,
———, new edition, with many additions, 4 vols. 1825.

CHANDLER's Travels in Greece, Oxf. 1776.—French, with notes, by Harald de Saranya. Paris, 1806, 3 vols.—Chandler, Revett, and Pars, sent by the Society of Dilettanti, 1764.

——— Inscriptiones Antiquæ. Oxon. 1771.

HAMILTON's Remarks on several parts of Turkey, 1809.

The Unedited Antiquities of Attica. By the Society of Dilettanti. London, 1819.

BARTHÉLEMY, Voyage du jeune Anacharsis en Grèce, 7 vols. 8vo. 1788.

CHOISEUL-GOUFFIER, Voyage Pittoresque de la Grèce. tom. I. fol. 1782, tom. II. 1809, tom. iii. 1822.

STRABO and HAWKINS, travelled in 1794 and 1795. Their Journal in Walpole's Memoirs. Lond. 1820.

PAPPEL and PALENT etc., travelled in Attica, &c. 1765. Their Papers in the Paris Library.

OBELISK, Grain Antiqui Monumenta emis illustrati prima Unae. Argent. 1788.

LORD ELGIN in Greece, 1797.

Elgin Marbles transported to England, 1811.

Memorandum on the Earl of Elgin's Pursuits in Greece, 1815.

LUSIERI's Plans, Drawn for Lord Elgin, 1800, and following years. Now in the British Museum.

Dr. E. D. CLARKE's Travels. 1810—14, 8 vols. 8vo.

DODWELL's Classical and Topographical Tour, 2 vols. 4to. London, 1819.

SIR W. GELL's Ithaca. 4to.
——— Argolis, 1811, 4to.
——— Itinerary of the Morea, 1817.
——— Itinerary of Greece, 1819.

COLONEL LEAKE's Researches in Greece, 1814.
——— Topography of Athens, 1821. Translated into German by Baimeister, with notes by Müller. Halle, 1829.
——— disputed Positions in the Topography of Athens, 1833.
——— Outlines of Greek Revolution, 1826.

WILKINS' Atheniensia, 1816.

POUQUEVILLE, Voyage dans la Grèce. Paris, 1820.

BARBIÉ DU BOCAGE, Carte de la Morée, 1811.

CHATEAUBRIAND, Itinéraire de Paris à Jérusalem. Paris, 1812.

HOBHOUSE, Journey through Albania, &c. Lond 1813, 4to.

HOLLAND's Travels in the Ionian Isles, Thessaly, Macedonia, &c. Lond. 1815; 2d. edit. 2 vols. 8vo. 1819.

WALPOLE's Memoirs relating to European and Asiatic Turkey, containing Papers by the Earl of Aberdeen, Dr. Sibthorp, Mr. Hawkins, Col. Leake, Col. Squire, Mr. Canterwell, Mr. Wilmot, Mr. Haifes.

STANHOPE, Topography of Platæa, 1817.
——— Olympia, 1824.

PORTER, Voyage dans le Levant. Paris, 1818.

TURNER, Tour in the Levant, 1820.

GOSSELIN, Positions Géographiques, in the "Connaissance de Temps," 1821, 1822, 1823.

MANNERT, Geographie der Griechen, 1822.

MÜLLER, K. O., Geschichte Hellenischer Stämme und Städte. 1820—1824. Orchomenos, with Map of Bœotia. The Dorians, with Maps of Northern Greece and the Peloponnesus. Geographical Appendices to both works.
——— Æginetica, 1817.
——— Aristie on Athens and Attica, in Ersch and Gruber's Encyclopädie, Translated by Lockhart.
——— Brief nach Athen, 1835.

HUGHES (T. S.) Travels in Sicily, Albania, and Greece: 2 vols. 4to, 1820; 2d edit. 2 vols. 8vo.

WADDINGTON's Visit to Greece, 1824.

KENDRICK, Ionian Islands, 1822.

THOMPSON, Ionian Islands, 1823.

St. VINCENT, Iles Ioniennes, avec un nouvel atlas, 1827.

BOBLAYE, Voyages et Recherches dans la Grèce, 1836.

EARLE's Hellas, 1825—1827, ? vols.; contains Aristie Magerie, Bœotia, Phocis, Doris, Locris, Ætolia, Acarnania.

WACHSMUTH, Hellenische Alterthumskunde, 4 vols. Halle, 1826.

Sketch of Greek Geography, vol. I. pp. 1—29.

CRAMER's Geographical and Historical Description of Ancient Greece, 3 vols. 8vo. Oxford, 1828.

COLONEL LEAKE on the Demi of Attica, in Transactions of Royal Society of Literature, 1829.
——— Travels in the Morea, 3 vols. 8vo. Lond. 1830.
——— Travels in Northern Greece, 4 vols. 8vo. 1835.

The Author of the following pages cannot mention these works of Col. Leake without expressing his obligations to them.

GORDON's History of the Greek Revolution, 1832.

THIERSCH, F. État Actuel de la Grèce, 2 vols. 8vo. Leipz. 1833.

POSTLETHWAITE'S Poëtische Reträume in Greece and Italy, &c. 1831.

PIGEON'S Sailing Directory, London, 1831.

Charts of the Coast of Greece, published by the Admiralty, sold at No. 32, Fleet Street, London.

VON MURALT, Das Griechische Volk, 3 vols. Hentzberg, 1835.

THIRLWALL's Greece; Geographical Outline, pp. 1—31 of vol. I. 1835.

PITTAKYS' Ancienne Athènes, 8vo. Athènes, 1835.

Voyage de la Commission Scientifique de Morée, Paris, 1836.

WORDSWORTH's Athens and Attica, with Maps, &c. 2nd Edit. 1837.

FORCHHAMMER, P. G., Hellenika, Berlin, 1837.

ROSS, L., Das Freistilum bei Athen und seine Metamorphosen Kunstblatt, 1837, Nos. ii.—iv. Other numbers contain papers on subjects connected with Greek topography and antiquities.

FINLAY's Remarks on the Topography of the Oropia and Diacria, Athens, 1838.
——— on the Battle of Marathon and position of Aphidnæ, &c. in Transactions of Royal Society of Literature, vol. III.

LEAKE, Col., Peloponnesiaca, Supplement to Travels in the Morea.

MURRAY, Handbook for Malta, Ionian Islands, and the East.

RAVLAND, A. R. Antiquités Helléniques. Athènes, 1842.

ROWAN, G. P., M.A., President of the Ionian University; "Ithaca," 1850.

Descriptive Catalogue of Sketches of Greek Scenery. By W. Linton, Esq. M.A. For Private Circulation, 1851.

Sketches in Greece and Turkey. 1852.

STATE OF SCULPTURE.

TABLE OF CONTENTS.

HISTORICAL OUTLINE OF GREEK ART.

State of the Arts in the time of Pausanias—Plan of developing the Subject—Importance of Date and of Coins in ascertaining the different Eras of Art—Monumental Remains—Ancient Practice of hoarding Money—Tombs the Depositories of Works of Art—Early Vases—Primitive Origin of the Greeks—Cyclopean Architecture—Ancient Pottery and Vases—Early Bronze Figures—Painted Vases—Selographny—Silhouettes—Objects of Early Worship—Representation of Form by Outline—Ancient Coins—Assyrian Hunt—Terra-cotta Figure found at Samos—Origin of Modelling—Early Workers in Bronze—Ancient Knowledge of Mechanics—Early Figures in Metal—Artists of mythical Antiquity—State of the Arts in the Homeric Age—Working of Gold—Cyclopean Architecture of Mycenæ and Cadyanda—Gate of the Lions—Sculptures of Thebes, Nineveh, Egypt, and Asia Minor—Art of Casting in Metals—The Early Communications of Greece with Egypt—First Introduction of Coinage—Art of Tempering Metals—Origin of the Ionic and Doric Orders—Ancient Inscriptions—Early Adoption of the Arch—Structure of Temples, and the peculiar Characteristics of the Doric and Ionic—Early Painted Vases—Monographs—Greek Art under Dipœnus—Paintings—Fountain of Callirrhoe?—Earliest Use of Marble in Architecture—First Erection of Temples at Athens—Draperies of Greek Sculpture—Acroliths—Dedication of Statues—Vase Painting—Portrait Statues—Invention of Foreshortening—Early History of Bas-reliefs—Centaurs—State of Greek Art from the Battle of Marathon—Public Games conducive to the Arts—Coins of Athens—A Greek Warrior—Names of Artists engraved on Sculptures—Ancient Mode of representing Hair—State of the Arts from the Defeat of the Persians—Marbles of Ægina—Sculptured Heads—Vase Painting—Rebuilding of Athens—Temple and Sculptures of the Theseum—Progress of Painting and Sculpture—Onatas—Important Changes in Vase Painting—Polygnotus—Subjects painted by him—Architects of the Parthenon—Pericles, and his glorious Works at Athens—Commencement of the Parthenon—Temples and Sculptures at Athens—The Erechtheum—Sculptures of the Parthenon—Battle of the Centaurs and Lapithæ—Section of the Parthenon—Drapery of Phidias—State of Art from the Death of Pericles—Polycletus, Myron, and Alexander—The Phigalian Marbles—Commerce of Athens—Greek Statuary—Celebrated Statues of Venus—Corinthian Order—Niobe—The Temple of Apollo Nudatus— Pediment of the Temple of Minerva at Ægina—State of Art from the Accession of Alexander—Art has reached its Culmination Point—Statues and Coins of Philip and Alexander—Temple of Lysicrates, and its Sculpture—Style of Drapery—Roman Period of Greek Art—Time of Hadrian—The Laocoon, Achilles at Scyros, Dirce tied to the Bull, and various subjects of Greco-Roman Art—The Age of Constantine, and the Degradation of Ancient Art .   .   .   .   .   .   Pages 1—17

GEOGRAPHICAL FEATURES OF GREECE.

Higher Tablet of Aristagoras—Herodotus - Sketch of the Geography of Continental Greece—FIRST STATION, Zyge, the ancient Larissa, on Mount Pindus; Panoramic View thence; Its Peculiarities; the Five Rivers which take their rise there—Virgil—Milton—Communication by these Rivers to every Part of Greece—The AOUS: Apollonia; Corinthian Colonies; Augustus; his Connexion with Apollonia; Actium—The Gulf of Ambracia—The ARACTHUS—Northern Frontier of Free Greece—HALIACMON—Macedonia—Berrhœa—Thessalonica—St. Paul—PENEUS—Olympus—Ossa—TEMPE—Mountain Boundaries to the Basin of Thessaly; Cambunian Hills; Pindus; Othrys—The History of Thessaly the Result of its Geography—Level Surface of the Soil; Fertility—Centaurs; Cavalry; Thessaly the Theatre of War—Pharsalia, Scodrasse, Crannon, Cynoscephalæ—ACHELOUS; why the Stream so far Water; its Course—SECOND STATION, on Mount Tymphrestus, at Belucki—Divergence of Mountains from this Point, as of Rivers from Zyge—ŒTA to the Sea, ŒTA to the South-east, and the Agræan Hills to the West of the Pindus—The PINDUS Chain continued in Parnassus, Helicon, Cithæron, Parnes, Brilessus, Pentelicus, Hymettus, Laureium, Sunium; thence to the Cyclades, and to the Asiatic Coast—The various Roads to Attica: 1, by Œnoe; 2, by Phyle; 3, by Decelea; 4, by Rhamnus—LAST STATION: HYMETTUS—View from Hymettus—Milton—Limits of Course of Mountains—Triangle of Sunium—Lucian's Contemplator—Geographical Sketch of the Peloponnesus—Station at Zakhouha on Mount LYCÆUS—Panoramic View—Mount Lycæus, Erymanthus, Cyllene, Mænalus, Parnon,—Mount Taygetus—Plain of Elis—Olympia—Physical Form and Characteristics of the Peloponnesus—Arcadia: surrounded by a natural Circle of Mountains; Hedli from this Circle to the Coast form the other Provinces of the Peloponnesus—Peloponnesus an Amphitheatre, of which Arcadia is the Arena, its Mountain circle the Podium, the other Provinces the Cunei, their Mountain Divisions the Vir, the Vale of the Alpheus the Vomitorium, Bay of Greece the Velarium—Political Results of Natural Causes—National Antipathies—Messenia and Laconia—No Centralization—ACHÆAN LEAGUE; its Origin; how far it was successful—Causes of its Dissolution—Rome united Greece—No general Coinage—Coins of different Provinces of the Peloponnesus—Restlessness of its Inhabitants—The Arts of Peace and Commerce little Cultivated—Pleasing Contrast offered by the Province of Elis—Arcadian—Olympic Games—Mythological Traditions produced by Character of Soil—Enimarion—Switzerland, Italy, Bœotia, ARCADIA—Nymphalus—Worship of Hercules—Natural Origin of Greek Mythology—founded not on Laws but Powers—Origin of Greek Music; why derived from Arcadia; its Influence on the Arcadian Character—Cymnius—The Pastoral Ideas of Virgil derived not so much from Italy as from Arcadia—Migratory and precarious Character of Arcadians; how produced: Mantis, how far unwalled; Lycurgus; its Mountains were its Walls—Laconia the Medium of the Peloponnesus—Picturesque Scenery of the Vale of the Eurotas—Sceva on Taygetus—Palladium the Cradle of Rome—Antoninus Pius—Phidippides and Pan, before the Battle of Marathon—View from the Citadel of ARGOS—ARGOLIS: Eroalinus, Lerna—Argos Amphilochicum a Colony from Argolis; National Connexions and Sympathies, shown in an Identity of Names .   .   .   Pages 84—139

ATTICA

Socrates and Alcibiades—Extent of Attica—Influence of Attica on Language, Literature, Arts, and Religion—Causes of this Influence—Form and Site of Attica—Benefits incidentally arising from its Defects—Barrenness—Rocks, Mountains—their Productions—Consequences of these Defects—

Limits of Attica—Chains of Parnes and Ægaleos on West, of Pentelicus and Hymettus on East—the Long Walls of the Country—Order of our Observations—Salamis; Site—Battle—View seen by Xerxes from his Silver-footed Throne on Mount Ægaleos—Digression to Eleusis—Mystic Procession to Eleusis—Sacred Way thither; its present and former State—Sacred Ways of Rome and Athens contrasted—Characteristic of these two Cities respectively—Approach to Eleusis—Temple of Eleusis—Description of the Eleusinian Mysteries—Return to Ægaleos—Phyle; its present and former Condition—View seen by Thrasybulus from the Fortress Walls of Phyle—Campaign of Thrasybulus against the Thirty Tyrants—View of Acharnæ—The Acharnians of Aristophanes—Return to Mount Parnes—Parnes the Barrier of Attica and Bœotia—Comparative View of Attica and Bœotia, physically and intellectually—"The Clouds" of Aristophanes—View of the Athenian Plain and Lycabettus—Decelea—Alcibiades—Agis—Decelea a Spartan Camp in Attica—"The Birds" of Aristophanes—Contrast between Decelea and Aphidna—Theseus—History of Attica to the Age of Theseus—Ostropa—Strife of Minerva and Neptune—Explanation—Areopagus; Origin of—Meaning of Attic Traditions—Cranaus and Pedias the Parents of Atthis—Deucalion's Flood—Amphictyon—Erichtheus—States of Society represented by them—Visits of Ceres and Bacchus to Attica—Theseus—Pisistratus; his Homeric Apotheosis of Theseus—Theseus a Personification (made by themselves, with an Historic Basis) of the Athenian People—Ariadne—Life and Death of Theseus—Temple of Theseus—His Civil Polity—Panathenaic Festival—Theseus and Pirithous; Meaning of their Friendship—Theseus and Hercules: their Rivalry; how an expression of National Feeling—Why Theseus and his two Hippolytus are made to pass their Youth at Trœzen—Bœotia represented by Hercules; Attica by Theseus—Illustration of this—View on the Route from Aphidna to Rhamnus—Two Temples at Rhamnus—Sacred Inclosure containing them—Description of the Temples—Architectural Terms applied to Ancient Temples—Plans—Larger Temple—Both the Temples were dedicated to Nemesis—Scenery of Rhamnus—Religion of Sacred Inclosures—Rhamnus to Marathon—Plain and Harbour of Marathon—Battle—The Battle illustrated by local Considerations—The different Advantages enjoyed by the Athenians at Marathon—Fresco Painting of the Battle—Tumulus at Marathon—Trophy of Miltiades—Different Treatment of the Battles of Marathon and Salamis—Why no Pictorial or Sculptural Record of Salamis as well as of Marathon—Poetical Commemoration—Walk up Mount Pentelicus—View of Marble Quarries—Character of the Marble—Reflections on the Quarries—Contrast of Rome and Athens in their respective Materials for Sculpture—Scenery of Cephissia—Villa of Herodes Atticus—Plato's Farm—Diogenes—Preservation of Ancient Names: Cephissia, Marousi, Herodes—Lycabettus—Hymettus—Perfume of Hymettus compared with that of Pentelicus—Grottoes of the Nymphs and Graces on Hymettus—Plato in this Cave—Port Raphti—Thoricus—Triangle formed by Thoricus, Amphiarus, and Sunium—Mines of Laurium—History of Mines—Peculiar Properties of Athenian Coinage—Temple at Sunium . . . . Pages 131—166

ÆGINA.

ISLAND of Ægina—Its Maritime Greatness attributable to its Harbours—Ruins of an Ancient Temple—Ancient Inscription—Ancient Tumulus—Site of Panhellenium—Volcanic Appearance of Ægina—Mount Pante—Mountain of Oros—Legend of Æacus, king of Ægina—Temple at Panhellenium—Remains of Antiquity on the Panhellenian Mount—Doric Inscription—Interior of the Island . . . . Pages 167—183

ATHENS.

REQUISITES for a Description of Athens—Suggestions from a Sight of its Ruins—Contrast of the Spirit which produced its Buildings with their Material Elements—Permanence and Extension of the former—Advantages of the Modern over the Ancient Spectator of Athens—Map of Athens drawn by Damochus for Philip—Physical Sketch of the Site of Athens—Its Harbours—Its Limits—Idea of Athens as it existed in Ancient Times on the Day of the Celebration of the Panathenaic Festival—

The Centre of that Procession followed—Ascent to the Acropolis—Propylæa described—Restoration of—Temple of Victory—Its Frieze—Doors of the Propylæa thrown open—First Sight of the Interior of Acropolis—The Acropolis was the Temple, the Fortress, the Museum, and the Treasury of Athens—Statues—Colossal Bronze Statue of Minerva Promachus—The Parthenon—Its Frieze, Metopes, and Pediments—Shields on the Eastern Front—Its Architectural Mouldings painted—The Ophthalmogenes—The Eastern Division of the Temple—Panathenaic Frieze, Idea of—Erechtheum—Its Two Divisions—The Eastern consecrated to Minerva Polias; the Western to Pandrosos—Architectural Description of—History—The Four principal Sacred Objects contained in it—Subterranean Passage to the Grotto of Aglaurus—Use of the Aglaureum—Grotto of Pan—Temple of the Winds—Different Uses of the Temple—Districts of Athens North of the Acropolis—Dionusion—Cynosarges, Colytus, Melite—Temple of Theseus—History and Ornaments of—Reliefs and Political Objects of the Temple—The Pnyx or Parliament of Athens—Its Site, Size, and Features—Idea of an Athenian Assembly—Picture of an Orator addressing an Assembly in the Pnyx—Objects before his eyes—Influence of the Local Peculiarities of the Pnyx on Athenian Eloquence—Description of the Areopagus—The Areopagus, why associated with the Temple of the Furies—The Agora, as it existed in Ancient Times—Its Principal Objects—View of the Agora from the Western Side of the Acropolis—Real Character of the Agora—Its Influences—Theatre—Its Site and Natural Scenery—Consequent Advantages enjoyed by the Athenian Dramatist and Spectator—Street of Tripods—Its Object—Odeum of Pericles—Temple of Jupiter Olympius—Choragic Monument of Lysicrates—The Ilissus, Lyceum, Stadium, Callirrhoë—Mountains of Attica—Not mentioned by Athenian Tragedians—Attic Tragedy silent about Attica—Italian Notion of Attica—Policy of Themistocles to isolate Athens—The Piræus—His Designs promoted by (?) and Pericles—Third Long Wall of Athens . . . . Pages 194—229

PHOCIS, LOCRIS, AND BŒOTIA.

RIVER Sperchius—Lamia, Demosthenes, Lamian War—Trachis—Hercules and Deianira—Trachinia of Sophocles—Trachinian Province and History of Hercules: his Apotheosis on Mount Œta—Pilgrimage thither—Leonidas at Thermopylæ—Influence of Hercules on the Spartans at Thermopylæ—Defence of the Pass at different Periods—Alterations in the Coast—Thermopylæ survives only in Herodotus—Amphictyonic Council House—at Anthele—Why?—Reflections on this Epicnemidian Locrians—Ajax Oïleus—Tabaea. Pantocomoli: Scamm whence derived—THIRD STATION, on Mount Parnassus—Panoramic Views—Daris; Elatea, Abae, Daulis; their early History—The Triple Way—Œdipus—Ancient Roads and Carriages—Delphi; Hill; Buildings—Ion of Euripides—Theatre, Temple, Oracle, Omphalos, Stadium—Castalia—Cirrha—Circle; Milton—Dorycleia Cave—FOURTH STATION: HELICON—Ascraippus, Hippocrene—The Grove of the Muses—Helicon and Cithaeron compared—Names of Objects on Helicon (Libethra, Pimplea, Pierides); Why of Macedonian Origin—Lebadea: Sirens, Harina, Sources—Oracular Cave of Trophonius—Lake Copais—Choronea, Battle of—Treasury of Minyas—Lebadea to Thebes: Coronea, Alalcomenae, Corallus, Tilphossa, Haliartus—Thebes: Dirce, Ismenus—Road from Thebes to Plataea—Plataea and Thebes—BŒOTIA—Homer's Catalogue—Comparison of Maritime Force of Attica and Bœotia—Station at Orchomenus—Course and Vale of the Cephissus—Plain of Orchomenus, or Northern Basin of Bœotia—Two important Cities on its Margin, at equal Distances from each other—Lebadea—Technical Arrangements and Phraseology of Astronomy and Geography compared—Basin of Orchomenus the natural Theatre of Bœotia—Chæronea, Plain and Battle of—Coronea, Battle of—Haliartus, Battle of—Mountain Circle of Bœotia—Commencement at Aulis—Mounts Messapius, Ptoum, Acraetium, Helicon, Cithaeron, Parnes—Thespiae, Oropus, Delium—Helicon and Cithaeron—Legend of—Their natural Scenery compared—Grove of the Muses on Helicon—City of Thespiae—Character of the Thespians—Road from Bœotia by Thespiae to the Corinthian Gulf—Zethus and Amphion—Legends of Mount Cithaeron—Dionysus, Pentheus, Œdipus, Sphraxidian Nymphs—Plataea—Campaign of Mardonius—Force of Mardonius—Topography of the Battle of Plataea—Three successive positions of the Greek Force—Narrative of the Battle—inconsistent Banquet of Pausanias; his Presence of Mind—Death of Mardonius—Various Moral and Political Results from the Physical Properties of Boeotia—Climate of Boeotia; how produced—Exertions of Nature to remedy the Evil—Embanking of the Copaic Lake—History of—Influence of the Copaic Lake on Boeotia—The Asiatic Road—Minstrelsy of Boeotia—Description of the City of Orchomenus—Its History—Basin of Thebes—Topography and Climate of Thebes—Theban Character affected by Climate of Boeotia .... Pages 228—275

THESSALY

Entrance at the North of the Pass—Frontiers of Thessaly—Basin of Thessaly—Its Rivers—Character of Thessalian Legends—Egress of the Sea through Tempe—Marriage of Peleus and Thetis—Signification of—Views of the Sea from the Mountains of Thessaly—Their Influence on Thessalian Mythology—Ceyx and Halcyone—Jason and the Argonauts—Centaurs and Lapithae; what they represent—Illustration of the Natural Properties of Thessaly from its Coins—Meaning of the Name of Thessaly—Alluvial Plains of Thessaly—Commencement of our Survey from Zeitun in Eastern—Pass over Mount Pindus—Roads and Bridges of Ali Pasha—Ascent to Metzovo—Klepts—Etymology of Metzovo—Present State—Greenhouse—Ascent to Zygos—View of the Monasteries of Meteora—Ascent to one of these—Church and Library—Kalabaka—Ancient Inscriptions—Aid of Inscriptions to Topography—Omission of Julian Caesar—Tricca—Ancient Thessalian Cities in the Vale of Peneus—Their Ruins—Larissa—Present State—Seized there—Influence of the Soil on the Thessalian Character—Ancient Inscriptions—Turkish Cemetery—Vale of Tempe—Military Character of Tempe—Scenery of Tempe—Sources of its Beauty—Pompey and Pharsalia—Road from Tempe to Pharsalia—Present Aspect of Pharsalia—Battle of Pharsalia—Contrasts between the Accounts of Julius Caesar and Lucan—Crannon—Pherae—Alcestis—Road from Pherae to Volo—View on Approach to Volo—Mount Pelion—City of Demetrias—Iolcus, Anaurus, Cave of Chiron on Mount Pelion—Bucolic School of Greece—Botanical Fertility of Mount Pelion—Consideration of it in Ancient and Modern Times .... Pages 276—366

EPIRUS, ACARNANIA, AND ÆTOLIA.

Bay of Actium—Present Appearance—Battle of Actium—Plan of the Battle—Temple of Actian Apollo—Coast of Ætolia—Bay of Missolonghi—Castle and Straits of Lepanto—Town of Prevesa—Turkish Scenes—Route to Nicopolis—Plan of Nicopolis—Theatre, Aqueduct, Architecture—Object of Nicopolis—Theatre—Architecture emblematic of Population—Ancient Fountain—Road from Nicopolis to Arta—Arta the Ancient Ambracia—Present State of Arta—Bazaar—Churches of Arta—Paintings in them—Ancient Coins of Ambracia—Ruins at Rogus—Ruins at Rastel—Rogus Identified with Charadra—Rastel with Ambracus—Scenery of the Charadrus—Ancient Fortress—Justice—Palace and Tomb of Ali Pasha—Mosque—Tomb of Turkish Saint—Tepeleni—River Arta—The Acheronusian Promontory—Where was Dodona?—Search for It now rendered more difficult—Dodona not merely a city but a country—Oracle of Dodona—their Fate, Extent, and Peculiarities—War Dance at Premiluna?—Bishop of Dodona—Road from Premiluna to Suli—City and Plain of Dramisius—Scenery of Suli—Homeric Inferno—The Acheron, Cocytus, and Acherusian Lake—Oracle of the Dead—Port of Glykys—Scenery of the Acheron—Ascent to the Gorge of the Acheron—Castles of Suli—Shrine and Plains of Epirus—Kakosuli—History of Suli—Ancient Geography of Ætolia—Trichonian Lake—Amgyathus—Zygos—Thermus—Pleuron—Calydon—Evenus—Dimmitza—Battle of Lepanto—Passage across the Mouth of the Gulf of Corinth .... Pages 367—459

IONIAN ISLANDS

ANCIENT and Modern Corcyra—Coins, Name, Esplanade of Corfu—Corcyrean Traditions and Customs—Homeric Phaeacia—Corcyra of Thucydides—Temple of Neptune—Nausicaa—Paxo—Milton's Ode on the Nativity—Leucas or Santa Maura—Leucadian Apollo—Lovers' Leap—Modern Ithaca—Is it

TABLE OF CONTENTS

the Ithaca of Homer?—Contrary Theory—Difficulty from a Passage in the Ninth Book of the Odyssey—Reflections on the Geographical Theories about Ithaca—Geographical Limits of the Fabulous Region in the Odyssey—Contrast between the Description of Phæacia and Ithaca—The Meridian Line of the Odyssey passes through Ithaca—Object of the Odyssey—Are the Ruins on Aëtos the Remains of the Palace of Ulysses?—Evils of discovering too much—Grotto of the Nymphs—Asteris—City of Ulysses at Polis—Cephallenia—Vale of Rakli - Herakles—Ithaca of Prosti—Colne—Herculeo—Samo: Ruins, Tombs, Gates, Walls—Cranii; Ruins—Pale—Zarynthus: Same, Meaning of—Town of Zante—Ancient Wine-vat—Pitch-wells—Herodotus—Cannabyte of Philip III. from Cephallenia into Ætolia—Sunium, the Acarnanian Capital—Thermus, the Capital of Ætolia—Site of Thermus—Island of Crithern—Isle of Scio—Town and Island of Sotra—Islet of Deles . . . . Pages 343—369

THE PELOPONNESUS.

Contrast between Arcadia and Achaia—Commercial Discriminations of the latter—Epithets, the ancient Name of Achaia when inhabited by Ionians—Political Results of its natural Character—Achaibn, whence called Achaia—Ionians of Achaia settled in Asia—Ionia the Asiatic Achaia—Aristocide, physical and political, between the two Countries—Name of Achaia—Why the Achaeans were neutral in the Peloponnesian War—Their Quiescence explained—Achaia the last in the Lamomodorion of Greek Nations—Domestic and Foreign Policy of Achaia—Its History from B.C. 280 to B.C. 146—Patræ—Feline—Sicyon—Ægira—Phligathaon—Polybius—Monastery of Megaspelion—The Corinthian Gulf—Mount Chelmos—Bouverie and Valley of the Styx—Sisi and Rivers of Elis—Why few Antiquities in Elis and similar Countries—Olympia; Mount Cronius—Rivers Alpheus and Cladeus—Altis—Olympic Games—Particular Care used in Greece—Origin and use of the Olympiad—Characteristics of, and national Benefits derived from, the Olympic Games—History of the Olympiads—Length of Stadium—The Olympic Stadium the national Element both of Distance and Time—Present Aspect of Olympia—Pelion—Xenophon there—His Description of the Place and his own Parental there—Lycannum—Magalopoli—Messenian Country—River Gortyn—Phoroeus and Phigaleia—Temple at Bassæ—Its Site and History—Mount Cotylæum—Architectural and Sculptural Descriptions—Pausanias . . . . Pages 369—398

MESSENIA.

Contrast between Messenia and Laconia—The River Neda—The Fortress of Ira—Aristomenes—The River Pamisus—Ancient History of Messenia—Result of Messenian Wars with Sparta—Return of the Messenians—Rebuilding of Messenia; Construction, Music—Expolitation—Present Aspect of Messenia—Forum, Walls, and Towers of Messenia—Aright Gate—Ancient Road—Greek and Roman Roads—Theatre and Stadium—Later History of Messenia—Philopœmen—Damocles—Harbours of Messenia—Pylos—Harbour of Pylos—Two Castles—Island of Sphacteria—Navarino—Messenian Pylos, the City of Nestor—Homeric Scenes at Pylos—Bay of Modon and Coron, compared with Amphilytus and Tharicus—Gulf of Coron, or Kalapaki . . . . Pages 398—411

SPARTA.

Journey of Telemachus to Sparta—Lacedæmon of Homer—Mistra—Sparta—Roman Ruins and Roman Appearance—Natural Position and Qualifications of Sparta and Athens compared—Results—Their System of Education—Bay of Laconia—Village of Marathonisi—Pellastium . . . Pages 411—430

ARGOLIS.

Route from Sparta to Argos—Artemisium Mountains—City of Mycenæ—Thucydides and Pausanias—Its Present State—Ancient Remains at Mycenæ—Treasury of Atreus—Idea of the Treasury as it formerly existed—Ruins of Mycenæ—The Argolic Plain—The Iliad contemporary with Mycenæ—

Gate of Lions—Mycenaean Heraldry—Herseum, or Temple of Juno—Walls of Tiryns—The Argolic Plain—Nauplia—City of Troezen—City of Argos—Citadel and Theatre—Mycenae absorbed in Argos—Ærobyrios—Town of Tripolitza—The Lernaean Lake—The River Inachus—Roads from Argos to Corinth—Nemea—The Nemean Lion—Temple and Stadium—Nemean Games,
Pages 420—433

CORINTH.

ACROCORINTH—Lechæum—Cenchreæ—Geographical Advantages of Corinth—Ancient Temple—Ascent to the Acrocorinth—Pelasgic Remains—Peirle-Bhomphia—Temple of Venus—Fountain of Peirini—Ancient Inscriptions and Architectural Decorations there—Three Fountains at Corinth—Which is the Ancient Peirini?—Pegasus—Why he appears on the Coins of Corinth and of her Colonies—Analogy between the Horse and the Element of Water—Advantage enjoyed by Corinth as "well-watered"—Road to Schœnus—Site of the Isthmian Grove and Temples—Isthmian Games—Stadium and Theatre—Remains of the Isthmian Wall—Nero's Intended Canal across the Isthmus—Ancient Amphitheatre at Corinth—Corinthian Theatre, Stadium, and Amphitheatre referred to by St. Paul in his First Epistle to the Corinthians—Local References in St. Clement's Epistle to the Corinthians . . . . Pages 433—448

INDEX Pages 449—452

(illegible caption)

STEEL PLATES

AND

PAGES OF WOOD ENGRAVINGS,

WITH THE NAMES OF THE ARTISTS.

Engravings on Steel

	DRAWN BY.	ENGRAVED.	PAGE
Frontispiece.—MISTRA, FROM THE THEATRE OF SPARTA	C. Radclyffe.	E. Radclyffe.	
Vignette in Title.—CASTALIAN SPRING—from a Sketch by ARUNDALE	T. Creswick.	E. Radclyffe.	
MAP OF GREECE	J. Dower.	J. Dower.	28
MAP OF NORTHERN GREECE			72
SCENE ON THE INACHUS—from a Sketch by HEAVE . . .	D. Cox, Jun.	W. Radclyffe.	128
MAP OF SOUTHERN GREECE			106
THE GULF OF SALAMIS	Major Irton.	E. Radclyffe.	142
MAP OF ELEUSIS			146
ATHENS, FROM MOUNT HYMETTUS	Major Irton.	E. Radclyffe.	163
TEMPLE OF MINERVA AT ÆGINA	Copley Fielding.	J. C. Bentley.	169
RUINS OF THE TEMPLE OF MINERVA AT ÆGINA . . .	F. Arundale.	J. Wrightson.	163
PLAN OF ATHENS			178
SOUTH FRONT OF THE PARTHENON	Major Irton.	J. C. Bentley.	248
MOUNTS OLYMPUS AND OSSA, FROM THE PLAINS OF THESSALY	W. Purser.	J. C. Bentley.	270
THE ISLAND AND CASTLE OF CORFU	W. Purser.	J. C. Bentley.	248
THE ISLAND OF SANTA MAURA (THE ANCIENT LEUCADIA)	W. Purser.	J. Woods.	254
THE PLAINS OF OLYMPIA	Railton.	R. Brandard.	263

	DRAWN BY	ENGRAVED BY	PAGE
TEMPLE OF APOLLO EPICURIUS AT BASSÆ	C. Radclyffe.	E. Radclyffe.	94
SCENE IN THE ARACHNÆAN MOUNTAINS NEAR ARGOS	D. Cox, Jun.	S. Radclyffe.	127
SCENERY ON THE ROAD FROM NAUPLIA TO CORINTH —from a Sketch by Hanen	J. C. Bentley.	R. Brandard.	134
THE CITY OF CORINTH	F. Arundale.	J. C. Bentley.	140

Pages of Engravings on Wood.

DRAWN BY G. SCHARF, JUN., ESQ.; AND ENGRAVED BY MR SAMUEL WILLIAMS
AND MESSRS G. AND E. DALZIEL.

	PAGE		PAGE
I.—EARLIEST SPECIMENS OF THE ARCH	29	VIII.—MARBLES OF THE PARTHENON	66
II.—VASES	34	IX.—SPECIMENS OF SCULPTURED DRAPERY	71
III.—ÆGINETAN MARBLES	47	X.—GREEK STATUARY	71
IV.—SCULPTURES FROM THE THESEUM	57	XI.—THE NIOBE AND ÆGINETAN MARBLES	
V.—VASE PAINTINGS	59	COMPARED	72
VI.—IONIC ARCHITECTURE	63	XII., XIII., XIV., XV.—ROMAN PERIOD OF	
VII.—THE CENTAURS AND LAPITHÆ	65	GREEK ART	90, 91, 94, 95

ENGRAVED AND PRINTED BY DAY & SON.

LIST OF ENGRAVINGS ON WOOD,

EXECUTED BY THE FOLLOWING DISTINGUISHED ARTISTS.

DESIGNED BY :—		ENGRAVED BY :—	
ARMSDALE.	BURTE.	BAPTEY.	PLAIDER.
BAGG.	BETET (PAUL).	BONIFR.	PAT.
BLENY (FELIX).	DETMR.	BRANSTON.	SMITH.
CHEVITE.	JAQUES.	DALZIEL (G. and E.)	SMITH (GREEN).
CM WERELL.	KEQmusDLER.	EVANS.	THOMPSON.
DANIEL.	PINELLI.	GRAY.	WILLIAMS (T.)
DAUBIGNY.	PITTS.	GREEN.	WILLIAMS (D. A.)
NICHEN.	FWELER.	JACKSON.	WILLIAMS (BIRS.)
FRANCAIR.	HARBENT.	BIETICLES.	WILLIAMS (R.)
GARVEY.	STANLEY (MONTAGU)	GILBY.	WHEELER.
HAMONT.	TAYLOR (P.)	GAXINELLE.	WHYMPER.

WOODS.	PAGE
Ancient and Modern Greeks	iv
The Emperor Trajan making his Will, attended by the Empress Plotina	v
Mount Parnassus	viii
Coast of Epirus from the Sea	ix
Death of Sertorio	xi
Anaxagoras at the Door of the Palace of Pericles	xvii
Island of Santorin	xviii
Ruined Aqueduct at Mitylene	xix
Theramenes dragged from the Altar by order of Critias	xx
Monument of Philopappus,—from a Drawing by Major Irton	xxiv
Athens restored	1
Four Illustrations of Primitive Architecture	5, 6
Cyclopean Walls of Tiryns and Calynda	6
Two Vases in the British Museum	7
Six Bronze Figures found in a Tumulus at Sardis	8

GREEK	PAGE
Stone Figure—Silhouette—Three Figures from an Early Painted Vase	8
Four Painted Vases from Athens, and one from Italy	9
An Ancient Herma—Terracotta Figure from Agrigentum	10
Four Representations of Form by Outline—Assyrian Head, Greek Coin, Coin of Athens, and Figure of Terracotta found at Sardis	11
Profile Eye—Head from the Dionysiac Vase	12
Figure from Vulci	13
Bronze Warrior; Nicoli	14
Interior of Doorway	16
Marbles found at Mycenae	16
Sculptured Lions of Mycenae	16
Lion Sword from Nineveh	17
Polygonal Walls of Mycenae and Cadymnda	17
Egyptian Workmen, From Thebes, in Egypt	18

ENGRAVINGS ON WOOD.

	PAGE			PAGE
Winged Bull, from Khorsabad	19	Illustrations of ancient Drapery—Coins of Antiochus and Pyrrhus	63
Mythological Figure, from Khorsabad	19	Ancient Modes of representing the Hair	61, 62
Tomb of Midas, in Phrygia	20	Monument of Philopappos	62
Four Coins—of Boeotia, of Ægina, of Epidamus, and of Corinth	22	Coin of Antimous—Statue of Julia	66
Ionic Columns of Persepolis—Aqueducts of early Ionic Columns of Persepolis	23	Bas-relief of Two Goddesses—Roman Sarcophagus	67
Triblichum, from Samothrace	24	Pass of Phyle	69
Doric Temple at Corinth	24	Heights of Hymettus and Town of Melasso	69
Ancient Greek Inscriptions	25, 26	Alinaticus, Costume, Scenery, &c.	91
Ichnographical Illustrations of ancient Temples	29	Argyro-Castro on the Aous	92
Doric Triglyph, Metope, and Fluting	30, 31	Acroceraunian Promontory	93
Three Figures of early Sculpture	33	Doric Pillar at Apollonia	94
Early Sculpture—Daedalus's Pointed Vase, and Flight of Danaus	34	Mouth of the Arta	96
		Mouth of the Hellenicus	96
The Fountain of Callirrhoë, from Mr. Rogers's Painted Vase	36	The Thermaic Gulf	96
Fragment from the Acropolis	37	River Peneus—looking towards Mount Pindus	97
Three Figures, Illustrative of the Drapery of early Sculpture	38	Isthmus to the Gulf of Corinth	99
		Phocis	100
Perseus cutting off Medusa's Head; from the Sculptures of Selinus	39	Grotto of Antiparos	101
Three early Bas-reliefs	41	Restoration of the Grove of the Academy	102
Costume, from an ancient Vase	41	Ancient Ships off Cape Sunium	103
Early Bronze Statue	42	Cape Sunium, from the Sea	104
Greek Warrior	43	Laurium and Cape Malapan	106
Figure from Kammako	44	Mountains of Arcadia near Phenaeos	106
Coin of Athens	44	Mount Taygetos, from the Plains of Sparta	107
Ancient Modes of representing the Hair	45	Taenarian Promontory, from the Sea	108
Laomedon, from the Eastern Pediment of the Æginetan Temple	49	Messenia, and Valley of the Nisy	109
Assyrian and Egyptian Heads	49	Bridge over the Alpheus	110
Greek Head, from Ægina	50	Mount Ithome	111
Greek Head, from a Vase Painting	50	Monastery of Megaspelion	112
Front Elevation of the Theseum	51	Town of Ægium in Achaia	113
Two Figures from the Frieze of the Theseum	53	Ruins of Megalopolis in Arcadia	114
Ornamental Panelling	51	The Plains of Nemea	116
Three Subjects painted by Polygnotus—Menelaus and Helen, Flight of Æneas, and Ajax and Cassandra	57, 58	City of Patræ in Achaia	116
		Sacrifice to Jupiter at Olympia	117
Sculpture from the Parthenon—River God Ilissus and Theseus	53	Valley of the Alpheus in Elis	129
Horse's Head	64	Mount Cyllene, and Lake Stymphalus	122
The Western Pediment, in 1674	64	Plains of Mantinea in Arcadia	121
The Eastern Pediment, in 1674	64	City of Orchomenus in Arcadia	122
Section of the Parthenon	66	Pastoral Scene	123
Ionic Callirrhoë	66	Mount Taygetos, from the Walls of Messene	123
Two Figures Illustrative of the Drapery of Phidias	67	Island of Cythera	124
Head of Juno, from a Coin of Argos	69	Valley of the Eurotas, from Mistra	125
Three Statues of the Apyrumpath	70	Modern Greek Costume	130
The Discobolus	70	Temple of Minerva in Ægina, Restored	130
Sculptures from the Phigaleian Marbles, and from the Temple of Victory	71	Vignette—Athos	131
Coin of Athens—A Group of the Graces, clothed	73	Coast of Attica and Ægean Sea, from Epidaurus	134
A Statue and a Coin of Venus	73	Quarries of Pentelicus	135
A Corinthian Capital	76	Plain of Athens from the Acropolis—from a Drawing by Arundale	135
Seal of Alexander	78	Athens and the Coast of Attica, from the Entrance to the Piraeus	135
Two Heads of the Alexandrine Period	79	Quarries of Pentelicus	130
		The Gulf and Island of Salamis	140
		Tomb of Ajax	143
		Athenians taking Refuge in their Ships—after PINELLI	146

	PAGE
View on the Road from Eleusis to Athens—from a Sketch by Henry	161
Eleusis—from a Sketch by Allason	162
The Pass of Phyle	163
Athens, from the Road to the Piraeus—from a Sketch by Henry	164
Daphne, near Athens	165
Mountain Scenery on the Road from Megara to Athens—from a Sketch by Henry	166
Defile near Drienza, in Mount Parnes—from a Sketch by Henry	167
The Acropolis, from the Fountain of the Areopagus—from a Drawing by Allason	167
Fancy Design	168
Temple of Theseus	169
Group of Elgin Marbles	169
Peninsula of Methana, Bay of Trœzen, and Town of Poros	182
Coast of Methana, from the Attic Shores	189
Port of Egripos, and Channel of the Euripus	191
Small Temple of Rhamnus Restored	192
Fountain near Marathon, from a Sketch by Henry	193
Tumulus, or Mound, at Marathon	193
Theseus-icles, inscribing the Trophy of Victory—restored from Stuart	193
Monastery of Pentelicus	196
Strata at the Source of the Cephissus	198
Scene near Cephissia—from a Design by Henry	192
Convent at Mount Anchesmus—from a Sketch by C. R. Cockerell, R.A.	196
Siege of the Huns on Mount Hymettus	199
Cave at Bari, on Hymettus	202
Port Raphti, and Statue	203
Ruins of a Theatre at Thoricus	204
Temple of Minerva at Sunium	205
City of Egina	207
Entrance to the Old Part of Egina	208
Coast of Epidaurus, from the Ancient Temple	209
Coast of Attica, from the Island of Egina—from a Sketch by Henry	168
Scene in Mt. Oros, near the Town of Egina	171
View in the Interior of Egina—from a Sketch by Henry	183
Restoration of the West End of the Acropolis	184
The Erectheum, the Propylæa, the Gate of Hadrian, and the Gate of the New Agora	185
Athens, from the Valley of the Ilissus	186
Athens, from the Ilissus—from a Sketch by C. R. Cockerell, R.A.	188
Athens, from the Gardens of the Academy, near Colonus	190
Part of Portico of the Propylæa	192
Programma from the Parthenon	198
Restoration of the North Side of the Acropolis	196
Restoration of the East End of the Parthenon	203
Portions of the North-east End of the Parthenon—from a Sketch by C. R. Cockerell, R.A.	204
The Parthenon from the East End—ditto	205

	PAGE
Raised Programmata of the Parthenon—from a Sketch by C. R. Cockerell, R.A.	206
Sepulchral Vases from Athens	206
North-east Side of the Parthenon—from a Sketch by C. R. Cockerell, R.A.	207
The Parthenon and Erectheum	208
The Pandroseum—from a Sketch by C. R. Cockerell, R.A.	209
Grotto of Pan	210
Temple of the Winds, Restored—from a Design by C. R. Cockerell, R.A.	211
Portico of the Temple of Theseus—from a Sketch by C. R. Cockerell, R.A.	211
Temple of Theseus—ditto	212
Stone Drum of the Pnyx—ditto	212
Vase from the Pnyx	213
Mountains of Phocis and Eleusis, from Salamis	214
Reservoir of the Ilissus—from a Sketch by C. R. Cockerell, R.A.	216
Gate of the so-called New Agora, called also Hadrian's Arch	218
Epidaurus and Isthmus of Corinth, from Ægina	220
Athens, from the North-west—from a Sketch by C. R. Cockerell, R.A.	221
The so-called Tomb of Euripides	222
Ruins of the Temple of Jupiter Olympius	223
Temple of Jupiter Olympius, from the Ilissus—from a Sketch by C. R. Cockerell, R.A.	224
Monument of Lysicrates	227
Fountain near Athens—from a Sketch by Henry	228
Houses in Modern Athens—from a Sketch by C. R. Cockerell, R.A.	227
Lake of Thomistocles	228
Tomb of Themistocles—from a Sketch by Allason	229
Thermopylæ	230
Parnassus	231
Female Peasants of Modern Greece	232
View near Daphnus	233
Plumæce of Mount Parnassus	235
Convent at Delphi	236
Village of Castri, near Delphi	238
Mount Parnassus	239
Cave of Trophonius—Acropolis of Lebadea	240
Town and Acropolis of Orchomenus	241
City of Thebes	244
Plain of Thebes	245
Hyram by Moonlight	246
Homer's Cave on the Island of Naxos	247
Plain of Chæronæa, from the Walls of Pananeus	248
Mount Parnassus, from Delphi	249
Mosque at Lebadea	250
Plain of Chæronæa	251
Battle of Chæronæa	253
Offering at the Temple of Delphi	254
Mountains of Bœotia, from the Bay of Aulis	255
Scene on Mount Cithæron	256
Bridge of the Euripus, from the North	257
Grove of Olive Trees	259

SUBJECT	PAGE
Bas-relief of the Muses	256
Ruins of Thespiæ—from a Sketch by Daniel	258
Ancient Seminary of Pentheus attacked by Bacchantes	263
Mount Cithæron, and Tomb of Plataea	269
Reception of the Ambassadors of Macedon	264
Hermes Karyatolil and Helicon, from the Bay of Crissa	268
City of Orchomenus	270
Lake Copais, and Katakothra	271
Coast of Bœotia near Aeantium	273
Plain and City of Thebes	273
Valley of the Ficinius, in Pæris	275
Vignette—Thronalis	276
Plains of Thessaly	277
Argos building the ship Argo—from Millin's Galerie Mythologique	278
Bridge at Larissa	279
The Lake and City of Jannina	283
The Pæneus, and Banks of the Peneus	283
Mount Ossa, from the Plains of Thessaly	285
General View of Meteora	289
Cliffs of Meteora	291
Monastery of Meteora	295
Bridge over the Peneus, at Larissa	294
Meteora at Larissa	297
Mount Olympus, from the Plains of Thessaly	297
Vale of Tempe	298, 306
The Peneus	301
Pharsalia—from a Sketch by Daniel	308
View on the Pagasæan Gulf	309
Pheræ	311
The Pagasæan Gulf and Mount Othrys	313
Mounts Ossa and Pelion, from the Pagasæan Gulf	314
Castle and Town of Tricheri	315
Modern Greek Priests	316
Vignette—Coast from Santa Maura	317
Coast of Epirus	317
Initial I	318
Western Coast of Greece, from the Ionian Sea	319
Coast of Ætolia, from Patras	310
Castle of Lepanto	311
Entrance to the Corinthian Gulf	313
Turkish Horsemen	314
Cyclopean Walls at Leucadia	315
Church at Arta	317
Valley of the Anactus	319
Town and Lake of Jannina	323
Town of Tepeleni	324
Mount Chimara, from the Gulf of Arbona	323
Banks of Linguetta	334
Source of the Drinus	337
Island and Convent of Jannina	338
Course of the Achorus	311
Mountains of Suli, from the Castle	337
Fortress of Suli	333
Island of Santa Maura	354
Valley of the Achorus	333

SUBJECT	PAGE
Raft of the Achorus	349
Ancient Sarcophagus	337
Castle of Kako-Suli	353
Missolonghi	339
Mountains of Ætolia, near Naupactus	340
Entrance to the Gulf of Corinth	341
Fanry Vignette, and Distant View of the Citadel of Korfou	343
Bridge at Korfou	344
Distant View of the Island of Korfou	345
Greek Priests in Costume	345
Citadel of Korfou	347
Destruction of a Greek City by Fire	348
Convent in the Interior of Korfou—from a Sketch by Prout	349
Ulysses and Nausicaa	350
Santa Maura, from the Coast of Epirus	351
Harbour of Phanyrio	353
Port of Ithaca	355
Cephallonia, from the Sea	354
Lovers' Leap	357
Cyclopean Walls in Ithaca	354, 350
Medals and Coins of the Ionian Islands	361
Cyclopean Walls in Cephallonia	363
Town of Zanyathus	364
View in Zanyathus	365
Isle of Scio	367
Town and Isle of Syra	367
Emblematical Headpiece to "The Peloponnesus"	369
Mountains of Pharis, from Corinth	370
Northern Coast of the Corinthian Gulf	371
Plain of Iamia, and Course of the Mæander	373
Ruins at Ephesus	373
Mountains of Achaia	375
Pharæ	376
Acro-Corinth	377
Church at Patras	378
Sicyon, from the Theatre	379
Convent of Megaspelion	381
Megaspelion	382
Mountains and Valley of the Styx	383
Valley of the Alpheus, from Erymanthus	384
The Alpheus in Elis	385
Plain of Olympia	387
The Coast of Elis	391
Coast of Arcadia, from the South	393
Bridge over the Carryalus	394
The Alpheus, with Karitena and Trapezus	395
Phigalia	396
Temple of Apollo at Bassæ, Restored—from a Design by F. Taylor	397
Ruins of the Temple of Apollo at Bassæ	399
Valley of Messenia	400
Source of the Neda	400
The Pamissus	401
Convent on the Site of the Temple of Jupiter, Ithome	403
Mounts Ithome and Evan	403

	Page			Page
Fountain of Chrysydes	404		Plain of Argos	424
Walls of Messene	405		Treasury of Atreus	424
Stadium at Messene	406		The Argolic Coast, near the Junction	424
Harbour of Pylos	407		Remains of Mycenae	426
Sphacteria and Pylos, from Navarino	408		Posture of Mycenae	426
Navarino, from the Sea	409		Gate of Lions at Mycenae	427
Isle of Sapienza and Castle of Modon	409		Ancient Olive Grove	428
Castle of Modon, from the Sea	410		Walls of Tiryns	429
Bay and Castle of Coron	411		Nauplia, from the Sea	430
Mounts Evas and Ithome, from the Laconian Shore	412		Castle of Tiryns	430
Stenyclarian Mountains, from Kalamata	413		Bay of Nauplia	431
Cardamyle	414		Bridge between Dasmala and Tiryns	432
Bridge over the Eurotas	415		Lernaean Marsh	433
Village of Mistra	416		Pass on the Road from Argos and Corinth—from a Sketch by Heath	434
Mount Taygetus	417		Ruins of the Temple of Jupiter at Nemea	435
Plain of Sparta	418		Corinth and the Acrocorinthus	436
Coast of Laconia—from a Sketch by Heath	419		Gulf of Corinth, from the Acrocorinthus	437
Village of Marathonisi	420		The Isthmus of Corinth, from the Gulf	438
Tripolitza	421		Mount Parnassus, from Corinth	444
Artemisian Mountains, near Olmos, Argos—from a Sketch by F. Heath	423		Coast of Olympic and Phocis, from the Aegean Gulf	441
Plain of Argos, from the Gate of Lions	423		Fancy Sketch	448

CHARACTERISTICS OF GREEK ART.

BY GEORGE SCHARF, F.S.A.

WHEN Pausanias travelled through Greece, during the age of the Antonines, about 1690 years ago, he found every city teeming with life and refinement; every Temple a Museum of Art; and every spot hallowed by some tradition which contributed to its preservation. The ruthless destruction of these works of art, in subsequent ages, has reduced them to a small number; and the Traveller now pauses, with a melancholy interest, to reflect upon the objects described by Pausanias, but which no longer exist. It is true that in our Museums many fine Monuments of ancient art have been preserved; but their completeness and unity as works of art cannot be appreciated under such circumstances. In order to comprehend the design of the artist, the surrounding scenery, to which it had reference, as well as the distance from which it was intended to be viewed, are to be borne in mind. Where an object of art is removed from its original site, the Scholar and the Antiquary must be combined with the Artist and Historian before the imagination can be carried back to the realities of a more classic period of its existence. It is therefore the object of these introductory pages to attempt a combination so necessary and important; and thus to illustrate some of the more striking characteristics of the different eras of Greek art;—to compare them with each other, to assist in chronologically arranging the more important examples still remaining to us, so as to

B

facilitate their comparison with the Historians, and to prepare the reader for the classic descriptions contained in subsequent portions of this volume.

Independently of the actual beauty and style of execution in works of art, it is important to trace the historical period at which they were produced. The process by which this information may be obtained is highly interesting, and in most instances quite conclusive. The known locality of a city, as described by ancient writers, frequently affords sufficient evidence to identify its ruins. The sculptured decorations which formed a part of its buildings, may also be historically associated with it. In this way the date of their execution can sometimes be ascertained; but, unfortunately, few Greek edifices remain which have their sculptures thus connected with them. With the exception of the PARTHENON, the TEMPLE OF THESEUS at Athens, the TEMPLE OF MINERVA at Ægina, and those of OLYMPIA in Elis and PHIGALEIA in Arcadia,—all of which contained sculpture most important towards a history of art,—few other instances are known where the identity is perfect. In many instances a new temple has been erected on the site of a former one,— portions of the ancient foundation having been left, and the old materials frequently used for the new structure. Bas-reliefs and inscriptions have thus been built into plain walls, with the sculptured sides turned inwards, as at Nineveh and Xanthus, where the bas-reliefs were only discovered on the demolition of the walls, by which they had been thus protected.

As guides to the different eras of art, coins, from having inscriptions upon them, are also of great importance. They are generally impressed with the portrait of the existing ruler, or with the religious emblems of the town in which they were struck; and they frequently bear allusion to some circumstance, the date of which is well known. In early times, coins bore the symbol of the presiding divinity of the city, and the issue of money was regulated by the priests as a matter of religious care. We may therefore assume that the first talent within reach was employed in their execution. Monarchs subsequently introduced their own features upon the coinage; at first under the semblance of divinity; but at length they represented themselves with all their personal characteristics and the usual insignia of power.

It was also customary to introduce upon coins reduced copies of the most celebrated works of art, especially statuary; thus furnishing transcripts of many fine groups, such as the Venus of Cnidos, the Venus of Cos, and the reposing Hercules,—works which have since perished. Being smaller in size, and of a material not easily broken, and, moreover, being of metal impervious to rust, many specimens of bronze coins have come down to us as perfect as when first produced. We are thus enabled to judge accurately of the beauty and delicacy of their execution. Many of our finest bronze medals have been preserved by a peculiarly hard coating, termed patina, which forms over the metal in the earth like a varnish upon the surface; and this being harder than the metal itself, has served the better to protect it. Iron, on the contrary, is destroyed by the rust which forms upon it,—a fact which accounts for the entire disappearance of many useful implements which the Greeks are known to have possessed.

Besides the enduring nature of the material of which coins were formed, other circumstances have tended considerably to their preservation. The practice of hoarding money by burying it in earthen jars was common in ancient times; the owner seldom communicating to any one the place of its concealment. In the event of his violent or sudden death, the secret would thus perish with him. History affords many instances of men becoming suddenly rich by the discovery of such hidden treasure. This was said to be the case with Herodes and Timon of Athens; and many similar hoards have been laid open in our own day. It was formerly a custom also to bury money with the dead; and the coin which was intended to pay the ferryman over the Styx, has in more than one instance been found adhering to the jawbone of the dead body. In very early times, tombs, called Hypogæa, were constructed beneath the level of the ground; which, from this circumstance, were more likely to escape desecration. Other tombs were also built of a more conspicuous form, serving for monumental purposes, and displaying fine architectural conceptions. These, as well as the Hypogæa, contained, besides the remains of the deceased, articles of great value, such as vases, bronze and gold ornaments, and even domestic utensils,—for the ancients paid great respect to the dead, and frequently buried with them all the articles they valued most during life. Tombs of distinguished persons were also protected by inscriptions engraved on the portal, imprecating curses upon any one venturing to disturb them. These inscriptions seem to have been effectual in early ages, for many such monuments have remained buried in accumulated soil, and have only been brought to light in our own days. During a later period all the tombs which offered any temptation to plunder were rifled by the Romans, especially during the time of Theodoric, when the plunder seems to have been carried on systematically. In more recent times the value of articles found in these tombs has been so great as to encourage a regular system of excavation, which has been attended with successful results at Athens, Milo, Corinth, and various parts of Italy, where some of the finest painted vases and ornaments have been found in connection with funereal structures. These vases, and the golden wreaths and other decorations found with them, were probably trophies of victory in the public games.

The custom of writing the name over the principal figures in the early vases has been serviceable in interpreting the subject of the painting. A uniform style of costume and personal appearance has been adopted in the representation of particular individuals which enables the initiated to trace with some certainty the intention of the artist. In early sculptures of heroic subjects, the names were also frequently engraved upon them.

Again; portraits, statues, and busts of individuals, often bore their names; by which means the artist has become familiar with the physiognomy of the statesmen and philosophers of ancient times, and has thus been enabled to associate their features with their thoughts and actions.

Historians have also left us some account of the changes which have taken place in art,—recording the name of the artist as well as the period at which such changes occurred. Pliny occasionally names artists who introduced new modes of treatment; but he is more careful in enumerating their works, and his writings thus offer us little more than a catalogue of names. Quintilian, Lucian, and Pausanias, give more particular descriptions of their works, and from these authors it is discovered that we are in possession of copies, or imitations at least, of some of the great works of former ages whose destruction is certain.

Historians also assist us in the study of ancient writing. From them we learn the period at which certain letters were introduced; and when one of these letters appears on a monument, we are certain that its date is posterior to the period of the introduction of that form of letter. The same changes extend to the spelling of words.

In the middle ages, when art degenerated into an hereditary trade, we find the very worst specimens employed upon public monuments. It would seem that the exclusive privilege of employment was bestowed as a personal favour upon certain individuals, irrespective altogether of their capacity. During this period many of the monuments of private individuals display more originality and refinement than the embellishments employed on public trophies, or the arches of the emperors themselves.

We shall now close our general remarks, and proceed at once to point out in detail the progressive stages of art, from the rudest phase to its most refined development, both in what are generally termed the works of the *artist* and in those of the *artisan*.

Whatever may have been the origin of the Greek nation, which, like most others, is lost in the dark recesses of time,—whether the Hellenic or Pelasgic element prevailed at the outset of its career,—is of little moment to our immediate purpose. We are content to repeat the traditions recorded by one of the earliest Greek poets, which were commonly received as truth in his day.— (Æschylus, Prom. 442, *seq.*) The *Hellenes*, according to this authority, preserved many traditions respecting their earliest state, which represented them to have been on a level with the savage tribes we now find wandering in the extensive forests and wilds of America. They had then no agriculture, but lived on the spontaneous produce of the woods ; and at that period not even fire could be appropriated to the service of man till it had been stolen, as Æschylus tells us, from heaven.

I.—THE ARTS TO THE ACTUALITIES OF PHIL- TRATUS. B.Q. 165.

In primitive times, the construction of human habitations acquired the distinctive title of *chief art;* and hence the Greek word Ἀρχιτεκτονία (Architecture).

Next in order to this *chief art* may be ranked Sculpture, originating in the use of clay for the formation of bricks and the construction of vessels for domestic purposes. Sculpture, properly so called, however, could not exist until after the introduction of tools by which marble and other hard material could be fashioned. Painting is of much more recent date; although it is probable that in very remote times colour was employed as a dye.

It may be fairly assumed, then, that the early Greek in his habitation accommodated himself, like other primitive races, to the rude shelter afforded by caverns and hollow trees; and that, as the race increased and wants multiplied, constructed habitations were attempted,—at first consisting of a mere roof, composed of boughs and skins spread from tree to tree, and serving as a protection against inclement weather. Primitive shelter of this kind may still be seen in some of the less frequented parts of Asia Minor, where trunks of trees, supporting a mass of interwoven boughs hung with the skins of beasts of the chase, keep off the wind, and form a temporary refuge.

Fig 1.—Primitive Shelter.

The primitive Temple of Apollo at Delphi, as Pausanias informs us, resembled a hut or cabin, and was composed of laurel trees.

Fig 2.—Hut Mrv.

In the course of time buildings became more permanent. Mud was added to the material of which the roof was formed, and the sides strengthened with clay. The trees forming the props were cleared of all lateral branches, and they were mounted on pieces of stone to prevent their rotting from contact with the earth. At this stage the structure began to assume the character of a complete building.

But this mud roof was found to retain moisture in winter, and in the summer heat it was liable to crack. It was found also that wood could be conveniently hewn into planks, and fitted together with some degree of nicety; and, following the idea, thus suggested, the flat sloping roof, such as is still common in Italy, was next devised. The double slope, however, which is more familiar to our habits, was also employed at an early age. In both these cases the roof was made to extend far beyond the walls, so as to form a shade from the summer sun, as well as effectually to throw off the water. Walls of stone, to protect man from his fellow-men, were next constructed. Originally these consisted of ponderous stones, heaped together without any attempt at form, but with smaller fragments fitted into the interstices; as may be seen in the still existing ruins of Tiryns and also at Calynda. These rude walls can hardly be distinguished at first sight from the masses of broken rock which lie heaped together in a limestone country, and which have so often misled the eager traveller in quest of ancient remains.

Pliny quotes a saying of Praxiteles, an ancient sculptor, that pottery was the mother of all the arts both in stone and metals. It is obvious that the softest and most easily-wrought materials would be first selected for experiment. The use of wood and clay, therefore, long preceded any attempt to work in stone or metal; and a modern writer has laid down a system of the progress of civilization among northern nations, from the nature of the materials in use among them. This system is divided into three periods :—Period 1. Implements and arms of stone, of wood, and of bone, and clothing of skins; 2. Arms of copper and gold, no silver or iron; 3. Arms of iron, articles of silver, and inscriptions.

We are at present treating of the first period, in which no other implements and arms than those of stone, wood, and bone, were in use—an age in which the bow and the arrow had just been added to the javelin; and when a stone adze was employed for shaping timber. Gourds were the vessels used in such a state of society; and Acorn-cups and Flowers naturally suggested some of the beautiful forms observable in pottery even of the earliest times. Moreover, clay being so easily moulded by the hand, it is easy to imagine that patterns would be traced, by way of ornament, upon these vases, while still in a soft and yielding state. At first these devices would naturally be imitations of the geometric lines of the spider's web, of a ring, or palm-branch, and the simple series of angles, known as the zig-zag pattern, VVVV. Two vases are here given, to show the simple pattern scratched upon them. The originals are made of coarse black-brown clay, and are

Fig. 1.—Vases of the Stone Period.

classed among the earliest specimens of Italian fictile art,—the form of the one being copied from a very primitive water vessel, the skin of an animal, and is called Askos. Such skins are still used in Italy, as well as Greece, for containing wine. The potter's art early acquired great importance, both from its utility and the scope it afforded to the arts of design by way of enrichment. From the superiority of the native clay, the best manufactures were established at Athens, Corinth, and Ægina, and the most finished and beautiful forms eventually became peculiar to these places.

With the discovery of a material so plastic as clay, man's imitative power expanded, and produced various attempts to represent the human form, in which the distinctive characters of the race, at least, were exhibited. Man's upright position, the head poised on the columnar neck, with projecting nose and chin, and eyes looking straight forward,—these at first engaged the artist's attention; and we must not be surprised that these peculiarities were exaggerated.

When the use of the hammer and anvil were discovered, it led to the formation of similar figures in metal, as being much more enduring than clay. In confirmation of this opinion, some very early bronzes have been preserved, which were discovered in a tumulus at Sardis, and which have traced on them the simple line patterns, such as we find on the earlier specimens of pottery.

These lines are also frequently found upon other ancient metals. The primitive clay figures also appear to have been imitated in stone, as may be seen in some curious specimens discovered by Lord Aberdeen among the earth-sunken tombs of Attica. Such figures are called SIGILLARIA, and are evidently of a very early fabric. In these fragments the deep grooves separating the

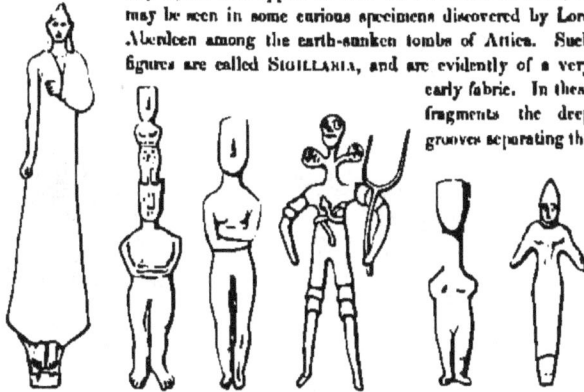

Fig. 1.—Bronze Figures from a Tumulus at Sardis.

limbs from the body exhibit the formality of line natural to inexpert workers in a hard substance, but in all other respects their style is exactly that which an unskilled hand would adopt in moulding a figure from very soft material.

Fig. 2.—Bronze Figure.

Painting, which in its early state was peculiarly historic, has been called the art of deception; but to this purpose it has been more especially applied in later times. The earliest and most ready pigment was undoubtedly blood,—a thin and colouring liquid, which dyes a dark brown colour, and which might, during sacrifice, have occasionally assumed, while flowing, the recognisable forms of objects, as we see in shadows which are cast upon the flat ground. Shadow certainly led to painting, and gave the name of SCIAGRAPHY to one particular style of art, which has always been retained—namely, the SILHOUETTES, a name given to pictures in one flat colour, usually black. By such shadows a vast number of subjects could be represented, and whole histories in a short time actually expressed. We find this art first employed

Fig. 3a.
Bronze Figure.

Fig. 3b.
Figure on small Painted Vase.

to decorate pale earthen vases with figures of flowers, leaves, and animals ;

but no attempt at figures occurs in the very earliest examples. Specimens of the earliest painted vases from Athens are now in the British Museum. They exhibit

great simplicity of form, and are made of a pale dull clay, with simple patterns and figures of animals coarsely painted upon them. Fig. 12 espe-

cially displays the elements of nearly all the Greek ornaments in the small patterns with which the whole ground is strewn. The drawing is rude in the extreme, and the colours somewhat pale,—a peculiarity also observable in the other two examples, and indeed in nearly all the vases of this period. There is no attempt at precision of form, such as distinguishes a subsequent style, in which we find a careful outline given by incised or deeply-scratched lines. The colour appears blacker and more glossy, and the clay ground of the vase, moreover, is covered with a kind of varnish, which gives a richness and polish to the whole surface. In the present specimens none of these peculiarities present themselves.

Passing from early painting to statuary, and from the traditions by which its history is cherished, we find, in the earliest times, a block of stone or wood worshipped as the symbol of bodily presence. In this form Mercury and Apollo received divine honours; Jupiter Casius was represented by a heap of stones; the Sidonian goddess appeared as a great block drawn about in a cart; and the Paphian Venus was shrined in her temple as

a cone. These symbols remained unchanged during a long course of pagan history. They are represented on medals struck by the Roman emperors. Sometimes the human head was placed upon a square column of a man's height; and as this form was most frequently employed for representations of Mercury, it was called HERMES, from one of his names. The Hermes was much used in later times for portraits of philosophers and learned men, of whom Mercury was the protecting deity. This ornament is peculiarly adapted to library decorations. Some-

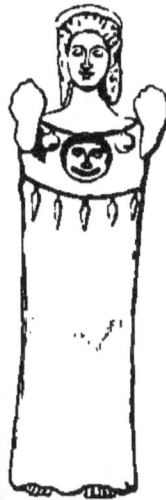

times hands and feet were added to the upright block; and in such cases the extremities were made of a more refined material, frequently of white marble. Pausanias describes thirty quadrangular stones at Pharæ, which he says the Pharæans venerated, calling them by the name of some particular god. The same author informs us that at Thespiæ, afterwards celebrated for its beautiful statue of the God of Love figured in Plate VIII., the oldest symbol of that deity was a rude representation in stone.

But although sculptors had by this time attained the power of imitating the human form, the ability to convey its expression and other niceties of character was still wanting. It was, moreover, opposed to the natural convictions of mankind to worship the images of ordinary beings like themselves. In order, therefore, to overcome this feeling, a terrible aspect was bestowed on the deities by the artist, who thus attempted to horrify the senses, where he could not command veneration. In common with all savage nations, hideousness and extravagant proportions characterized

the earliest gods of Greece. Traces of these monstrosities lingered, through the whole progress of Greek art, in the Gorgons and Furies of theatrical representation. In later times the Gorgon's head decorated the coinage of Athens, and was a favourite emblem on the shields of her heroes.

The art of expressing form by mere outline partakes of difficulties which those can scarcely estimate to whom practice has made it familiar. But although the modern artist begins his work with an outline, we feel assured that this discovery followed the laying on of colours. Patterns composed of lines, such as have been already described, were in previous use; but they were merely employed as lines to gratify the eye. The difficulty of comprehending forms by these means is often

experienced, even among ourselves. Take a map, for instance, in pure outline, where a lake may be taken for an island. Until the shading is added, there is nothing to distinguish the land from the sea, or the solid body from empty space.

Pliny informs us that Cleanthes of Corinth was the first who represented

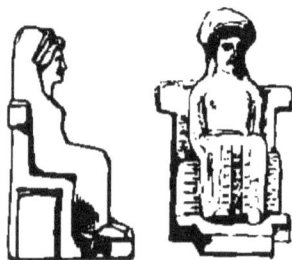

form by lines. The name of the originator is of little importance; but it shows that this was recognised as a separate and essential stage of the art. The use of colour was not confined to vases, but was evidently extended to sepulchral monuments. Many of the clay images found in the Greek tombs retain traces of paint. Some of these even appear to have been gaudily decorated with gold and a profusion of the brightest colours.

A curious specimen from a tomb at Samos is now preserved in the Museum at Canterbury; and many others, discovered by Mr. Burgon and the Baron von Stackelberg in Attica, exhibit similar instances of enrichment. In the Wisdom of Solomon, chapter xiii. 11—14, and chapter xv. 8, will be found a curious description of the manufacture of woolen and clay images,—"laying it over with vermilion, and with paint colouring it red, and covering every spot therein."

It may have seemed easy to represent the shadow of a profile face; but more than this was required. The eye and ear must be added. The latter could be tolerably represented; but with the eye greater difficulties present themselves,—difficulties which those only who have undergone the trial can appreciate. To represent the eye in side view requires a complicated knowledge of foreshortening, such as the Greeks of that period had not acquired; they therefore began by inserting the shape of a full eye; thus giving a bird-like character to the profile. A curious method of representing the eye, on painted vases of an early period, was to draw a circle and carry a line through it. In some instances a ball was placed within the circle, and the corner lines somewhat shortened, as in fig. 21, from a vase in the Museum Disneyanum.

Pliny traces the origin of drawing and modelling portraits to Dibutades, a potter of Corinth, whose daughter, seeing the shadow of her lover's profile cast upon the wall by a strong light, traced the outline. The father's attention being called to this sketch, he pressed clay into it, and placed it in the furnace to harden. In all probability some such event first originated the *bas-relief*, which has always been regulated by shadows; and it will be found that those bas-reliefs are most perfect which are still intelligible upon being reduced to mere shadows, as sciagraphs or ombres chinois. Dibutades, according to the same author, was the first to decorate architecture with sculptured ornaments made of clay. He is said to have placed figures in the gable-ends, and ornaments along the ridge-tiles of the temples—an application of his art very natural after the discovery just attributed to him. In the same passage we are told that the sculptor found the means of colouring the ornaments in red.

In sculpture of this period figures were generally represented with the limbs close together. Very frequently neither the hands nor the arms were indicated, the whole being supposed to be wrapped up in a tight, painted garment, and with the feet alone projecting. Figures of this kind had little to distinguish them from the columnar Hermes already described; but a slight advance on this is seen in the curious statue of white marble, found at

Polledrara, a part of the Necropolis of Vulci. In general attitude the columnar character is here preserved; but the arms from the elbow are made to project, and the hands in proportion are enormously large. The dress is also distinguished into an upper and under garment; but there is no attempt to indicate a fold in the drapery. Remains of elaborately-designed borders and ornaments are traceable in this drapery in black, red, and white colours; and these strongly resemble the minute interlacings found on the neck of some of the vases of an early but refined period.

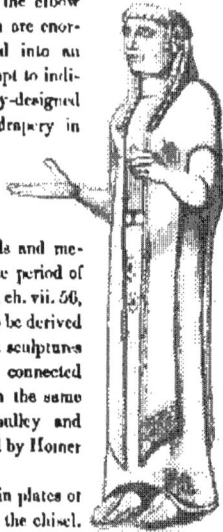

The ancients were well acquainted with tools and mechanical contrivances for moving weights at the period of which we are treating. The saw—said by Pliny, ch. vii. 56, to be the invention of Dædalus or Perdix, and to be derived from the teeth of a serpent—is to be seen on the sculptures recently brought from Nineveh. The wheel connected with carts and chariots frequently appears upon the same monuments, on which also is observed the pulley and battering-ram. The potter's wheel is mentioned by Homer in the Iliad, xviii. 375, 600.

The earliest metal figures were formed of thin plates of bronze hammered into shape, and finished with the chisel. In this manner was formed the brazen statue of Jupiter on the Acropolis of Sparta; the parts being firmly united together with nails. Pausanias describes this (iii. 17) as a very ancient work of art, the production either of Dædalus or Learchus of Rhegium. It is also recorded that the arts of sculpture and architecture are indebted to Dædalus for their first development among the Athenians and Cretans. Diodorus Siculus gives a long history of the works and adventures of this artist; but it will suffice here to state, that he was regarded as a native of Athens, who dwelt a long time in Crete, from whence he fled into Sicily. He is said, also, to have worked in Egypt, and to have copied many of the works of art of that country; his labyrinth in Crete having been a copy from the Egyptian. The whole story may be purely mythical; but it coincides with our belief of a friendly intercourse having been established, at this early period, between the Egyptians and the Asiatic Greeks. Dædalus is said to have made his figures walk, and to seem as if endowed with life, because he was the first to separate the limbs, which suggests movement. Hence wooden figures of the greatest antiquity were called by his name—Dædalus.

The name of the mythical artist Smilis was derived from σμίλη, a knife
for carving wood. The names of the artists who accompanied Tarquin
from Corinth to Italy are Euchiros, Diopus, and Eugrammus (Pliny, xxxv.
12, 43), which names signify the dexterous, the overseer, and the correct
designer. The qualities which these names imply have a special reference
to the purely Greek vases found so abundantly in that part of Italy first
occupied by Tarquin.

Such we may assume was the point of excellence to which the arts had
attained in the time of Homer. All descriptions beyond this must be traced
to the poet's imagination. In the Homeric poems little knowledge is gained
of the actual state and quality of art, beyond the use of certain materials
and their application. Copper tempered and hardened is chiefly employed
for armour, both offensive and defensive; whilst iron is rarely mentioned, and
then only in connexion with agriculture. All applications of this metal for
the purposes of war belong to a subsequent age.

In the ODYSSEY the value of material is often particularised,—the halls of
Alcinous and Menelaus glitter with gold, copper, and electrum; and large
stores of metal yet unemployed are laid up in the treasure chambers. Precious
woods are specially named. The carriage in which Priam goes to seek Achilles
is made of cedar; and the grotto of Calypso is fragrant with it. Penelope
received a rich veil from her suitors, and Hecuba dedicated the handsomest
embroidered garment, selected from her rich store, to the tutelary goddess,
whose statue was enthroned in the temple of the sacred city. The Phœnicians
had already introduced ivory, purple, and incense from Arabia, and byssus
and costly robes from the east.

Silver is rarely mentioned in these poems, whilst both bronze and gold are
familiar metals. Homer does not appear to have known either the compass
or the saw.

Articles of furniture, such as chairs and bedsteads, seem to have been
made of wood, hewn out of the rough block with an axe; then carefully
wrought with finer instruments, and afterwards adorned with gold, silver,
ivory, or amber, inlaid and inserted into the bored and depressed portions.
Ivory is described as adorning sword sheaths, keys, and caskets.

By the door of Alcinous, as described in the Odyssey, stand rows of dogs
in gold and silver. In his hall, upon pedestals, are golden statues of boys
holding torches, whilst the whole palace shines like the sun. Its walls are brass,
and the cornice gilt, with portals of silver and gold. In these halls rise pillars
of silver, surrounded by clustering vines, dazzling the eye with all the glitter of
an oriental city. But this condition of the arts, as represented in the Homeric
poems, must be accepted with many qualifications. The poet appeals to our

imaginations by the exercise of his own. How easy for him to describe a degree of excellence in the arts, which never existed. The same words which describe a single group of figures on a shield might extend the subject to an army, and, at the expense of words only, swell the whole into a universe. Such, in effect, was Homer's description of the shield of Achilles. It had no real existence so far as the artistic description is concerned; but it communicates the important fact, that groups of figures in metal had already been attempted.

Homer is very particular in enumerating the various details of armour and equipments for war. The construction of these always continued the same, and each part can be recognised upon the ancient figures, although the works of art which exhibit them are of a much later period.

The Laisiion, or shield-curtain, which Homer occasionally refers to, has been only recently determined. The form was frequently seen on vase paintings, but was not known to be represented on sculpture until the discovery of the Lycian monuments. The gorgon-headed shield of Agamemnon may be quoted as an elaborate specimen of various metals.

The use of money seems to have been utterly unknown to Homer; nor does he make any direct mention of the stone statue. That of Athena in the Trojan Citadel seems to have been one of the wooden statues called Xoana (Ξόανον), and in a sitting position; for Hecuba lays the tributary garment upon its knees.

Fig. 30.—Bronze Warrior, Micali.

Gold, we find, was beaten extremely thin for the purpose of gilding; of this Homer gives an instance in describing the preparations for a sacrifice (Odyss. iii. 437), when Nestor produces gold which is applied to the horns of the ox, "Ἵν' ἄγαλμα θεὰ κεχάροιτο ἰδοῦσα." The same process may have been applied to the doors and columns in the palaces before mentioned. The solid walls of the Treasury, still existing at Mycenæ, were plated inside with some metal, probably bronze; for the nails by which it was

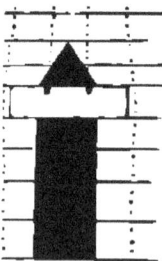
Fig. 31.—Interior of Treasury.

fastened yet remain, and the same metallic lining may have been used for the brazen chamber in which Danäe is said to have been confined by Acrisius of Argos.

Although Homer does not describe marble as decorating any of his stately palaces, we find that he was aware of the difference between that material and common stone; for he tells us

that Paris was struck on the mouth with a marble stone. Green and red marble, however, are found casing the front of the Treasury at Mycenæ.

Another very remarkable relic of Homeric times, if not much older, is seen in the walls and sculptured lions on the gate of Mycenæ. The blocks which form the walls are square-hewn, and laid in horizontal courses. Over the portal are two lions, executed in very rude sculpture, but much resembling those seen on the painted vases of the period, being probably derived from the early Assyrian type exhibited in some of the sculptures from Nineveh. Mycenæ was destroyed by the Argives soon after the battle of Thermopylæ; and Pausanias, who wrote in the reign of the Antonines, describes the ruins of the city as a wonder still existing in his day. He says (ii. 16, p. 170): "Among other parts of the inclosure which still remain, a gate is perceived with lions standing on it; and they report these were the works of the Cyclops, who also made for Prœtus the walls of Tiryns."

Walls composed of enormous stones, which still remain in many parts of Italy, Greece, and Asia Minor, are called Cyclopean, because the ancient authorities describe the Cyclops as having occupied themselves with such constructions.

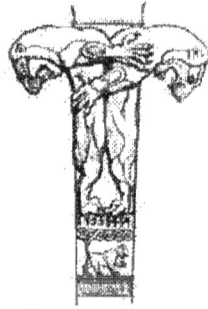

Fig. 25.—Lion's Gate at Mycenæ.

Strabo especially informs us that they came originally from Lycia, and that they were working men who lived by their labour (viii. 373).

A more refined mode of building succeeded, in which the surface of the wall was carefully smoothed, and the edges of the stones accurately fitted. Where strength and exactness were required, the stones were not cut square, but formed into every possible variety of angles. Beautiful

Fig. 26.—Polygonal Walls of Mycenæ.

specimens of this polygonal style may be seen at Mycenæ, and also at Cadyanda in Lycia, where the joints are so exact as scarcely to admit the point of a pen-knife between them. The walls of Mycenæ, according to Euripides (Herc. Fur. 948), were formed by means of the measuring-line and stone-axe. By a

Fig. 27.—Polygonal Walls of Cadyanda.

common error, these walls have received the appellation of Cyclopean; but this designation applies only to constructions by means of great blocks, and of rough execution, which accorded with the supposed character of that fabulous race.

The vast genius of the Greeks, and their natural predisposition for all matters of science and art, could not remain long uninfluenced by the matured experience of older countries. Important events occurred, which opened communications with two of the most ancient nations in the world—Egypt and Assyria. These circumstances arose whilst Amasis and Crœsus ruled in Egypt and Asia Minor, and Cyrus the Great held dominion over Persia. The Egyptians had long exercised a style of art peculiarly their own; but they rejected all improvement. We are told by Plato that the priests never suffered painters or statuaries to introduce any novelty into their art; so that what was

Fig. 37.—Egyptian Workmen. From Tombs, in Egypt.

produced yesterday was the same as that which had been produced a thousand years previously.

The characteristic features of Egyptian art, as seen in the specimens which remain, are the exquisite finish bestowed upon colossal proportions, general delicacy of form, absence of muscular exaggeration, angularity of action, and parallel arrangement of the limbs. The feet placed close together in mummy fashion is generally employed to express repose. The peculiarities alluded to can be well seen in the annexed figures, which are copied from Egyptian paintings, and which represent sculptors, polishers, and painters finishing two sculptured figures.

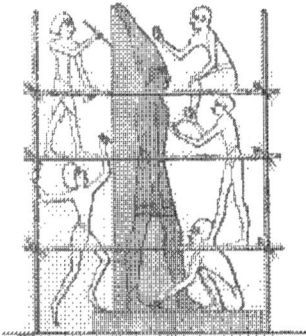

Fig. 38.—Egyptian Workmen. From Tombs, in Egypt.

The sculpture of Asia was less stupendous and massive than that of the Egyptians, although still distinguished by a certain grandeur of scale. The natural materials of the country determined the peculiarities of each. In Egypt vast blocks of granite led to gigantic propylæa and towering obelisks; whilst the clay soil of Assyria produced bricks, which were built into great masses, and then cased with slabs of alabaster, which was a soft and easily-wrought material in comparison with the harder stone. Muscular development and an indication of strength, sometimes amounting to brute force, are

peculiar to the Assyrian; and, generally speaking, there is a greater degree of roundness about all their sculptures. Both nations used bas-relief; but the Egyptian bas-reliefs always display a flatter surface with sharper edges to their figures. Projection is a characteristic of the Asiatic, while what is technically termed under-cutting is rarely to be seen among the Egyptians. The accompanying figures, from Khorsabad, the residence of Sargon, king of Assyria, and also to be seen at the palace of Sennacherib, at Kouyunjik, exhibit many distinctive peculiarities, in action, proportion, muscular development, and expression of the face. That many of the sculptures from Nineveh present greater refinement, as well as infinite variety of style, must be evident to all who have seen Mr. Layard's grand work upon Nineveh, or examined the treasures themselves in the National Museum; but the characteristics above alluded to are distinctly traceable in all. Layard quotes some curious passages illustrative of a direct influence exercised by the Assyrians upon the arts in Greece and Asia Minor. Sardanapalus, he says, had already founded Tarsus and Anchiale on the southern coast of Asia Minor; and in Eusebius he finds the curious statement that Sennacherib built a temple at Athens, and placed brass monuments in it, upon which his deeds were recorded.

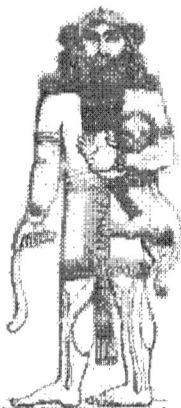

The influence of Persia and Assyria could only be transmitted to Greece through Asia Minor and Phœnicia,—an extensive tract of

country which separated these countries, and in the mountain inclosures of which
a distinct and original style of architecture already existed. Among the high
rocks of Lydia and Phrygia may still be seen many curiously-sculptured tombs,
all excavated in the natural rock, and adorned with ornaments chiefly composed
of squares and circles. Mr. Steuart thinks these widely-spread patterns were
intended as imitations of carpet work, for which these countries were anciently
celebrated. Another district, lying more towards the southern coast of Asia
Minor, the almost inac-
cessible Lycia, possesses
many tombs and monu-
ments of remarkable pecu-
liarity. The inhabitants
of the country, whenever
they appear in history, are
conspicuous for their independence; but from the
natural barriers which separated them from other
countries, their native art
seems to have exercised
no influence upon con-
temporary nations. They
fell at length, however,
under the dominion of
Persia; hence their monu-
ments in several instances
are devoted to Persian
subjects.

Fig. 14 —Tomb of Midas, in Phrygia.

Shortly before the time of Homer a great change appears to have taken
place in the settlements of the Grecian race. The scanty and unequal provision of nature drove many states to establish colonies in more fertile
countries. A large tribe had already descended from the northern plains,
and settled in the milder and more productive countries on the shores of the
Corinthian Gulf. Driving many of the primitive occupants to other lands,
they finally spread over the Peloponnesus.

From Athens, numbers spread to the coast of Asia Minor, and there
established themselves, living in communities and occupying towns which
seemed willing to adopt their customs, whilst the religion, which they
found already established, accorded with their own views. The Ionians
occupied twelve cities on the coast, of which the principal were Smyrna,

Miletus, and Samos. Most authorities now agree in regarding Smyrna as the birth-place of Homer. This opinion is confirmed by the preference and veneration with which he speaks of Athens, and of the divinities Neptune and Minerva.

The Ionian settlement in Asia Minor exercised a very important influence upon the arts in general. It was a means of establishing communications between the Asiatic and peninsular Greeks, which was kept alive by the civil and religious institutions common to both. In Caria and Lycia the inhabitants appear long to have enjoyed uninterrupted peace and security; and the arts of Sculpture and Painting, free from any of those retarding events which shook the nations around them, appear to have steadily advanced. We shall find, at a subsequent period, that, when talent was required, artificers returned from those colonies, and mainly contributed, by their skill and fertility of invention, to the grace and beauty of the Athenian city. Great changes soon took place in Metallurgy. The art of casting was discovered. The process of smelting, in which the ore was separated from the less pure substances, had long been known; but to run the molten metal into a previously formed mould was first devised by the Samians; for both Pausanias and Pliny agree in ascribing the invention to Rhœcus and Theodorus, natives of Samos. The casting of metal hollow, by means of a core, must however have been a much later invention.

Pliny (xxxiv. 4, 24) mentions a solid gold statue of Diana Anaïtis, which was hammered out of one piece. The ordinary mode of producing metal work on a large scale was to hammer plates of metal to the required thickness, and finish them upon a mould of wood or baked clay, riveting the different pieces with nails, or welding them in the ordinary way.

The enterprising spirit of the Greeks, even before the time of Homer, had led to many adventures by sea and land. Herodotus, in his first chapter, shows the early communication that Greece held with Egypt and Assyria. The Phœnicians, having exported Egyptian and Assyrian merchandise, carried it to Argos, at that time the most civilized of all the Grecian states; and this spirit was strengthened and regularly applied to commerce by the Milesians. Certain natives of Ionia and Caria found their way into Egypt, and were serviceable to Psammetichus, the king of that country, who allotted them lands and settlements near the mouth of the Nile. They remained under the protection of his successors during three generations, when a new dynasty arose, which confirmed to them the city of Naucratis. The people of Ægina, Samos, and Miletus erected Temples there to their particular Gods; and Amasis, the Egyptian king, to strengthen their friendship, dedicated statues and paintings of himself at Cyrene, Lindus, and Samos. Under these circumstances, unrestrained intercourse was maintained, and the venerable and more ancient art of the Nile poured its influence upon the character of an infant nation in Greece.

Pheido, tyrant of Argos, first introduced coinage. The earliest coins were lumps of copper and silver, stamped with a single device, in the same way as

signet seals were put upon pieces of lead or wax, and affixed to deeds. Of this practice some curious instances are recorded by Mr. Layard, who discovered sig-

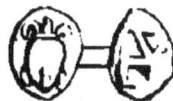

net seals in one of the Assyrian palaces, consisting of lumps of clay stamped with a ring, and which, judging from the impression still left of the texture on the other side, seem to have been attached to linen or canvas.

In the process of coining, the metal was melted and cast into an oblong roundish form; then laid upon a hard roughened surface or anvil, when it received the stamp of the distinctive emblem of the place where it

was struck,—the impression of the rough anvil on which it was placed still remaining on the back. Coins of Argos and Bœotia were distinguished by the form of a shield, Ægina by the simple form of a turtle, Ephesus by the effigy of a bee, and Corinth by a winged Pegasus.

The art of hardening metal had been discovered long before this time, even as early as the days of Homer; but a certain Glaucus, who appears to have lived much later, is said to have possessed the art of tempering iron by plunging it into water, and to have been the inventor of the process of laying one metal on another. A bowl wrought by him was dedicated to Apollo at Delphi by Alyattes, king of the Lydians, and father of Crœsus. In entering upon the historical period of Herodotus, we find Crœsus, king of Lydia, to be the centre around whom all Grecian events then turned. The geographical position of his country placed him equally in relation with the Greeks on both sides of the Ægean and the islands, on the one hand, and to Egypt on the other; and, as his wealth was enormous, he became master of all Asia Minor, except Lycia. He was of the race of the Mermnadæ. His ancestor, Gyges, on assuming the monarchy, sent many offerings to Delphi both of silver and gold, with iron inlaid,—the work of Glaucus of Chios, the inventor, as we have seen, of that art. In power and opulence Crœsus exceeded all who had preceded him; and having brought the Greeks under his sway, the rising power of the Persians, under their young king Cyrus, engaged his attention. He sought means to check its growth; and with this object strengthened his alliance with the Egyptians and Babylonians. Having provoked the hostility of the Persians by an incursion made into the territories of Cyrus, that monarch drove him back to his own capital, which, after a siege, was reduced, and Croesus himself fell into the hands of the enemy. Lydia thus became a Persian province. A satrapy was established at Sardis, and communications were opened between the empire of Cyrus and the western nations, the civilizing influence of which was felt, not only in Greece but in Sicily and all the Grecian colonies.

The scarcity of stone in Assyria rendered the employment of wood and clay in their buildings inevitable. Their brick walls were square and remarkably solid; but the only wood at hand being the date, the palm, and the poplar, the columns of wood were necessarily very slender. According to Herodotus the houses of Sardis were of reeds; and such of them as were built of brick had thatched roofs.

In a country where vegetable life has a tendency to develop itself, the eye of a workman, in using wood, becomes naturally accustomed to curves and curls in the young shoots, and in the graceful tendrils of various clinging plants. Peculiar curves and tendril forms are to be seen in the architecture of Khorsabad and

Fig. 38.—Ionic Channel.

Fig. 40.—Ionic Detail.

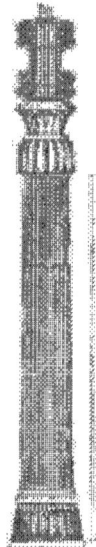

*Fig. 42.
Ionic Base.*

Persepolis, identical with those features which are now regarded as distinctive of the Ionic order (Fig. 39), 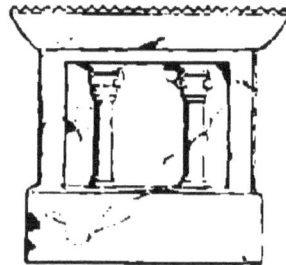. This is strengthened by many other shapes and mouldings connected with the same order, but especially by the volute and the beautiful pattern called the guilloche, ███████ . These Asiatic forms were various, and expressed with great natural truth (Figs. 41 and 42). Indeed

Fig. 41.—Ionic Column of Persepolis.

the beautiful features of the Ionic order may be said to have originated in the varied forms of the vegetable kingdom.

In many parts of Greece, where trees were comparatively rare, a different material was employed for building temples. The durability of stone accorded with the permanence of shelter required for their gods; and, as soon as tools were discovered adapted to rough-shape them, huge blocks were brought together, forming constructions not unlike our Druidical temples of Stonehenge and Abury. Within such buildings whole communities, forming an association resembling the Panhellenium, might assemble for worship. The Doric order, therefore, may be considered to have sprung from the use of stone. Buildings of this magnitude were permanent; the principle was recognised, and a marked style of architecture arose, distinguished by its massiveness and simplicity of ornament. The luxurious curves we have just traced in the Asiatic building are wanting, and the whole character becomes significantly reversed,—solidity and permanence being the leading characteristics. The two leading styles or orders of architecture,

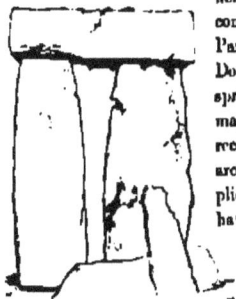

Fig. 43.—Tomb near Phigaleia.

Doric and Ionic, were thus established. The former developed itself among the fixed inhabitants of a stony country; whilst the latter arose in the vegetable luxuriance of an Asiatic land.

The Greeks, who left their native country to establish themselves on the coasts of Asia, thus found the germ already existing in the towns that sheltered them. Their taste improved and perfected it; and by their means it was transferred to Athens with their own name, by way of distinction.

Admitting a less remote date than that assigned by Colonel Leake to the oldest temple of Corinth (Fig. 44), we still find that the Doric order was fully developed, and exhibits all its characteristics in perfect detail long before the Ionian settlement in Egypt.

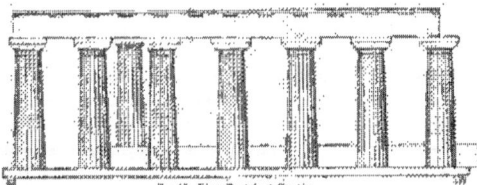

Fig. 44.—Doric Temple at Corinth.

The form of letters and modes of writing are important in determining the period at which a work of art was produced. After the establishment of the Greek alphabet, the form of its letters underwent a series of changes, the dates of which are sufficiently known to establish a parallel variation in the progress of sculpture and painting.

Pliny expresses his belief that the Assyrians had always known the use of letters; and recent discoveries seem to bear out this remark; for almost every fragment of remote antiquity recently discovered at Nineveh bears characters perfectly expressed. At the same time there is no good reason to suppose that writing was generally employed in the time of the Trojan war. The few instances mentioned by Homer, as indicating even an approach to writing, do not extend beyond mere signs. In the Iliad (vii. 175), each hero marks his lot, and they are all collected in a helmet. The first taken out is handed round by the herald, until Ajax recognises the sign as his own. Again, the treacherous messages given to Bellerophon (σήματα λυγρά—Il. vi. 168), appear to have been mere signs which could only have been understood by Iobates to whom they were addressed. In Assyria, writings on stone and metal passed from left to right, while those written in ink or colour upon a smooth surface passed from right to left, or retrograde. The Greeks at first employed the latter method, especially in inscriptions of a single line, like the following, found by Colonel Leake on a helmet at Olympia.

It records the name of the workman; and is interesting as exhibiting the letter Koppa, ρ, originally contained in the Greek alphabet, but disused at a very early period. This letter, the first in the inscription, reading backwards, answers to our letter K, and occurs in the most ancient coins of Corinth and Croton. At this period the long O, Omega (Ω), was not known; therefore the common O was used on every occasion. The variations in art agree with this; for the earliest coins in the island of Cos are stamped with a rude figure, accompanied by the name written ϘΟΣ. The next stage exhibits improvement in the form, with the name spelt ΚΟΣ; and, lastly, great freedom and mastery of art is seen, and the Omega (Ω) substituted in the name ΚΩΣ. An inscription from right to left occurs on a vase, the letters of which are painted very thick.

In most of these genuine early inscriptions there is great inequality of size in the letters; the O is generally very small, and the first stroke of the A and N very much longer than the rest of the letter; the second leg of the former being generally wanting. The short lines of E usually slope downwards, and indeed there is almost invariably a slope forward of the whole letter E.

The next variety in early inscriptions is a double course given to the letters. The lines read in alternate directions. If the first reads from right to left, the next will read from left to right, and the third again from right to left, and so on. This style of writing is called Boustrophedon—Βου-στροφη-δόν, or ox-turning-wise, because oxen thus draw the plough. A good example of this arrangement is seen in an inscription brought from Leucadia. In this example, the direction of each line can always be perceived by observing which way the letter E is turned. But the best specimen is the Sigæan inscription, now in the Elgin room of the British Museum. Although scarcely legible now, it was copied, in a more perfect state, by Chishull and Chandler. The stone has, since their visit, been supposed to possess healing powers, and the characters upon it to be talismanic. Hence the people afflicted with rheumatic pains have

```
Ǝ MOTOΔIΑ⌐
NEΣIⱭΔA TOΣTO
Ǝ ϘO,TIƎ ◁O Ϙ
OϘAϘΑ ΔΣIΜΕ Α
ΜO JJ OꞀΑ⌐OꞀO
OΣ PΑΙꞀOEΕΙΛ
·AM O ΥOOΜO
ꞀΕΙΝ Μ ΑΤΕΕΛOↃ
ƎΥΑΤΑΣ,Γ\ƎϘ
Μ ꞀoⳆLΕ◁ϘΑꞀOↃ
```

been made to roll upon it by the Greek priests, to the serious injury of the inscription, the middle parts of which have by these means been almost obliterated. The form of the stone is tall and narrow. It contains two inscriptions, the lower of which is considered to be the more ancient, and is here given. The darker letters show what still remains visible; and the lighter ones are copied from Chandler's work. Visconti thought that the marble was actually a herma intended to support a bust, as the inscription begins, "I am of Phanodicus,"—"the gift" being understood. (Icon.

Greeque, p. 5.) He substitutes "the portrait," instead of "the gift," between the words I am of Phanodicus, and considers it a dedication, by Phanodicus, of his portrait to his native town. This monument is regarded as one of the most ancient specimens of palæography. Its celebrity far exceeds that of any other known. Louis XIV., in the fulness of his power, made several attempts to obtain it; but in vain. Another Boustrophedon occurs on a very early coin of Agrigentum. An ancient letter, the digamma, which imparted a sound like an f, and was written F, also disappeared at a very early period; but it is seen on the Elean tablet, and also on an inscription on a coin of Elis,

The Egyptians imparted to the Greeks the use of papyrus, the most easy and convenient material for writing known to the ancients. It was originally called *Hyblos*: hence, probably, the Greek word βίβλος, a book.

Long before historic times a colony passed from Lydia, a province of Asia Minor, to the northern coast of Italy, where the Pelasgi, a people celebrated for their skill in building walls like those of Tiryns and Argos, were already established under the name of Ombrici. (Plin. Hist. Nat. iii. cap. v. 8.) The new comers called themselves Rhasena, while the Greeks called them Tyrrheni, and the Romans Tusci. Among these people the arts flourished; and some of the most important specimens of early architecture are to be found in this country. They appear always to have maintained a close intercourse with Greece; and it is within *their* sepulchres that the most beautiful specimens of the pure Greek vase have been found. Indeed, the vases commonly called Etruscan are of pure Greek workmanship, inscribed with genuine Greek characters, and very different from the real Etruscan productions, which are much less refined, and often border upon the grotesque.

Etruria contains many examples of solid masonry and ponderous walls, rivalling those of Greece in magnitude and antiquity. The distinctive character of the architecture of this nation is the use of the arch, formerly regarded as a Roman invention; but History has corrected this opinion, and informs us that the artists who accompanied Tarquin (a Tuscan Lucumo of Corinthian descent) to Rome, aided him in adorning the city with temples and statues, besides forming roads, quays, and sewers. It teaches, moreover, that in the latter the arch was employed as the best means of support. A yet more ancient origin must be claimed for the arch; it was known to the Persians, and existed in very early times among the Assyrians; for Mr. Layard informs us that the arch is found in a position which renders it certainly coeval with the most ancient portions of the Nimroud palaces. Nor was it unknown to the Egyptians, as we learn from Wilkinson's great work, vol. iii. p. 316, *et seq.* It was in use among the Egyptians in the reign of Amunoph I., as early as the year 1540 before our era. It has been inferred, because not seen in their buildings, that the Greeks were ignorant of the principle of the arch; but this will hardly seem probable, when we reflect that in Egypt and Assyria the arch had long been employed, and that the people of Asia Minor derived their knowledge of it from the Persians, and, in all probability, transferred it to a nation beyond Greece itself. Nor is it likely that a people so remarkable for their perception and spirit of inquiry should have been ignorant of its advantages, had it suited their tastes to make use of it. The first arches known, both in Egypt and Assyria, are of brick. In early Greece, as well as Etruria, there are many examples of arch-shaped apertures being cut through walls, and even low arch-topped galleries excavated in massive walls built in horizontal courses. This pseudo or false arch must always be carefully distinguished from the real wedge-made construction. The true arch here noticed, of which we give examples in Plate I., is seen in an Egyptian building at Thebes; in the remains of an Etruscan cloaca on the Marta; and in the Gate of Volaterra.

Instances of apertures cut through the wall, and represented in the same Plate, are taken from Negni, Mycenæ, and Alindæ in Asia Minor. The excavated arch form is from Cervetri, in Etruria, which precisely resembles a tomb discovered in Rome by Sir William Gell, and bears also a strong resemblance to the Treasuries of Mycenæ and Orchomenus. The example here selected also exhibits the horizontal courses of stone. Among the oldest sculptures discovered at Nineveh are several representations of arched gateways in city walls, of which Fig. 54 is an example.

Before leaving the architectural examination of this period, it may be useful to pause, and consider the varieties of form and arrangement observable in the temples of antiquity, as well as the terms used in the work.

The early temple was constructed like ordinary habitations, but with greater care and of more solid materials. The chief part of the building was a four-walled chamber or CELLA, having a door at one end. This inclosed the symbol of divinity, and was for the most part adorned externally with columns which supported the roof when it extended beyond the upright walls.

The arrangement of columns is highly important, because, according to their character and position, all buildings are named and classified. We sometimes find that the side walls of the cella are prolonged beyond the door, and these projections are termed παραστάδες, or ANTÆ. The roof is carried forward, and extends over them with the occasional support of two columns placed before the jambs of the door.

When the roof was so long as to extend in front of these, a row of columns was required, thus, This arrangement is called PROSTYLE; and, where this is repeated at the back also, the temple becomes AMPHI-PROSTYLE. Large temples, of necessity, had entrances at the back as well as at the front.

The roof most generally projected on all four sides beyond the walls, and then side rows of columns became necessary, and caused the arrangement called PERIPTERAL.

These rows of columns were sometimes doubled, thus, and in this way the temple becomes DIPTERAL; but where the temple was too large for the beams of the roof to span, a square range of columns was added within the cella, thus, The roof then only extended from these columns to the walls, leaving space in the centre open to the sky; from which circumstance the build- ing was called HYPÆTHRAL. The inclosure, or

PLATE I.—EARLIEST SPECIMENS OF THE ARCH.

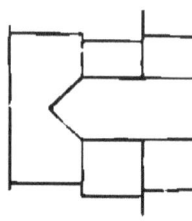

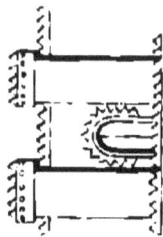

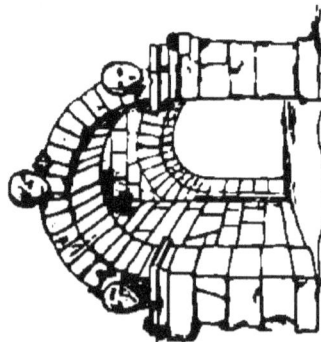

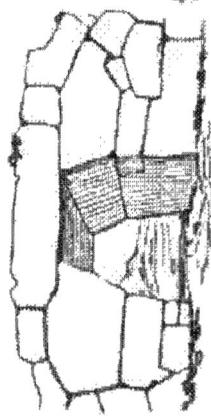

close in which the temple stood, was called ΤΕΜΕΝΟΣ (τέμενος). It was frequently planted with trees, surrounded by a colonnade called PERIBOLUS (περίβολος). The importance of columns in ancient times may be gathered from the fact, that at the building of the Ephesian Temple of Diana, each of its one hundred and twenty-seven columns was presented by an Asiatic prince. The columns of the temples at Aphrodisia and Euromus, in Caria, still existing, bear inscribed tablets, which exhibit the names of the various persons who contributed them.

The number of columns in the front of **a temple is an important means of** distinction, and temples are described accordingly. The most ordinary number in front seems to have been eight, OCTOSTYLE; the greatest ten, DECASTYLE; and the least four and six, TETRASTYLE and HEXASTYLE. The interior of the cella they termed NAOS (ναός); and that part of the building without the front door PRONAOS, or PRODOMOS (πρόδομος), whilst that at the back was called POSTICUM, or OPISTHODOMUS (ὀπισθόδομος). The walk round the outside, between the columns and the wall, was termed PERISTYLIUM, or AMBULATORY.

The column itself is divided into various parts, the principal of which are the shaft, capital, and base. With the exception of the base, all orders of columns have these divisions in common; but in early times only two **orders or styles** were distinctly marked. Colonel Leake makes the important observation, that the Ionic order was almost always employed for buildings upon a level surrounded with hills; whilst the massive and majestic Doric was best displayed **on a lofty rock. The columns** of the Doric temple at Nemea, he observes, situated in **a narrow plain,** have proportions not less slender than some examples of **the Ionic order.** It was, in fact, situation that determined the Greeks in all the varieties of their architecture. "So far," he says, "from being the slaves of rule, there are no two examples of the Doric, much less of the Ionic, that perfectly resemble each other either in proportion, construction, or ornament." (*Leake's Asia Minor*, p. 259.)

The Ionic is distinguished by elegant mouldings, and by the volutes already described. The Doric, on the contrary, is characteristically heavy in proportion, and is marked by a peculiarity in that portion of the building which rests immediately upon the columns. This remarkable feature is a square tablet fluted with upright grooves. It is repeated at equal distances in a row all round the building, and is called the TRIGLYPH (τρίγλυφος). The square space left between the triglyphs is called the METOPE (μετόπη). These form the distinctive features of the Doric, as the volute and base characterise the Ionic order. The Doric column, be it observed, has no base. The shafts of both styles present a varied surface by fluting or long upright channeling; but

those of the Doric are larger and shallower in proportion to the circumference of the column. Their form also varies remarkably. The section of a part of the Doric shaft will show that the flutes or channels are immediately close together, leaving only a sharp edge between them. In the Ionic, on the contrary, these hollows are deeper, leaving some of the curved surface of the extreme circumference, as shown in the other section. The beautiful patterns, the honeysuckle and palmette, are frequently seen upon buildings of the Ionic order; but we are most familiar with them in vase paintings. The horizontal portion of a temple, which rests upon the columns, is called the ARCHITRAVE.

The next and more richly adorned course is the FRIEZE; whilst the CORNICE hangs over and crowns the whole, connecting itself, at the same time, with the roof. These three horizontal members together are called the ENTABLATURE. The triangular space in front, between the sloping roof, is termed the AETOS (ἀετός), or TYMPANUM; and was made use of for the display of sculpture. The framing, or cornice, which inclosed these triangular spaces is not uncommonly named the PEDIMENT, or FASTIGIUM.

Few examples remain to us of the very early period of architecture. That of Corinth has been already noticed; and there are also temples of a very remote antiquity at Præstum, the ancient Posidonia, in Italy : but, as our object in these pages is to examine works more especially pertaining to Greece Proper, we must forbear further mention of them.

The oldest example of the Ionic order is at Sardis. Two columns yet remain, and they are supposed to have formed part of the Temple of Cybele, which was destroyed when the city was burnt by a band of Greeks who invaded it, B.C. 499. The Temple itself was most probably erected under the last dynasty of Lydian Kings, which terminated B.C. 546; and it is certainly older than the Ionic Temple of Juno at Samos, built by Polycrates.

The same object which we had in view, in comparing the varieties in architecture, renders necessary a few remarks on the more leading shapes of VASES. To these are added the names by which each particular form is recognised. It must, however, be here borne in mind, that these illustrations are for shape alone, and altogether irrespective of size.

The painted vases of this period are of a very pale tint and dull surface. The figures on them are of a reddish or purple colour, adorned with simple patterns. Perhaps the most ancient vase, of which the purpose is known, is an Amphora, discovered by Mr. Burgon, at Athens, in 1813. It was found buried in the earth outside the ancient wall of the city, close to the Portæ Acharnicæ.

PLATE II.—VASES.

Fig 36.—Pyxis

Fig 38.—

Fig 37.—Aryballus

Fig 39.—Lecythus

Fig 40.—Lecythus

Fig 41.—

Fig 44.—Cylix

Fig 42.—Hydria

Fig 43.—Amphora

ΤΟΜΑΘΕΝΕΟΝΛΟΝΕΙΜ

Fig 45.—Minerva, from a Panathenaic Vase.

Fig 46.—Alabastrum

Fig 46.—Œnochoe

Fig 47.—Cyathus

Fig 48.—Pithos

Fig 49.—Rhyton

It contained burnt bones, a Lecythus, and five smaller vessels. The extreme antiquity of this vase is proved by the details of the painting, the form of the letters, and by the condition of the burnt human bones still remaining in it. The figure on the front of the vase is given in Fig. 64. It is painted in black, red, and white; and the inscription down the left side (Τον Αθενεθεν αθλον: εμι,—"I am one of the prizes from Athens," the short ε being used for η, and the o for ω,) shows that the prize served afterwards for the tomb of the victor. Other instances are known, in which a prize vase has been buried in the earth without any building near it; but in every case, except the one before us, an outer vase of a coarser material was added for protection. The figure here represented is the Goddess Minerva. The serpents of the ægis appear on her right side. The owl cannot be seen, but is painted upon the neck on the other side of the vase. Her round shield is filled with a dolphin, such as appears on the early coins of Zancle, afterwards Messene.

Another early representation of the Goddess occurs in a sitting figure lately discovered at Athens. It is of stone, but apparently copied from a wooden statue,—from the Minerva

Polias itself,—according to the opinion of the late C. Ottfried Müller. The ægis hangs like a tippet round the neck, and the boss in front was originally painted with the Gorgon's head; but all traces of colour have now disappeared from every part of the statue. The arrange-

Fig. 70.—Minerva.

Fig. 70.

ment of the hair in plaited tresses is very similar to that of the Polledrara statue (Fig. 22). Another attempt at the human form is shown in the fragment of a statue recently found at Athens (Fig. 71). It is characterised by extreme anatomical ignorance, but still exhibits peculiarities which are traceable throughout the whole course of early Greek art: these are—narrowness at the hips, broad chest, a peculiar physiognomy arising from a cat-like arrangement of the eyes, and great breadth of the lower lip. The head is better seen in the enlarged drawing (Fig. 72); and the peculiarities of the face are more strongly developed in the standing figure holding a pigeon (Fig. 77).

The ombre chinois, here given from the lid of a vase discovered by Mr.

Dodwell, at Mertem, near Corinth (Fig. 73), is an interesting sciagraph, representing a boar hunt, with a multitude of figures; the names, in addition, being written over each figure. Dodwell assigns the date of its execution to about 700 B.C. The names next to the two human-headed winged sphinxes at the bottom—AΓAMEMNON and ΘΕΡΣΑΝΔΡΟΣ—are known in heroic history. The general form of the letters is very like that seen in the inscription on a coin of Agrigentum (page 20). The names all read from left to right; but the letter E is made like a Ⅾ, and the Σ like an M. There is a genuine character about the composition, very different from those prepared at a later period in imitation of this style. The drawing, indeed, is laboured, and executed with evident difficulty; but the attitudes, especially of the four figures next to Agamemnon, are excellent, if considered with regard to the restrictions of a flat black colour upon a light ground. In all the sciagraphs referred to, traces may be seen of a fine

Fig. 73.—Drawing of the Dodwell Vase.

Fig. 74.—Chimæra by Archael. Painting from Etruscan Vase.

white outline here and there upon the black figure. This was produced by scratching with a sharp point into the clay, after the colour was dry. Such lines are technically called INCISED. The last peculiarity to be remarked of this period is, that the skin of the females is always painted white, whilst that of the males remains black. The white painting was subsequently added just before the incised lines. This is seen in the Burgon vase. Many other parts, such as patterns and borders on drapery, were heightened with red, and old men's hair touched on with white. All these peculiarities—pale ground, white skins, black skins, red spots, and incised lines—are to be found united in the accompanying group, representing the flight of Æneas from Troy. (Fig. 74.) The story is well told, and the action of the children displays all the peculiarity of this style of art.

Deities and heroes, on painted vases of this period, are all invested with the same type of humanity. We do not, as in later art, distinguish Mercury from Neptune by his more graceful form, but by the name written over the figure, or by his well-known attributes—the caduceus, the petasus, and the chlamys; just as in early poetry an especial distinctive epithet is appropriated to each particular hero or divinity.

74.—FROM THE ACTUAL AGES OF PISISTRATUS, B.C. 560, TO THE PERSIAN INVASION, B.C. 490.

The rule of Pisistratus over the Athenians was contemporaneous with that of Tarquin Superbus at Rome; and we find, as a remarkable coincidence, that both their descendants were expelled from power in the same year. Pisistratus died in the quiet enjoyment of power, B. C. 527; but his son Hipparchus, who succeeded him, was slain at the very period when Tarquin was obliged to quit his kingdom. Hippias fled to Persia, as Tarquin fled to Clusium.

Pisistratus, like Tarquin, seems to have greatly favoured literature and the arts, but more especially architecture. We read of his commencing the great Athenian temple dedicated to Jupiter Olympius. This building appears to have been originally Doric; but at a later period—that of Antiochus—it was altered to the Corinthian style. He built a temple to the Pythian Apollo at Athens, in which tripods were placed; and also constructed the fountain at Athens with nine streams, called Enneacrunus (ἐννεάκρουνος), through which the stream Callirrhoë supplied the inhabitants with purest water. Fountains of this kind are frequently represented on early vases. A painting from one of them, in the collection of the late Mr. Rogers, a portion of which is copied in Fig. 75, shows the porch, with one of the streams flowing from a lion's mouth. Women are seen passing to and fro with pitchers or hydriæ on their heads, and engaged in conversation, while the foremost woman is filling her pitcher.

Fig. 13.—Fountain of the Woman's Painting Vase.

This vase painting, which represents the fountain of Callirrhoë, with the inscription ΚΑΛΙΡΕΚΡΕΝΕ (καλλίρρη κρήνη.—"the fair flowing fountain,") has been shown as an illustration of the architecture of this age. The Minerva also (Fig. 64) deserves a passing notice, as regards style and treatment. A much greater freedom of action and drawing will be observed; but as respects treatment, everything remains as flat as possible. The draperies are pressed so flat, that not a line of the pattern on any dress is discomposed. The eyes are drawn at full length, a peculiarity before remarked on, and existing in the works of the Egyptians and other oriental nations. The mouths, even where the women are conversing, are quite closed, and indicated by a single line only. There is no attempt at foreshortening.

During this reign (B.C. 548) the temple at Delphi was burnt, and in the account of its rebuilding we trace the first record of marble being used for architectural purposes. Herodotus tells us that the Alcmæonidæ built the frontage of the temple at Delphi of Parian marble, and found it a more beautiful material than had been expected; for they had contracted to make use of common stone. Dipænis and Scyllis, natives of Crete, are described by Pliny as distinguished for their statues in marble. They were already famous, he says, when Cyrus ascended the throne of Persia; so that their date is tolerably fixed. He tells us, moreover, that an oracle spoke in their favour, when they refused to complete some works (xxxvi. 4). They always used the purest white marble from Paros (xxxvi. 5). Long before their time, he adds, a man of Chios, named Melas, was a worker in marble; and he was only compared with them from the similar nature of the material used.

Pisistratus is said to have erected a temple to Minerva upon the Athenian Acropolis, which was afterwards replaced by the Parthenon of Pericles. Hesychius says, that the former building measured fifty feet less than the other. He does not state expressly that it occupied the same site; but he speaks of them comparatively. Remains of a previous building have been discovered beneath the Parthenon; but it is probable that the temple of Minerva Polias was the original one, and that a second building was commenced by the side of it on a grander scale. The sacred well, the olive tree, and the tombs of Cecrops and Erectheus, could not be removed. Hence the lesser edifice, throughout the most flourishing times, retained a peculiar sanctity; and we find that the most solemn rites were performed in that building rather than in its more stately neighbour, the Parthenon.

Fig. 76.—Fragment from the Acropolis.

A relic of sculpture belonging to the Parthenon of Pisistratus, or at least to a building of his period, has been recently discovered at Athens. It seems, by its proportions, to have originally adorned one of the metopes of a Doric temple (Fig. 76). The subject is a female stepping into a car. The form of her drapery and the arrangement of the hair precisely resemble the sculpture from the Harpy Monument at Xanthus. We know that many portions of the Hecatompedon were built into the north wall of the Acropolis; and numerous frag-

ments of columns, and a range of triglyphs, are observable there to this
day. In the execution of this metope, great attention
has been paid to details of the folds;
and a nearer approach to movement
than in the Xanthian monument is
evident.

Similar to the above are two figures,
displaying great carefulness of execution, although of different materials.
(Figs. 77, 78.) The one of clay, brought
by Lord Strangford from Greece, and
now in the Museum at Canterbury,
represents a female with hair plaited,
somewhat resembling that of the Minerva Polias (Fig. 70). The drapery is
carefully modelled, although still very
formal. The other figure, holding a
pomegranate, represents a female, probably Proserpine.

Hitherto every indication of drapery
that we have met with in Greek sculp-
ture consists of a tight-fitting dress, or a vague marking of the limbs under a
cloak; but no attempt to firmly express a fold. The early Greeks covered the
naked form in their statues with coloured pat-
terns, evidently to suggest the idea of clothing.
They afterwards began to mark the edges of the
garments more clearly, and at last succeeded in
imitating the zig-zag lines caused by the bottom
of a series of plaits, as in the back view of the
Canterbury figure (Fig. 77 a). In these figures,
however, for the first time we observe an attempt
beyond this. The dress of the figure (77)
displays a curved fold as her left hand raises it.
The plaits on the back of the metope figure
(Fig. 76) are curved; but in the sitting female
(Fig. 78) there is no bend in the drapery from
knee to knee, as would be natural, and as we
might expect, from the zig-zag and folds of
the rest of the drapery being so well done and cleverly arranged. This figure
was found at Chiusi. The limbs are of separate pieces, and attached to the

body by metal pins; even the head is moveable, and the body having been hollowed out was found to contain ashes. A bright red colour was traceable on the drapery, on the sandals, and on the sides of the seat.

The sculptures of Selinus in Sicily, supposed to have been executed a few years previous to the accession of Pisistratus, demand our notice, as being the most important architectural sculptures yet discovered, and ranking second only to those

of Athens and Ægina. They formed the metopes of two temples, and were discovered in 1823 by Messrs. Angell and Harris. The principal subjects are, —Hercules carrying off two robbers; and Perseus, in the presence of Minerva, cutting off the head of Medusa (Fig. 70). Since that time other metopes have been discovered by the Duke Serra di Falco, in the same place. The material of which they are composed is a calcareous tufa, the coarse grains of which are filled up with cement and a coating of paint; the extremities, however, are of marble. Statues so formed were called ACROLITHS. The proportions of these figures are very short and broad, and the muscularity of the joints, especially in Hercules and Perseus, is very remarkable. The faces have all the ugliness which has hitherto characterised the sculptures exhibited on these pages, and the physiognomy is a violent exaggeration of the face seen in Figs. 71 and 72. Minerva is represented clothed in a peplos. It is quite simple and plain. All accessories must have been added in colour alone; and no Gorgon's head or helmet is indicated. In the other metope Hercules appears without either club or lion's skin. The figures are in high relief. The heads are presented in front, whilst the feet and legs are turned sideways, in a manner resembling the figure from Nineveh (Fig. 33; see also Fig. 89, postea). The limbs are remarkably broad, and much flattened externally; their outline presents equally convex lines on the opposite sides. There is little feeling or attempt at anatomical accuracy to be perceived in these groups; and the hair is very remarkably expressed; there is also a curious parallel between these works and the early coins of Macedonia. In both the same clumsiness of proportion and breadth of limb are visible, but more especially on the coins of Lete and Orescos. The early coinage of Thasos displays very clumsy figures, which is the more remarkable, as this city produced Polygnotus, the painter,—one of the greatest artists of his age,—at a period not very distant from that to which these coins belong.

Portraiture, both in painting and sculpture, had already acquired sufficient importance to be deemed an honorable testimonial of friendship. Solon, the relative of Pisistratus, when he visited Crœsus, told him that the Argives had caused statues to be made of the youths Cleobis and Biton, and had dedicated them to the god at Delphi, in commemoration of their piety. (Herod. i. 31.) Crœsus himself dedicated to the same divinity a golden statue, said to be the portrait of his baking woman. Amasis, king of Egypt, sent to Polycrates two statues of himself carved in wood at Samos, as an assurance of his friendly disposition; and to his father-in-law Arcesilaus, king of Cyrene, he sent his own portrait.

There is, in the French collection, a remarkable vase painting, which represents Arcesilaus, king of Cyrene, surrounded by slaves and attendants, packing silphium,—a celebrated article of commerce in that country. The king's name is written over his head; and, although this picture cannot have any value as a likeness, it is important as a production of antiquity. The first instances of portrait statues being dedicated at the Olympian Games occur about thirteen years after the accession of Pisistratus, and at the time when the Persians captured Sardis (Pausanias, vi. 18, 5), when statues of the victorious athletes—Praxidamas of Ægina and Rhexibius of Opuntia—were dedicated in Olympia. The statue of Rhexibius was made of the wood of the fig-tree, that of Praxidamas of cypress wood (B. C. 548, Olymp. 59). On the expulsion of the Pisistratidæ, Antinor was employed to make statues of Harmodius and Aristogiton, which were afterwards carried off by Xerxes to Susa, but restored by Alexander of Macedonia.

Pliny speaks of Cimon of Cleonæ, who invented foreshortening, and who attempted to represent the features of the face viewed in every possible direction. (Pliny, xxxv. 8, 34.) The period when Cimon lived is not known with certainty; but his invention and method of study are eras in art too important for his name to pass unmentioned.

A remarkable bas-relief, probably of this period, was discovered at Samothrace, which exhibits very fairly the combination of the pictorial with sculpturesque treatment. The relief is very low; and but for the description affixed to it, this outline might be supposed to represent a vase painting. (Fig. 80.) The Homeric names of Agamemnon, Talthybius, and part of the name of Ebour, the maker of the Trojan horse, are inscribed close to the figures. The first name reads from right to left, but that of Talthybius from left to right. The form of the Theta, in the latter name, is worthy of observation. It is an O with a cross within it,—a form not at all uncommon in inscriptions of this period. These names, and those on the Dodwell vase (Fig. 73), are fair examples of the kind of inscriptions Pausanias saw on the chest of Cypselus—"winding characters, difficult to be understood." The age had its grotesque characters as well as its more dignified features; and certain strange combinations of the human form with that of the brute first appeared about this time. From such monstrosities sprang that noble conception the Centaur, which stands in rivalry with the human form among the finest sculptures of the Parthenon—the animal form representing brute force—irresistible strength,—as the rushing impetuous bull best expresses headstrong might; for we find a bull frequently used as the type of a rushing river,—the Achelous for instance. The coin (Fig. 81) bears a representation of the river Gelas, with the name written over the figure, which is a combination of the human head with the horns and body of an ox. The eye also is here shown in full length. Another figure of the period (Fig. 82) exhibits a man with a horse's ears,

tail, and hoofs. This may bo taken as a Centaur; for a similar figure appears on early Macedonian coins; and in later times a similar group occurs, but with greater equine develop-

Fig. 83 is a form of the Centaur by no means rare upon vases of this period: in fact, the next stage to the conception so beautifully executed by Phidias, and seen by Pausanias upon the chest of Cypselus, who thus describes it:—"In the next place, a Centaur presents him-

Fig. 83

self to the view, whose hinder feet are those of a horse, and his front feet those of a man." (Paus. v. 19, p. 57.) Chiron, the Centaur, is also so represented on the celebrated vase Clitias; a winged female figure, holding a lion and leopard, being also on the same vase,—a description which perfectly corresponds with a Diana upon the same chest. Pausanias describes every figure upon the chest very minutely; being assisted by the name written over each character "in Boustrophedon fashion," as well as by the twisted words already alluded to.

In reviewing the leading features of Greek Art, in the age of which we have been speaking, let us avail ourselves of the words of Flaxman:—"The early arts of Greece," he says, "were interrupted in their progress by a succession of political commotions and destructive wars; and we scarcely perceive any improvement in them until the time of the Seven Sages, of Pythagoras and Æsop, who were all contemporaries about 130 years before Phidias." "The benign influence of their example," he adds, "was felt in the arts of design, and prepared them for that beauty and perfection with which they were subsequently graced in the time of Pericles, Alexander, and his successors."

ILL — FROM THE BATTLE OF MARATHON, B.C. 400, TO THE DEFEAT OF THE PERSIANS, B.C. 464.

The reader may feel some disappointment at the want of beauty in the illustrations hitherto presented to him; but it must be remembered that the most refined period of art was of comparative short duration, forming only one step of an extensive series, the whole of which course we propose to follow. Greater attention is required, in treating of this rising period, than is needful in the corresponding changes which took place when the arts were hastening to their extinction. The public games of the ancients and the constant habit of bodily exercise must have greatly tended to increase the knowledge of the human form, and to facilitate its representation. The athlete, or contenders in these games, were then as closely observed and judged of as horses are in our modern races. The build of the man, his bones, sinews, and proportion of limb, and, above all, his action, were the primary objects of attention; and this study would enable the artist to express the sinews, muscles, and bones with reference to motion, whilst the expression of the face, or general physiognomy, would seem to have received little or no attention. We accordingly find, in works of art of this period, the limbs clearly delineated, with only muscle enough upon them to perform the functions of motion without overloading the joints,—characteristics different from those observed in the sculptures of Selinus, and on the coins of Northern Greece, where the limbs were so encumbered with flesh as to destroy all possibility of motion. Examples, after the change had taken place in the proportion of the limbs, will be seen in the annexed figures. Figure 84 (a bronze statue in the early style, now preserved in the Louvre, and supposed originally to have held a torch in the left hand) is curiously inlaid with silver, both in the eyebrows, nipples, and lips. The foot also bears an inscription in silver letters, thus,

AΘAΝΑ
ΔΕΚΑΤΑΝ

The eyes are hollow. Fig. 85 is a very interesting figure in low relief, discovered near Marathon, and is one of the finest specimens of tinted sculpture yet discovered. The figure still remains at Athens, and represents a Greek warrior in full armour, named Aristion, as we learn from the inscription in large letters beneath. The dress perfectly coincides with that which we observe on the painted vases of the period. The same costume was, however, retained with very little variation in the time of Pericles, and is exhibited among the horsemen on the frieze of the Parthenon. The feet of this figure are remarkably large, the toes strongly pronounced, the hair very formally arranged, and the same slope in the eye formerly observed. The muscles of the arm are extremely well marked, and there is a general truthfulness in the joints, although the action is stiff and formal. The same remarks

apply to the bas-relief seen and copied by Dodwell at Homaiko, near the Cephissus. (Fig. 86.) It was lately discovered that the name of the artist had been inscribed on lead, and inserted into the body of the first of these three figures,—an expedient evidently adopted by the artist to perpetuate his fame. History mentions several other instances in which artists made use of similar expedients to preserve their names from oblivion—expedients which would seem to intimate a jealous reluctance on the part of their patrons to make their names known. On the foundations of a Pharos, one architect engraved his name in large letters which he covered over with cement, on which more perishable material he inscribed the name of the monarch in whose honour the monument was erected. In the course of time the cement has disappeared, and with it the external inscription, while the name of the architect is permanently displayed. The architects, Saurus and Batrachus, introduced into the capitals of their buildings the figures of a lizard and a frog,—these being symbolic of their respective names. The Marathon figure (Fig. 85) has the name of the artist, ("Εργον Αριστοκλεος,—"The work of Aristocles"); from which it may be inferred that the prohibition against artists appending their names applied more especially to statues of the gods.

The coins of this period correspond with the larger sculpture, in exhibiting increased delicacy in the execution of the figures. They now bear elaborate compositions on both sides. Those of Athens, however, retain their old type and general appearance. The archaic head of Minerva, with all the peculiarities exhibited in the annexed engraving, (Fig. 87,) remained upon her money till the times of Pericles. There seems to have been a great variety in the coins

of other states during this period; but the coins issued from Magna Græcia and Sicily far surpass those of the States of Greece Proper in their execution.

The manner in which the hair was represented in different eras is curious. At first no attempt was made to distinguish it; the features of the face being all-important. Round lumps in front were sometimes added, to suggest curls, or to mark a particular arrangement; but the first definite indication may be seen in parallel lines slightly waved, thus, This perhaps expressed the delicate flowing hair; but a crisper and more knotty kind suggested a number of round dots strewn closely over the head. These were afterwards employed in a row, to represent long plaited hair, such as we have seen in fuller detail in Figs. 22 and 70. These are to be seen on an ancient coin of Terpilla, in Macedonia, or in larger masses, as in the clumsy figures upon coins of Lete, also in Macedonia. The two methods are united in the coin of Gelas, already shown in Fig. 81, where the human beard is marked by lines, and the bull's head and neck covered with globules. A more graceful undulation was introduced in the hair of the nymph Arethusa, upon the coins of Syracuse, where the lines are wavy, and strongly bent, both at the back of the head and over the brow. In the coins of Athens, the hair seen under the helmet of Minerva is marked with parallel lines, thus, but lapping over one another, as in Fig. 87. A conventional formality thus arose, in which artificial plaits are introduced, as in the sitting figure of Minerva, which were more easily represented than flowing tresses. The female stepping into a chariot has the hair marked by a series of crisp undulating lines, such as are used in the same sculpture to represent the texture of the stuff of which her sleeve is made, and which looks very like the chain armour worn by our own early knights in church monuments. This last peculiarity is especially observable in the hairy figures from the monument at Xanthus. The bronze statue (Fig. 70) has the hair in parallel lines, except on the forehead, where they terminate in a row of long-drawn locks; not what we term corkscrew, but with a round curl at the end of each. These constitute the leading peculiarities, at this period, of one of the most difficult branches of art—the representation of human hair. Flaxman has observed most truly, that the first essays of Grecian art, in the heroic age, prove that they were neither stronger nor swifter than other nations; but their improved imitation of nature, founded on the sure principles of science, left their competitors at a distance not to be recovered; and the ability and zeal with which they pursued the advantage thus gained gave them beyond dispute possession of the palm.

IV.—FROM THE DE-
FEAT OF THE PER-
SIANS, B. C. 446, TO
THE DEATH OF
PERICLES, B. C. 429.
Ægina was the bitter enemy of the Athenian State; and she was, after a disastrous war, compelled to surrender her independence, B. C. 455. At a still later date, namely, in 431, her entire population was expelled by the Athenians, and replaced by settlers from Attica. From that period the island never regained its former importance. Early Æginetan art was characterized by a peculiar rigidity of style, a sharpness resulting most probably from the frequent use of

metal, which produces that effect until the artist has completely mastered his
material. Other peculiarities belonged to the early Æginetan works of art.
Their figures were more slender, and sharper in form, than other contemporary
works. They exhibited a great disposition towards angularity, with lines producing a formal effect. Among other productions of art, the island was also
celebrated in early times for the manufacture of candelabra. Pliny records the
existence of a peculiar style of art, spread over various countries in his day, which
he calls Tuscan, because he believed it to proceed from Etruria. It appears to have
been the general name given to certain statues among wealthy Romans; and the
works of the Æginetan sculptors, Callon and Hegesias, are referred by Quintilian to this Tuscan style. Now, as the first of these artists flourished in the 66th
Olympiad, at which time the Pisistratidæ had been expelled, we may imagine
that this was the prevailing character of Æginetan art before the Persian war.

Among the most important discoveries, with reference to art, in modern
times, must be ranked that of the Ægina marbles. For this we are mainly
indebted to Professor Cockerell, whose restoration of Athens in its glory stands
at the head of the present Introduction. They can hardly be regarded,
however, as works exclusively of the Æginetan school; for everything relating
to the Temple is peculiarly distinct from the known Dorian character of the
early inhabitants of the island. It seems more than probable that the Temple,
among the ruins of which these sculptures were found, was dedicated to Minerva;
for the subject of one of the sculptures is an heroic combat, over which the
Goddess presides in the centre of the pediment. These sculptures are entire
statues under life-size, and seem to have occupied the pediments of each end
of the Temple.

The difference between the sculptures of the two ends of the Temple is so
great, that they are evidently executed by different hands, and most probably at
different times. The figures of the eastern pediment are larger, and executed
in a manner so superior to the western group, that Mr. Cockerell was led to
think the latter might have been the work of pupils. The style of Minerva
and the combatants in the western pediment perfectly accords with that which
has been called Tuscan; and it is probable that in these figures we see the
peculiarities of Calon and Hegesias. The Athenians, when they expelled the
inhabitants and destroyed their works, might have respected this group, which
bore reference to their own Goddess, and might have spared the Temple and
its western sculptures for her sake. In all probability they completed the
building, and added the figures on the eastern pediment,—a notion not inconsistent with their style and execution, for they form the next stage in art to
the sculptures of the Temple of Theseus, and they occur at the very moment
when they might have been expected.

PLATE III.—ÆGINETAN MARBLES.

Fig. 86.—From the Western Pediment.

Fig. 86.—Minerva, from the Western Pediment.

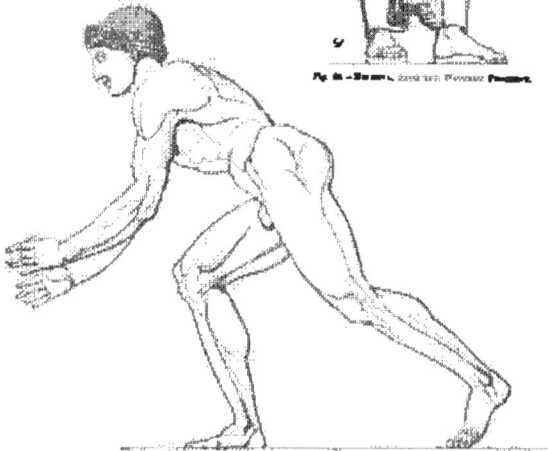

Fig. 87.—Advancing Figure from the Eastern Pediment.

The temple itself was of the Doric order, hexastyle and amphiprostyle. No traces of sculpture in the metopes have been discovered. The statues on the eastern pediment are the more valuable from being sculptured all round; having been, in fact, chiselled as carefully at the back as they were in front. The triangular outline of the cornice, which bounded the tympanum in the western pediment, being still in existence, the arrangement and extent of the figures of that group can be fixed with tolerable accuracy; but the eastern group having suffered, the subject, from general mutilation and the absence of many of the statues, cannot now be determined with any degree of certainty. The western pediment certainly represented the fight between the Grecians and Trojans for the body of Patroclus. This has been a prolific subject with early artists; many of their compositions having been found in vase paintings of nearly the same period, in which the identical archers and general characteristics of costume are introduced. The figure of Minerva, in the centre, displays great elaboration; but there is no feeling of art exhibited in the folds of the drapery. The feet are turned sideways; and, but for the formality and stiffness of the other figures, she might represent a statue. The other figures, with the exception of their armour, are all nude, and their proportions remarkably short. The joints are most carefully defined, and show a great advance in anatomical knowledge; but the execution is feeble. The waists are small; the eyes are very round and projecting; and there is a smile on every mouth. The hair is wiry, and most elaborately curled in regular rows over the forehead. The projection of bone at the pit of the chest, in Fig. 88, is very remarkable. Holes in the marble indicate that bronze armour was attached in several places; and remains of colour are perceptible on the garments, lips, eyes, and weapons, but not on the flesh. Some portions of the hair on the heads and beards were originally represented by wire.

The sculptures of the eastern pediment, five only of which were found, are in many respects admirable. Sir Richard Westmacott regards them as the production of the best masters before the time of Phidias. The careful marking of the muscles shows a complete attainment of anatomical knowledge. The execution is good, and the heads alone show the mannerism of the earlier style. The figure advancing with outstretched arms is very excellent, and remarkable for the truth with which the bones and sinews are exhibited. It is a perfect model of minute care in every part, and most worthy of study. Scarcely less excellent, both for feeling and composition, is the wounded figure called Laomedon (Fig. 91). The limbs of this figure—placed in the angle at the left end of the pediment—spread out easily, without the slightest feeling being awakened in the spectator that the narrow-pointed corner was a difficult space for the artist to fill. The Laomedon forms a wonderful contrast to the statue on the left hand of the western pediment, where the same space is occupied by a grossly angular figure.   In the figures of the western pediment no attempt is made to express the veins, which Phidias afterwards contrived so triumphantly to introduce; and which are delicately indicated in the larger figures of the eastern pediment: but all the lesser accessories of skin and its creases are carefully attended to.

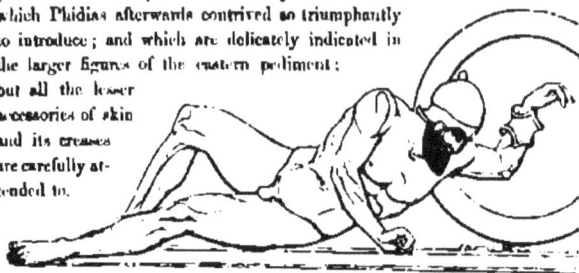

Fig. 91.—Sleeping, from the Eastern Pediment

On comparing the head, as it has now become developed in Greek art (Plate III.), with those of Egypt and Assyria (Figs. 92, 93), we see a strong resemblance; but, on the whole, perhaps the archaic peculiarities of the Greek more nearly resemble those of the East.   The full aquiline nose and strongly distending nostril, and the full round eye with long projecting lids, sloping downwards and inwards, and covered with bushy eyebrows meeting over the nose, strongly characterise the Assyrian type. (Fig.92.) On the other hand, the Egyptian

Fig. 92.—Assyrian Head.

Fig. 93.—Egyptian Head.

displays less prominence of eyelids or brow, less convexity about the nose, and altogether no fulness of flesh about the cheeks or face generally.   Their is often a peculiar sweetness about the mouth (Fig. 93), as we see in some of those colossal heads now displayed in the British Museum.   The Grecian countenance of this period exhibits a greater affinity to the Assyrian in the brow, the nostril, the projecting eye, and full lower lip. They have a peculiar prominence also between the lower eyelid and the nostril ; and the space between these two points is always greater in the Egyptian than in the other two. The treatment of the hair, marked in parallel lines and elaborately curled, is only found in Assyria and Greece; while the pointed beard seems to have been peculiar to the Greeks only ; hence one of the early epithets of Mercury, who in olden times wore a beard, was σφηνο-πώγων (the wedge-bearded). As a parallel to

Fig. 93.—Greek Head, from Ægina.

the head here given from the Ægina marbles, we add one (Fig. 95) from a vase painting to show how the two branches, painting and sculpture, kept pace, preserving each the character of their era. The painted tresses probably show what were supplied in the sculpture by means of wire.

The political events of this period had great influence upon Athenian art. The Persian invasion roused the Greeks to their true interests, and convinced them that without unity there could be no hope of success ; and for a time it is probable that art was only employed for private tributes of affection ; and we may regard the warrior Aristion, whose name and monument we have so recently criticised, as one of the heroes who fell at Marathon, and who was commemorated by the art of his own time.

Fig. 95.—Greek Head, from a Vase Painting.

When the Persians destroyed all the buildings on the Acropolis of Athens, they probably laid the foundation for the future prosperity of the arts in Greece. The glory obtained by the victors, in defeating the enemy in such overwhelming numbers, was not sufficient in itself to call forth the energies of the artists to record it;—it was, in addition, the destruction of the buildings themselves, which was viewed in a religious light. They were to be restored, as a matter of necessity, for the continuance of their religious rites; and the utmost magnificence was to be bestowed upon them, as a compensation to the Gods, whose temples had been thus desecrated.

Thus the new town of Athens was rapidly rebuilt; the houses arose in an incredibly short space of time; and, prompted by the prudence of Themistocles, the whole was encompassed with a new wall, sixty stadia in circumference. These circumstances produced most important effects upon the Athenians, in their intercourse with the neighbouring States. They were already beginning to feel the want of excitement, when one of those events happened, which are sometimes devised by clever rulers for political purposes;—the Athenians heard with wonder that the bones of their great ancestor Theseus had been discovered.

During fourteen years the Athenians, with the assistance of their allies, were occupied in driving the Persians from the Ægean Sea, and from the strong positions they possessed on the coast. In the course of this contest the Athenians possessed themselves of the stronghold of Syros. This acquisition had followed the decisive victory at the Strymon; and an oracle in the same year (B.C. 476) desired the Athenians to bring home the bones of Theseus. They were found, or pretended to be found, by Cimon, immediately after he had taken the island. The remains were brought

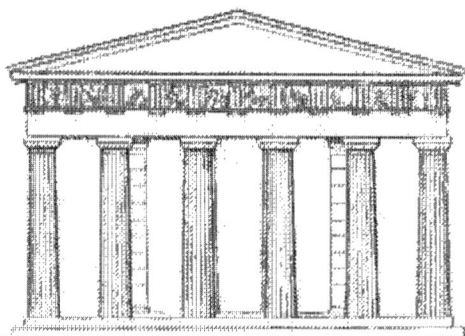

Fig. III.—Front Elevation of the Theseum.

to Athens in the year B.C. 469; and, after being welcomed by the people in grand procession, as if the hero himself had come back, they were deposited in the interior of the city. The temple monument, called the Theseum, was erected to receive them, and the building was invested with the privilege of sanctuary. It was finished about B.C. 465,

PLATE IV.—SCULPTURES OF THE THESEUM AND PARTHENON.

Figs. 97 and 98.—Metopes from the Temple of Theseus.

Fig. 99.—Metope of the Temple of Theseus.

Fig. 100.—Metope of the Parthenon. Western Front.

Fig. 101.—Fragments of the Eastern Frieze of the Theseum.

and was probably the first great architectural work, completed for religious
service, since the Persian devastation.

The Temple of Theseus most probably furnished the model for the Parthenon.
The Theseum, although only half the size, resembles the Parthenon in its more
essential points, and impresses the beholder more by its symmetry than its
magnitude (Fig. 96). The cella within is forty feet in length, and twenty
in breadth. The width of the ambulatory along the sides is only six feet.
The entire height, including the two steps on which it rests, is thirty-two feet
and a half. The tympanum of the eastern pediment alone was adorned with
sculptures; and of those the cramps and sockets are all that now remain.
The metopes at the east end only, and the four adjoining ones on the flanks,
were executed in sculpture (Figs. 97, 98, 99). The rest may have been originally

painted, but are now quite plain. A
frieze (Fig. 101), in very high relief, is
placed at each end of the cella, which,
passing over the ambulatories and
joining the inside of the entablature
that rests on the outer columns,
extends north and south beyond the
antæ. The position of this frieze, with
respect to the cella, is very different
from that of the Parthenon, which was
sculptured about thirty years later.
From the extreme projection of the
figures in the Theseum, it is hardly

possible to see the sculptures from below. This defect seems to have acted as
a warning to those who executed the works of the Parthenon; for there we find
the lowest possible relief adopted, and the objection entirely obviated. Moreover,
the ground of the Parthenon figures was hollowed out deeper in many places, so
as to give the effect of projection to the figures without affecting the general
surface. In the Theseum there is scarcely any difference between the relief
of the frieze and that of the metopes. In some instances the figures project
as much as six inches from the stone surface. In the execution of some of these
figures, there is a close resemblance to those of the Parthenon, especially in
Fig. 100, taken from the western frieze. The straight lines of the mantle of the
horseman, as it floats on the wind, remind the observer of the examples of
drapery from the Theseum given in the same plate.

No sculptures have been removed from the Theseum; but there are casts
in the British Museum of the finest portions still remaining. The subjects
sculptured on the metopes are the labours of Hercules and the exploits of

Theseus. The ten metopes, over the principal or eastern part of the temple, were occupied by the Labours of Hercules; while the less important ones on the two flanks, eight in number, relate to the exploits of Theseus. The subject of the eastern frieze, or pronaos, is supposed to represent the battle between the Gods and the Giants,—a contest usually termed Gigantomachia,—in which the latter are hurling great masses of rock. Some other divinities are seated; but no attributes remain to characterise them (Fig. 101). The subject sculptured on the western frieze is a fight between the Centaurs and the Lapithæ,—called Centauromachia,—in which Theseus is supposed to have taken part. Here, for the first time, we see the Centaurs completely formed with graceful equine proportions. The sculptures all bear traces of colour; and we are taught, by this building, that the marble surface and other portions of the columns were enriched with painted patterns, delicately applied in the same manner as we have seen the graceful ornaments introduced on the earthen vases already described. The ground of the figures, in all these instances, seems to have been blue; and Mr. Hawkins explains the subject of the metopes to be the deeds of Theseus, from finding the representations of similar subjects, with their names, on vases in the British Museum.

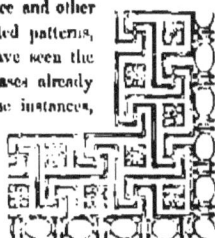

The Temple was formerly decorated with paintings, as well as with sculptures, illustrative of the exploits of Theseus, the Centaurs, and the Amazons. According to Pausanias, the name of the artist by whom they were executed was Micon. The stucco upon which they were painted still remains; and each picture, like the great Italian frescoes of modern times, must have covered an entire wall. The names of the sculptors employed in the building we have now no means of knowing. The most celebrated artists living at the period were Ageladas, the master of Phidias, Onatas of Ægina, and Calamis; the last of whom became afterwards known by his statue of Apollo Alexicacus.

Onatas practised painting as well as sculpture, and was intimately associated with Polygnotus in the former branch of art. His most celebrated work, besides a brazen chariot of Hieron at Olympia, was a series of statues forming a group of the Homeric heroes, taken at the moment when Nestor, holding the lots in a helmet, is surrounded by the Grecian chiefs, who had accepted Hector's challenge. Agamemnon's statue only is inscribed, and with retroverse letters. That of Ulysses was removed by Nero; and upon the shield of Idomeneus, in addition to the device of a cock, the artist had inscribed his own name, "Onatas, the son of Micon." An inscription beneath intimated that the

Achaians dedicated these statues to Jupiter. In the same place was a brazen Hercules, dedicated by the Thasians, which was also inscribed with the artist's name; and Pausanias concludes his chapter with the words, " we regard this statuary of the Æginetan, in respect to his art, as not inferior to any of the school of Dædalus, or the workshops of Attica." The nature of the subjects he executed at Delphi and other places accord so well with the embellishments of the Theseum, that his connexion with that work is rendered highly probable.

We have thus traced, by slow and cautious steps, every improvement in the motion of the limbs, balance of the figure, and representation of drapery. Great labour and anxious imitation of nature were everywhere perceptible. The remains of the Hecatompedon, as well as the statues from Ægina, evince the same characteristics; but in the Temple of Theseus the aspect is changed. The genius of the plastic art now bursts forth, and displays itself in composition, equipoise, action, anatomical truth, and perfect execution. A breadth of style, in which all trifling details are rejected, becomes the prominent characteristic of the whole. Broad folds, and boldly arranged lines of drapery, take the place of formally disposed plaits and zigzag lines. The hair, no longer wavy or wiry, with a multitude of small curls, is now represented by a compact mass, which is smooth, and almost fitting to the head like a cap; thus returning, in some measure, to the original style of Egypt. The beard, which was wedge-shaped in the Aristion and Æginetan warrior, has now become a graceful mass, projecting from the mouth and chin, and confined principally to the Centaurs. The artist, on examining these marbles, will find a very peculiar treatment of the human body. From the pit of the throat downwards it is divided horizontally, by well-defined lines, into three equal portions; the first at the end of the pectoralis, or chest-muscle, and the second at the navel. These horizontal divisions are carefully marked, while the perpendicular lines are neglected. There is little indication of the arch of the ribs on the termination of the sternal bone, which was a powerful characteristic in the figures of Ægina. The anatomy of the back, as displayed in two instances, is most excellent. All the figures are remarkably fleshy, but well proportioned, and suggestive of a race totally different in form from that which we have hitherto seen. Of all modern writers, Dodwell is the only one who awards that meed of praise which the sculptures of the Theseum seem to merit. When we consider their vast improvement upon what had preceded them, and, again, that they were thirty years in advance of the sculptures of the Parthenon (with very little difference, comparatively speaking, in point of excellence), it seems surprising that the pen should hitherto have been engaged merely in critical investigation of the subjects they were intended to represent.

An innovation peculiar to this building still requires to be particularized.

Hitherto the draped figures we have commented on have been in perfect repose, with the exception of the Hecatompedon figure, where a slight intimation of movement was given; but in the painted Minerva and water-carriers no such attempt was visible. Of all drapery, that which is technically called *flying* drapery—that is, when the folds of the stuff float in the air—is the most difficult. The movements are so varied and transient, that nothing can arrest them for a moment; and a perfect knowledge of the principles of motion is required to produce a correct representation. Execution must be combined with experience, and taste with judgment, in order to secure what is called the best *throw* or adjustment. In the Theseum we find the attempt not only made for the first time, but effected in the most successful manner. It is, however, more flowing than floating. In the Temple of Theseus we have a striking contrast of fold lines to the action of the limbs in the long dragging mantle seen in the eastern frieze (Fig. 101). On turning to the vase paintings we find no instance of flying drapery at this or any previous time. In the Alexandrian period, however, the fashion of an arched scarf behind the figures was not uncommon.

A striking change also took place in vase painting about this period. Hitherto we have seen the figures dark upon a light ground. The arrangement was now reversed;—the background became black, and the figures light. As a natural consequence the figures became larger in proportion to the surface of the vase, and the compositions were no longer crowded with objects. In fact, the spirit of grandeur not only appeared in sculpture, but also manifested itself in vase painting. In the old paintings, so long as the black figures were painted upon the vase, the artist felt himself to be superadding to his work; but in later times his process became more closely allied to that of the sculptor; for, with his black paint-brush, he seemed to be clearing everything away from around the figures, leaving them standing out, just as the figure comes out of a block of marble under the chisel of the sculptor. Nobleness and grandeur of form always accompany vase paintings with a black ground. For a long course of years no other colour than a greenish black was employed, except red in the letters; for the names still continued to be inscribed upon the black ground. Afterwards other colours were introduced,—a style which marks a declining age. All incised lines disappear, and the outlines of the figures are henceforth drawn with clear black lines upon the light forms. The colour of the clay itself, as seen on the figures and ornaments, now became a beautiful yellow, inclining to a reddish tinge, which was heightened by the polish of a brilliant transparent varnish, laid over the whole by way of finish.

The most brilliant name on the records of antiquity, as a painter, is that of Polygnotus. His works stand alone and apart from all previous attempts of the kind,—at least if any faith is to be placed in Pausanias, who has left a minute description of his paintings, both at Athens and Delphi. Like the paintings of Micon, they seem to have covered the walls themselves, and consisted of a *series* of subjects, which require to be viewed in regular order, if the spectator desires to understand the story.

Polygnotus was a native of Thasos, which island was reduced by Cimon, B.C. 463, about three years after the completion of the Theseum and the victories at Eurymedon. Cimon most probably brought Polygnotus to Athens, and immediately employed him upon the building in which he himself had most interest. In this Temple, however, he could only have acted as assistant to Micon. He painted the destruction of Troy (Paus. i. 15) in the decorated building (the Stoa) at Athens; this being one of the many colonnades, or places of shelter, provided as a resort for the citizens from the midday sun, so oppressive in eastern cities. The greatest works of Polygnotus, however, were in the lounging-room, or Lesche, at Delphi. One side of the apartment was occupied, according to Pausanias, by a painting of the Greeks at the conclusion of the Trojan war, and the other by the visit of Ulysses to the infernal regions. Ulysses is represented as holding a sword, and in the act of summoning Tiresias. His

mother stands near, and Theseus and Pirithous are sitting on a throne *beneath* Ulysses; so that we may presume the groups to have been painted flat upon the ground, one over the other, as is constantly seen in vase pictures of the best time,—for instance, in the Edwards, Stewart, and Meidias vases. Upon the first of these paintings Polygnotus thus inscribed his name and the title of the

Fig. 80.—Ulysses and Ships.

work—"Polygnotus, a Thasian born, son of Aglaophon, designed the capture of Ilium." (Plutarch de Orac. defect. p. 436.)

Polygnotus was enamoured of Cimon's sister Elpinice, and took her as a
model for his picture of Laodice. He seems to have been the first to throw
expression into the countenance, and showed the teeth by opening the mouth,
which before this time was closed, as may be seen on comparing the annexed
with the water-carriers (Fig. 75). He showed the form of the limbs clearly
through the drapery, and Lucian admired a blush that suffused the face of
Cassandra at Delphi. Lucian also particularly mentions the drapery, which
he describes as being executed with the utmost delicacy,—the parts required to
show the limbs beneath fitting close and straight, but the greater part hanging
loose, and fluttered by the wind. Most of the subjects painted by Polygnotus
seem to have been imitated by others; for we find subjects and groups of
figures painted upon vases which are minutely applicable to the descriptions
of Pausanias.

The vase paintings here given represent Menelaus leading back Helen,
the cause of the Trojan war, to Sparta (Fig. 104). In Fig. 105 the subjects
are the flight of Æneas and his family,—a contrast to the former painting of the
same subject (Fig. 74),—and the story of Ajax and Cassandra, who is clinging
to an ancient *represented* statue. Fig. 106 is a continuation of the same
subject, and represents the death of Priam, who is seated upon an altar. The
drapery in all these figures retains somewhat of the archaic manner, especially that of the female in the centre (Fig. 106), where the hanging folds
remind us of the Hecatompedon relief (Fig. 76). The other subject of
Plate V. (Fig. 107), is a rich specimen of vase painting from the Louvre, which

Fig. 48. — Scènes diverses sur un vase.

illustrates the condition of the arts, and shows elaborately the varieties of dress and equipage at a later period of art.

Polygnotus worked with the brush; and this probably contributed more than anything else to the greater freedom of his drawing. He refused payment for his painting in the Lesche, and it was decreed, in the Amphictyonic Council, that he should be maintained, as a reward, at the public expense. Micon was paid in money for the part he performed in the decorations. (Plin. xxxv. 0, p. 227.) Polygnotus also practised statuary,—a combination with painting to be found in Onatas, Phidias, Raphael, Michael Angelo, and many great artists. He painted the actions of the Dioscuri, in their Temple at Athens (Paus. i. 18); among them the Rape of the Daughters of Leucippus. These subjects are also admirably illustrated by vase paintings; but especially by one, the work of Midias, now in the British Museum. Among his lesser works we find his name attached to two pictures in the vestibule of the Acropolis at Athens; one of Achilles among the daughters of Lycomedes, the other of Ulysses and Nausicaa with her maidens washing garments. The first subject frequently occurs in sculpture, and is found among the Pompeian paintings; the second is shown on a vase at Berlin. Cicero (Brut. 18) tells us that Polygnotus only used four colours; and Aristotle (Poetics, ii. 2) calls him a painter of good manners (vi. 15), probably meaning good style, adding that his works were preferable to nature. A vase in the British Museum is inscribed with the name of Polygnotus.

Pausanias omits to give any minute account of the Parthenon, because much had already been written upon the subject. In the present instance the same reason fully justifies us in confining our attention to a personal account of its chief sculptor, Phidias. He was the director of those decorations by which Pericles imparted to Athens a majesty such as had never belonged to any other Grecian city. The architects of the Parthenon, and other buildings of the same period, were Ictinus, Callicrates, Corœbus, and Mnesicles; all of whom acted under his superintendence. He had, besides, a school of pupils and assistants, to whose management was confided the mechanical part of his labours. The expense incurred in the Athenian works of this time is computed at no less a sum than £690,000 of our money.

Pericles first appeared in public life about 459 B.C., in the same year that Mycenæ was destroyed and Socrates born. The date is also remarkable as that in which Sophocles produced his first tragedy. He adopted the popular party, and as such became the opponent of Cimon, the friend of Sparta, and the zealous adherent of the old institutions of his country. He saw that Athens was already at the head of the Grecian states; and it became his object to add to this pre-eminence, by rendering her, by perfection of the fine arts and in the cultivation of dramatic literature, the most brilliant city in the world. In the 84th Olympiad, he commenced the Parthenon and other works of the Acropolis; and by his zeal and energy the artizan population were kept in constant occupation and excitement till their completion. The picture drawn by Plutarch of the employments entailed upon persons of all classes, in procuring and transporting material, is lively in the extreme. But for defraying the expenses thus incurred, Pericles had recourse to a very dubious act,—he unhesitatingly employed the money-store which all the states had contributed as a general fund for defence against their common enemy, the Persians. This fund was by general consent deposited at Delos; but when the Athenians attained the ascendancy, it was removed to Athens. This transfer was made, unknown to the other States, and Pericles had to defend himself against the charge of misapplication of the public property. He defended himself with that brilliant eloquence for which he was renowned, and attempted to show that the Athenians were perfectly justified in what they had done.

The buildings in Athens, and on the Acropolis, formed the glory of the Periclean age. A new theatre, termed the Odeon, was first constructed for musical and poetical representations at the great Panathenaic solemnity; next, the splendid Temple of Minerva, called the Parthenon, with all its masterpieces of decorative sculptures and reliefs; lastly, the Propylæa was erected to adorn the entrance of the Acropolis, on the western side of the hill, through which the solemn processions were conducted on festival days. It appears that the Odeon and the Parthenon were both finished between B.C. 445 and 437; the Propylæa somewhat later, between B.C. 437 and 431. Progress was also made in reconstructing the Erectheum, which had been burnt by the Persians. The Peloponnesian war, however, seems to have delayed its completion. When finished, it became the most perfect example of the Ionic order. Dr. Wordsworth has so fully described this great work, that further remarks, beyond directing the attention to the annexed beautiful restoration and the accompanying capitals (Plate VI.), are rendered unnecessary. In all these structures the sculpture was no less memorable than the architecture. Three statues of Minerva, all by the hand of Phidias, decorated the Acropolis; namely, the colossal figure of ivory in the Parthenon, forty-seven feet high; a second of bronze, called the Lemnian Minerva; and a third, of colossal magnitude, also in bronze, called Minerva Promachus, which was placed between the Propylæa and the Parthenon. This was visible from afar off, even to the navigator approaching the Piræus by sea. His last and greatest work was the colossal statue of Jupiter in the great temple of Olympia.				•

Of the statues executed by Phidias no copies or even probable imitations have been preserved. Elaborate descriptions of them are given by Pausanias

PLATE VL.—IONIC ARCHITECTURE.

Fig. 84.—The Erechtheion, Athens.

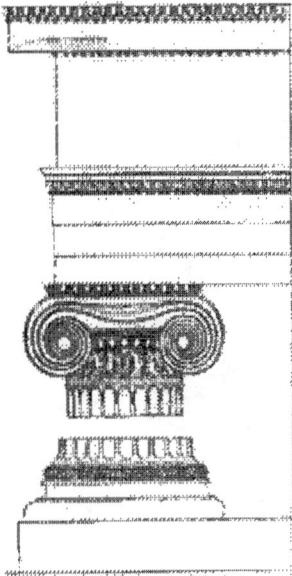

Fig. 85.—Capital of the Erechtheion.

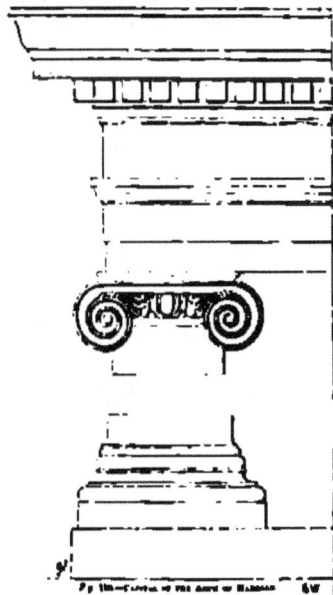

Fig. 86.—Capital of the Arch of Hadrian.

and other classic writers; but little is known of the life of Phidias. The best authorities agree that he died at Elis, about the year B.C. 432, and it is generally believed that his death was a violent one. Pliny (xxxvi. 5) includes him in his chapter on stone-workers, but states expressly that he worked in marble —"*marmora sculpsisse.*"

The sculptures of the Parthenon are the productions not only of the best age, but of that school of art which the ancients themselves most esteemed.

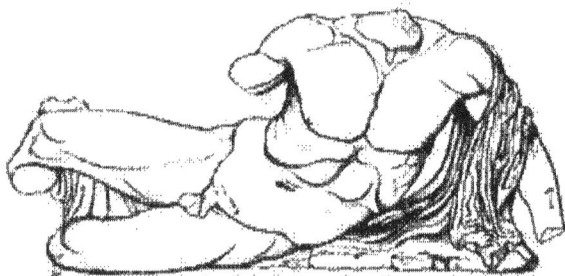

Fig. 111.—River God Ilissus. From the Western Pediment.

They were not executed to gratify individual caprice; nor were they given on so small a scale as to be inadequate representations of a style. They are not of uncertain date, as is sometimes the case with vases, coins, or gems; they are pre-eminently national monuments and historical documents, and are therefore of inestimable value in fixing the standard by which all specimens of ancient art may be measured and classified. They may be regarded, in fact, as Mr. Newton has shown, as a poem, each separate sculpture tending to one great purpose, unity. Respecting the sculptures themselves, Flaxman says:—"The horses appear to live and move, to roll their

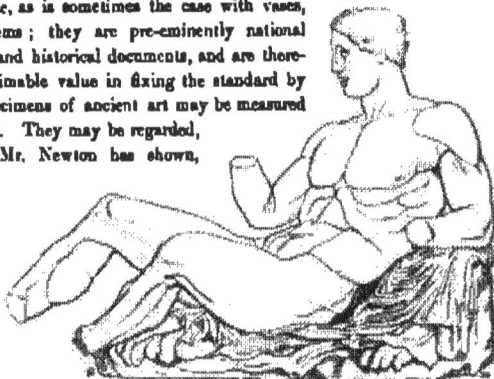

Fig. 112.—Theseus. From the Eastern Pediment.

eyes, to gallop, prance, and curvet; the veins of their faces and legs seem distended with circulation; in them are distinguished the hardness and decision of bony forms, with the elasticity of tendon and the softness of flesh. The beholder is charmed with the deer-like lightness and elegance of their make; and although the relief is not above an inch from the background, we can scarcely suffer reason to persuade us they are not alive."

Our limits will not permit us to dwell at any length even on these gems of Greek art, or even to detail more minutely the points in which they excel the sculptures of the Theseum, or in which each of these differs from the sculptures of the Temple of Apollo at Bassæ. To point out these differences would involve a great amount of mere technical phraseology. The finest figures and compositions, therefore, have been selected from each and arranged in Plates VII., VIII., and IX. The position occupied by the Parthenon marbles can be best ascertained by a reference to the pediments and section represented in Figs. 114, 115, and 121. By thus at once addressing the eye, it is thought that a better estimate may be conveyed of the points in which they differ from the sculptures that preceded them, or which were executed subsequent to the Periclean age.

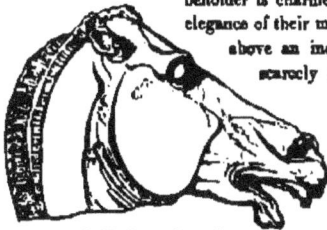

Fig. 113.—Prom the Eastern Pediment.

Fig. 114.—The Western Pediment, in 1674.

The two pediments of the Temple (Figs. 114 and 115) show the earliest record preserved of them by a French artist, Jacque Carey, in 1674. How

Fig. 115.—The Eastern Pediment, in 1674.

much they had then suffered is here shown by the drawings themselves; how

PLATE VII.—THE CENTAURS AND LAPITHÆ.

Figs. 116 and 117.—Reliefs from the Western Frieze of the Parthenon.

Fig. 118.—From the Sculpture of the Centaur of the Temple of Apollo Epicurius.

Figs. 119 and 120.—Reliefs from the Western Frieze of the Parthenon.

K

lamentably, since that period, may best be seen by a visit to the British
Museum. The Parthenon was described by Spon and Wheeler in 1676; at
which time it had been used as a Christian Church, and the central figures of
the eastern pediment had been removed for the introduction of an eastern
window. Hence the gap now seen in this precious composition (Fig. 115).
By the assistance of Stuart and Cockerell we have become familiar with the
architecture of the Parthenon; but the most important discovery in connexion
with it in modern times is the fact, that the outline of the building, instead
of being square, as it appears to the eye, is in reality curved. This was first
discovered by Mr. Pennethorne, and has since been demonstrated by Mr.
Penrose in his superb work.

A section of a portion of the Parthenon is here introduced (Fig. 121) to
show the relative position of the frieze and metopes. The latter will be recognised between the tri-
glyphs; and it will be
seen that the frieze was
placed on the wall of
the cella close behind
the columns, and at
the same height as the
metopes. No light,
therefore, could fall di-
rectly upon them; in
fact, all the light they
received was reflected
from the sides of the

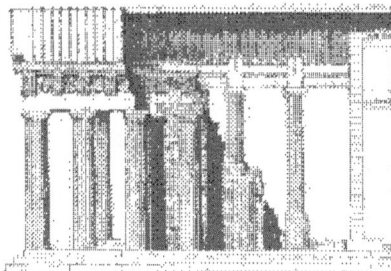

Fig. 121.—Section of the Parthenon.

columns and from the floor of the ambulatory. Here, for the first time in
Attic art, we find the Ionic order introduced; the columns within, which support the roof of the western chamber, being of that order. It was also combined
with the Doric in some of the internal parts of the Propylæa. The Ionic
order was very prevalent in the settlements made by the Athenian colonists in

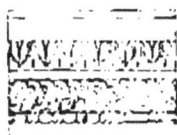

Fig. 122.—Ionic Capitals.

Asia Minor; but with one important difference. In
the Ionic of Asia Minor, including the ancient Temple of Sardis, the band which crosses the capital from
volute to volute, and which, in fact, forms a
part of them, is straight. In the Athenian
Ionic, as seen in the capitals of the Propylæa, it
hangs down like a festoon. An Asiatic exception
occurs in the Temple of Minerva Polias, at Priene,
which is pure Ionic. The arch of Hadrian is an exception to the Athenian

Ionic, the band being straight (the capital and base of which is placed as a parallel by the side of a capital and base from the Erectheum, Plate VI.). A specimen of the guilloche, with the bead and reel ornament, is added (Fig. 122).

Among the perfections of the sculptures of the Parthenon may be observed

several examples of draped figures. One on the western frieze may be mentioned, which presents the finest specimen known of flying drapery (Fig. 123). It is not floating, but actually fluttering; and by this example we can understand the attainments of Polygnotus. Among the metopes, an examination of the originals will show that some are executed in a less bold and harder manner; and this proceeds, it is supposed, from less expert artists having been employed, owing to the urgency for its completion. In the works of Phidias, as in those of Raphael, whose genius was the culminating point of modern Italian art, we perceive the first indications of that which,

when a little in excess, becomes a fault, namely, roundness of line and consciousness of attitude. In Figure 124 we find, perhaps, the nearest approach to perfection in the beautiful curve of the limbs, combined with much firmness and purity. Nothing can exceed the dignity of the females from the frieze in Plate VIII., Fig. 127; and in the metope (Fig. 126) we find the same grandeur of drapery, but still with traces of the archaic folds, that contribute to a feeling of firmness and stability, and which probably characterised the great ivory statue that stood in the Temple. On the other hand, the magnificent drapery of the sitting females in Fig. 128, realizes the ideas of art attributed to Polygnotus; the folds being here gracefully thrown about, but at the same time properly displaying every part of the limbs which it was necessary to exhibit.

In the year B.C. 484 Pericles died, having, by his taste and magnificence, placed Athens in a position of unequalled glory. Phidias, the sculptor, who had so largely assisted by his great genius, died, as we have seen, two years earlier. In the same year Athens was visited by one of the severest plagues that city had ever known.

PLATE VIII.—MARBLES OF THE PARTHENON

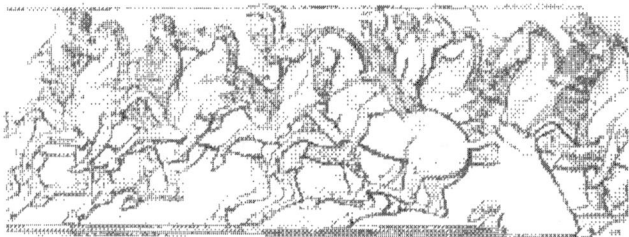
Fig. 172.—Panthenon Frieze. North End

Fig. 173.—Metope. South End

Fig. 174.—Part of Panthenon Frieze. East End

Fig. 175.—Theseus or Ilissus. From the Eastern Pediment

When the ravages of this terrible plague had ceased, the Athenians in gratitude dedicated a statue, executed by Calamis, to Apollo Alexicacus, "the averter of evil." Calamis was associated with Onatas before the appearance of Phidias; and we now find him surviving his great patron, and employed in embodying the gratitude of a whole nation. He produced one statue of ivory and gold; but his most celebrated work was the Sosandra, one of the masterpieces of antiquity. He was celebrated for his horses; it is therefore very probable that he was employed on the Parthenon.

No period in the history of art presents greater difficulties than that which includes the age of Praxiteles and Scopas, the chronology of which is involved in considerable obscurity. Pliny and other authors have handed down the names of these artists and their contemporaries, with incidental notices of their productions; and there are works of art in different museums which correspond in subject with these notices; but we have no great historical monument like the Parthenon,—no satisfactory record even of the main features of their productions; and we seek in vain to gather, from mere verbal description, the marks of genius—the spirit of original art—which, in process of copying, has passed away.

The name of Polycletus stands high as a sculptor,—the more so, perhaps, on account of his successful competition with Phidias; his statue of an Amazon having been preferred before all the artists who competed to produce a bronze statue for the Temple of Diana at Ephesus. The chryselephantine statue of Juno at Argos, which he executed, afforded an admirable opportunity for the display of his talents. We learn from Pausanias that the figure was colossal, in a sitting posture, and holding a sceptre and pomegranate. Pausanias particularizes the crown, "στέφανος," and we at once recognise the same head of Juno on a coin of Argos,—a subject very frequently introduced on the Argive coins at this period (Fig. 129). The full character of the countenance and expression displays the peculiarities attributed to Polycletus, which consisted in his representing the full female form in its perfect maturity, unimpaired by age. The Doryphorus, a manly youth, holding a spear, was so celebrated among artists for the justness of its proportions, that it was universally adopted as a standard, and called the

Fig. 129.

CANON. Polycletus himself wrote a treatise upon it. He excelled in throwing the weight of the body on one foot so as to vary the outline; this also occurs in the sculptures of the Theseum (Plate IV.), and on the Parthenon (Plate VII.). He also executed a figure in the act of using the strigil (ἀποξυόμενος, apoxuomenus), which gained great celebrity with the Romans.

In the absence of known copies of this figure, representations of three recognised

statues of the apoxuomenos are here adduced by way of
illustration. The first (Fig. 130) is from
a gem, and the finest in point of composition ; the second (Fig. 131) is from a
sketch made on its discovery at Athens,
and is probably more like that attributed
to Polycletus than the preceding. The
third (Fig. 132) is from a statue discovered
at Rome ; but, as there were two other
apoxuomeni of great celebrity in ancient

times, this may for many reasons be assigned to a later period. Polycletus,

like many other great artists, was also an architect. He
acquired great fame by his theatre at Epidaurus, a great part
of which still remains. In statuary he was distinguished for
the softness of his style, in which, however, Myron rivalled
him. In this respect he excelled Calamis, without being perfectly true to nature. Myron was the fellow pupil of Phidias
and Polycletus, all three being pupils of Ageladas, whose celebrity is chiefly derived from them. The genius of Phidias rose
high above all. Myron, notwithstanding his great industry,
never could thoroughly divest himself of the peculiar style of
their common master. Polycletus, gifted with genius, imparted
originality to his style.

Quintilian has bestowed great praise on the Discobolus
or quoit-player of Myron, and we may obtain a general
idea of the figure from a statue in the British Museum,
of which several repetitions are to be found in other galleries. One of those, now in the Vatican, and from which
our illustration is taken, is inscribed MYPΩN EΠOIEI
(Fig. 133). It is remarked, that in this inscription the
second letter is I ; and the second letter of the next
word is a rounded P instead of Π, and seems to have been
inscribed by a Roman, who used the Roman P instead
of the Greek. Myron produced many of his works in
bronze, and elaborated his figures so much as to be
called " operosa." He represented animals with a won-

derful fidelity to nature. The last contemporary of Phidias we shall mention is
his pupil Alcamenes, whose most celebrated work, the Garden Venus, received
its last touch from the hand of his great master. He adorned the tympanum

of the temple at Olympia,—fragments from the metopes of which only remain. Alcamenes rashly entered into competition with his master, and failed, as might have been expected, from his want of experience.

Another work of this period, to which only slight allusion has hitherto been made,—the Temple of Apollo at Bassæ,—deserves mention. Ictinus, the architect of the Parthenon, was also the architect of this building, and the sculptures are presumed to have been designed by Phidias; but they breathe a totally different feeling, both in composition and execution, to the marbles of the Parthenon. Like the sculptures of the Theseum, they are in bold relief, but in execution very unequal. The back-ground, unlike that of the Parthenon, is open between the figures; and the space is filled up by waving drapery, consisting frequently of curved lines or flourishes, by way of ornament.

Many of the drapery folds are very peculiar (Fig. 134). The form of the limbs are round and fleshy; but with the exception of

Fig. 134.—Phigaleian Marbles.

some female figures and a group of wounded Amazons, they are deficient in the characteristics of a refined period of Art. Some of the figures and groups are similar to those on the frieze of the Theseum, but inferior in execution. These sculptures are also treasured in the British Museum, and are known by the name of the Phigaleian marbles. A smaller series of sculptures, very different in character to the preceding group, belongs to the temple

Fig. 135.—From the Temple of Victory.

of the Wingless Victory, which has generally been attributed to the time of Cimon. In style these figures have a great resemblance to the monument of Lysicrates. One group, which has been chosen for illustration here (Fig. 135), is unquestionably a battle between Greeks and Persians; the latter being easily distinguishable by their peculiar costume. In front of this little temple, which faced the great ascent to the Propylæa, was a series of sculptures larger and in higher relief. Of these a specimen is given in a Victory tying her sandal, in Plate IX. Fig. 138, and, on a smaller scale, two Victories leading a bull, as delineated in the same Plate, Fig. 141. The rich and admirably-arranged draperies of these figures, combined with elegant female forms, may suffice to associate them with the peculiarities which characterise the productions of Scopas;—at least they fairly serve to illustrate his style, as it has been handed down to us by verbal description. The beautiful figure of a Bacchante in bas-relief, from the Towneley Collection in the British Museum (Plate IX. Fig. 140), is generally referred to the same artist. The stately Caryatis (Plate IX. Fig. 139), from the temple of Pandrosos at Athens, is another specimen of exquisite finish, with every combination of female grace, combined with fitness for architectural purposes. It nearly resembles some of the females on the eastern frieze of the Parthenon, especially in the fluted character of the dress, which covers her feet. About this period the head

of Minerva was altered on the coins of Athens. The old type gave way to the irresistible grandeur of the Phidian conception (Fig. 136), and a blooming countenance, covered by a helmet richly adorned with sculptured representations of griffins

Fig. 136—Coin of Athens.

and prancing horses, took the place of the grim Gorgon's head, to which the Athenians, in spite of their refined taste, had clung with superstitious veneration, and which remained in use as long as any freedom remained to Athens. The owl, standing on a vase, surrounded by a magistrate's name within an olive wreath, continued to be the type of the reverse. Among others practising the art of sculpture in this age was the great Socrates, the son of Sophroniscus,—himself a statuary. Pausanias saw, at the entrance to the Athenian Acropolis, a group of Graces clothed, which was executed by the Philosopher. Three small figures on the reverse of a coin represent the Graces, who are draped; and there is every reason to believe that, until the age of Praxiteles, both Venus and the Graces were represented clothed. A celebrated

Fig. 137—The Graces.

piece of sculpture in the early style, containing figures of the twelve Gods,

PLATE IX.—SPECIMENS OF SCULPTURED DRAPERY.

Fig. 120.—A VICTORY TYING HER SANDAL. FROM THE TEMPLE OF VICTORY.

Fig. 122.—CARYATID. FROM THE PANDROSEUM.

Fig. 121.—BAS-RELIEF OF A BACCHANTE.

Fig. 123.—TWO VICTORIES LEADING A BULL. FROM THE TEMPLE OF VICTORY.

PLATE X.—GREEK STATUARY.

Fig 141.—Venus, in Rome.

Fig. 142.—The Graces.

Fig 143.—Venus, From the Vatican.

Fig 144.—Cupid of Praxiteles.

the Fates, the Seasons, and the Graces, confirms this belief. The Graces from
that sculpture are shown in the accompanying illustra-
tion (Fig. 137).

When the inhabitants of Cos applied to Praxiteles
for a statue of Venus, he exhibited two, offering them
the choice of a naked or draped figure. The Coans
being accustomed to see the goddess clothed, preferred
the latter, whilst the former was eagerly purchased by
the Cnidians, and exhibited by them in a separate building, open on all sides for the better view. Lucian,
who saw this statue, gives a minute description of it in
one of his Dialogues. So great was the celebrity it
attained, that strangers came from all parts for the sole
object of beholding it; and King Nicomedes offered to
forgive the Cnidians an enormous debt if they would
transfer their Venus to him; but the statue being an
important source of their revenue, they rejected all
overtures of the kind. Unfortunately we have no
satisfactory trace of this wonderful piece of sculpture.
The Venus di Medici, here introduced (Fig. 146), can
only be a feeble version of the original. The nearest
resemblance is a bronze Roman coin in the French
cabinet, which bears on the reverse a statue of Venus,
corresponding more nearly with the description of
Lucian than any other. This coin has often been
represented in a perfect state, and in beautiful con-
dition. We present it here in its actual state, to show the amount of authority

attachable to it (Fig. 147). The legend on it is
"KNIΔIΩN;" hence, being money "of the Cnidians,"
there is great probability that the figure is a reduced
copy from the statue of which we are treating. Another
statue in the Gardens of the Vatican, however, of
which a copy is given in Plate X. (Fig. 144), would
seem to have greater claim to be considered an imitation of the Cnidian Venus than the famous Medi-
cæan statue. This figure, though inferior in art, corresponds more exactly with the figure on the coin.

The other figure of Venus, given in Plate X. (Fig. 142), is from a bronze, and
represents her as Anadyomene, that is, "coming up" out of the water.

The Graces (Fig. 143, Plate X.) are from a gem, and present the best contrast to the draperies in Fig. 137, while they illustrate the style of a sculptor, Praxiteles, who did not hesitate to unveil the naked charms of the goddess herself. The most beautiful of the many repetitions of a Cupid which have come down to us, is given at Fig. 145, Plate X. The original statue was, in all probability, the Cupid which Praxiteles gave to Phryne, who in her turn dedicated it at Thespia. In this statue the flesh is admirably imitated; but the wings and hair do not indicate the Praxitelean touch. Another celebrated work of this sculptor was the Sauroctonus, or Lizard-killer; many repetitions of which, of various degrees of excellence, are to be seen in different galleries.

The name of Callimachus was one of great celebrity among the ancients. He was, according to Vitruvius, the inventor of the Corinthian order. The origin of this order arose from his accidentally seeing some leaves growing up round a basket, and it is too graceful a legend not to be generally known. The golden lamp, dedicated in the old temple of Minerva on the Acropolis, was

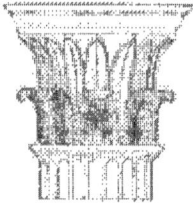

Fig 146 Corinthian Capital

probably composed of leaves and tendrils such as are seen on the Corinthian frieze and capital. The simple form of leaves growing round a basket, or what is technically called the bell of the capital, is best shown in this example (Fig. 146), taken from the Tower of the Winds at Athens.

The style of Callimachus seems to have been too artificial. The figures of his dancers were so elaborated that their beauty was destroyed. A very indifferent relief, inscribed with his name, is preserved in Rome.

Among the uncertain works of this period are the sculptures representing the dying children of Niobe, once in the temple of Apollo Sosianus at Rome. The ancient authorities are divided on the question whether this was the production of Scopas or Praxiteles. It is now impossible to decide; but from much finer fragments existing in other places, and from numerous repetitions, of varying degrees of excellence, we may infer that the statues at Florence have no claim to be considered as emanations from the studio of either of these masters. The Pediment of the Temple of Apollo is given in Plate XI., to show the style of art peculiar to this age, and also as a contrast to the more primitive arrangement of the Western Pediment of the Æginetan Temple, given in the same Plate. At this period a tendency to exaggerated expression, especially in sculpture, began to develop itself. The group of Niobe is an instance in point. The sufferings of the mother, and the dying agony of the children, are here painfully apparent. This is also observable in the Jocasta of Silanion, who is represented as dying; a deadly colour being

PLATE XI.—THE NIOBE PEDIMENT AND EGINETAN MARBLES COMPARED.

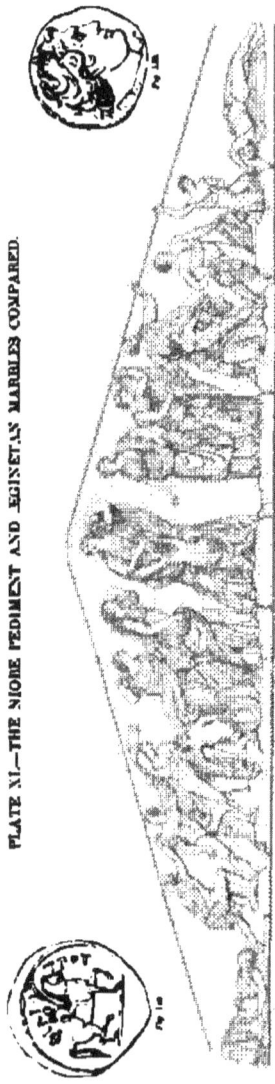

Fig. 58.—Pediment of the Temple of Jupiter Panhellenius.

Fig. 59.—Restored Pediment of the Temple of Minerva. From Müller.

given to the face by an infusion of silver. Some great names of this epoch occur, which we can only enumerate. Among these are Euphranor, both painter and sculptor, and the painters Zeuxis and Parrhasius. Aristides of Thebes was a remarkable painter of this age. He excelled in depicting the passions, and painted a picture of the plague, and a battle with the Persians, containing one hundred figures. His picture of Bacchus was taken to Rome by Mummius after the capture of Corinth.

SI.—FROM THE AC-
CESSION OF ALEX-
ANDER, B. C. 336,
TO THE TIME OF
CONSTANTINE, A. D.
330.

Art had now reached its culminating point. An inferior style had already made some progress, and the genius, which in the better days of Greece was employed in honouring heroes and statesmen, was in this era devoted to flattering the vanity of monarchs. Philip of Macedon, the father of Alexander the Great, commemorated his victories in the Olympic games by introducing chariots and horses upon his coins. Fig. 149 (Plate XI.) commemorates the race won on the day Alexander was born. Alexander himself was no great patron of the fine arts. Lysippus the sculptor, Apelles the painter, and Pyrgoteles the gem engraver, were the only artists suffered to represent his person. Lysippus, we are told, was most exact in his likenesses, even to a peculiar bearing of the head which is represented rather hanging down on one side (Fig. 154). Apelles painted Alexander holding lightning in his hand; but the monarch's complexion being remarkably fair, the flesh-colour was thought to be too dark. The eye is said to have had a remarkably sweet expression,—that they were large is clear from existing busts and gems. His successors introduced the portrait of Alexander upon their coins, and this is the first instance of portraiture used for the purpose. He was represented by Lysimachus as Jupiter Ammon with the ram's-horn; but more frequently, by others, as Hercules, from a Macedonian notion of his descent from the Heraclidæ.

ΑΛΕΞΑΝΔΡΟΣ
ΦΙΛΙΠΠΟΥ
ΜΑΚΕΔΟΝΟΣ

Fig. 154

Pliny observes that Lysippus first reduced the size of the head to a proportion with the rest of the body. His chief work was a group of equestrian statues, representing the Generals who perished at the Granicus. He worked in brass, and executed statues of Alexander at every age, from his childhood upwards. The brother of Lysippus is recorded as the first person who moulded the figure in clay.

The most satisfactory example of Sculpture, of the age of Alexander, is the frieze of the Choragic Monument of Lysicrates, of which we give two separate

slabs, which will suffice to show the changes wrought by Lysippus (Plate XII. Figs. 157 and 158). The graceful form of the capital (Plate XIII. Fig. 164), in which stalks and tendrils are beautifully combined with leaves, seems to have prepared the way for the more permanent Corinthian employed at Athens.

The countenance of Alexander the Great pervades all the heroic statues of this period. Certain peculiarities, which we now find for the first time, were retained and reproduced in a subsequent age, when sculptors confined themselves to copying former productions. The hair rising on the forehead like horns, and then falling over, is a peculiarity well seen in the bust (Fig. 154), and also on the coin of Lysimachus (Fig. 155), in which the large eyeball is also characteristic. The same eye is to be seen in the head of his relation, Ptolemy the First (Fig. 152), and in many others of the Ptolemaic gems. The prominence of forehead over the nose, ending with a deep line which divides it horizontally (Fig. 156), is an important feature of the Macedonian family. It appears in the Farnese Hercules, the head of which is remarkably small, and the original of which is attributed to Lysippus. It is also seen in a small bronze representing Hercules

returning with the apples from the Garden of the Hesperides (Plate XII. Fig. 162), which seems to combine all the peculiarities of the Lysippus school.

Two colossal marble statues, curbing horses, stand on the Monte Cavallo at Rome. One of these figures has been copied in bronze, and placed in Hyde Park. These two statues now stand as the Dioscuri; but the lineaments of Alexander are unmistakeable. The small head, rising hair, projecting forehead, large eye, full neck, and snaky locks, are all peculiarities of the Macedonian race. The violent expression of the face is very unlike Phidias, although his name is affixed to the modern pedestal, and rather indicates the style of Aristides. The costume of Phidias may be easily seen in the examples we have given from the Parthenon frieze and painted vases of the best period, and also from the bronze figure from Falterona of an early time (Plate XIII. Fig. 163), which forms a strong contrast to that of the age of Alexander. In Architecture, the last phase of Greek art to be recorded is a more slender style of Doric,

PLATE XII.—ROMAN PERIOD OF GREEK ART.

Fig. 158.—The Pirates of Tyrrhenus. From the Monument of Lysicrates.

Fig. 159.—Bacchus. From the Monument of Lysicrates.

Fig. 160.—Venus and Cupid.

Fig. 161.—Coin of Caracalla.

Fig. 162.—Coin of Fabius.

Fig. 163.—Hercules Farnese.

PLATE XIII.—ROMAN PERIOD OF GREEK ART.

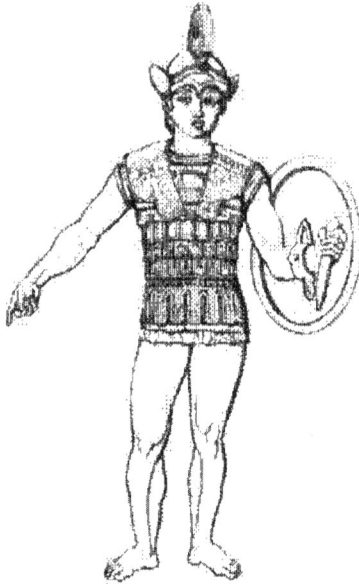

Fig. 159.—Roman Statue.

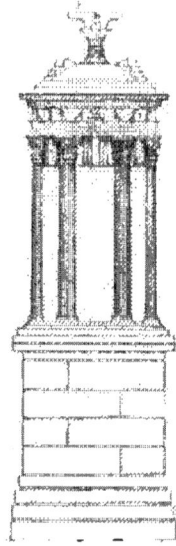

Fig. 160.—Monument of Lysicrates.

Fig. 161.

Fig. 162.—Doric Temple of Paestum.

as instanced in the fragment from Delos (**Plate XIII. Fig. 160**), inscribed with the name of a Macedonian Philip.

An artificial style of drapery is first traceable in the coins of Alexander's successors, Antigonus and his son Demetrius Poliorcetes. The drapery hangs over the arm, or from any other point of attachment, instead of falling by its **own** weight, and forming what Flaxman termed cascade drapery. The folds are made to turn up in the most unnatural manner, as in the coin of Antigonus (Fig. 167), and in a fragment from a coin of Demetrius Poliorcetes. Many archaic-looking sculptures, executed after this time, may

be detected by these peculiarities; for the early **works** are always characterised by a minute attention to the **laws** of Nature.

This artificial taste seems to have spread to other countries; for we find one beautiful coin of Pyrrhus, king of Epirus, of most elaborate workmanship and with flowing drapery (Fig. 169); while another coin of the same monarch (Fig. 170) exhibits all the peculiarity of

curves, although more artistically managed than those of Demetrius.

The Greeks were now to feel the effects of their want of union among themselves in their national degradation. In the year B.C. 167, the Greek power fell under the Roman arms, at the battle of Pydna; and, in B.C. 146, the conquest was completed by Mummius. Some of the finest objects of Greek art were carried to Rome to grace his triumph; among which was the celebrated group, by Lysippus, of horsemen slain at the Granicus. **Numerous** works of art were removed to Pergamus and other parts of Asia; **but their** transport to Rome was only temporarily delayed. The Romans soon became masters of Asia Minor,—Attalus, the last king of Pergamus, having made the Roman people his heirs.

From coins of this period we have the best means of judging of the various changes that took place in the mode of representing the hair. Bristly hair was confined only to the satyr and brute creation, thus: The snaky Alexandrian curl may be seen elaborated upon many coin

portraits, especially those of Thrasymachus and Mithridates. A head of
Neptune on a coin of Antigonus shows the rising hair and
divided locks of this period. In course of time a heavier
and more isolated mode of marking the locks was adopted
on many coins of Antiochus, and to his country must
be referred the bronze Hercules (Plate XII. Fig. 102).
The Trajan coin of Paphos (Fig. 101) is peculiar.
The coin of Caracalla (Fig. 100) represents the Farnese Hercules.

The Corinthian order of the Jupiter Olympius is so beautiful and pure, that
we may attribute the design of it to an earlier period than Hadrian. Vitruvius,
one hundred and seventeen years before that reign, states that it had already
been changed to Corinthian; and he names Cossutius as the architect, B.C. 174.
Hadrian, however, completed the Olympium, and dedicated it. Pausanias saw
within the temple two statues of Hadrian. Before the columns were brazen
statues of him; and the inclosure surrounding the building was full of similar

emblems, each of which
had been dedicated by a
city of Greece; Athens
surpassing all others by
a colossal statue.

The ruins of an archi-
tectural monument of
great curiosity, of which
a restored elevation is
given (Fig. 171), still exists on the hill of the
Museum at Athens. It
was erected to the memory
of Philopappus, a Syrian,
who lived in the time of
Trajan, and was intended
for the reception of sculpture. This structure most

Fig. 171.—Monument of Philopappus.

probably belongs to the reign of Hadrian; but the capitals of the Corinthian
order, although carefully executed, are very inferior in design to those on the
arch of that emperor, and on the Olympium.

The arch of the aqueduct built at Athens by Hadrian indicates the departure
from the early horizontal principle among the Greeks. The entablature is here
altogether curved into an arch, and may be regarded as the beginning of many
architectural monstrosities. These are to be seen combined in the ruins of

PLATE XIV.—ROMAN PERIOD OF GREEK ART.

Fig. 175.—The Laocoön.

Fig. 176.—Relief representing the Dionysiac Mysteries: the dance of the Bacchantes.

PLATE XV.—ROMAN PERIOD OF GREEK ART.

Fig. 113.—Farnese Bull, now in the Museum at Naples.

Fig. 114.—Roman Sculptures. (Alto-Rilievo.)

Diocletian's Palace at Salona. Nevertheless, art flourished under Hadrian, and to this period may be assigned the statue of Antinous in the Capitol. The coins of Antinous. however, were provincial. Of works executed in Rome, during the interval between the conclusion of the Carthaginian war and the accession of Augustus, it

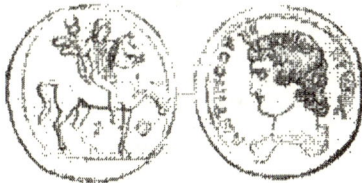

Fig. 170 of an of Antinous

will suffice to mention two compositions—Laocoon and his Sons (Plate XIV. Fig. 172), and Dirce being fastened to the Bull (Plate XV. Fig. 174). Although both these subjects were executed in Asia Minor, they best represent the arts of this period. The latter was a Rhodian production; the former was of Tralles, in Asia Minor. The Laocoon was actually found among the ruins of the very place where the ancient historian Pliny had seen it. Two bas-reliefs, each representing the same subject, namely, Achilles at Scyros (Plate XIV.

Fig. 190.

Fig. 173. and Plate XV. Fig. 175), afford a good opportunity of seeing how both—reproductions in all probability of some older and far superior work—deviate from each other with regard to design. The first, in the Louvre, is of the period of the Antonines, and exhibits Achilles—a fine figure —standing boldly forth, surrounded by the daughters of Lycomedes (Fig. 173). The other, of a later time, shows the hero lost behind a female figure and two soldiers, who are unnecessarily introduced into a prominent place, without contributing immediately to the story. The figures themselves are correspondingly inferior. Another statue of the Antonine age is given in Plate XIII. (Fig. 165) as a specimen of the mechanically-arranged drapery of the period.

A curious piece of sculpture is a statue of Julia, daughter of the Emperor Titus (Fig. 177), where the ideal and the portrait treatment are most absurdly blended. A taste for antique and affected drapery prevailed strongly even in the reign of Claudius: for we find, in a bas-relief (Fig. 178), two goddesses—the one in flowing folds and other refinements of art, while the other exhibits all the formality of wilful ignorance.

Our last subject shows an elaborately-decorated sarcophagus, with a
reclining statue introduced
lying upon it. The multitude
of subjects corresponds with the
overloaded images in the Latin
poetry of the period. There
is a violent contrast in the size
of the figures; large and small
are brought into immediate
juxtaposition; and not unfrequently small figures are placed
in front, or at the feet of larger
ones. Exuberant architectural
decoration, curiously perforated, mixes the back-ground

Fig. 159.

and accessories with the figures, producing only confusion. In this, and also
in the portrait of Venus and Cupid (Plate XII. Fig. 150), we may, indeed,
trace the imitation of previous works of excellent conception and composition;
but marked by the most ignorant execution and barbarous forms.

The age of Constantine affords so many examples of utter barbarism, that
the eye can with difficulty be brought to dwell upon them. Indeed the condition of the arts has now reached the extremity of neglect and worthlessness;
and the reader will turn with satisfaction from this subject to the descriptions of
nature, and freshness of thought, which will be met with in the succeeding pages.

Fig. 178.—Reni Bettas Rumford, etc.

GREECE

GREECE.

WHEN Aristagoras, governor of Miletus, came to Sparta to request assistance from Cleomenes, the king of that city, he brought with him a tablet of bronze, on which was engraved an outline of the Earth, and whereon the circuits of Seas and courses of Rivers were traced. This Map was probably the work of Hecatæus, the historian of the Asiatic city. It is the earliest effort of geographical delineation which we read of in the annals of Greece. Although rude and imperfect, it served the purpose of conveying to the mind of the spectator a general idea of the leading features of the countries which it portrayed, and was therefore thought worthy of being brought from Asia into Greece, and of being exhibited by an ambassador to a king.

In this our Geographical Introduction to the present work, we shall endeavour to present to the reader a rapid sketch of the geography of Greece, similar in execution to that of the bronze tablet which Aristagoras put into the hands of Cleomenes. We shall attempt to exhibit, in a comprehensive and general outline, the forms of its lands, and seas and rivers. This difference, however, will be observed: we design to construct a Map from a view of the Country, rather than to communicate an idea of the Country from the contemplation of a Map.

For this purpose, let us take our station on one of the most commanding heights of that long range of mountains, which, running from north to south in an uninterrupted line, nearly bisects the Continent of Greece. This chain, formerly known by the name of PINDUS, is, as it were, the spine or back-bone of that country. Its successive vertebræ are distinguished by different appellations. That which we have chosen as the point to which we shall now refer, is at present termed ZYGO, resembling, in name, the Helvetian JUGU, which

separates the valley of Engelberg from that of Meyringen. It was formerly called Lacmos, and stands in 39° 50' north latitude, and 21° 20' east longitude. It hangs over the town of Metzovo, which is familiar to all travellers who have passed from Iannina over Mount Pindus, in an eastward course, on their road either to Larissa or Thessalonica.

The height of Zygo is one of the most remarkable in the geography of Continental Greece. It is the centre and focus, as it were, to which different radii converge from all the shores, by which, on three sides, that country is

bounded. What the Milliarium Aureum, or
gilded Milestone, which stood in the Forum of
Rome, and from which the Roads of Italy
were measured, and what the Altar of the
Twelve Gods, which was erected in the centre
of the Agora of Athens, and at which those
of Attica commenced—what these two grand
central points were to the routes of those two
countries respectively, such is this eminence to
the rivers—the liquid roads—of Greece. It is
what the glacier of the Rhone is to Switzerland.
At its foot, Five Rivers, the largest in the terra-
firma of Greece, take their rise, and connect this
central spot with the ADRIATIC and IONIAN SEA
on one side, and with the THERMAIC GULF and
the ÆGÆAN on the other, and with the mouth
of the CORINTHIAN GULF, between these two,
on the third. The rivers of which we speak,
are the AÖUS, the ARACHTHUS, the HALIACMON,
the PENÈUS, and the ACHELOUS.

It may reasonably be supposed, that, when
Virgil conceived in his mind that noble and
original picture, which he has presented to his
readers at the close of the fourth Georgic, of
the subterranean grotto, in which all the Rivers
of the earth arose, and from which they
issued, by hidden channels and silent courses,
into every quarter of the globe, that the idea
was suggested to his mind by this spot, in
which, with respect to the continent of Greece,
his poetical vision may be said to be realized.
This conjecture derives support from the consideration, that the scene which he is then

describing is laid in Thessaly, and indeed at the source of the Peneus itself, one of the rivers which rises from this mountain-reservoir at our feet.

The reader will also remember the use which our own Poet, in the Paradise Regained, makes of the *roads* of Italy in his description of the city of Rome, from which they all start, and to which they all return. He will recollect how Milton sends, as it were, his thoughts from that spot, to travel by those routes to the most distant points of the Roman Empire—how, for instance, by the Æmilian Way, he penetrates, in imagination, into the forests of Germany, and traverses the British West; how he thence crosses to the Sarmatians, and beyond the Danube to the Tauric Pool: and how again, by the southern communication of the Appian Way, he migrates downward to Syene, and wanders eastward to India, and the golden Chersonese.

So it is with the Grecian traveller who stands on the point of which we have been speaking. By means of these Five Rivers which we have named, all starting from this point, he holds converse with noble Cities, and thick Forests, and rich Valleys, and Fields of Battle, upon their banks, which crowd together in his mind; and with the seas themselves into which they fall, and with the

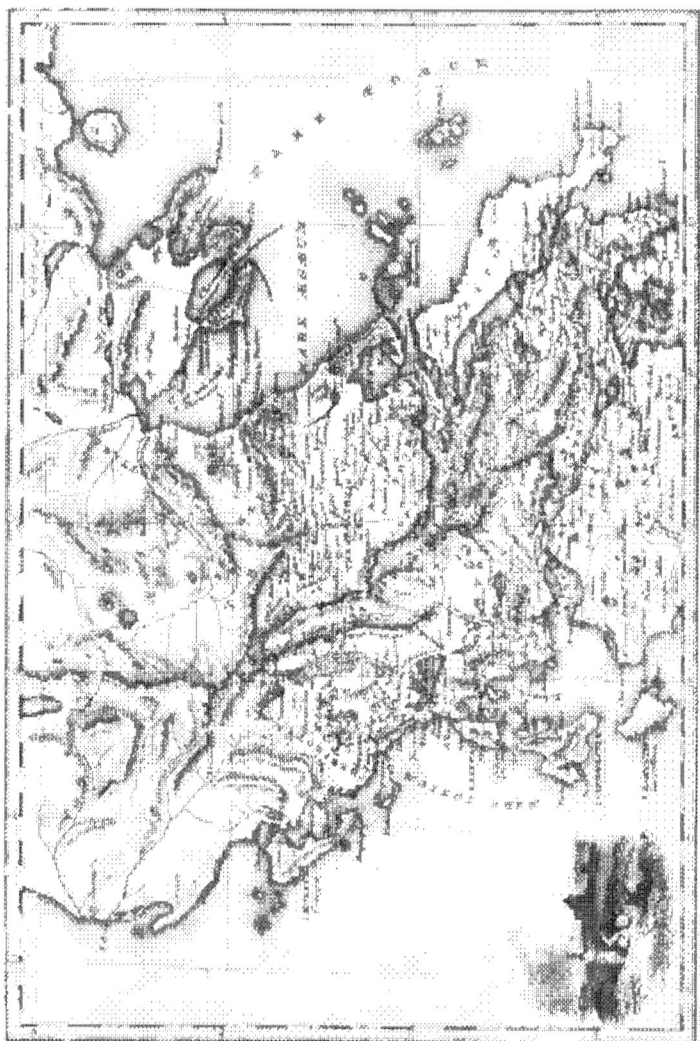

Islands which hang upon their coasts. Let him therefore rest for a while, after the toil of his ascent, on some clear day of summer, on one of the limestone rocks in this place; and beneath the shade of the beeches and the pines which wave over his head, let him indulge in such reflections as these.

First of all, let him turn his thoughts in the direction by which he himself has probably come. The river Αὅος, perhaps so called by a Doric or Æolic form, because it flows from the EAST, now the Voioussa, which is a corruption of the same word, issues from the earth at this spot. If he follows its course in his imagination, he will pass through a solitary tract of sterile and rugged country, broken by defiles and ravines, which were formerly inhabited by the Parsvæi, so named from their neighbourhood to the river of which we speak. He will trace the progress of the stream through a long and narrow gorge, called the straits of the Aöus, once traversed by a Roman army of 9,000 men, under the guidance of their young leader the Consul T. Q. Flamininus, in pursuit of the Macedonian King, whose defeat by that General was speedily followed by the extinction of the liberties of Greece. This is the only spot of historical interest which he will discover in his course through this bleak and lonely country, until he arrives, after a route of more than a hundred miles, within sight of the hill APOLLONIA, the coast of Epirus, and the shining waters of the Hadriatic.

MOUNTAIN PASS PERSPECTIVE

He is here brought into immediate contact with that long and famous line of Corinthian Colonies, of which Apollonia is one, which stretched along the western coast of Greece from Corinth upwards to this point. Bearing in his mind the wise and beautiful custom by which those Colonies derived the Fire, which they kept ever burning in their Prytaneum, from the sacred Hearth of their Mother State, he may regard these Cities, on their own hills, as a system of Beacons, burning along the coast, and communicating in a telegraphic series of national communion from the summit of the Acrocorinth to the borders of Illyria.

From this point the passage to Italy lies open before him, and on a bright day he will descry the harbour of Brundusium, so often wished for by those who were caught by tempests on this gulf, when the passage was rendered perilous by the stormy gusts sweeping down upon it from the Acroceraunian rocks.

Apollonia was the retreat of Augustus Cæsar when he was a student and a philosopher, before he became Emperor : as Rhodes was afterwards that of Tiberius. Here the great nephew of Julius resided in tranquillity and retirement for several years. A few huts, a monastery and a church, some ruinous remains of two temples, and some fragments of ancient inscriptions, are all the vestiges that survive of the polished city which initiated in literature and arts the future master of the world.

It is worthy of notice, that the scenes of the two most remarkable events in

the life of the Emperor Augustus, lie at the mouths of the two rivers of Greece, which, issuing from the same spot, flow downward into the sea which washes the western coast of that country. At the entrance of the Aöus into the Hadriatic, he passed some years, as has been said, of his early life in the peaceful pursuits of literary leisure at Apollonia. Near the mouth of the

Arachthus, or river of Arta, which rises by the side of the Aöus, and flows down in a southern course by the city of Ambracia, the modern Arta,—where it passes under a handsome bridge, one of the few now remaining in Greece, into the Ambracian Gulf,—we see him no longer a student clad in his peaceful toga, and walking on the sea-shore in conversation with philosophers of Greece, but dressed in the military sagum, with one hundred thousand men and two hundred and fifty ships at his command, and, as Virgil expresses it, bringing the "Gods of Italy, with the Senators and people of Rome, the Penates and great Gods," to that battle which ended in giving him the empire of the world.

As its name indicates, the city of Apollonia was under the special tutelage of Apollo; and in the descriptions of this decisive victory, Apollo is represented as standing on his own promontory of ACTIUM, with his quiver on his shoulder, his bow drawn, and his arrows pointed against the foes of the favoured Augustus; and thus the same deity is associated with the same man,

BAY OF THE ARTA

near the mouths of these two great rivers, which rise at the same point, and fall—the one after a course of a hundred, the other of sixty miles—into the same sea.

There are two spots—one on the east, the other on the western coast of Greece, both nearly in the same latitude—which are both famous for the great battles fought near them, in causes very different, and very dissimilar from each other in the character and feeling of the combatants. These are THERMOPYLÆ and ACTIUM. They are now remarkable, as being the most distinguished sites near the two terminations of the frontier line which separates Free Greece from Turkey. The horizon of Greek liberty stretches from a point on the western coast, a little to the south of Actium, to another on the eastern, a little to the north of Thermopylæ.

We return to the position which we had chosen on Mount Pindus,—namely, the spot from which the two rivers, of which we have spoken, take their rise. Let us now turn our thoughts eastward. A third river, rising in the same spot, and flowing in that direction, is ready to accompany us in this excursion. This is the HALIACMON.

The Thermaic Gulf, into which it flows, would indeed hardly have been considered, in the best times of Greek history, as possessing a claim to be reckoned among the bays which washed the coast of Greece, properly so called. In that age, the name of Greece did not extend beyond the barrier of the

CAMBUNIAN Mountains; but the successful arms of Philip of Macedon, and the more brilliant conquests of his son Alexander the Great, conferred the rights of Greek citizenship on the country which he ruled, and made it as honourable for Greece to claim Macedonia, as it was for Macedonia to be admitted into Greece. To Macedonia,—a province which Greece had long refused to acknowledge as an integral part of the Hellenic nation,—she stood afterwards indebted for the diffusion of her language and literature, by means of those conquests, to the remotest corners of the globe. And it is worthy of remark, that the same district, which was regarded as *barbarous* by the statesmen and philosophers of the most enlightened age of Greek civilization, was the *first* to invite and welcome that *better Philosophy*, to which Greece has owed, after the lapse of so many centuries, her own revival from national degradation and decay. It was not an inhabitant of Corinth or of Athens, but "a man of Macedonia," who stood by the side of St. Paul as he slept, and called him from Asia into Greece, and said, "Come over and help us." To us, therefore, the country intersected by the Haliacmon presents an object of attraction and interest peculiar to itself, as being that region of Greece which was first visited by Christianity. At a little distance from the left bank of this river, and not far from its entrance into the sea, stands, amid luxuriant plane-trees and well-watered gardens, the town of DERRHŒA—still preserving its ancient name, whose inhabitants "were more noble than those of Thessalonica, because they searched the Scriptures daily," and therefore receive so honourable a testimony from the inspired companion of St. Paul, who visited that city on his first journey into Greece. A little further to the east, and on the shores of the Thermaic Gulf, is THESSALONICA (a name now changed from its ancient form to Saloniki), which was favoured by the earliest personal ministrations of the Apostle, and by the first effort of his pen in the Christian cause.

More celebrated than the Haliacmon in the pages of Greek Poets and Historians, is another River which rises at the same spot, and flows for several miles in the same direction. The valley of the PENEUS,—the stream to which we now allude,—is separated from that of the Haliacmon by a chain of mountains, which, commencing near the spot in which these rivers rise, runs off from the PINDUS in an easterly direction, and, under the name of the Cambunian Hills, stretches away to the coast of the same sea, into which they fall. The snowy eminence which there terminates their range on the left, is OLYMPUS, the fabled residence of the Homeric Deities. A little farther in the distance, on the right bank of the same river, rises the conical peak of OSSA; placed, as Poets feigned, on the ridges of Pelion by the hands of the giants when they aspired to scale heaven.

Parallel to the Cambunian Hills, at about sixty miles to the south, and branching off in the same manner, from Mount Pindus to the east, and also extending to the sea, is Mount OTHRYS. These are the three rocky barriers,— namely, the Cambunian Hills on the north, Mount Othrys on the south, and Mount Pindus on the west,—which form, if we may so speak, a mountain Triclinium, bounding the rich and fertile table-land of THESSALY. On the east it is fed with plentiful resources by the sea.

Nearly through the centre of this plain, and in the direction above specified, sweeps the Peneus, in a semicircular course. As it declines to the south soon after it has quitted the mountain of its birth, so as it approaches the sea, it verges upwards in a northerly direction, and enters a rocky gorge five miles in length, which is formed by two mountains—namely, OLYMPUS on the north, and OSSA on the south. This is TEMPE.

The history of the river Peneus is that of THESSALY. Its origin on the summit of Mount Pindus speaks of the rocky bulwark by which that country is fenced from the western half of Greece: its slow and winding course, after its descent from that mountain, tells of the level and extensive plain of which Thessaly is formed. Again, that vast area of flat soil reminds the spectator of the results which these physical elements produced, especially if considered in contrast with the rugged surface of the rest of the continent of Greece. They call to his recollection the historical facts, that Thessaly was a land of corn-fields, of flocks and herds, of horses and of battles.

Of its fertility, the name of CRANNON, which is not far from the river's bank, with its records of the rich court of the Scopadæ, the friends of Simonides, and of their oxen, which, as the Sicilian poet Theocritus says, in some most musical verses, lowed as they went to their stalls, and the ten thousand sheep which were driven under the shade, along its plain, will afford sufficient evidence. And the appearance of the Centaurs in the fields of Thessaly, and their mythological appropriation to this country, would be sufficient proof of its equestrian superiority to the rest of Greece, if others of a more recent date were not supplied by the conquests achieved in international warfare by the cavalry of Thessaly. Lastly, the tributary streams which flow into the Peneus, bring with them thither the names of cities by which they flow, and beneath the walls of which those warlike feats were done, which gained for the Thessalian plain the name of the "Orchestra of Mars." Thus, for instance, the APIDANUS bears along with it into the river of which we speak, the fame of the battle of the plain of PHARSALIA, which it laves; and the ONOCHONUS contributes to the same channel the names, scarcely less memorable in the history of war, of SCOTUSSÆ and CYNOSCEPHALÆ.

We have reserved, for our final excursion, the course of a stream, which, even in the strains of the Italian muse, was celebrated as the first-born of all the rivers. The ACHELÖUS was generally considered, in Greece, as the symbol and synonyme of water; and this is probably to be ascribed to its superiority in magnitude to the other streams of the Greek Continent; and it was also a more remarkable object to all visitors from the western world, than any other of these, not merely from its size, but because it came under their notice in the passage, either up the Gulf of Corinth, or in their course to the southward,

ENTRANCE TO THE GULF OF CORINTH.

round the Peloponnesian Peninsula. In tracing its progress from its source, we are led through a rude, mountainous, and thinly-peopled country, the fastnesses of which have never been cleared of robbers, from the earliest times to the present—after a course of one hundred and thirty miles, we witness its union with the ocean, at the point where the Ionian Sea may be said to end, and the Gulf of Corinth to begin.

Quitting our station at Zygo, near Metzovo, on Mount Pindus, but still remaining upon the same ridge of mountains, we pursue our course southward, following the line which is made by the successive links of this long and continuous chain. We proceed in this direction for a distance of sixty miles. Here we arrive at an eminence formerly called Mount TYMPHRESTUS, but now termed Beluchi. As Mount Zygo is the central point from which the *rivers* of Continental Greece take their origin, and thence diverge towards all the shores by which that country is bounded, so may Mount Tymphrestus be regarded as the centre from which its *mountains* radiate in the same manner.

From the north, the range of Pindus descends to this point; on the east, the ridge of Othrys branches from it to the sea; the Œtæan chain stretches to the south-east, towards the same coast; to the west it extends itself, from this central spot, along the northern frontier of ÆTOLIA and ACARNANIA, under the name of the AGRÆAN Hills, until it arrives at the shore of the Ambracian Gulf; southward, is the continuation of Mount Pindus, which, shortly after it has passed by this point, changes both its name and direction.

Diverging gradually to the south-east, it assumes different titles as it goes through the various stages of its course, and forms the barrier which separates one valley or province from another. Thus, it divides the southern half of

PHOCIS from the vale of the CEPHISSUS, and is then called PARNASSUS: in BŒOTIA, it becomes HELICON; as CITHÆRON and PARNES, it severs the Bœotian vale of the ASOPUS from the plain of ATTICA; thence, pursuing its course southward, it bisects the Attic Peninsula; and having raised its head

in divers summits, and borne the
illustrious names of BRILESSUS,
PENTELICUS, and HYMETTUS, it
gently subsides into the declivities of Mount LAUREUM, and sinks
into the sea at SUNIUM.

It does not terminate here:
but may be supposed to emerge
again in the rugged and lofty
crags of the Island-chain which
hangs from this promontory. It
may be recognised in the cliffs of CEOS, and in the
citadel of THERMIA. We may trace it to the white
quarries of PAROS, in the CYNTHIAN hill of DELOS,
and in the crystal grotto of ANTIPAROS. We may
pursue its course to the TRIOPIAN promontory in
CNIDOS, and the PANIONIAN hill at EPHESUS, by
means of the rocky group of the CYCLADES and
SPORADES of the ÆGÆAN Sea, which serve as
natural stepping-stones to conduct us across the
Archipelago, to the continent of Asia from Greece.

In order to obtain a general view of the country
of Attica, the traveller will pass from the eminences
of Cithæron to those of Parnes; he will then ascend
the summit of Pentelicus, whence he will pass southward to that of HYMETTUS.

From the other points he will enjoy magnificent
prospects of hill and plain, and beyond these, of the
waters of the seas which wash the shores and pene-
trate the creeks of the Athenian peninsula. But
from the eminence of Hymettus he will obtain the
noblest view of the immortal CITY itself. Thence
he will see ATHENS, placed on the central rock of
its Acropolis, whose form and colour are exquisitely
beautiful, lying under a clear sky, and still surmounted by the marble temples of its ancient gods;
he will see the city lying at its feet; he will follow
with his eye the long line of the SACRED WAY to
Eleusis; on this, the eastern side of the City he will

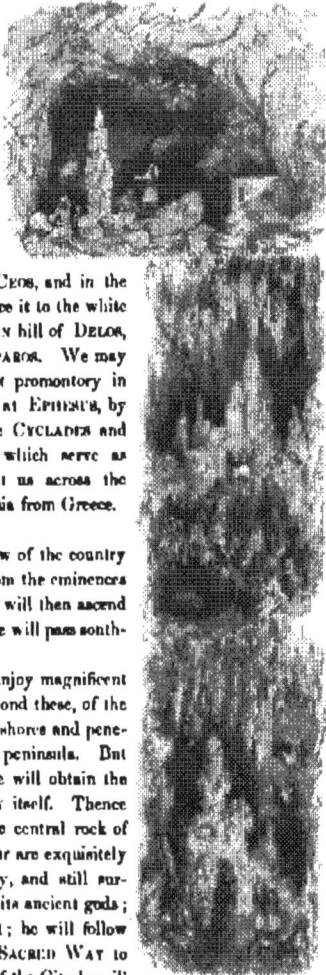

" Look once more, ere we leave this specular mount,
Westward, much nearer by north-west behold ;
Where on the Ægean shore a City stands,
Built nobly ; pure the air, and light the soil ;
ATHENS, the eye of Greece, mother of arts
And eloquence, native to famous wits,
Or hospitable, in her sweet recess,
City or suburban, studious walks and shades.
See there the olive grove of ACADEME,
Plato's retirement, where the Attic bird
Trills her thick warbled notes the summer long ;
There flowery hill HYMETTUS, with the sound
Of bees' industrious murmur, oft invites
To studious musing ; there Ilissus rolls
His whispering stream : within the walls then view
The schools of ancient sages ; his who bred
Great Alexander to subdue the world,
Lyceum there, and painted STOA next."

Remaining in the same position on the heights of Hymettus, let him now cast a glance *eastward*. Immediately beneath him extends the MESOGÆA or INTERIOR of Attica, sprinkled over with numerous villages : to the north-east he will see the cape CYNOSURA, which projects into the sea from the northern extremity of the plain of Marathon : further to the south-east are the lofty summits of CARYSTUS, concealing in their recesses their rich streaked veins of cipollino, and the GERÆSTIAN promontory, in the island of Euboea : beyond it to the south-east are the rocky cliffs of ANDROS and TENOS, and the cluster of the Cyclades grouped around their central islet of DELOS ; and in a line between that spot and himself, he will pursue with his eye the range of hills which proceed onward from the mountain on which he stands, and run in a southerly direction over the silver mines of LAUREUM, sinking into the sea at the SUNIAN promontory.

Where *Rivers* discharge themselves into the Ocean, there Cities are built, harbours are formed, and commerce flourishes. *Here*, at Sunium, where this *Stream of Hills*, which we have now followed for three hundred miles, falls into the sea, stands an object not unworthy to mark the close of its career. The solitary and beautiful TEMPLE, once dedicated to Minerva, which crowns the summit of the Sunian Cape, is the goal of their long and continuous course, which connects the central heights of PINDUS with the last promontory of ATTICA.

CAPE SUNIUM FROM THE SEA.

ITHOME AND CAPE MATAPAN

I F Lucian, in his dialogue which derives its
title from their Contemplations, had desired
to direct the attention of Mercury and Charon
to the portion of Greece which is called the
PELOPONNESUS, he would probably have adopted
an expedient similar to that here employed in
order to give them a more extensive prospect.
The wish of one of those two personages whom
we have mentioned was not merely to be presented with a view, as he
expresses it, of Cities and Mountains, but to behold the inhabitants, and to
learn what were their occupations and conversation. For this purpose he
chose an eminence to which he and his companion ascended, and which
commanded a sight of the objects he desired to contemplate.

Our present design is not so extensive as that which was entertained by
the philosopher of Samosata. From the imaginary summit where they stood
he exhibited to his two spectators a comprehensive panorama, which embraced
the islands of Ionia and the coast of Lydia on the east, Sicily and Italy on the
west, and stretched from the Danube, southward, to the shores of Crete. Our
view is limited to the district which lies nearly in the centre of these points.

P

He showed to Mercury and Charon, a prospect of the known world from an ideal summit : we would exhibit to the spectator, from a real mount, a view of the Peninsula of Greece.

The spot most suitable for this purpose is the apex of a mountain on the western frontier of ARCADIA. Its peaked and isolated crest is crowned with a ruined castle ; its slopes are sprinkled with groups of cottages and sheepfolds, and thinly clad with low forests of oaks and mountain pines. It rises on the western side of Mount LYCÆUS, the hill sacred of old to Pan and to the King of the Goats. It is now called Zakkouka.

From this point the spectator beholds the Map of the Peloponnesus unrolled before his eyes. Looking northward, he sees the lofty range of the Arcadian hills, which, commencing with the heights of the woody ERYMANTHUS, run in an easterly direction to the central eminence of CYLLENÉ, thus dividing the coast-land of ACHAIA from the inland territory of Arcadia.

From the rocky pile of Cyllené his eye moves southward, and traces the

continuation of the same ridges in that direction, till they arrive at the hill of MÆNALUS, whose pine-tree groves have been celebrated in the pastoral poetry of Greece and Italy. This rocky barrier separates Arcadia on the west from the Argolic peninsula on the east.

Mount Mænalus, at the south-east angle of Arcadia, connects itself with a long chain of hills, which stretch from that point further to the south-east, till they terminate in the Ægean Sea. They form the eastern boundary of the plain of Sparta: their most remarkable mountain is PARNON. The snow-capped summits of this ridge are visible from the point where we now suppose ourselves placed, the summit of Lycæus.

A line drawn from Mount Mænalus towards the west, and terminating in this point, forms the southern limit of Arcadia: from this summit, the magnificent range of Mount TAYGETUS, which runs in a parallel line to that

MOUNT TAYGETUS, FROM THE PLAINS OF SPARTA.

of Parnon, and bounds the Spartan Valley on the west, as Parnon does on the east, branches off to the south-east, and goes on in an uninterrupted course till it at last arrives at the southern coast of LACONIA, where it ends in the TÆNARIAN promontory, the most southern point of the Grecian Peninsula. This noble chain of hills is seen from our station on Mount Zakkouka. Nearer to us are the verdant and cultivated declivities of the Lycæan mountains of Arcadia.

On the west of that chain, the spectator from this eminence beholds the rugged and irregular surface of MESSENIA, which is separated from Laconia by the long and lofty range of Taÿgetus. Further to the south he perceives the coast of Coronè, and the waters of the Messenian Gulf.

Turning his eyes to the north-west, he sees the fruitful plains of ELIS stretching themselves along the western shore of the Peloponnesus; and, being fatigued by a monotonous view of rude and rugged mountains, some bare and uncultivated, some capped with snow, others thinly clad with the meagre produce of a stunted vegetation, and seeming to refuse all recompense to the industry of the husbandman, his eye will rest with delight on the wide and luxuriant plain of Olympia, refreshed and beautified by the waters of the Alphèus, winding through it to the sea.

From the rapid survey which our view from this eminence has enabled us to make of the Greek peninsula, we may derive some general inferences from its physical conformation and local peculiarities, with reference to the moral, social, and political consequences which may be considered as the result of these characteristics.

It is impossible to avoid the reflection, which such a view as the present suggests, that the PELOPONNESUS was intended by nature to be the seat of different tribes of inhabitants, varying in manners and government. The Alps have formed the Cantons of Switzerland; and in the Peloponnesus, whose greatest length is one hundred and fifty miles, the greatest breadth being one hundred and thirty, similar causes were in operation to produce similar results.

The central province of Arcadia resembles a large natural Camp, fortified by a lofty and impregnable circumvallation of mountains.

MAENALUS, AND VALLEY OF THE HELISSON.

Around this circular bulwark lie the other provinces of the Peninsula: they abut, as it were, upon this central wall, which serves as a defence to them from the interior, while their external frontier is formed by the sea, which supplied them at once with an outlet and protection. Each of these Provinces is separated from its neighbours by mountain radii thrown out toward the sea from the mural circle of Arcadia.

If we may be allowed to illustrate its local peculiarities by such a com-

parison, we may regard the entire Peloponnesus as a vast natural Colosseum,
of which Arcadia is the Arena, surrounded by its Podium, or
parapet of high mountains. The other provinces, separated
from each other by mountain Viæ, which diverge from this
podium, are the Cunei, bounded externally by a wall of
sea. We shall have occasion to remark hereafter, that
the Arcadian Arena of which we speak possesses but one
outlet, or Vomitorium, namely, that through which the
Alpheus flows away to the Ionian Sea. There is also

one entrance or Corridor, which leads to the interior of the whole. This is
the Isthmus of Corinth.

If we were to form an opinion from the stern features which characterise
the external appearance of this natural arena and cunei, it might be supposed
that there was little probability of their offering the charms and allurements
of a refined and pleasurable existence; and this would certainly have been
the case, had they depended for their principal recommendations on their
physical structure.

But while these were of the character we have attempted to describe, the
air and climate which were combined with them served to mitigate the
asperities of their other attributes. The arena and cunei of the Peloponnesus
were formed of rugged and bleak mountains, but a clear and brilliant sky,
such as hangs over few other countries in the world, was their Velarium.

The description of physical elements, then, which is applicable to Greece in
general, is especially appropriate to that part of it which we are now describing.
The great kingdoms of Europe are not more distinctly severed from each other
by their natural boundaries, than the small provinces of the Morea are by

theirs. Each of these possesses, as it were, its own Alps and Pyrenees. Hence there was little unity among them. Each of them was self-sufficient and independent. Hence, too, their history is that of separate countries, rather than of one; and of countries opposed to, as well as divided from, each other. In looking down as we have done from the heights of Lycæus on the two southern provinces of the Peninsula,—Messenia and Laconia,— separated from each other by the long Apennine of Mount Taygetus, we are reminded of the bitter enmity which exasperated the ancient inhabitants

of these two districts against each other, and which raged the more fiercely in consequence of the opportunities for military aggression, which their contiguity afforded, and which was only terminated by the national extinction of one of the belligerent parties.

It would have been fortunate for Messenia if no barrier had existed between itself and its more powerful neighbour. It might then have been incorporated in Laconia as a part of that country, instead of being subjugated by it; its inhabitants might have risen to be Spartans, instead of being depressed into Helots.

Thus locally isolated from, and opposed to, each other, the provinces of the Peninsula never organized among themselves a national confederacy for mutual protection, or for the attainment of any great political object. The battles of Greece were never fought against a national foe within the limits of the Peloponnesus. In the pass of Thermopylæ, upon the plain of Marathon, on the field of Platæa, in the Straits of Salamis, the cause of the Hellenic Nation was nobly defended; but not on the Isthmus of Corinth.

The PELOPONNESUS indeed has, by the Greek Geographer Strabo, been styled the ACROPOLIS of Greece: and as such it might seem to offer within itself the best means for the defence of the national cause. The character

which he has assigned to it might reasonably appear to arise from its position and local advantages: but, in fact,- from its possession of numerous mountain passes and isolated piles of rock, such as those, for instance, which overhang the castellated monastery of MEGASPELION,—this Acropolis contained within itself too many minor and independent citadels, and these citadels were too well fortified in themselves, to render their inhabitants very solicitous about the general welfare and security of the great national fortress, whose legitimate defenders were too often engaged in besieging the castles of their neighbours, to regard the defence and safety of the whole as an object of much interest or importance to any of them in their individual character.

Hence it arose, that all attempts to unite and concentrate the nations of the Peloponnesus in one federal body, however prudently devised, and with whatever zeal, integrity, and sagacity they might have been prosecuted, did not meet with the success which under different circumstances would have attended them.

The Achæan League, framed by the deliberate wisdom of a people who were distinguished by the excellence of their civil institutions, consolidated as it was by the political and military prudence and energy of Aratus, and animated by the vigour of Philopœmen, was not able to overcome the difficulties which Nature seemed to have thrown in its way to impede and thwart its progress.

The influence of this confederacy was felt along the level coasts, and over

the extensive lowland of Achaia: it reached the walls of Ægium, of Sicyon, and the Isthmus of Corinth; and thence descended, embracing within its grasp the city of Argos and some other towns of the Argolic Peninsula: it was enabled to conquer the geographical obstructions which there embarrassed it: it passed with difficulty over the mountain chains of Erymanthus and Cyllené, and reached the walls of the Arcadian Megalopolis; but it met with a hostile power which arrested its career, on the frontier of Laconia; and, though it succeeded for a time, by measures of vigorous coercion, in reducing the Capital of that country, and attaching it to the league; yet this forced union produced so much of national antipathy among the parties thus intended to be cemented together, that it furnished the circumstance which ultimately led to the dissolution of the whole, and ended the national struggle by combining the antagonists,—not indeed in a confederacy among themselves,—but by reducing them to the common condition of subjects to the foreign despotism of Rome.

An illustration of this national disaffection of these provinces among themselves, and of their subsequent amalgamation under the levelling domination of the Roman power, is supplied by the numismatic history of the Peloponnesus.

SITE OF ORCHOMENUS IN ARCADIA.

While each of these possessed in its coinage its peculiar symbol, derived from its own history or mythology, or from its various productions either of nature or of art,—while, for instance, Achaia exhibited on her medals the effigy of her own deities, Jupiter and Ceres,—while Argolis referred to the temple of Juno and the games of NEMEA as the peculiar glories and ornaments of her own soil,—while the forms of the tutelary Dioscuri appeared on the coins of Laconia, and Elis displayed her national cognizance by appealing to her popular solemnity in honour of the Olympian Jove, these several States never united together in any such expression of their common sympathy among themselves, or of their social attachment—either to the soil of the Peloponnesus as their common country, or to one another as joint members of the same national family. They never emblazoned their union in any such

THE PLAINS OF TROY

device, so long as they were enabled to do so from the spontaneous dictates of civil freedom and unfettered choice. They were not combined until they were conquered. It was left for Rome to unite the States of Greece. The first coin which expressed the feelings of amity and relationship which a community of soil, sea, and sky seemed likely to inspire in the minds of those who shared them, was struck under the auspices of the Roman Consul, Titus Quintius Flamininus.

The absence of union alluded to was the main cause which led to this subversion,—a result for which it would otherwise have appeared difficult to assign any adequate reason. Placed in a central position between Asia and Italy, admirably adapted for facilitating the communication between them, washed on three sides by a frequented sea, not ill supplied with harbours for the reception of shipping such as was used in the commerce of those days, and with abundance of timber for the building of vessels, the Peloponnesus possessed ample natural qualifications for becoming the seat of a flourishing trade, and the scene of mercantile activity. This source of prosperity, however, was in fact never reached. The states of the Peninsula were too much occupied in the struggles of international warfare, to devote their attention to the more useful and humanizing pursuits of peace. Few ships were seen in its ports; there was little interchange of its own produce with that of foreign lands; nor could it boast any great skill or success in domestic manufactures for the advantage of its own inhabitants. The exceptions to this assertion are

CITY OF PATRE IN ACHAIA

found in the instances of PATRÆ, SICYON, and CORINTH, which enjoyed the advantage of possessing the most desirable situations for mercantile purposes, and which were removed from the pernicious influence of the intestine broils which distracted the more central cities of the Peloponnesus.

In considering the civil disorganisation, which prevailed in the earlier ages of the history of the Peloponnesus, and amid the social convulsions produced by it, it becomes more interesting to remark, that a desire of tranquillity, and a longing—natural to man in his better moods—for that gratification which arises from peaceful repose and friendly intercourse, did not fail to stamp some impress, in visible characters, on the face of the Peloponnesian soil. While the other districts of the Peninsula, with their stern and rugged forms, seemed to resist all attempts to blend and fuse them together,— while their mountain defiles and fastnesses offered the most favourable sites for the exercise of military skill,—while their limestone rocks afforded facilities and supplied materials for surrounding their towns with walls, hewn from its quarries, and of fortifying their citadels with the massy bulwarks of polygonal masonry, which still crown the summits of their precipitous cliffs; while thus, under the influence of evil passions, the Peloponnesus appeared formed to be a workshop of War, yet, on one small portion of this country, Nature shed a more peaceful influence; and Man, acting from the dictates of gentler feelings, after the storm of warlike passions had subsided, was not reluctant to give a visible character and expression to

this genial and softer power. While the other provinces were so many Theatres of War, *that* which surrounded the city of ELIS was consecrated by the united voices of the peninsular population, as a TEMPLE OF PEACE. The land itself was considered holy and inviolable. The sound of arms was not permitted to cross its frontier. It was the Delos of the Peloponnesus. Here was a perpetual armistice; and not only was the influence of this asylum felt within its own limits, but at stated periods it extended itself to the other parts of the Peninsula.

The full Moon which succeeded the Summer solstice, and gave the signal for the celebration of the OLYMPIAN GAMES,—which were under the direction and control of the citizens of Elis, and were celebrated once in four years, —was like a natural Herald, proclaiming peace to the inhabitants of the neighbouring provinces of Greece, who, however bitter their enmity at other times might be, and within the frontiers of other provinces, resorted with feelings of a different kind to the hallowed limits of Elis, and stood as friends and brothers, at that season, on the banks of the Alphēus, beneath the shade of the olive-grove of OLYMPIA.

We have endeavoured to show how the political state of the Peloponnesus received its tone and character from the physical form and features of the soil itself; and it would not be an uninteresting speculation to examine how the religious faith, the mythological traditions, and the social manners of its inhabitants, were affected by influences arising from the same source.

There is no country, of the same dimensions, in Europe, which has been the scene of so many and such varying natural revolutions, as that which we are now describing. It has been the arena of conflicts, not merely between man and man, but of even fiercer struggles, in which the elements of nature have been the combatants. The "loss of the Rhone," which dives into a subterranean channel beneath the rocks of the Ecluse, has attracted the notice and excited the wonder of the Swiss traveller; and in Italy, the stupendous works by which the waters of the Alban and Fucine lakes have been reduced from their ancient level, and conducted through the centre of high hills, by means of long, deep, and broad emissaries, serve as proofs of the power and ingenuity of man to rival the operations of nature. The Copaic lake, in the continent of Greece, presents examples of a similar kind. But the single province of Arcadia, in the Peloponnesus, exhibits wonders of this description which may vie with all these. From the sides of the mountains by which this country is encircled, numerous torrents descend into the hollows of the rocky crater of which Arcadia is formed; and there is little reason to distrust the ancient tradition which records that this basin itself was originally a large lake.

At present there is one valley through which these streams discharge themselves, and one only. It is at the northern foot of the mountain which we have chosen as the centre of our panoramic view of the Peloponnesus, namely, Mount Lycæus. Through this gorge, which tends to the north-west, the rivers which flow westward from the centre of Arcadia find their way into the Ionian Sea, having united themselves to the stream which receives the waters of nearly all the rivers of the west of the Peloponnesus, namely, the Alphēus.

But on the eastern side of Arcadia no such outlet exists for the discharge of its streams as is found in the valley at the roots of Mount Lycæus. The waters there are left either to stagnate in the hollows of the valley, and to expand themselves into lakes, or to force their way by subterranean chasms through the rocky barrier of the hills. By a benevolent provision of Nature, the geological formation of these mountains is such as to admit of the latter alternative. The limestone strata of which they consist allow of easy perforation by the agency of the rushing waters. Hence, these streams, which seemed destined to be pent up within their rocky prisons, have opened for themselves valves and sluices by which the inland country has been rescued from inundation, and the ulterior provinces fertilized as if by a process of artificial irrigation. The lake or rather the river of STYMPHALUS, at the southern foot of the Arcadian mountain of Cyllené, discharges itself from its channel at the

VALLEY OF THE SUPREME OF TIME.

bottom of a limestone precipice, where it enters the earth and passes by a hidden course under a range of mountains to the south-east side, till at last it emerges from its dark bed in the recesses of Mount CHAON, and flows in a rapid stream, which bears the name of ERASINUS, into the Argolic territory.

To the lively imagination of a Greek, these struggles of nature presented something more than the phenomena of physical causes producing their effect by known laws. To him, they were the acts of Supernatural Powers. It was not the river which, by the impetuosity and pressure of its waters, mined its way through the opposing strata of calcareous rock till it found an issue on the opposite side of the mountain precipice, but it was the arm of some living and all-powerful Agent, who grappled with his antagonist, and achieved a conquest, which was alike glorious to himself and beneficent in its consequences to man. The Agent, by whose power, in popular estimation, the

aqueous revolutions were effected, was Hercules; and the establishment of his worship in Arcadia may be traced to the sub-terranean passage of the Stymphalian lake into the Erasinus.

We may refer to like causes as influencing the character, pursuits, and tastes, of the inhabitants of the country. The soil of this division of the Peloponnesus was such as to afford little encouragement to the agriculturist. Its mountain tops are covered with snow for the greater part of the year, and its plains themselves, such as those of Tegea, Mantinea, and Megalopolis, are rather flat surfaces on the elevations of hills, than warm and fruitful lowlands. In these plains no rich alluvial soil is deposited by fertilizing streams, nor are they sheltered by umbrageous forests, nor refreshed by the mild breezes of the sea, as in more favoured parts of this country. The temperature and soil of such provinces as Bœotia and Thessaly, were almost without a parallel in the Peloponnesus; much less could they be rivalled within the limits of Arcadia. From the circumstances which have been detailed, the life of the inhabitants of that country was necessarily pastoral. The same leisure, the same freedom, and familiarity with grand and beautiful scenes, which the pastoral life in a fine country supplies in abundance, and which has produced the mountain melodies of Switzerland and the Tyrol, made the land of Arcadia, in earlier times, the cradle of the pastoral music of Hellas. On the summit of Cyllené, Mercury found the lyre; and it was Pan, the deity of Arcadia, who invented the pipe—the favourite musical instrument of the swains of Greece.

The social character of the Arcadians was beneficially affected by these influences. They were beguiled, by their means, of the rudeness which they would otherwise have derived from the ruggedness of their soil, and from the inclemency of their climate; and thus, by a happy and beneficent compensation of nature, the same causes which gave them impulses towards a rigid and savage mode of existence, supplied the most efficient means for reclaiming them from those tendencies, and leading them to habits more refined.

It is said, by the native historian Polybius, that the inhabitants of the village CYNÆTHA, who alone, of the people of Arcadia, resisted the influences which were supplied by the national music, owed to that circumstance the sternness and inhospitality by which they were distinguished from their compatriots.

Such, then, were some of the results produced by the soil and climate of this country.

As an illustration of the fact, that whatever was connected, in the mind of antiquity, with the occupations and enjoyments of a country life, was produced and cherished in Arcadia, it is not unworthy of remark, that even the pastoral Poet of Italy, when he is commencing his didactic poem upon the

affairs of rural life, is carried away from his own country into Greece, and derives his inspiration, not from the rivers and mountains, from the meadows and the vineyards, of his own beautiful land,— not even from those which adorned the fairest part of it, in which he was then writing,—but from the rude hills and barren sheep-walks of Arcadia. Not the majestic steeps of the Apennines, nor the vine-clad slopes of Vesuvius, but the Arcadian mountains of Mænalus and Lycæus, supplied the landscapes from which Virgil drew his pastoral scenes. When he commenced his Georgics, he invoked their deities.

There is another result, derived from a source similar to that of which we have just spoken, and which is not to be neglected in an attempt to form an

estimate of the social character of the inhabitants of this country, and of the natural causes which led to its development.

The life of shepherds is usually of a migratory kind. The temporary abandonment of old pastures, and the selection of new, are the familiar duties of their calling, and the constant condition of their existence; and the continued exercise of these habits has a tendency to weaken their attachment to particular spots, and to produce a restlessness of character and an impatience of the same objects, which renders a change from one scene to another, not merely agreeable, but almost necessary.

Hence was produced a feature in the character of the Arcadians, which obtained for them less respect than they derived from their probity and hospitality, and from the exercise of those other virtues which are generally associated with the idea of a pastoral life. The Arcadians were not unwilling to serve as mercenary troops, in whatever country, and under whatever commander there seemed to be a prospect of the greatest personal advantage to themselves; and instances are not wanting of contests, in which some of them were ranged on a different side from others of their fellow-countrymen. Thus as Arcadia was the Switzerland, so were the Arcadians the Switzers of antiquity.

O pass, however, from Arcadia to the province which bounded it on the south;—it was a part of the policy of the great legislator of LACONIA, to dissuade his compatriots from surrounding their Capital with Walls. He did this, no doubt, from the conviction, that "men, and not walls, make a city," and that the best way to secure for a city the best walls—namely, the bravest men,—was to leave it unfortified. Sparta was most secure, when she had no walls; and she was least safe, when she erected them.

We have spoken above of the whole peninsula of the Peloponnesus as bearing a resemblance in form to an AMPHITHEATRE; and from what has been just stated, it will appear that the country of Sparta,—the *hollow* Lacedæmon, as it is called in the Iliad and the Odyssey,—being flanked on the east and on the west by two long parallel ridges of mountains, which were connected together by a similar but much shorter barrier at the northern extremity, may be compared in shape to an ancient STADIUM, of which Mount Parnon and Mount Taygetus are the two sides, and of which the end is formed by the northern abutment, already described, of the Arcadian hills; so that the physical characteristics of his country alone might well have suggested to Lycurgus the policy which he advocated. Nature herself had, in truth, already surrounded, not indeed the capital city, but the whole region of Laconia, with bulwarks. The Walls of Sparta were her Mountains. From them she gained the appropriate title of "unassailable." On the west, she was fenced in by the lofty range of Mount Taygetus; on the north, all entrance within her limits was blocked up by the huge hills of the Arcadian frontier; on the east, her territory was protected by the sea; and within its coast line, and parallel to the ocean, it was walled off by the steeps of Mount Parnon, which run from the heights of Mount MÆNALUS to the MALEAN promontory, and terminate in the insular cliffs of CYTHERA.

The bed of this natural stadium was the valley of Sparta. The approach to it was from the Bay of Laconia at the south. Along it flowed the river EUROTAS, which has its source above the northern termination of the valley, and which was believed to run in the same channel as the Alpheus, till these rivers separated themselves in the bowels of a mountain not far from that point, —the Alpheus diverging northward toward the centre of Arcadia, while the Eurotas issued from the same chasm into the territory of Laconia. The city of Sparta stood in the middle of this valley, on the right bank of the stream.

The Mænalian summits are a central point to which the mountain chains of Arcadia, Laconia, and Argolis converge. Beneath them, on the south-

VALLEY OF THE OLYMPIA FROM BELOW.

west, in the modern town of TRIPOLITZA, which stands on the site formerly occupied by one of the oldest and most venerable cities of Arcadia. This was PALLANTIUM, the city of Pallas and Evander.

It is interesting to trace the first footsteps of Rome, the Mistress of the World, on this rude mountain of Arcadia; and to pass, in imagination, from the sylvan scene before us, while we look upon the pine-tree groves of Mænalus, and on the castle-hill of Pallantium, to the gorgeous pile of imperial splendour which glittered on the top of the Roman PALATINE. We are pleased also with the reflection, that one of the best of Roman Emperors, ANTONINUS PIUS, did not scorn the tradition which deduced the primeval colony of Rome from the Mænalian mount; and that he showed to the humble Pallantium the respect and gratitude that was due to the old city, from which Evander, the friend of Æneas and father of Pallas, was believed to have come to that Roman hill, which derives its name from Pallantium, and on which the Roman emperor dwelt.

The road from Tripolitza to Argos passed along a narrow defile between the

hills of ARTEMISIUM on the north, and PARTHENIUM on the south. It was
near this spot, that the Athenian Courier, Pheidippides, in his way from
Athens to Sparta, whither he went to implore her succour before the battle of
Marathon, was accosted, as he said, by the Arcadian deity Pan, who desired
him, on his arrival at home, to assure the Athenians of his good will towards
them, and to signify to them his regret that his favourable dispositions had not
been acknowledged by them with due honour and gratitude, and he was further
to apprise them of his intention of being present to assist them in the great
conflict in which they were about to engage; a promise which, having been
duly fulfilled by the pastoral deity, obtained for him a shrine in the grotto consecrated to his honour at the north-west corner of the Athenian Acropolis.

The best view of the ARGOLIC plain, to which we now pass, is that which is
obtained from the citadel,—anciently called LARISSA,—of ARGOS, its capital city.
This Acropolis stands on the summit of a lofty and insulated hill, about four
miles distant from the northern shore of the Argolic Gulf.   Here the spectator
may contemplate the sites which have rendered the soil of Argolis illustrious
for more than a thousand years in the history and poetry of Greece.

To the south of him, is the bay in which Danaüs landed from Egypt with
his suppliant daughters—the subjects of one of the earliest dramas of the
Athenian stage.   On the western edge of the same bay, is the LERNÆAN pool;
at a point nearer the city, the river ERASINUS falls into the sea, having passed
through a subterraneous chasm from the north of Arcadia, thus connecting
the lake of STYMPHALUS, in which it rises there, and which was the scene of
one of the Labours of Hercules, with the site of the Argolic Lerna, which was
also the witness of another feat of the same hero.

Nearer still to the citadel from which our view is taken, flows the famous
stream of Inachus, connected with Argolic history from the earliest times.   It
descends, in fact, from the frontier of Arcadia; but, according to the mythical
accounts of the Greek poets, who delighted in uniting distant lands with each
other by means of rivers, and who, therefore, scrupled not to give them the
course which was most convenient for such a purpose,—it was no other than a
stream of the same name, which flowed in the country of the AMPHILOCHIANS,
on the eastern shore of the Ambracian gulf, and which, having mingled its
waters with those of the Ætolian Achelöus, passed under the earth, and
emerged from a cavern at the roots of Mount CHAON, near the southern foot of
the citadel of Argos.

In this fiction, we recognise the trace of a very natural and not unpleasing
attempt to connect the inhabitants of a colony with those of their mother city,
by such sympathies as would arise notwithstanding their distance from one
another, from the circumstance of their dwelling on the banks of the same river.

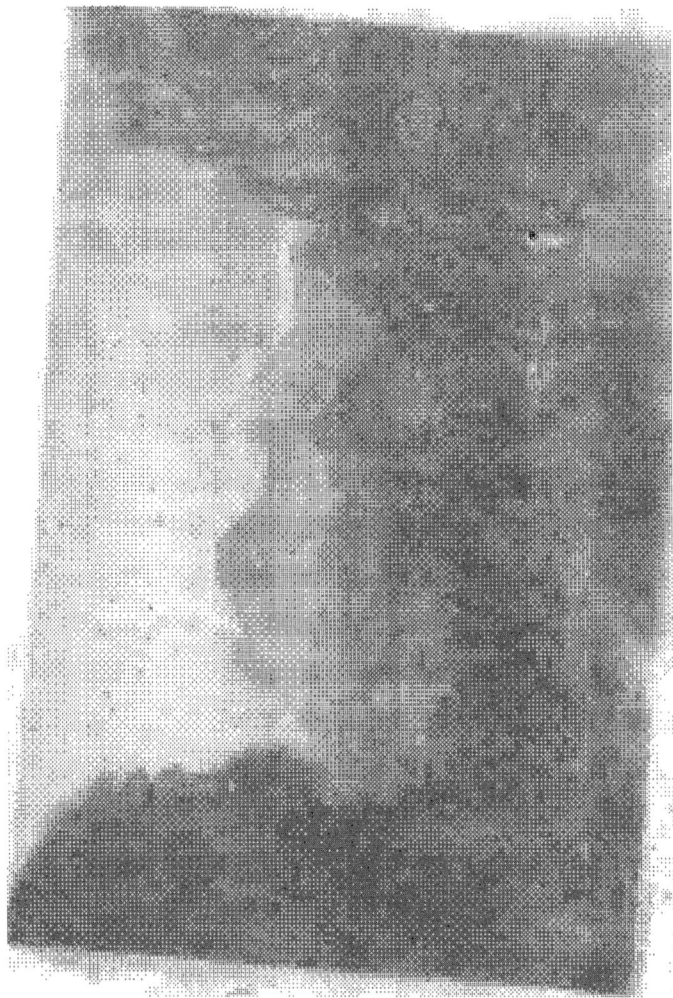

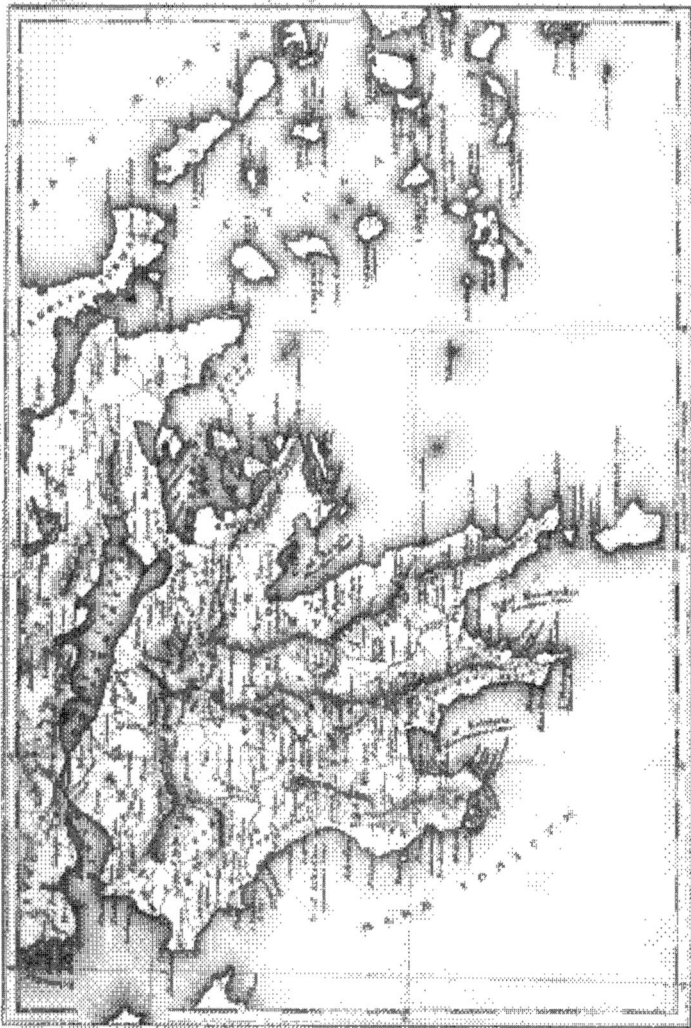

The *Amphilochian* Argos was peopled and named from the Argos of the *Pelo-ponnesus* ; and by the supposition above mentioned the two kindred Cities were held in alliance and communion with each other ; their hearts were tied to each other by the silver cord of the same stream.

Further to the south, and commanding the entrance of the bay of Argos, on the east side of it, and rendered conspicuous by the lofty eminence of its citadel, is the town of NAUPLIA. The rank which was held by Argos in the heroic times, was occupied by Nauplia in the middle ages ; and the natural advantages of its position will preserve to it an importance, which will long render the name of Nauplia—a name derived from a son of Neptune—a familiar word to the merchants and sailors of the Archipelago.

At the conclusion of this preliminary sketch—before we quit our position on the heights of the Acropolis of Argos,—we may be allowed to indulge in some speculations of a more general character, on the geography and natural peculiarities of the country which we are describing. These reflections are not ill-suited to the spot which exercised so powerful an influence, from the earliest times, over the conditions and fortunes of the continent and peninsular of Greece, and are naturally suggested by the localities of this their heroic metropolis. The geographical position of GREECE, properly so called, is evidently such as to favour the development of the physical and intellectual faculties of man. Under the temperate influence of its seasons and its climates, they acquired strength without sternness, and softness without effeminacy.

Its situation, again, with respect to other countries,—to ASIA and EGYPT, to ITALY and SICILY,—was such as to afford every facility for receiving the arts of civilized life, while it furnished the best opportunities for communicating to others what it received. In this respect, no country possessed greater advantages ; its long coast-line, indented by numerous bays and harbours, conduced to the same end. Nor was it possible for the inhabitant of Greece to forget the world beyond him, which the sea, ever presenting itself to his view as he crossed the lofty hills even in the inmost recesses of his own land, brought perpetually to his mind. Thus, the spirit of enterprise and ambition which distinguished his character was the natural produce of his soil.

Again : if we turn our eyes to the interior of the country, we are struck by the remarkable manner in which it is divided by the hand of nature into distinct provinces. The long ridges of mountains, by which it is intersected in various directions, have traced upon its soil the lines of a natural map, which no hand of man will ever erase. Hence that distinction of tribes, differing from each other in dialect, and in civil and religious institutions, with which the soil of Greece was peopled. The spirit of emulation and rivalry which was naturally roused among these different tribes produced important results, for good and evil. While the cause of the Greeks, as a nation, suffered from the disunion consequent upon it, yet a love of glory and distinction was excited among the individual members of which the nation consisted, which led to no ignoble results in arts or arms. The productions, too, of the poet and historian, gained life and vigour from the variety of dialects which were spoken by these different tribes, which were appropriated and consecrated, as it were, to the service of their several branches of literature; and the political philosopher of Greece was enabled to confirm and illustrate his speculations, by reference to the various forms of civil polity adopted by the numerous states, into which his country was divided.

We need not now pause to inquire what facilities and encouragements were given to the cultivation of the arts by the physical properties which characterised the land of Greece. That the imaginative faculties of its inhabitants were awakened and kept alive by the remarkable phenomena which presented themselves to their view, cannot be doubted.

The volcanic fires which agitated its soil, the earthquakes which shook the walls of its cities and convulsed the inmost depths of its valleys, the lakes whose inundations engulfed its plains, the rivers which forced their way by subterranean chasms through the barriers of rocky hills, the majestic forms of nature in repose which daily met his eye, a transparent ether and blue and cloudless sky, a sea studded with numerous islands, and a land clad with thick forests—the creations of *art* which so happily blended with and adorned these *natural* objects as to seem to be united and identified with them, the stately mass and the well-marshalled columns of the Doric temple rising on the hill, or the almost breathing statue in the grove;—these objects were to the imagination of the Greek like so many trophies of Miltiades to the mind of Themistocles; they haunted him like a passion by day, and disturbed his sleep by night: they carried him away from the region of blank abstractions, and from the contemplation of objects of sense, to dwell in the presence of living Powers, by whom, in his creed, all the motions of the Universe were impelled and controlled.

It was the geological formation of its mountains—the durable limestone

rock of which they consist—to which Greece owed those magnificent works of
military Architecture, the solid wall and massy tower of polygonal masonry by
which she defended the cities which still stand upon her hills, and which
seem to rival, in strength and permanence, the mountains themselves from
which their materials were hewn.

Again: the rich and varied veins of marble, which she possessed in
exhaustless abundance, in the quarries of Paros, of Pentelicus, of Hymettus, and of Carystus, supplied her with materials for the noblest works of
her Sculptors and her Architects— for her PARTHENONS, her PROPYLAEAS, and
her THESEUMS, and for her friezes of PHIGALEIA and of ÆGINA.

It was the wealth of her soil to which she was indebted for the existence
of these beautiful creations, and it was the purity of her air which preserved
them. This latter element allowed her to attract the popular eye, to inform
the national taste, to inspire the faith, and evoke the gratitude of her sons, by
statues and pictures of her Gods and her heroes, of her good and great men,

which she placed, not only beneath roofs or within walls, not merely in the enclosures of her halls and of her fanes, but on the lofty pediments of her Temples, in the open spaces of her Agoras, at the doors of her houses, and in the crowded avenues of her streets.

This permitted her also to decorate her buildings with the vivid and varied hues which Painting lent to her Sister-Art, and to imitate the clearness of her own sky, and the freshness of her own sea, by those architectural embellishments which Art could not venture to adopt, except in a country where Nature has eclipsed, in brilliance and vivacity of execution, everything that Art can conceive.

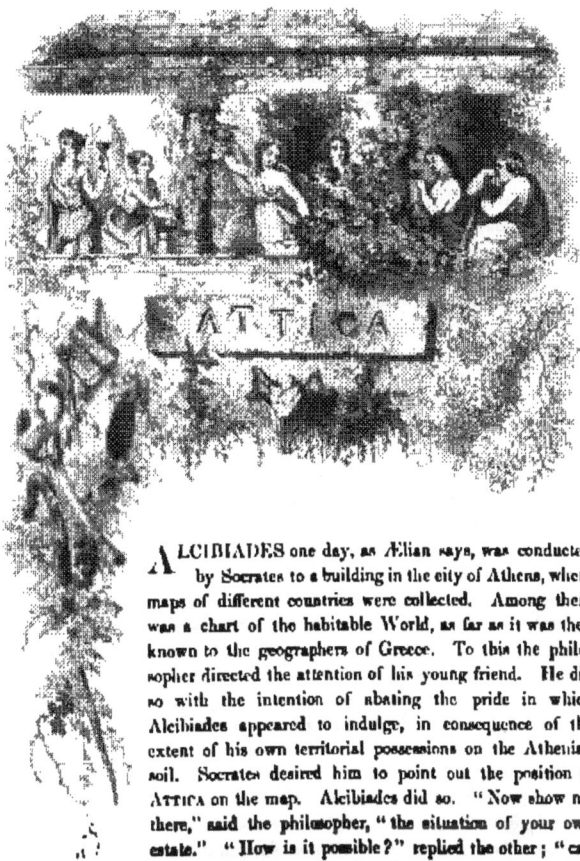

ATTICA

ALCIBIADES one day, as Ælian says, was conducted by Socrates to a building in the city of Athens, where maps of different countries were collected. Among them was a chart of the habitable World, as far as it was then known to the geographers of Greece. To this the philosopher directed the attention of his young friend. He did so with the intention of abating the pride in which Alcibiades appeared to indulge, in consequence of the extent of his own territorial possessions on the Athenian soil. Socrates desired him to point out the position of ATTICA on the map. Alcibiades did so. "Now show me there," said the philosopher, "the situation of your own estate." "How is it possible?" replied the other; "can you expect that my domains should appear there, where even Attica itself occupies so small a space?"

Whatever effect this comparison of the extent of his own possessions with that of the country in which they were contained, might have produced upon the young pupil of Socrates, a contemplation of Attica itself, and of its geographical dimensions, as contrasted with those of other countries of which the World, as then known, consisted, will not fail to suggest reflections of no uninteresting kind, to an observer of the parts which Nations have played as well as Men,—of the achievements which they have performed, of the influence which they have exercised, and of the position which they occupy in the History of the World.

The superficial extent of Attica is estimated at not more than seven hundred square miles: its greatest length is fifty, and its breadth thirty miles. If it is compared in *size* with some of the provinces of Europe, and much more with the wilds of Africa or the forests of America, it sinks into the insignificance of some baronial estate, or of a private allotment in a colonial dependency.   This, it is evident, is the case if we look at its *physical* dimensions.

But from a consideration of these we pass to another view of the subject. While, strictly speaking, it occupies a space in the Map which is hardly perceptible, to how many square miles, or rather thousands of square miles, in the social, moral, metaphysical, and political Geography of the World, does Attica extend?

This is, in truth, a contemplation which fills the mind of man with a feeling of triumph and exaltation, and with an ennobling sense of its own dignity, as compared with that of the accidents and qualities of the *material* objects of the world; it inspires him with a sublime sense of the energies of the intellectual and moral, and may we not add, of the divine and spiritual part of his own nature. It presents to his sight a small Province, confined within those narrow bounds which have been specified, yet stretching itself, like a living Agent, from its contracted limits, by the vigorous growth, elastic energy, and expansive activity of those powers, to a comprehensive vastness, nay, even to a kind of intellectual Omnipresence, upon the surface of the earth.

There is no region of the civilized world which is not breathed on by the air of Attica. Its influence makes itself felt in the thoughts, and shows itself in the speech of men; and it will never cease to do so: it is not enough to say that it lives in the inspirations of the Poet, in the eloquence of the Orator, and in the speculations of the Philosopher. It exhibits itself everywhere in visible shapes; it animates the most beautiful creations of Art. The works of the Architect and of the Sculptor, in every quarter of the globe, speak of ATHENS; even our manufactures are imprinted with her ornaments; the galleries of Princes and States, the temples and palaces, the libraries and council-rooms of Capital Cities pay homage to Athens, and will do so for ever.

Above all, it is due to the intellectual results produced by the inhabitants of this small Canton of Europe, that the language in which they spoke and in which they wrote, became the vernacular tongue of the world. The genius of the Athenians made their speech universal: the treasures which they deposited in it rendered its acquisition essential to all: and thus the sway, unlimited in extent and invincible in power, which was wielded by the arms of Rome, was exercised over Rome herself by the arts of Athens. To Attica, therefore, it was due, under the blessing of Divine Providence, that when a channel of general communication was most needed, there existed a common language in the world; and that this language was Greek; or, in other words, that there was, at the time of the first propagation of the Gospel, a tongue in which it could be preached to the whole world; and that Greek, the most worthy of such a distinction, was the language of Inspiration, the tongue of the earliest preachers and writers of Christianity. Therefore we may regard Attica, viewed in this light, as engaged in the same cause, and united in a holy league, with Palestine; we may consider the Philosophers and Orators and Poets of this country as preparing the way by a special dispensation of God's providence, for the Apostles, Fathers, and Apologists of the Christian Church.

Such was the influence exercised on the destinies of the world, and such the manner and degree in which the highest interests of mankind have been, still are, and will for ever be, affected, by a small province whose physical dimensions may be said to bear the same ratio to those of Greece, which the estate of Alcibiades did to the territory of Attica itself.

This is a fact well worthy of attention; nor is it a matter of vain or idle speculation to examine the causes which led to so remarkable a result.

The land of Attica is a peninsula; from this circumstance it derived its name (the *Coast-land*): it is an irregular triangle, of which the base or northern side is *applied* to the Continent of Greece; with its eastern face it looks towards Asia; from its apex on the south it contemplates Egypt; and on the west it directs its view to the Peloponnesus, and to the countries of Italy and Sicily lying beyond it.

By this combination of the advantages of inland communication with those of an extensive and various intercourse with all the civilized countries of the world, it was distinguished from all the other States of the Peninsula and Continent of Greece.

It should not be omitted, that on the coasts of which we speak, and by which Attica was bounded on the east and west, it was furnished with commodious harbours for the reception of shipping: and this will appear more clearly to have been the fact, if we consider the nature and requirements of the vessels of antiquity. When, also, we bear in mind the peculiar practice by which the navigation of the ancients was distinguished from that of modern times, and which gave to their voyages the character of cruising and

coasting expeditions, rather than that of adventurous passages from one continent to another, the islands which hang like links in a continuous chain from the promontory of Sunium, and connect it with the Asiatic shore, will then assume the character of ports or emporiums of Attica.

As Greece was the centre of the civilized world of antiquity, so was Attica the centre of Greece; and as the climate and temperature of Hellas was considered to be more favourable than that of any other country of Europe or of Asia for the healthy and vigorous development of the physical and intellectual faculties of man, so did every Hellenic province yield in these respects to the superior claims of the Athenian territory.

Again; it was not merely aided by these natural advantages, which arose from its form, its position, and its climate: the very *defects*, also, under which this country laboured, the very *difficulties* with which it was compelled to struggle, supplied to Attica the motives, and afforded it the means, for availing itself in the most effectual manner of those benefits and privileges with which Nature had so liberally endowed it. One of these deficiencies was the barrenness of its soil.

The geological formation of Attica is primitive limestone: on its northern frontier, a long ridge of mountains, consisting of such a stratification, stretches from east to west: a range of similar character bounds it on the west, and in the interior of the country it is intersected with hills, from north to south, which belong to the same class.

Hence the geographical dimensions of Attica, limited as they are, must be reduced within a still narrower range, when we consider it as far as it is available for the purposes of cultivation. In this respect, its superficial extent cannot be rated at more than one-half the value assigned to the whole country.

These mountains of which we have above spoken, are either bare and rugged, or thinly clad with scanty vegetation and low shrubs. The mountain pine is found on the slopes of Laurêum: the steeps of PARNES and PENTE-LICUS are sprinkled over with the dwarf oak, the lentisk, the arbutus, and the bay. But the hills of this country can boast few timber-trees; they serve to afford pasture to numerous flocks of sheep and goats, which climb among their steep rocks, and browse upon their meagre herbage, while the brushwood furnishes fuel to the inhabitants of the plain.

DEFILES OF PENTELICUS

While such is the character of the mountainous districts of the province, its plains and lowlands cannot lay a much better claim to the merit of fertility. In many parts of them, as in the city of Athens itself, the calcareous rock projects above the surface, or is scarcely concealed beneath a light covering of soil: in no instance do they possess any considerable deposit of alluvial earth.

The plains of this country are irrigated by few streams, which are rather to be called torrents than rivers; and on none of them can it depend for a perennial supply of water. There is no lake within its limits. It is

unnecessary to suggest the reason, when such was the nature of the soil,
that the Olive was the most common, and also the most valuable, production
of Attica.

Such, then, were some of the physical defects of this land. But these
disadvantages, for such in fact they were when considered in themselves, were
abundantly compensated by the beneficial effects which they produced.

The sterility of Attica drove its inhabitants from their own country. It
carried them abroad. It filled them with a spirit of activity, which loved to

PLAIN OF ATHENS, FROM THE ACROPOLIS.

face danger, and to grapple with difficulty: it did for them, what Virgil says
was done for the early inhabitants of the world by its Supreme Ruler, who,
in his figurative language, first "agitated the sea with storms, and hid fire,
and checked the streams of wine which flowed abroad in the golden age, and
shook the honey from the bough," in order that men might learn the arts in
the stern School of Necessity; it told them, that if they would attain the
dignity which became them, they must regard the resources of their own land
as nothing, and profit by those of other countries as if they were their own.

The same cause, also, while it inspired them with an ardent desire for
bold and adventurous enterprise, and thus detached them from the tranquil enjoyment of their own homes, and made them cosmopolites; yet, by

another influence which it possessed, called them back with a feeling of
patriotic devotion to the scenes and recollections of the country of their birth.

By reason of the barrenness of her soil, as her greatest historian observes, Attica had always been exempt from the revolutions which in early
times agitated the other countries of Greece;—which poured over their
frontiers the changeful floods of migratory populations, and disturbed the
foundations of their national history, and confounded the civil institutions
of the former occupants of the soil.

But Attica, secure in her sterility, boasted that *her* land had never been
inundated by those tides of immigration. She had experienced no such
change: she had enjoyed a perpetual calm. The race of her inhabitants had
been ever the same; none could tell whence they had sprung; no foreign
land had sent them. She traced the stream of her population in a backward
course, through many generations, till at last it hid itself, like one of her own
brooks, in the recesses of her own soil.

This belief, that her people was indigenous, was expressed by her in
different ways. She intimated it in the figure which she assigned to Cecrops,
the heroic Prince and Progenitor of her primæval inhabitants. She represented him as combining in his person a double character: while the higher
parts of his body were those of a man and a king, the serpentine folds in
which it was terminated declared his extraction from the earth. The Cicadæ
of gold, which she braided in her hair, were intended to denote the same idea;
they signified, that the natives of Attica emerged from the soil upon which
they sung, and which was believed to feed them with its dew.

The attachment of the inhabitants of this country to their own land was
cherished and strengthened by this creed; they gloried in being natives of
hills and plains which no one had ever occupied but themselves, and in which
they had dwelt from a period of the remotest antiquity: and thus the barrenness of their soil, while it urged them to foreign lands on adventures of
commerce or of conquest, brought them back to their own home with emotions
of patriotic enthusiasm; it led them to regard themselves as citizens of all
the civilized countries of the globe; but it also made them consider those
countries as tributary colonies of Attica.

Such, then, were some of the circumstances which gave to this small province the dignity and importance which it enjoyed among the nations of the
world. Occasions will arise hereafter of noticing some other particulars which
conduced to the same end, in the course of the observations which will be
made on the principal sites and geographical features which distinguish it.

For this purpose we may turn our attention to that mountain which we
have already described as the northern frontier of Attica. This is Mount

PARNES. It separates the Athenian plain from the valley of BŒOTIA by a rocky barrier, which extends from the eastern termination of Cithæron to the coast of the Euripus. On the west, this plain is bounded by a ridge of which the principal summit is Mount ÆGALEOS, and which stretches southward from Mount Parnes to the Bay of Salamis: its eastern limit is formed by two mountains, Pentelicus on the north and Hymettus on the south; the latter of which sinks into the sea on the east, in the same manner as Mount Ægaleos does on the west.

Thus, as the CITY of Athens was protected from external aggression, and connected with the sea by means of its Long Walls,—as they were called,— which stretched from the town to its harbours, so was the PLAIN of Athens defended from invasion and maintained in communication with the coast by its own LONG WALLS—that is, by its mountain bulwarks,—namely, by Parnes and Ægaleos on the west, and by Pentelicus and Hymettus on the

ATHENS AND THE EDGE OF ATTICA, FROM THE ENTRANCE TO THE PIRÆUS.

east; and thus the hand of Nature effected for the Plain what was done for the Capital of Attica by the genius of Cimon and of Pericles.

In our survey of the Geography of Attica, we propose to pursue this mountain range from its south-western extremity on the coast, and to trace its course in a northerly direction till we arrive at the point from which it begins to descend to the south. We shall then follow the eastern ridge in a contrary direction till we reach the sea again, at the south-east corner of the Athenian plain. In other words, we shall ascend northward from the sea by the western, and descend to it southward by the eastern of these two Long Walls of Hills which have been described.

With this view, we may take our station at the southern declivity of Mount Ægaleos.

From this point we overlook the Gulf and Island of SALAMIS, which lie beneath us on the south. The hill, on which we stand, is now bare and desolate; the gulf is vacant and still; the island presents no objects to attract the eye, except a few cottages, and one or two small churches which are scattered among the vineyards of Ambelakia, the village which now occupies the site of the ancient city of Salamis.

On this spot, where we now are, in the month of September of the year

B.C. 480, on a day of momentous importance to the fortunes of Greece and of the civilized World, the great King of Persia, Xerxes, sat and looked down upon the island and upon the gulf, and all the natural objects which we now see. It was here that he viewed the BATTLE of SALAMIS.

In the Straits below him, on the eastern side of the Gulf, or that nearest to himself, was drawn up in three lines, and in all the pageantry of Oriental splendour, with all their variety of national equipment, and in all the pride of anticipated victory, that immense Armada which he had mustered from the shores of the Persian Gulf and of Ionia, from Cyprus, and Caria, from Phœnicia and from Egypt, and from every quarter of his vast dominions. The whole maritime force of the East was there, lying at the feet of their sovereign, and about to engage in his cause.

Opposite to them, on the western side of the Strait, and lining the eastern coast of the Island of Salamis, lay the combined navy of Athens, Ægina, and

THE BAY AND ISLAND OF SALAMIS

Sparta. It consisted of three hundred and ten ships, while those of their
opponents amounted to more than one thousand vessels. But the Greeks
had amongst them men second to none, in wisdom, genius, and valour.
While Xerxes sat and encouraged his Persians, Themistocles fought and
commanded the Greeks. On the islet of Psyttaleia, at the southern entrance
of the Straits, was Aristides; mixed in the battle were men such as Amcinias
and his brother the poet Æschylus, who afterwards celebrated in his dramatic
poem, the PERSÆ, the deeds of his country at Salamis. The eye of imaginative
faith beheld the majestic forms of the old Æacidæ, the divinized heroes of
Ægina and of Salamis,—of Ajax and Teucer and Achilles,—who had been
implored with solemn entreaties to assist their descendants; and they were
seen coming to the conflict, clad in the armour with which they fought at
Troy, animating their own countrymen, and striking terror into the hearts of
the Barbarians.

The Sea, too,—the Wind, and even the Place itself, in which, on account of its narrow and confined limits, the vast numbers of the Persian army embarrassed themselves,—all these elements of nature were powerful allies which fought for Athens and for Greece.

These, then, were the objects which Xerxes saw from the station which he occupied on the southern slope of Mount Ægaleos. He sate there, attired in his royal robes, on a throne of gold supported by silver feet : around him,

while he viewed the battle, were his princes and courtiers from Susa, Babylon and Ecbatana ; on each side stood the Secretaries of the King, with pens and tablets in their hands, noting down the names of those Persian combatants who were observed to distinguish themselves by any act of remarkable courage in the conflict, and recording them as worthy of future honour and reward, to be received at the hand of the Monarch, who relied on victory as sure.

From this spot, on the morning of the battle, Xerxes heard the war-song of the Greeks proceeding to the fight, and the echo of the island rocks responsive to the martial pæan. This sound was followed by the splash of their oars beating the waves in regular order, and by the unanimous voice of the whole navy moving onward in a compact body, cheering the Sons of Greece, with one heart and tongue, and exhorting them to go to the battle and "free their country, their children, their wives, the temples of their gods and the tombs of their ancestors; for all was now at stake."

In the evening of the same day, he saw the surface of the Gulf covered with the wreck of his vessels and with the corpses of his men; he beheld the flower of his army mowed down before his eyes in the little island of Psyttaleia, at the southern extremity of the channel, where he had placed them for the purpose of preventing the escape of the Greeks.

This sight he could not endure : he groaned deeply, rent his clothes, and rushed from his throne of gold in an agony of grief. Such was the conclusion of the battle of Salamis. The throne of the Persian King became the spoil of the conquerors, and was dedicated as a thank-offering to Minerva, and was preserved in the Acropolis of Athens, together with the sword which was taken from Mardonius the Persian General at the battle of Platæa.

We proceed from this point, about five miles northward, along the same ridge, till we fall into the road which crosses the mountain of Ægaleos in its way westward to ELEUSIS, which lies on the coast, and is situated at a distance from Athens of about eleven miles. At a short space before its arrival at Eleusis, it pursues the southern edge of the Thriasian plain.

A few days before the battle of Salamis, when the terra-firma of Attica was deserted by its inhabitants, who had taken refuge in their ships, or had fled for an asylum to the shores of SALAMIS and TRŒZEN, and when their country was occupied by the forces of Xerxes, two persons in the Persian army, who were then standing in this plain, beheld a cloud of dust coming from Eleusis. It appeared to them to be issuing from that city, and to arise from a procession which they supposed might amount in number to thirty thousand men.

APPEARING PAGAN CHORUS OF THEIR DEAD.

Presently they heard a sound, as if uttered by a chorus of voices proceeding from the same quarter. One of them who was acquainted with the strains used on such occasions, declared to his companion that the sound which they then heard was no other than the hymn which was usually sung in honour of the

mystic Bacchus, when his statue was carried—as it was on this anniversary—from Athens to Eleusis, and again from Eleusis to Athens, at the time of the celebration of the Eleusinian mysteries; and that this procession, from which the dust now floated along the coast, and filled the air before them, and whose united voices rose to the sky, was coming from the city of Ceres, on its return from Athens, after the celebration of that ceremony. As Attica was now abandoned by the Greeks, this appearance seemed more than human. He foretold, at the same time, that if the dust and sound moved toward Salamis, the Gods themselves were coming to fight against the Great King, and that the destruction of his host was inevitable.

The road on which this procession then seemed to move, and to which we shall digress from our mountain position for a short time, in our way to Eleusis, the place from which it appeared to come, is in some respects the

ROAD ON THE GULF FROM ELEUSIS TO ATHENS.

most remarkable in Greece. It witnessed, year by year, in the autumnal season, the solemnity to which we have just alluded. Along it at that time, on the sixth day of the Eleusinian mysteries, the figure of Bacchus,—not the Theban deity, but the youthful son of Ceres and the giver of the vine to man,—crowned with a chaplet of myrtle, and holding a torch in his hand, was carried in procession; he was followed over hill and plain by thousands of worshippers, clad in festal attire, wearing garlands of ivy leaves, and chanting his praises in strains of harmonious adoration.

The stone pavement of the ancient road which this procession followed, still remains in some parts of the plain near the sea-coast; on its surface the tracks of the wheels which passed over it in former days are yet visible. They remind us of the slow trains of Eleusinian cars in which the women of Athens were conveyed along it from their own city to Eleusis.

But not merely the women of Athens,—the mothers of Miltiades, of Cimon, of Themistocles, and of Pericles,—not only the youth and men of that city have passed over this paved way, to visit and participate in the most august ceremony of the heathen world; these stones have also been trodden by the feet of her poets, her statesmen, and her philosophers, tending to the same place, and on the same errand; and not merely have they been traversed by them, but also by Kings and Princes, by Satraps of Asia and by Monarchs of Egypt, by Consuls and Prætors of Rome, and by her wise, and eloquent, and learned men,—by her Augustus Cæsars, her Ciceros, her Horaces, and her Virgils,—going on their way to Eleusis to pay their homage to the awful Deities of that place, and to receive, as they believed, by initiation into the mysteries of their worship, a clearer knowledge of the most abstruse and perplexing questions which could be presented to the intellect of Man, and also a fuller assurance of their own felicity in the present and future world.

This road on which we are now travelling presents a remarkable contrast in character, scenery, and circumstances, to that of the Capital of Italy which bore the same name as this which leads from Athens to Eleusis. Let the SACRED WAY of Athens be compared with the Sacred Way of Rome. These two roads are, as it were, representatives of the peculiar character, genius, and influence of the people to which they respectively belong. Each of them exhibits to the eye and mind of the spectator traversing them, the objects which would be selected as the most appropriate characteristics of the pursuits and tastes, the qualifications and the achievements, by which those two Nations were distinguished.

The Via Sacra of Rome starts from the Colosseum; it passes under Arches of Triumph; it traverses the Roman Forum, and terminates in the Capitol. Thus it begins its course with pointing to the scene of the gladiatorial shows which afforded a savage pleasure to the assembled thousands of the imperial city in that vast Amphitheatre, that splendid shame of Rome. By the triumphal Arches which span it, it refers to the military conquests which gained for Rome the title of Mistress of the World; it speaks of the cars of the conqueror, of the chains of the captives who passed over it; of the triumphal processions of victorious armies which moved along it, laden with spoil and decorated with trophics won from the most distant regions of the earth. Again, the Rostra and Senate House of the Forum through which it passes, supply a memorial of the grave eloquence and dignified wisdom which controlled the people and guided the senate of Rome; of that eloquence and wisdom which governed provinces, and ratified peace, and dictated laws, and indited rescripts to foreign kings and nations; and, lastly, from the summit of the Capitol,—whither all these triumphal processions tended, as to the goal and limit of their course, to offer prayers and spoil and thanks, after their victories, to the Capitoline Jove,—a voice seems audibly to declare that the consummation of the hopes and aspirations of Rome was Military Glory;—that conquest and empire were *her* Mysteries; that they were the Temple to which she marched along her Sacred Way; that this was the initiation by which she raised herself above the nations of the earth,—this the Apotheosis by which she became partaker of the immortal dignity of her own Deities.

But the Sacred Way which led from Athens to Eleusis was of a very different character. It issued from the western and principal gate of the Athenian city into the most beautiful of her suburbs; there, in the Cerameicus, as it was called, were the monuments of her great men,—monuments decorated with the ornaments of poetry and of sculpture. Amid these monuments those funeral orations were spoken over the graves of them who had fallen in their country's cause, which made their fate a subject of congratulation rather than of sorrow to their friends. It then pursued its course through the Olive Groves of Plato and the Academy; it crossed the stream of the Cephissus; it mounted the hill of Ægaleos; it passed by the temples of Apollo and Venus, and descended into the Sacred Plain; it traversed a long avenue skirted by tombs of priests, poets, and philosophers; it coasted the Bay of Eleusis, which,—girt as it is on all sides by majestic mountains, except where two narrow channels on the east and west side of the Bay forms the Island of Salamis,—presents the appearance of a beautiful lake. At length, in the termination of its course, the Sacred Way of Athens arrived at the foot of the hill of Eleusis, crowned with marble porticoes and spacious courts, and with the noble pile of the temple of Ceres, celebrated as the work of the most skilful architects, alike venerable for its sanctity and its mysteries, and claiming for Eleusis the title of the religious Capital of Greece. In its course it had passed within sight of Colonus on the right, and of Salamis on the left, one the birth-place of Sophocles, the other that of Euripides; and it ended at Eleusis, the native city of Æschylus.

Thus did the Sacred Way, in its commencement, its career, and its conclusion, make an appeal to those peculiar objects both of nature and of art which obtained for Athens a moral, intellectual, and religious supremacy over the nations of the world, of greater extent and permanence than that military sway which was exercised over them by the invincible arms of Rome.

Few vestiges now remain of the temple of CERES at ELEUSIS. It stood on an elevated platform at the eastern extremity of the rock on which the city was built. It was approached by a portico similar to that at the western side of the Acropolis of Athens. Thus these two PROPYLÆA, which were due to the administration of Pericles, looked towards each other. The entrance through this vestibule led to another of smaller dimensions, which opened into a vast inclosure, in which the temple itself stood, which was one of the largest in Greece. It was faced on the south by a portico of twelve columns, and the interior of the cella was divided by four rows of pillars parallel to each other and to the portico, and on which the roof of the fabric was supported.

Æschylus was summoned before the religious tribunal of the Areopagus at Athens, on a charge of having divulged, in one of his dramas, the secrets which were revealed to the initiated in this place; the traveller Pausanias was cautioned in a dream, not to communicate the information he received here respecting the mystical signification of some of the objects of adoration at Eleusis; and the expressions of Horace on the same subject appear to be another indication of the awe with which men shrunk in those days from the sacrilege, of which he who made such revelations was supposed to be guilty.

BAY OF ELEUSIS

ELEUSIS

It would, therefore, be a vain and presumptuous enterprise to attempt to describe at this time what they who could best tell were least willing to disclose.

But some of the external circumstances which attended the celebration of the Eleusinian Mysteries are not involved in the same obscurity. We are still enabled, while standing within the sacred inclosure, and on the marble pavement of the temple of Ceres, to revive in our minds and describe some of the scenes which gave to this place, in ancient times, a solemnity and a splendour, the impression of which was never erased from the memory of those who had once felt its influence.

The fifth day of the Sacred Festival was distinguished by a magnificent procession of the initiated, who were clad in purple robes, and bore on their heads crowns of myrtle: the Priests led the way into the interior of the temple through the southern portico which has been described. The Worshippers followed in pairs, each bearing a torch, and in solemn silence. But the evening of the tenth day of this august pageant was the most remarkable: it brought with it the consummation of the mystic ceremonies. On this day the initiated were admitted for the first time to a full enjoyment of the privileges which the Mysteries conferred. Having gone through the previous rites of fasting and purification, they were clad in the sacred fawn-skin, and led at even-tide into the vestibule of the Temple. The doors of the building itself were as yet closed. Then the profane were commanded by the priests, with a loud voice, to retire. The worshippers remained alone. Presently strange sounds were heard; apparitions of dying men were seen; lightnings flashed through the thick darkness in which they were enveloped, and thunders rolled around them; light and gloom succeeded each other with rapid interchange. After these preliminaries, the folding doors of the Temple were thrown open. Its interior shone with one blaze of light. The votaries, whose senses were entranced in a visionary ecstasy, were led to the feet of the Statue of the Goddess, which was clad in the most gorgeous attire; in its presence their temples were encircled by the hands of the priests with the sacred wreath of myrtle, which was intended to direct their thoughts to the myrtle groves of the blessed, in those happy isles to which they would be carried after death: their eyes were dazzled with vivid and beautiful colours, and their ears charmed with melodious sounds, rendered more enchanting to their senses by their contrast with those appalling and ghastly objects which had just before been exhibited to them. They were admitted to behold visions of the Creation of the Universe, to see the workings of the divine agency by which the machine of the world was regulated and controlled, to contemplate the state of society which prevailed upon the earth before the visit of Ceres to Attica, and to witness the introduction of agriculture, of sound laws, and of gentle manners, which followed the steps of the goddess; to recognise the immortality of the soul, as typified by the concealment of corn sown by her in the earth, by its revival in the green blade, and by its full ripeness in the golden harvest; or, as the same idea was otherwise expressed, by the abduction of Proserpine, her daughter, to the region of darkness, in order that she might pass six months beneath the earth, and then rise again to spend an equal time in the realms of light and joy. They were then invited to view the spectacle of that happy state in which they themselves, the initiated, were to exist hereafter. These revelations displayed the greatest happiness to which, it was imagined, man could aspire in this life, and assured him of such bliss as nothing could exceed or diminish, in the next.

We retrace our steps eastward to our station on Mount Ægaleos, and, pursuing its range in a northerly direction, arrive at the north-west angle of the plain of Athens, and at the road which leads from it into Bœotia through a narrow defile formed by Mount Ægaleos on the south, and Parnes on the

THE PASS OF PHYLE.

north. The pass of PHYLÉ is one of savage grandeur:—rocks and trees, and torrents, mingled in wild confusion.

The fortress which guarded this pass, still preserves its ancient name; it hangs over one of the numerous precipices of the defile, adding not a little to the natural beauty of the scene. Its walls and towers still remain in nearly the same state as when, in the month of September, B.C. 404, it received the future deliverer of Athens, Thrasybulus, who was here besieged by his opponents, and sallied forth from its gates with a small force to eject the Thirty Tyrants from the city, and to raise Athens from the state of degradation to which it had been reduced by the Lacedæmonians at the close of the Peloponnesian war. From the lofty eminence on which this castle stands, the eye enjoys a magnificent prospect of the Plain and Citadel of Athens,—from which Phylé is distant about ten miles—objects which, then presented to their gaze, doubtless inspired Thrasybulus and his followers with patriotism and courage, and stimulated them with an enthusiastic desire to liberate their country from the unworthy bondage in which it was enthralled.

From Phylé, Thrasybulus descended into the Athenian Plain, with a band of seven hundred men. His first aim was the town of ACHARNÆ, which lies at the south-east of that fortress. It is six miles from Athens, and was the

ATHENS, FROM THE ROAD TO THE PLAIN.

largest and most important of the one hundred and seventy-four DEMI, or Boroughs, of Attica. Here he defeated his antagonists; this victory enabled him to proceed without interruption to the harbour of Athens, the Piræus, from which he expelled the forces of the Tyrants, and was thus furnished with the means of effecting an entrance into the city, and of rescuing it from their hands.

The name of Acharnæ is connected with one of the earliest and most agreeable of the surviving productions of the great comic Poet of Athens, Aristophanes. Its size and its situation—the former placing it, as has been said, at the head of the municipal towns of Attica, the latter exposing it to aggression from all the routes which led the Lacedæmonians across the Athenian frontier, and which converged, as it were, to the walls of Acharnæ— were no doubt the reasons which suggested to Aristophanes the choice of inhabitants of Acharnæ as fit representatives of the sufferings which were undergone by the agricultural population of his country at the commencement of the Peloponnesian war, and which the citizens of this place were so eager to avenge. The view which is presented to us from our position at Phylé, reminds us very significantly of the particular privations which were sustained by them, when compelled, as they then were, to quit their farms and homes, and to take up their abode in confined dwellings within the walls of Athens. It shows us, beneath this hill, the vineyards that they cultivated, which supplied them with occupation and refreshment, and which were rudely laid waste by the violence of the invader: it exhibits to us the farms which furnished them with the necessaries of life; it shows us the site of the rural shrines and altars before which, at the season of the vintage, or of harvest, they paid their grateful homage to the protecting Deities of the soil; and we look upwards to the mountain which they often ascended, to collect among its thickets the freight of holm-oak, lentisk, and other brushwood, which formed, when converted into charcoal, an important object to the Acharnians of traffic and of use.

Resuming our position on Mount Parnes, we pursue our course along the ridge of that mountain in an easterly direction. We are now following the line of the northern frontier of Attica. To compare smaller things with great, Mount Parnes was to this country what the Alps are to Italy. But not merely was this mountain range a line of natural demarcation, which severed the land of Attica on the south from the vale of Bœotia on the north—so that in all the political revolutions which this country underwent during the period of its independence, this distinction was never erased—but also, what is more remarkable, it served, if we may so say, as one of the degrees or parallels of latitude which were drawn on the surface of the intellectual Map of Greece. It was like a long and lofty Wall built in a beautiful garden, and stretching from east to west, along and up the *south* side of which fruit-trees and flower-

ing plants are trained, which deck it with their bright blossoms of white, red,
and purple, and with luxuriant foliage, and golden produce, all of which
are rendered more beautiful by the cheerfulness of the sun beaming upon them
in full lustre; while the *north* side of the same wall is cold and blank. So,
while in Attica, on the *south* side of Mount Parnes, the intellect of man
flowered and ripened, as it were, in a Phœacian garden, teeming with mental
produce, and flourishing with perennial fruitage,—on the other side of the
same hill the picture was reversed. Bœotia, the country on the *north* of Mount

DAPHNE, NEAR ATHENS.

Parnes, was as remarkable for its intellectual barrenness, as Attica was for its
intellectual fertility: Attica was synonymous with intelligence, Bœotia pro-
verbial for the reverse. But in respect of physical fecundity, Attica was far
inferior to Bœotia. It seemed as if Nature, which made Attica a country
of sterile hills and cliffs, and gave rich fields and pastures to Bœotia, had
desired to adjust the balance, by denying intellectual wealth in the one case,
where she had conferred physical, and by compensating for the absence of
physical, by the abundance of intellectual, in the other.

Aristophanes, in his Play of the NEPHELÆ, brings his goddesses, the
CLOUDS, from the heights of Mount Parnes, when, in compliance with the
invocation of Socrates, they descend to visit the earth. Quitting their aërial

station on this lofty mountain, they soar over the Athenian Plain, they float
across the peaked hill of LYCABETTUS, at the north-east extremity of the
city, and above the town itself, and the rock of the Acropolis, they fly over
the Parthenon, and at last alight on the stage of the Theatre, on the south
side of the citadel.   Before they commence their flight, they join their voices
in a choral strain, replete with poetical beauty, and furnishing clear evidence that the poet who composed it might have been as distinguished for
lyrical, as he was for his dramatic excellence; that he might have been a
Pindar, if he had not been an Aristophanes.

While listening to the beautiful language and melodious harmony of this
song, the audience might almost imagine itself to be placed in the same
elevated position supposed to be occupied by those who united in giving
it utterance; and thence it might seem to contemplate the noble and fair
spectacles which they there see and describe.   With the Chorus of Clouds,
it might suppose itself looking down upon the objects of which they speak
as then visible to themselves—to see the land of Pallas stretched out below
them, and the lofty Temples and Statues of Athens at their feet; to trace the
long trains of worshippers in festal array traversing the hills to the Sacred
Mysteries of Eleusis; to follow the sacred processions winding through the
streets to the Acropolis of the Athenian city; to witness the banquets and
sacrifices on solemn holidays; to behold the crowds seated in the Theatre
at the beginning of spring, witnessing the dances and listening to the melodies
which there gave an additional charm to that season of festive joy.

Mount Parnes was the natural barrier which protected the Athenian territory from foreign invasion on the north.   But, as a military fortress, when it
falls into the hands of an enemy, becomes the cause of danger to those whom
it was before accustomed to defend, so this mountain, when the foes of Attica
had obtained possession of a stronghold upon it, proved as much fraught with
peril to the Athenians, as it had before been productive of advantage.

Pursuing our course eastward along its heights, we arrive at a point, about
ten miles distant from the fortress of Phylé, above described, and discover the
ruins of some ancient walls on a circular and isolated hill, near the little
village of TATÓI, and which projects from the mountain where we now are.
It stands at a distance of twelve miles to the north-east of Athens, and is
clearly visible from it.   It also commands a view of the whole Athenian plain.

These ruined walls of which we speak are the remains of the celebrated
fortress of DECELEA.   In the year B.C. 413, the nineteenth of the Peloponnesian war, this hill was fortified by the Lacedæmonians, at the instigation of
Alcibiades, and under the command of their general, Agis.   From that time
forth to the conclusion of the war, they remained during the winter months

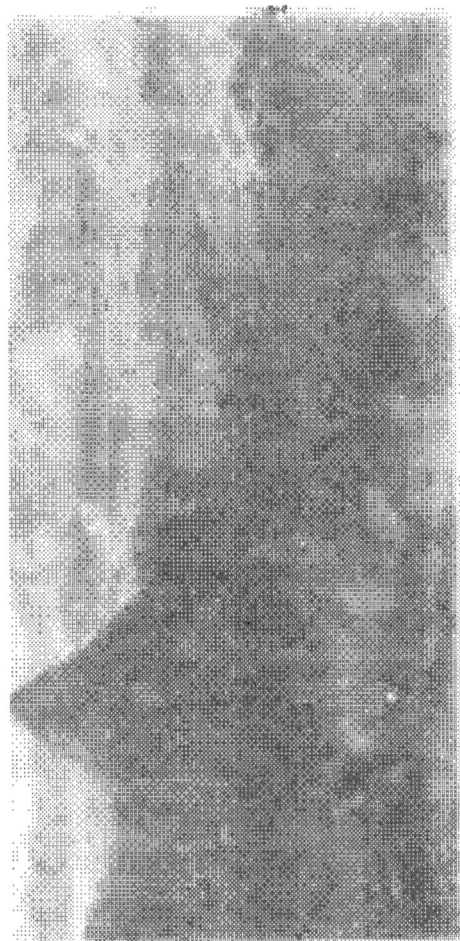

within the Athenian frontier, instead of retiring from it at that season, as they had formerly done with the intention of returning to invade it again at the commencement of spring.

The particular position also which they occupied on this eminence of Mount Parnes, furnished them with the opportunity of laying waste the most pro-

ductive parts of the Athenian plain, and of maintaining themselves with its resources: it enabled them also to intercept the supplies which were conveyed from Eubœa to Athens, and to reduce their enemies to the necessity of abandoning the direct and expeditious route across the mountain passes of Parnes, for the circuitous passage round the Sunian promontory. From these circumstances it arose that, nine years after its occupation by the Lacedæmonians, this small hill proved fatal to the liberty of Athens.

Decelea was a Spartan camp in Attica. A year only before its occupation, the comic poet of Athens, Aristophanes, had exhibited to an audience of his fellow-citizens a city built in the air by two Athenian emigrants, for the purpose of intercepting, in its passage from earth to heaven, the sacrificial steam which arose from the altars of men to the mansions of gods. When the inhabitants of Athens enjoyed the spectacle of this aërial town, presented to their eyes in that drama, little did they dream, that they were about to suffer in the same way from the erection of a similar barrier in their own territory. The Decelea of Agis and the Lacedæmonians proved to Athens

itself, what the Nephelococcygia of Peisthetærus and Euelpides was in the
fiction of the Aristophanic comedy to its Deities.

It is worthy of remark, that the two principal passes from Attica to
Bœotia, over Mount Parnes, were guarded by two forts, one at the north-west
and the other at the north-eastern angle of the Athenian plain, and nearly
equidistant from Athens and from each other. These are Phylé and Decelea.
The remains of both are still clearly visible. They are both distinguished
by the important figure which they make in Athenian history. Both have
now been noticed. The latter, as has been observed, was one of the main
causes of the decline and fall of Athens at the close of the Peloponnesian
war: by means of the former she was raised again from the degradation into
which she had then sunk. What she lost by Decelea and the treachery of
Alcibiades, she recovered by Phylé and the patriotism of Thrasybulus.

Not far from Decelea was the important town of APHIDNÆ, one of the
twelve independent and confederate cities of which the Athenian Republic
was composed before the age of THESEUS, who united them in one community, of which Athens was the head. It is not unworthy of observation,
that, while Decelea was connected with the calamities and subjugation of
Athens, and with the misfortunes and indignities which she suffered at the
hands of her rival Sparta, it was from the neighbouring town of Aphidnæ that
three individuals issued, who liberated from a state of bondage both of these
states. The same city, which gave TYRTÆUS to Lacedæmon, sent HARMODIUS
and ARISTOGEITON to Athens. They were all natives of Aphidnæ. It was also
at Aphidnæ that HELEN was concealed, when she was brought by Theseus into
Attica. Here she was discovered by her brothers Castor and Pollux, who were
guided to the spot by the inhabitants of Decelea. Thus these two places are
connected with each other, and with the earliest traditions of Attica.

Standing on a spot which derives from these circumstances an interest of
no ordinary nature, looking upon the soil and surrounding objects of a place
which has been honoured by the presence of persons whom Time has invested
with mysterious dignity, and whose names have been famous in the mouths of
men for three thousand years,—a scene which has been visited by Theseus,
by the Dioscuri, and by Helen,—and at the same time surveying the distant
Plain of Athens—which from this lofty eminence we command—stretching
from the hills of Parnes to the harbour of the Piræus, we are naturally led to
indulge in speculations on the aspect which this country wore at that distant
epoch, and on some of the most important vicissitudes, subsequent to that
time, which it has undergone. Blended with fable as the narratives of that
period are, and prone as the inhabitants of Attica were to enhance their
national glory by adorning its annals with fictitious embellishments, yet it

is not difficult to trace some footsteps of truth in those legendary records, which have been handed down to us, of the most distant ages of their history.

The earliest monarch of this country, whose name is preserved, is CECROPS. Backward, beyond him, historical tradition did not go. He was, therefore, an AUTOCHTHON or indigenous—the offspring of the earth. The form under which he was on that account represented has been above noticed. In his days, it is said, the Gods began to choose favourite spots among the dwellings of men for their own residence, or, as the expression seems to mean, particular Deities were worshipped with special homage in particular cities. It was at

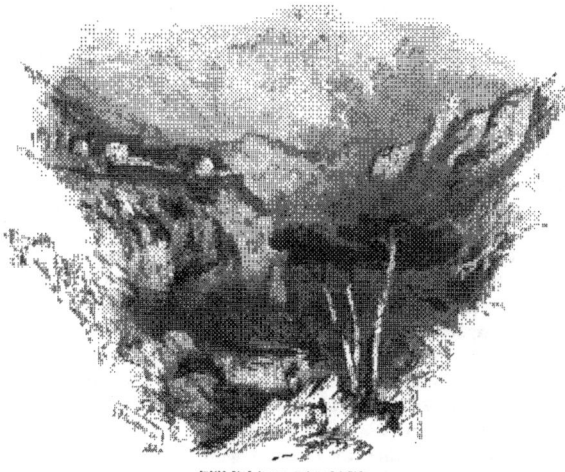

this time, then, that MINERVA and NEPTUNE strove for the possession of Attica. The question was to be determined by the natural principle of priority of occupation. Cecrops, at that period the King of the country, was called upon to arbitrate between them in this controversy. It was asserted by Neptune, that he had appropriated the territory to himself by planting his TRIDENT on the rock of the ACROPOLIS at Athens, before the land had been claimed by Minerva. He pointed to it there standing erect, and to the salt spring which had then issued, and was flowing from the fissure of the cliff which had opened for the reception of the trident.

On the other hand, Minerva alleged that she had taken possession of the country at a still earlier period than had been done by the rival deity. She appealed, in support of her claim, to the OLIVE, which had sprung at her command from the soil, and which was growing near the fountain produced by the hand of Neptune from the same place.

Cecrops was required to attest the truth of her assertion. He had been witness of the act: and he decided in favour of Minerva, who then became the tutelary Deity of Athens.

It is not difficult to perceive that in this tradition a record is preserved of rivalry—produced by the form and the situation of Attica itself—between the two classes of its population, the one devoted to maritime pursuits, and aiming at commercial eminence, the other contented with its domestic resources, and preferring the tranquil and unambitious occupations of agriculture and pastoral life, which were typified by the emblematical symbol of peace. The victory of Minerva, which it commemorates, is a significant expression of the condition of this country, and of the habits of its people, before the days of Themistocles.

Again as a settled form of religious Worship may be inferred from this tradition to have commenced at the period to which it relates, so we may reasonably conclude that the influence of Law was then felt, and that the sanctions of Justice were recognised, by a people whose king was called upon to decide a suit in which the parties at issue were two rival Deities, and who founded his decision upon that principle of equity, on which the safe tenure of property depends. The same inference is supplied by the mythological narration, that when, during the reign of Cecrops, another Deity, Mars, was accused of homicide, the court, before which he was brought to be tried upon that charge, was the Athenian tribunal of the AREOPAGUS.

We do not mean to assert that the legends to which we are alluding are the productions of the periods to which they refer; but, granting that they first made their appearance in a later age, still, if we trace them in the chronological order in which they are presented to our notice by the Athenians themselves, we may fairly regard these mythological legends as historical expressions of popular opinions, entertained by those who had the best opportunities of forming them concerning the different stages of their own history.

Much historical ore may be smelted from mythological minerals.

Proceeding further in our Mythical inquiries, we seem to recognise the trace of an attempt to unite the inhabitants of the Hills with those of the Plains of Attica,—who before this period had probably been at variance with each other,—in the tradition which records that CRANAUS, the successor of Cecrops, married PEDIAS, and that the issue of their wedlock was ATTHIS:—

in other words, that Attica was then formed by the union of the two districts which are aptly signified by the particular names, the one signifying *rugged*, the other, belonging to the *plain*,—which are there assigned to Cranaus and his wife.

This state of prosperity does not appear to have been of long duration; for Atthis is said to have died in early youth; and the flood of Deucalion is

related to have inundated the country during the reign of Cranaus, who was himself driven from the throne by the king next in succession, whose name Amphiction,—a collector of neighbouring people in one community,—appears to indicate an attempt made in this, the next age, to organize afresh the social elements which had been disturbed by the convulsions of the previous generation, and to combine them together in one body.

This design seems to have been attended with success, and to have produced results favourable to the cultivation of the arts of civilized life. For

the immediate successor of Amphiction, and the representative of the state of the Athenian nation, as it existed in that period, was Erichthonius. It seems reasonable to consider these Attic kings as personifications, if we may so call them, of the Athenian people, in the different eras of their early history. Erichthonius was, in the language of mythology, the son of Vulcan and Minerva; or, as that tradition may be interpreted, it was in this age and under its auspices that the manual labours and mechanical arts which enjoyed the patronage of those two Deities, began to attract the attention, and to assume the importance which afterwards rendered them the source of affluence and glory to the possessors of the Athenian soil.

Not inconsistent with this account is the other tradition, which ascribes to Erichthonius the honour of being the first to yoke four horses to a car,—a remarkable circumstance in the barren land of Attica, where the horse was reared with difficulty, and maintained at considerable expense, and which was therefore the most expressive indication that could have been adopted of the greater diffusion of wealth, consequent on the successful cultivation of those arts and manufactures which began to flourish at this period.

The tranquillity which then prevailed,—a tranquillity expressed by the fact that Erichthonius was succeeded by his son,—not only conduced to the progress and successful development of the Arts, but led to the adoption of new modes of tillage, which enriched the Athenian husbandman with a greatly increased variety and abundance of agricultural produce derived from his own soil.

Therefore it is that the visits of CERES and of BACCHUS, the givers of Corn and Wine, are said to have been paid to Attica at this time. Perhaps, too, we may be allowed to assume, as another result from the peaceful character of the period, that greater attention was given to the appearances of Nature, to the vicissitudes of the elements, and to the forms and character of the other objects of Creation, than had hitherto been the case; and that the legends in which the Monarch of that time, Erichthonius, is raised after his death to a place among the celestial constellations, as the HENIOCHUS, or Charioteer—an honour in which his contemporary, ICARUS, the entertainer of Bacchus on the occasion of his visits to Attica, as well as his daughter

ERIGONE, or, the Virgin, are admitted to participate,—are proofs of the observation with which the phenomena of the heavens were then regarded; while the story of Tereus and Procne and her sister Philomela, metamorphosed into Birds, suggests the belief that the more humble creatures of the animal world were not treated with neglect.

A new and important era of Athenian history commences with the reign of THESEUS, whose name gives rise to these remarks, to which we will now direct our thoughts.

Pisistratus, tyrant of Athens, in his revision of the Homeric Poems, is said to have interpolated a verse which characterized Theseus and his friend Pirithous as sons of the immortal Gods; and it is also alleged, by the historian who makes this assertion, that he expunged a line from the works of Hesiod, which mentioned a fact not very creditable to the memory of the Athenian hero, namely, the circumstance that he was induced, when returning from Crete to Athens, to abandon Ariadne on the island of NAXOS. That the Athenians themselves felt a personal interest in all that concerned the history and character of Theseus, would appear from these circumstances, as well as from other evidence. The incidents of his story which reflected honour upon *him* were subjects of national pride to *them:* they strove with him, as it were, in his struggles, fought by his side in his battles, and triumphed in his conquests. He was, in a word, the ancient People of Athens personified by itself. This being the case, the narrative of his adventures and exploits become an object of peculiar interest, not so much as presenting facts of historical value, but as exhibiting to our eyes a picture of the ancient population of Attica, as drawn by themselves, and retouched and embellished by the hands of their posterity.

It is not hereby intimated that all belief in the incidents of the biography of Theseus, as detailed in the popular records of Athenian tradition, is vain and groundless: it is, on the contrary, more rational to suppose, that a people eminently distinguished for its critical perception of propriety in all the imitative arts, would not have failed, in this national portrait, to adopt a real model, and to sketch from it an outline not inconsistent with the truth; and that subsequently it would have studiously endeavoured to fill up the lineaments thus correctly drawn, with lights and shadows harmoniously adapted to them, and have been careful to introduce nothing that was not in due keeping with the tone and character of the age to which the subject belonged.

As a proof of this assertion, we may refer to those particular circumstances in the life of Theseus, which exhibit him and his countrymen in an unfavourable light. His biography is not a mere panegyric. It records his ingratitude to Ariadne, and the ingratitude of his country to him. In it the Athenian hero abandons his benefactress on a desolate shore; and he is driven by the Athenians from his kingdom into exile on the barren rock of SCYROS. The heroine, indeed, is soon rescued from her distress by the appearance of Dionysus, the deity of Naxos; but Theseus is left to die in banishment; and it was not until many centuries had elapsed, that his bones were dug up and brought with triumphal honours to his own city, and deposited there in that magnificent building which still survives in almost its pristine beauty to this day, and thus unites the age of Theseus with our own, and was his Temple and his Tomb.

The character of Theseus, as exhibited in the surviving remains of Athenian tradition, appears to be founded upon the basis of the life and exploits of a real individual, and may justly be considered as a representation partly historical and partly ideal of the condition of the Athenian people, when the age of Mythology was drawing to a close.

Viewed in this light, it becomes, as it were, the Athenian theory of the state in which they were wont to contemplate themselves as existing at that early period of their history : and thus the fabulous legends of his heroic acts assumed a *practical* character. They became assertions of national power exerted for great and useful purposes in that age. His legislative enactments were expressions of their own civil polity at that time.

In these accounts Theseus is called the founder of the Athenian form of popular government. To him the statesmen and orators of later days ascribed the origin of the political privileges enjoyed by those whom they addressed. He was said to have organized the federal body of which the communities of Attica were members. He united them in a civil society, of which the old Cecropian town was the head. He gave to that city, which thenceforth became the capital of Attica, the name of Athens. He instituted the PANATHENAIC festival, to commemorate this act of union.

All these works attributed to Theseus seem to have been so ascribed to

him, as the personified representative of the State. And not merely may his *public* acts be thus identified, as it seems, with those of the national polity, but even his *private* relations appear to have been so modified as to express the connexion of the Athenian people with objects analogous to those which were contemplated by those relations. Thus the inviolable friendship which united Theseus and Pirithöus seems to have represented the ancient national amity which subsisted between the two countries to which these two heroes belonged, namely, Athens and Thessaly. Again, in the rivalries of the Athenian king was shadowed out the history of popular jealousies. The object of his ambition is represented as originating in a desire to emulate the deeds of his contemporary and relative, Hercules. If the latter destroyed the monsters which devastated the land of Greece, Theseus did the same. If Hercules sailed in the Argo, Theseus belonged to the same crew. If he joined the hunters of the Calydonian boar, Theseus was there also; if Hercules is clad in the skin of the lion of Nemea, Theseus wears the hide of the Marathonian bull; if Hercules bears a club, so does Theseus; if the Olympian Games are founded by him, Theseus institutes the Isthmian; if Hercules erects columns at Gades, Theseus does the same at the Isthmus of Corinth.

In all these particulars, the real competitors, whose emulation is expressed by them, are not so much Hercules and Theseus, as the *nations* of which these two heroes are the representatives. They are either Thebes and Athens, or Argos and Athens; and thus these legends are of value, as indicating the political relation which subsisted between these nations respectively at the period when the traditions in question originated.

The antiquity of a similar feeling of jealousy which estranged Athens from Sparta, is proved by the story which represents the Spartan Helen detained as a prisoner at Aphidnæ in Attica, and committed by Theseus to the custody of Æthra, his mother, till his country is invaded by her two brothers, Castor and Pollux, who rescue her from her captivity. A different feeling was entertained by Athens towards the people of Trœzen; and this is expressed by the tradition which leaves Theseus to pass his early youth under the tuition of his father-in-law Pittheus, the wise and virtuous monarch, as he is described, of that country; which sends him to Trœzen as a place of refuge during his temporary exile from Attica; and which consigns Hippolytus, the son of Theseus and the Amazon Hippolyta, for his education to the same place. In connexion with these accounts, it will be remembered, that Trœzen was the

FRONTIER OF ATTICA, BAY OF PHALEA, AND POST OF PIRÆUS

principal asylum of a part of the population of Attica, when driven from their country by the Persians before the battle of Salamis; and, perhaps, these Athenian traditions *themselves* are allusive to that fact, and are grateful memorials of it. It may be added, as a further indication of this intimacy, that Sphettus and Anaphlystus, two important cities on the western coast of Attica, are said, in mythological language, to be the *sons* of Trœzen.

Several instances have been referred to in which the superiority of Theseus over his rival Hercules is evinced. Hercules indeed remained without a competitor in deeds of physical force. The palm of greater excellence in athletic exercises was willingly conceded by the Athenians to Thebes; and the eminence of Thebes in this respect was regarded by its more intellectual neighbours as one of the causes that conduced to give its inhabitants a character which was neither to be envied nor admired. Hercules was no

statesman; he framed no laws, settled no form of government, organized
no religious or civil societies. But all these things were done by Theseus.
Above all, Hercules gave no encouragement to the arts, and he was often
satirized on the Athenian stage for his clownishness and gluttony. Theseus
was, on the other hand, the friend—he is called the cousin and brother—of
Dædalus, who formed the Cretan labyrinth for Minos, and who first endued
statues with the powers of motion and of sight: Theseus was also the
favourite, the son, of Neptune; he built ships and encouraged commerce:
he worked mines and coined money, he was the personification of an
accomplished citizen and enlightened statesman. In all these respects the
balance is greatly in favour of the Athenian hero; or, as it may be expressed
in other words, in all the arts and sciences which elevate the thoughts and
promote the welfare of man in social and civil life, the merits of Attica are
asserted by these traditions to have far eclipsed the pretensions of her
Bœotian neighbour.

To return from these excursions in the regions of the early history of this
country to a survey of the scenery which suggested them—We pursue our
course from Aphidnæ, in an easterly direction, over the high land of Mount
Parnes till we arrive at the sea-coast, which is distant about ten miles from
the ruins of that place. The cliffs above the shore present magnificent
views of the channel of the Euripus, and of the bold and rocky coast of
Eubœa, sweeping in a varied line, and terminating at the south on the bay

of Carystus, and in the noble summit of Mount Ocha. The country over which we pass in our way to the sea, and at a little distance from it, is covered with thick clusters of heath, arbutus, and lentisk: there are scarcely any trees, with the exception of the mountain-pine and the wild pear; and no human dwelling is now visible.

In this solitary scene, at about half a mile from the sea and three hundred feet above it, is a rectangular terrace, of which two sides, namely, those on the north and east, are faced with massive blocks of white Pentelic marble, fitted to each other with the nicest symmetry. The eastern wall is one hundred and fifty feet in length: it rises eight feet above the soil below it, which slopes gently to the sea.

This terrace was a Sacred Inclosure. On it two Temples formerly stood; they belonged to the city of RHAMNUS, which lay below them on a circular knoll upon the sea-shore. The direction in which they were placed was from north to south; and the remains of both are considerable. Whether they ever existed contemporaneously in a perfect state is uncertain. Had this been so, the buildings, as is clear from their actual foundations, must have presented a very irregular and un-symmetrical appearance, for which there was no reason, inasmuch as the area around them is large and spacious.

Of these two fabrics, that to the west consisted of a simple cella, built _in antis_, as it is called; that is, with but one portico, formed by two columns, placed between two pilasters, in which the walls of the cella terminate.

This temple was only thirty-five feet long, and twenty-one broad: it was constructed of polygonal masses of marble; some portions are still standing of the four walls which formed the cell. The entrance to the temple was on the south; on each side of it, under the portico supported by the two columns and antæ above-mentioned, was a marble throne, each having an inscription on the plinth, from which it appears, that the chair on the *right* hand of the door was dedicated to NEMESIS, and that on the left to THEMIS. Within the temple was a marble statue of ancient workmanship, which represented the Goddess to whom the temple was dedicated.

SMALL TEMPLE AT RHAMNUS RESTORED.

Adjacent to this temple, on the east, stood a second building of the same kind, but of a much more magnificent style and of ampler dimensions. It was a *peripteral hexastyle*, that is, it was surrounded on all sides with columns, having six at each end; namely, at the *pronaos*, or front, on the south, and at the *posticum*, or hinder porch, on the north: there were twelve columns on each flank; in both the temples, these were of the Doric order. This latter temple measured seventy-five feet in length and thirty-seven in breadth. Within it, some fragments of a colossal statue are still visible.

From the testimonies of ancient authors, especially Pausanias, and from the fact, that the town of Rhamnus, to which these temples belonged, was under the special patronage of the Goddess NEMESIS, and also from the language of an ancient inscription still extant in this larger temple, which speaks of an honorary statue of a young Athenian there dedicated to *her*, it appears that this latter building was consecrated to that Deity. This large and splendid building was the temple of Nemesis.

The smaller fabric first noticed has generally been supposed to have been the Temple of THEMIS; but there is no ground for this opinion, except the circumstance that one of the marble chairs, noticed above as standing in its vestibule, is inscribed to *her:* but it should be observed, that the chair on the *left* of the entrance is dedicated to THEMIS, while that on the *right* of it was sacred to NEMESIS. In addition to this,—since the awkward position of the buildings with respect to each other suggests the belief that they never *both* existed in a state of integrity at the *same time,* and it is just to conclude that the patron Goddess of Rhamnus was *never* without a temple in this place, from the time when the spot itself was first dedicated to her,—it seems reasonable to believe that the older and smaller temple was also consecrated to the same Goddess.

It appears, then, probable, that when this building fell into decay,—whether, from lapse of time, or, as is more likely, from hostile violence,—and when the inhabitants of Rhamnus had advanced in wealth and architectural skill, they then thought fit to erect another more magnificent and spacious temple in honour of their own Deity, while their respect for antiquity, and their veneration for the consecrated building, in which she had been worshipped by their forefathers, caused them to retain, in its actual state, the smaller and simpler fabric which stood by its side.

The ruins, too, of this ancient temple, if it had been laid waste by human force, were perhaps preserved in their dismantled condition for a particular purpose, for they appealed to the patriotic courage of the Rhamnusians against those who had thus treated them: and they conjured Nemesis, the Goddess of Retribution, by a silent and perpetual prayer, to aid them in repelling and chastising those enemies who had thus violated her dignity and profaned her worship.

It is impossible to contemplate the ruins of these temples, and the peculiar features of their site, without being impressed with a deep feeling of admiration for the intelligent spirit which set apart this spot for purposes of religious devotion. Let us imagine this scene as it existed in former days. These buildings then stood on an inclosed terrace, supported by long and high walls of pure marble. This was their pedestal. They were surrounded by a sacred grove of green and fragrant shrubs, among which were statues and altars. One of these two buildings reminded the spectator of the simplicity of earlier days by its chaste and severe style: the other charmed him by the size and beauty of its structure, by its long lines of columns, its lofty pediments, the richness of its sculptured decorations, and by the brilliancy of the colouring

with which they were adorned. Beneath them, at some distance, was the sea:
on its shore was the city of Rhamnus, one of the strongest and most important fortresses of Attica. The town stood on a low peninsula: it was surrounded with lofty walls of massive stone, and was entered on the west by a
gate flanked with towers; on the southern side was its port.

From contemplating the picture which these latter objects suggest to the
imagination,—from ideal visions of the military or naval preparations which
the town of Rhamnus, now lying in ruins before us, was wont to witness in
early days;—from sights such as it then presented, of seamen hastening down
to its port, and invited to embark there by a favourable gale; or of the crews
of Athenian merchant ships, transporting their freight to warehouses on the
quay; or of travellers entering the gate of the city, or issuing from it,—we
turn again to the contemplation of a quieter scene, to the view of these
beautiful temples, standing alone on their lofty platform amid the shadows
and the silence of their consecrated grove.

However mistaken its object, we cannot condemn, nay, rather, we cannot
but fervently approve and admire, the temper of that devotion which raised
these two buildings,—one of grave simplicity, the other of sumptuous splendour,—in such a scene as this. We reverence the feeling which removed
them from the turmoil of the city, sequestered them by a local consecration
from all buildings devoted to traffic and to toil, and placed them in this tranquil
spot, which invited the worshipper to them as a refuge from the stir of the
streets below, to taste the pleasure and enjoy the fruits, if not of devotion,
at least of meditation and repose; we venerate the principle,—a principle, not
of Paganism, but of a purer spirit speaking in a Pagan age,—which in the
dignified structure and in the hallowed and peaceful precincts of these temples
at Rhamnus seems to have conceived and realized the idea of what we may be
allowed to call an architectural sabbath, such as even a heathen could enjoy,
and no Christian can despise.

We recognise, therefore, in this place one of the most interesting specimens
to be found on the soil of Greece of those SACRED PRECINCTS, or INCLOSURES,
which, from their elevation and retirement, gave additional beauty, dignity,
and sanctity to the Temples contained within them, and which may suggest
instruction to our own Architects, and give delight to modern times. We find
the same idea, which suggested such an arrangement, developed in other places
on a grand scale, and with great magnificence. In a certain sense the
Acropolis of Athens was itself a hallowed TEMENOS, as such an inclosure was
called in the language of ancient Greece. The spacious grove of the Olympian Jove at Elis was another of the same kind. Another example is found
in the walled platform at Eleusis, on which the Propylæa and Temple stood.

We are presented with another specimen at Epidaurus in Argolis, where the Temple of Æsculapius and other consecrated buildings, and also the unrivalled Theatre of Polycletus, were grouped together within the same precincts. At Sunium, the fane of Minerva; at Patræ, that of Diana; at Corinth, that of Palæmon; at Megara, that of Jove; at Sicyon, that of Hercules,—were combined with other fabrics in the same way. Nor was this practice limited to Greece. We may discover it on the shores of Asia and of Sicily. At Priené it was seen in the sacred buildings dedicated to Minerva Polias: it exhibits itself at Selinus, where four temples stand side by side on a raised terrace inclosed by walls: and no one can view the line of magnificent fanes still standing at Girgenti on their elevated platform, looking over the sea on one side, and the site of the ancient city, from which they are removed, on the other, without feeling a share of the pleasure and veneration with which they were contemplated by spectators and worshippers of ancient days, and which they inspired by their position.

It is a distance of about six miles from Rhamnus to MARATHON. The road descends from the heights of Mount Parnes in a south-westerly direction. The plain of Marathon lies from north-east to south-west. It is nearly in the form of a crescent, the horns of which consist of two promontories, which project into the sea, and form its semicircular bay, which is of the same length as the plain—namely, six miles: the breadth of the latter, in the widest or central part of the crescent, is two miles. A line drawn from the middle of the arc of the bay, so as to cut the centre of the arc of the plain, will, if produced, pass upward along a valley in which is the modern Village of Marathóna, and down which a stream flows, which nearly divides the plain into two equal parts, and then falls into the bay: on all other sides towards the land the crescent of the plain is bounded by rugged limestone mountains, covered with pines, olives, and cedars, and low shrubs, such as lentisk, cypresses, and myrtles. Near each of the horns or capes of the northern and southern extremity of the plain are two marshes, overgrown with reeds and rushes: between the southern of these, and the central stream above mentioned, is a Tumulus—called Soró, or the Mound—of red sandy earth, and ten yards in height, two hundred in circumference, and a thousand from the shore.

The plain is dry and bare, consisting, chiefly, of arable land, and quite flat: there are no hedges nor houses upon it; here and there is a small white chapel, with a low door and narrow window, and in a ruinous condition; some oxen are seen feeding in the southern marsh, and others ploughing on the plain; rarely is a vessel discovered at anchor in the bay, which is entirely exposed on the east and south-east; its best anchorage is at the centre and at the north-west, where the depth is seven and eight fathoms, gradually decreasing to the shore. Such, now, is the aspect of the plain of Marathon. Its distance from Athens is twenty-two miles.

The battle of Marathon, which preserved the liberties of Greece, and perhaps of Europe, from the dominion of Persia, was fought in the month of September, B.C. 490. The numbers of the combatants on each side cannot be accurately determined; but the calculation seems most probable which estimates the force of Athens at eleven thousand heavy-armed men, while that of Persia amounted to two hundred thousand. The Athenians possessed neither bowmen nor cavalry, but the Persians were well supplied with both. The Athenian force was drawn up so as to extend from one side of the plain to the other, in order that the mountains on each flank of them might prevent the cavalry of the enemy from wheeling round to charge them in the rear. The right wing of the Greeks was commanded by Callistratus of Aphidnæ, who was the polemarch, or third of the nine Archons of Athens in that year: he was at the head of the troops of the tribe Æantis. The whole Athenian force was so disposed that the members of the same tribe might fight near each other,—a circumstance worthy of notice, and which conduced much to stimulate the exertions, and to increase the valour of all, by the honourable rivalry among the different tribes, and by the encouragement given by the members of the same tribe to each other; which were the results aimed at and naturally produced by such an arrangement. The tribe Œnëis was led by Miltiades; Aristides was at the head of his own, Antiochis; Themistocles commanded that of Leontis: these two latter composed the Athenian centre. Its left wing was formed of Platæans, amounting to one thousand men. The Athenian line was two miles in length, and about that distance from the sea-shore. That of the Persians coincided in extent with it, and was drawn up at an equal distance from it and from the sea.

The battle was commenced by the Athenians, who marched with a quick step over the mile of ground which separated them from the enemy. They were the first among the Greeks who dared to attack the Persians, or even to endure the sight of their armour, or to look them in the face on the field of battle: until that day, the very name of Medes had struck a panic into the hearts of the dwellers of Greece.

Both the wings of the Greek army were successful. The centre, which was the weakest part of the line, being necessarily stretched beyond the usual length for the purpose above mentioned, was broken by the Sacæ and the Persians, who held the corresponding place of the enemy's force. The battle lasted for many hours. Towards evening, the Greek wings returned from the pursuit of their opponents, and closed to intercept and attack the Persian centre in the rear. This they effected. In the meantime, their own centre

K

rallied, and having formed itself again, it joined with the two wings in a charge upon the Persians from different directions, at one and the same time. They drove the right wing of their opponents into the marsh, and their left and centre into the sea; and attempted to set fire to the Persian vessels in the bay, and succeeded in seizing seven of them. The greatest slaughter of the Persians took place in the two marshes; that of the Athenians in the plain between them: of the former, six thousand four hundred fell; the latter lost only one hundred and ninety-two men. Thus ended the battle of Marathon.

The plain of Marathon is described by Herodotus as one of the most favourable places in Attica for the operations of cavalry; and for this reason, he affirms, it was recommended to the Persian generals by Hippias, the exiled Tyrant of Athens, who was then in their army, both as the most convenient spot for the landing of their troops, and also the most advantageous for an engagement with the Athenians, whose force, at that time, consisted of infantry alone. It is clear that this character of the place must be qualified by certain restrictions; for, as was evinced by the result of the battle, the marshes at either extremity of the plain render it not merely unfavourable, but, on the contrary, very inconvenient for that purpose which he is said to have had particularly in view when he advised such a selection. It seems most probable that the Persians, whose course hitherto, on their way to Greece, had been little else than a succession of victories, little dreamt that they should experience any check or opposition worthy of the name, in landing on any point of the Athenian soil. They thought, as the same historian says, that those whom they saw marching rapidly against them, were impelled by a spirit of infatuation which drove them to certain destruction. They therefore directed their course to Marathon, as the nearest place of any importance after their conquest of Eubœa, not without reference indeed to the character of the spot, as more favourable for the disembarkation of infantry, and for its operations, than other parts of Attica, but imagining that, however this might be, there was but little chance of their meeting any resistance from its inhabitants, and none whatever of defeat. This confidence in their own strength, and the contempt of that of their adversaries, was as beneficial to their enemies as it was destructive to themselves.

Another disadvantage under which the Persians laboured, when compared with their antagonists, and which much contributed to their defeat, was the circumstance that they had a place of refuge, and one easy of access in case of their receiving a check from the Athenians: whereas, their opponents, on the contrary, had all the benefit of despair. If the Athenians were not conquerors at Marathon, from that time their cause was lost, and their country enslaved. Had the Persian leaders, Datis and Artaphernes, landed all their troops, and then set fire to their ships, the issue might have been different. In that case, Attica, and with it the Peninsula of Greece, might have become theirs, as the greater part of the Greek continent already was.

The arrangement of the Athenian forces on the field of battle, according to their respective tribes, has been already noticed. It was the same as that recommended by Nestor to Agamemnon on the plains of Troy. If we compare with this the fortuitous disposition of the Persian force, and the confused heterogeneous elements of which it was composed, varying in origin, habits, costume, language, and interests, not one among them fighting for liberty, but for an absent monarch, who had, perhaps, reduced their country to bondage, we recognise the important fact, that the Greeks had on their side a *moral* force, which made them, though few in number, superior to their adversaries.

The season of the year, also, at which the battle was fought, and the time of day to which it was prolonged, were favourable to the Athenians. In the month of September, the marshes at the two extremities of the plain, in which the greatest carnage of the Persians took place, had probably been saturated with rain; whereas, in the summer months they are nearly dry; and had the battle been fought at that period of the year, they would have been as serviceable to the Persians, in giving, by their flat area, a greater extension to the plain, and by affording more room for their cavalry, and greater facili-

BATTLE NEAR MARATHON.

ties for breaking through the enemy, and taking them in the rear, as they now proved pernicious to them. From the direction, also, of the plain, it happened that at the crisis of the conflict, which was in the evening, the Greeks had the sun behind them, while it streamed in full radiance on the faces of their opponents.

We have specified some of the moral and physical advantages which the Athenians enjoyed on the field of Marathon: they had also on their side certain religious ones, which are not to be forgotten.

The place in which they fought was consecrated ground: it was dedicated to Hercules. As the Greeks at Thermopylæ fought beneath the mountain, so at Marathon they contended on the plain, of that hero. Mount Œta was, as it were, a natural Altar, and Marathon a Temple, of Hercules. It was here that his daughter MACARIA had offered herself up to death, as a victim for the liberty of her people. The fountain which supplied the marsh that was so destructive to the Persians, bore her name. Her example could not have been absent from the minds of the Greeks who were about to engage near it in a similar cause. And it was near this stream that the sons of Hercules, by the assistance of the Athenian king of that time, had routed the army of their enemy, Eurystheus. Again, it was at Marathon that Theseus, the prince and guardian hero of Athens, had destroyed the monster which had been brought by Hercules from Crete, and which had ravaged Attica.

It is evident that these local recollections were not lost upon those who welcomed with great gladness the promise of the pastoral Deity Pan,—to whom a grotto on the rocks above the Plain of Marathon was subsequently dedicated,—that he would come from Arcadia to assist them in the battle in which they were now about to engage. In fact, these traditions were blended in after-times with the historical features, and became a part of the real scenery, of the battle of Marathon. This was shown by the fresco, in which the battle was represented by PANÆNUS, the cousin of PHIDIAS, on the walls of the Pœcilé, or Painted-porch, at Athens. In the back-ground were the Phœnician ships riding in the bay, and, nearer to the spectator, the Athenians were driving the Persians into the marshes and the sea; in the foreground of the picture, were Miltiades, Callimachus, and Cynægeirus, and near them the forms of MINERVA, of HERCULES, and of THESEUS rising from the earth.

To the traveller who visits the plain of Marathon at this day, the two most attractive and interesting objects are the TUMULUS, or Mound, which has been described as standing between the two marshes, and about half a mile from the sea; while at the distance of a thousand yards to the north of this are the remains of a square building, formed of large blocks of white

PLAIN, OR TOWER, OF MARATHON

marble, which now bears the name of PYRGOS, or the Tower. Beneath the former lie the remains of the one hundred and ninety-two Athenians who fell in the battle; the latter may be the site of the trophy of Miltiades.

It was a wise and noble thought to bury these heroes on the spot where they fell. The body of Callimachus, the leader of the right wing, was interred among them; and as they fought, arranged by tribes, in the field, so their ashes now lie in the same order in this tomb. Even the spectator of these days, who comes from a distant land, will feel an emotion of awe when looking upon this grand and simple monument, with which he seems, as it were, to be *left alone* on this wide and solitary plain; nor will he wonder that the ancient inhabitants of this place revered those who lie beneath it as Beings more than human,—that they heard the sound of arms and the neighing of horses around it in the gloom of the night, and that the greatest Orator of the Ancient World swore by those who lay buried at Marathon as if they were living Powers.

Not only was Miltiades the leader of the Athenians on this plain, but it was through his means that they fought there at all. To him, therefore, they erected the honorary monument of which the probable remains have just been noticed. This trophy of Miltiades would not suffer Themistocles to sleep. As he himself said, it disturbed his dreams, and stimulated him to imitate the deeds of the hero of Marathon. Such was the moral influence of this trophy on his mind. Such were the fruits of public honours in those times. By honouring greatness, they created it. The trophy of

Miltiades on the plain of Marathon produced the trophy of Themistocles on
the promontory of Salamis.

Of both of these great battles, there existed visible memorials on the spots
where they were fought. But with respect to the manner in which their
memory has been preserved by *other* records, their fate has been very different.
The battle of Marathon was represented both in painting and in sculpture,—
on the walls of the Pœcilé in the Agora of Athens, and in the Temple of
Victory on the Acropolis, on the frieze of which we still see the figures of the
Persian combatants with their lunar shields, their bows and quivers, their
curved scimitars, their loose trousers, and Phrygian tiaras. But this has not
been the case with the battle of Salamis. Perhaps this difference arose,
not from any pre-eminence of glory which the former enjoyed, for in this
respect Salamis did not yield to Marathon; but rather, as it seems, from the
dissimilar nature of the two battles themselves. While the variety of attitudes
and movements of combatants engaged in a conflict by *land* afforded ample
scope to the artist for a display of his powers of conception and of execution,
especially in his treatment of the human form—the features and scenery of a
sea-fight, such as the long ships, their erect beaks, and their parallel lines of
oars, were less tractable materials for the chisel and the pencil: their forms

were too rigid, and too little susceptible of that ideal grace which is the soul of art, to permit him to attempt a representation which would fail to enhance the glory of that memorable deed, and perhaps would even expose it to the disparagement of his fastidious countrymen.

The same refinement of taste and love of imaginative beauty, the same impatience of reality when inconsistent with his own conceptions of symmetry, which induced the Artist to exhibit, in the frieze of which we have spoken, the Athenians at Marathon with no other armour than their shields, and with no other covering than a loose and flowing drapery, compelled him, it would seem, to abstain from any representation of the sea-fight of Salamis, which might, if executed, have been probable without being picturesque, or picturesque without being possible.

But what Sculpture and Painting have not attempted, another Art has accomplished. Among the combatants, at Marathon and Salamis, was the tragic Poet Æschylus. He left the battle of Marathon to be celebrated in the frescoes of the Porch, and on the frieze of the Temple; but he immortalized Salamis in verses which retain their original freshness, when the painting of the Pœcilé has vanished, and the sculpture of the Temple has been mutilated by decay. The colours of the Painter have faded, the marble of the Sculptor is broken, and is banished to a distant land, but the work of the Poet lives everywhere. Æschylus, in his drama of The Persians, has painted a Portico in honour of Salamis which will never fade, he has erected a Temple of Victory which will never fall. So much nearer is the approach made to Immortality by what is spiritual, than by what is material, in man.

It is a walk of five hours from the Plain of Marathon to the heights of Mount Pentelicus, where the marble quarries are seen which have obtained for this mountain so much renown in the annals of ancient Art. The road ascends from the plain towards the south-west, and passes over elevated steeps clad with pines and olives, and through glens refreshed with clear brooks, and overhung with oleanders and myrtles. The quarries, of which there are two, lie to the north,—the one at a mile's distance, the other a little more than two miles, from the Monastery which derives its name from the mountain under whose summit it lies.

The larger quarry is open to the light: on the south it is bounded by the rock, hewn to a lofty and perpendicular wall. At the base of it is a wide cavern, which penetrates into the recess of the cliff, and is hung with stalactites of white marble glittering with the brilliance of alabaster: the incrustations, tinged with various hues, which shoot like branches from the rock, present the appearance, when seen at a distance, of groves and forests of stone. The mouth of the grotto is fringed over with tufts of ivy.

The marble of the Pentelic quarries resembles that of Paros in whiteness and splendour; in fineness of grain it excels it; in this respect it is very similar to that of Carrara, and it is free from the metallic stains with which the latter is frequently sullied. Let us contrast for a moment the present appearance of this vast quarry before us, with its former condition. About two thousand two hundred and ninety years ago, its sides, which are now deserted and silent, resounded with the din of busy workmen hewing its cliffs, or heaving with ropes and pulleys the huge masses which had been quarried from them, and letting them sink upon sledges which were to bear them down the steep mountain track into the plain and through the gates of the city of Athens. Others carried them to the harbour of the Piraeus, whence they were transported to distant lands.

We look with feelings of respect on the spots where great men were born: the palace where a king or a conqueror first saw the light is an object of veneration; we make a pilgrimage to the native place of the philosopher, and tablets are placed on the walls of the dwelling where a great poet first breathed the air. And surely we should be guilty of strange insensibility, if we could regard with indifference,—or without some feeling of veneration,—this, the *native place* of so many buildings and statues—the rocky cradle of so many Friezes and Temples, which have inspired the admiration, refined the taste, influenced the acts, humanized the manners, and elevated the thoughts of men;

which have even added dignity to the religion of cities and kingdoms for thousands of years. He would be little to be envied, who could look upon the quarries of Pentelicus without enthusiasm,—who could behold this vast and silent chamber of rock, from whose womb those immortal fabrics, the PARTHENON, the PROPYLÆA, and the TEMPLE OF THESEUS came forth, and whence issued that long train of beautiful forms which, sculptured in marble, have made the Panathenaic solemnity, that they represent, no longer a quinquennial festival, but an *eternal jubilee*, and the possession of which alone,—marred, as they now are, torn from their proper soil, and no longer breathing in their native freshness on their own Temple, but deposited, like mummies, in a foreign Museum,—have made England richer in the productions of sculpture than any other nation of the world.

Here, at least, on this spot, and with this object before us, we may be permitted to indulge in such emotions, and to express the sentiment, that in this marble mine of Pentelicus, when we thus consider it in connexion with the structures and forms which have proceeded from it, we see a faint picture,—to compare human things with divine,—of the operations of that architectonic and vivifying Power, by which the great fabric of the Universe was built, and by which all the forms and imagery, with which it is furnished, were educed from the lifeless quarry of Chaos.

Nor should we here forget the names of those who have employed their art in fashioning the materials which they derived from this place. The marble which was drawn from the spot before us was worked by the hands of the greatest Architects and Sculptors of antiquity. It was hewn and chiselled by Ictinus and Phidias; it was carved by Scopas and by Praxiteles; on it was exercised their skill, and by it have their names been made immortal.

Cicero, in one of his letters to Atticus, expresses a desire to receive some statues of Pentelic marble which his friend had promised to send him from this country; and the architraves hewn from the neighbouring mountain of Hymettus were used to decorate the palaces of Rome in the Augustan age. Rome borrowed her marble from Athens; and nothing indicates more forcibly the pre-eminence over the capital of Italy, which Athens enjoyed as the mistress of the world in arts, than a comparison of the materials for plastic and architectural purposes which Nature supplied respectively to each. While the resources of Rome were limited to the dark Peperine stone of Alba and Gabii, to the Tufo of the Campagna, and to the porous and encrusted Travertine of the Anio—materials not very favourable for architecture of a decorative kind, and still less serviceable for sculpture,—the wealth of Athens, for both purposes, was inexhaustible. On one side of the City lay the quarries of the

snow-white Megarian and of the grey stone of Eleusis; on the other, the blue
Hymettian, the veined Carystian, and the lucid Pentelic. In a word, (as her
language reminds us,) her stone was marble.

Returning to the monastery of which we have spoken, and descending
towards the plains of Athens, on the south-west, we cross one of the sources of
the river Cephissus. Another is seen at CEPHISSIA, a small village in the
plain, on the right of the road from Pentelicus to Athens, at about eight miles
distant to the north-east of the latter. The stream there rises from the earth
beneath a wide plane-tree and spreads itself into a broad and quiet pool of
clear water, which in the summer season is overhung with the leaves and fruit
of various trees. The houses of the village are sprinkled among gardens,
vine-yards, and olive-groves. Cephissia still preserves its ancient name.
It was the country of the comic poet Menander, and the summer retreat of the
learned philosopher of Athens, Herodes Atticus. This was his Tusculum.
To this spot he retired for health and study: hither he invited his friends and
the lovers of pursuits similar to his own. His villa at Cephissia, as we are
informed by one who enjoyed his hospitality here in the sultry season, was
refreshed by streams and shaded by a grove. On one side of it were long
porticoes, or arcades, beneath which he and his friends used to walk and
converse, and at its back were copious baths of cool and transparent water: the
gardens about it resounded with the murmuring of brooks and the warbling of

VALLEY OF THE SOURCE OF THE CEPHISSUS.

birds. This was the residence, and these were
the recreations, of one whose character bore
much resemblance to that of his Roman namesake
the friend of Cicero, and who was, from his
erudition, his public spirit, and his munificence,

worthy to have passed his days in peace, as he did, at Athens, at Cephissia, and at Marathon, in the comparatively tranquil age of Trajan, Hadrian, and the Antonines, notwithstanding the charges which have been made against him of literary vanity and idle display, and notwithstanding the foibles of an affected dilettanteism,—the vice of his age, rather than his own, from which he was not exempt.

We are carried from our mountain track still further into the plain, and in the direction of Athens, to visit a place which was connected in former times with the private life of another Philosopher. Between the two villages of CEPHISSIA and MAROUSI, is that of HERACLÉ. Near this spot, among those olive groves and vineyards, was the country-seat of PLATO. He speaks of it in his will,—where he bequeaths it to his son Adeimantus,—as lying near the road to Cephissia, which was on the north, and reaching on the south to the HERACLEUM, or Temple of Hercules. From this notice, its position is easily ascertained; for the names of both of these places are preserved to this day; that of the former in the modern Cephissia, while that of the latter survives in the village just mentioned of Heraclé. Perhaps it was from his orchard on this spot that the Philosopher sent a liberal present of figs to Diogenes, who had asked only for three, which drew from the cynic, instead of thanks, the sarcastic answer: "Thus it is, that when you are asked a plain question in philosophy, which might be answered in three words, you reply to the inquirer in ten thousand."

We have spoken above of the village of Marousi. As those of Cephissia and Heraclé preserve in their names a record of their ancient inhabitants,

their language, and their religious worship, so that of Marousi recalls to the
recollection a heathen Deity who was an object of devotion to the ancestors of
the villagers who dwell here, more than two thousand years ago. Cased in
the plaster wall of a small Greek chapel, near to this place, is a marble slab,
which, as the ancient Greek inscription upon it commemorates, served once as
a limit to mark the termination of the sacred inclosure of the Temple of the
AMARUSIAN DIANA, of whose appellation a vestige remains in the modern
name of the village of Marousi.

At the birth of Erichthonius, the ancient King of Attica, Pallas Minerva
is said to have come from her Temple at PALLENÉ to Athens, and to have
borne through the air, as a birthday gift, that remarkable conical hill which
stands at the north-east of Athens, and which was first named LYCABETTUS,
then ANCHESMUS, and, at present, the mountain of ST. GEORGE. The Goddess, it is said, dropped it from her arms on the spot where it is now placed,
in order that it might serve as a bulwark of Athens on that side. The
Temple at Pallené, from which she came, stood, it is probable, not far from
Marousi. It is a spot famed in history as the scene of the contests between
the sons of Peisistratus and their rivals the Alcmæonidæ; and in earlier days,
for the pursuit, by Iolaus, of the Argive Eurystheus, from the Plain of
Marathon to the Scironian rocks.

Between the southern foot of Pentelicus and the northern slope of
Hymettus is a level interval, two miles broad. This is the communication
between the two principal plains of Attica, namely, that of Athens on the

PENTELICUS AND MT. ANCHESMUS.

west, and that of MESOGÆA, or INTERIOR of Attica, on the south-east. At
the eastern foot of the mountain a lion sculptured in marble, of colossal size,
is recumbent on the plain; it is of Pentelic marble, and in good preservation,
except that the legs have disappeared. Near to the spot are other blocks of
marble, vestiges of some temple or other ancient building.

The view from the summit of Mount Hymettus will long live in the
memory of him who has beheld it, presenting to the eye, as it does, objects
and creations both of nature and of art, distinguished by their surpassing

loveliness of symmetry and colour, and of much interest in themselves, and in
the thoughts which they suggest. Their extent, variety, and beauty is such
that neither the lapse of time, nor the business of life, nor weariness of body
or of mind, can erase from his memory the pleasure which he felt when contemplating the scenery beneath him from this spot.

The produce of the neighbouring mountain of Pentelicus has been spoken
of. To compare with it that of Hymettus: while the vast *quarries* of the
former—worked with such laborious energy by generations of men who have
departed and left no posterity in the land—have remained untouched for many
centuries, there has been no cessation of industry, no interruption in the
succession of labourers in the humble *hives* of Hymettus, from the most
glorious days of Athens to the present hour. The storms which have swept
away cities and empires have spared them. The Cecropian Bees have survived all the revolutions which have changed the features and uprooted the
population of Attica: according to the poetical prophecy,

" Their race remains immortal, ever stands
Their house unmoved, and sires of sires are born."

On the southern slope of Hymettus, a little above the village of DARI, is a subterranean grotto, which well deserves to be visited. The visitor descends a few steps hewn in the rock, and enters the cave, which is lighted from the narrow adit: it is hung with stalactites, and bends itself into two apartments, the one nearly parallel to the other. This place was a natural Temple, dedicated to Pan and the pastoral Nymphs. It would have been a fit scene for an Idyl of Theocritus, and was worthy of inscriptions from the pen of Nossis or

CAVE OF PAN, OF MELETTE.

Meleager. In ancient days, the pipes and reeds of shepherds were suspended, as votive offerings, on its rocky walls; basins of stone, and cups of wood carved with figures and flowers, were here dedicated to the Deities of the place: here images of the Nymphs stood in their small niches; hither the first flowers of their gardens, the first ripe ears of their harvests, the first grapes of their vineyards, the first apples of their orchards, were brought as oblations by the shepherds and peasants of Attica. Even at this day there remain visible traces of their devotion, as well as memorials of the person who dedicated this grotto to the worship of the rural Deities. Engraved on the rock, at the entrance, is an inscription in verse, which announces that Archedemus, a native of Pheræ, in Thessaly, formed this "cave by the counsel of the Nymphs:" other records of the same kind inform us, that it was sacred to the Graces, to Apollo, and to Pan. Two verses, inscribed on a slab of marble, speak of a parterre planted here in honour of the Nymphs. In another part of the cave is the figure of Archedemus himself, rudely sculptured on the rock, dressed in his shepherd's coat, and with a hammer and a chisel in his hands, hewing the sides of the cave.

Plato, in early youth, was led by his parents to a grotto on Mount Hymettus, that he might present an offering to Pan, the Nymphs, and the

Pastoral Apollo, to whom it was dedicated. There is reason to believe that *this* cave, which, as the above inscriptions still existing on its walls assure us, was consecrated to those Deities, has been trodden by the feet of the great philosopher of Athens; and that his eye has rested upon some of the same objects that we now see in this simple pastoral temple, which has sustained but little injury from the lapse of ages, while many of the magnificent fanes of the Athenian capital have crumbled to decay.

At a distance of ten miles, in an easterly direction, from this spot, is the bay of PRASIÆ, one of the best harbours of the coast of Attica. At the centre of its entrance, which is a mile broad, is a small island, on which, at an elevation of three hundred feet from the level of the sea, is the fragment of a sitting statue of white marble, from the attitude of which, resembling that of a tailor at his work, the harbour derives its modern name of PORT RAPHTÉ, —an appellation not very complimentary to its sculptor, who is supposed to have intended it to represent a Roman Emperor.

About nine miles south of this place is another harbour, more celebrated in ancient times, that of THORICUS: it is a semicircular bay, a mile and a half in breadth: to the north of it, on a rugged hill, are the remains of the Acropolis of the city, of rude and massive masonry: at its foot is a Theatre, and near it a covered Gallery of very antique style. In the plain, to the west, are the ruins of a large and magnificent Building, which was adorned with a marble peristyle. Another vestige of the ancient Thoricus survives in the modern name of the place, THERICO.

If a line be drawn due west from the site of the ancient Thoricus, it will, after a distance of eight miles, meet the western coast of Attica, in a place formerly called ANAPHLYSTUS, and now, by a slight change, ANAPHYSO: if again, from these points, Thoricus and Anaphlystus, lines be drawn to CAPO COLONNI, the ancient SUNIUM, we shall then have a triangle nearly equilateral, at the three angles of which are three places all of considerable importance in the history of Attica, and whose sides inclose a space from which she derived the means of her former affluence and glory.

The *coined* treasure of Athens was preserved in the OPISTHODOMUS, or hinder apartment of the PARTHENON, or Temple of Minerva, in the Acropolis of that city. The Country, which we are now describing, at the southern extremity of Attica, was, as it were, a *natural* Opisthodomus to Attica itself. In it lay the *uncoined* wealth of Athens. In it were the Mines of Attica, that "fountain of silver, the treasure of the land," as Æschylus calls them. The district was called LAUREUM, a name probably derived from the shafts and passages sunk and pierced beneath its surface, many of which are still visible on the road between Sunium and Thoricus. The path here, near the sea-shore, is strewn with scoria, from which the silver ore was smelted in ancient times.

These mines were the property of the Athenian State. They were worked at a period of very early antiquity: in the days of Themistocles the supply from them was very abundant; when Xenophon wrote, they were beginning to fail; in Strabo's age they were exhausted; Pausanias speaks of them as a monument of the past. They consisted of large vaults, supported by columns, aired and lighted by vents, and divided into compartments. Many thousand slaves were employed in working them. From these dark cavities, now shaded with pines and overgrown with junipers and lentisks, was derived the wealth which enabled Athens to create and maintain the navy by which she first coped with Ægina and afterwards rescued Greece from the despotism of the East. Hence issued the coin which circulated in every part of the civilized world, and was nowhere surpassed in purity. For a long time Athens had no other term in her language for money than that which signified *silver*; whether she ever coined Gold is doubtful, but before she used it in her currency, her liberties were lost.

It was the boast of Athens that her coinage was so excellent that it was everywhere exchanged with profit by its possessor: and it is worthy of remark, that, in order to preserve its credit in foreign lands, she studiously retained upon it the antique type of the head of Minerva, which looked as if it had proceeded from Ægypt rather than from the most polished capital of Greece. Thus, while in the other arts of design she advanced from the rude outline to consummate symmetry, in Numismatics she remained stationary, and, while her other productions were unrivalled in elegance, her money was as inferior in beauty, as it claimed to be superior in value, to that of nearly all the other states of Greece.

The TEMPLE OF MINERVA, at Sunium, stands upon a raised terrace at the highest point of the cape; its direction is from east to west: it had six columns at each front; the number of those on the north and south cannot clearly be ascertained: nine are still standing on the south, three on the north, two and one of the *antæ* at the east. It was surrounded by a sacred *temenos* or inclosure, entered by a portico or Propylæa at its north-east corner. The walls of the fortress descend from the temple toward the north; and are still traceable for their complete circuit, which is half a mile. This temple—elevated on high above the Ægæan Sea, at the extremity of this promontory—stood like the Portico or Vestibule of Attica. Constructed of white marble, placed on this noble site, and visible at a great distance from the sea, it reminded the stranger who approached it in his vessel from the south, by the fair proportions of its architecture, and by the decorations of sculpture and of painting with which it was adorned, that he was coming to a land illustrious for its skill in the most graceful Arts,—a land set apart, as it were, from all others for their cultivation, and appropriated to their use; and inasmuch as this fabric was approached by a portico, and surrounded by a consecrated inclosure, so the whole land of ATTICA itself was a sacred TEMENOS, whose boundaries were Seas and Mountains, and whose PROPYLÆA was the Temple dedicated to Minerva on the promontory of Sunium.

The situation of this temple—on the summit of a rock projecting precipitously into the sea—is singularly magnificent, and the view it commands over the islands of Ægina and the other headlands is perhaps unrivalled. To the south and east is the group of islands called the Cyclades, studding the waters of the Ægean Sea ; more to the north is the coast of Eubœa, the lofty ridges of Carystos terminating at Cape Mandili in the Geræstian promontory. To the south-west, about ten miles off, the Scylæan promontory, now Cape Skylo, forms, with Cape Sunium, the entrance to the Ægean Gulf. Within this point the Island of Calaurea, the Town and Port of Poros, and the Isthmus of Methana are seen, with the coast of Epidaurus, deeply indented with gulfs and bays, while the volcanic mountains of the Argive coast rise dark and massive behind them. From this spot let us pass to Ægina and the other islands of the Saronic Gulf.

TEMPLE OF MINERVA AT SUNIUM.

THE island of Ægina—according to Aristotle the
eye-sore of the Piræus—is of the form of an irregular triangle, the western angle being the site
of the ancient port and city. The eastern angle
is distinguished by the remains of the Temple which has obtained such celebrity from the Æginetan Marbles, once attached to its pediments, and which
now enrich the Glyptothek at Munich; while at the southern corner of the
island rises a conical mountain, which, from its grandeur of form and its
historical associations, is the most remarkable object among the natural
features of the island.

   Remains of the maritime power of Ægina may be traced in the harbour

where we now are. From its size and beauty it once attracted the admiration of its Athenian neighbours and enemies. The entrance to it is through a narrow opening between the two moles which project from the shore, and then converge towards the opening. They terminated in two towers, by which the opening was flanked and protected. That on the left side has been succeeded by a small modern chapel, dedicated to St. Nicholas, whose name is dear to the Greek mariner. There are foundations near the shore of docks and basins, stretching for about a hundred and eighty yards to the north of this harbour, and connected with it. Toward the northern extremity of these substructions is the *scala* or wharf, which leads to the modern Lazaretto;

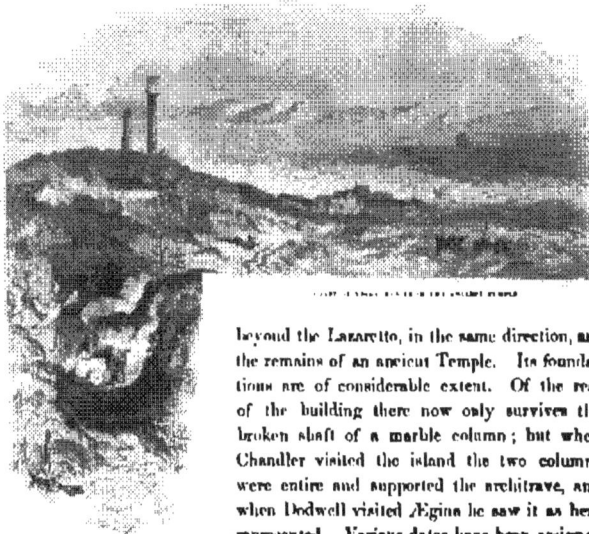

PART OF THE RUINS OF THE ANCIENT TEMPLE

beyond the Lazaretto, in the same direction, are the remains of an ancient Temple. Its foundations are of considerable extent. Of the rest of the building there now only survives the broken shaft of a marble column; but when Chandler visited the island the two columns were entire and supported the architrave, and when Dodwell visited Ægina he saw it as here represented. Various dates have been assigned to the erection of this Temple. To determine the question, the following circumstance is worthy of notice. The temple has been used by the modern Æginetans as a quarry, from which they have excavated materials for the construction of buildings, public and private, in the town to which, unhappily for its preservation, it is immediately contiguous. In hewing out the masses of the ancient fabric, several blocks were found to be inscribed with letters of red chalk, which were still distinctly legible. These blocks were drawn from the lowest foundation; the characters, therefore, which are inscribed upon them, are coeval with the building itself. These characters, from their form, may serve as authentic data for determining the time of the erection of the temple. The two names which they exhibit, Prothymius (ΓΡΟΘΥΜΙΟΣ) and Euphamides (ΕΥΦΑΜΙΔΙΣ), belonged perhaps to two builders employed in the construction of the fabric. From a comparison of the character of these inscriptions with others of which the date is known, it is probable that the foundation of this temple is not of an earlier date than the Peloponnesian war.

Following the coast in the same northerly direction, we find a tumulus on the shore, probably the same which Pausanias saw there, and which he believed to be the work of Telamon, who landed in the neighbouring port and raised a monument to Phocus. Near to this tumulus were the Theatre and Stadium, of which, however, no vestiges remain.

COAST OF ÆGINA FROM THE RUINS OF ÆGINA

The beautiful ruin of the Æginetan Temple, at the north-east corner of the island, has been the theme of the general admiration of travellers in Greece. It stands on a gentle elevation near the sea, commanding a view of the Athenian coast, and of the Acropolis at Athens, and beyond them of the waving line traced by the mountain ranges of Pentelicus and Hymettus. Its site is sequestered and lonely. The ground is diversified by grey rocks overhung by tufted pines and clusters of low shrubs, among which goats may be seen feeding, placing their fore-feet on the boughs of the shrubs and cropping the leaves. It is such a scene as this which proves that the religionists of Greece knew how to avail themselves of two things most conducive to devotional effect, Silence and Solitude.

There was perhaps another reason, besides a desire for solitude, why a site at the distance of eight miles from the city of Ægina was selected in preference to one in its immediate neighbourhood, for the position of this temple; it is probable that this building did not owe its origin to Æginetans themselves. It has, indeed, by many topographers been considered as identical with the Temple of Jupiter Panhellenius, and even as the same fabric which Æacus, the king of Ægina, erected to that deity. But not merely does the position of the temple itself, standing—not on a mountain as that temple did—but on a gentle eminence, forbid the inference; but the character of its architecture plainly indicates that it is not the Temple of Jupiter Panhellenius. The only evidence in favour of this supposition is furnished by the two words (ΔΙΙ ΠΑΝΕΛΛΗΝΙΩΙ) which are *said* to have been inserted on its portico; but if this inscription ever existed there, the dialect alone excites a suspicion that it was a forgery. Besides, there is another distant site, which can be proved to coincide with that of Panhellenium.

To whom, then, was this Temple dedicated? In order to answer this question, let us examine the groups of sculpture which once stood against the azure ground of its two pediments. They had no doubt an immediate reference to the object of that worship which was paid in the Temple itself. In both these groups one figure, that of Minerva, is more prominent than any other, which seems to intimate that the Temple was dedicated to that goddess.

The following circumstance leads to the same conclusion. Returning to the town of Ægina from the Temple, we pass a small Greek church, at the distance of a quarter of an hour's walk to the west of it. The spot is called Bilikada; the church is dedicated to St. Athanasius. The door of the church is surmounted by a large marble slab, inscribed "The limit of the sacred precinct of Minerva;" an inscription which probably defined the boundary of the consecrated inclosure around the Temple.

That it was dedicated to the Goddess of Athens, not by the Æginetans, but by the Athenians themselves, when in possession of Ægina, may be inferred from the site which it occupies, at a distance from the town of Ægina, and looking directly upon Athens. It may be inferred, also, from the language of the inscription itself, in which, it may be observed, the name of the Goddess is expressed, not in the Doric dialect of Ægina, but in the Attic form.

Some parts of the island exhibit the devastating effects of volcanic agency; rocks of lava piled in wild confusion, as here represented. These rocks are of a dark grey colour, resembling those of the Alban Mountains, near Rome.

The site of the Panhellenium was placed on the summit of the conical
mountain at the southern angle of the island, which has been noticed as so
prominent a feature in the scenery of Ægina. This hill is now called OROS,
THE MOUNTAIN. The name is derived from the ancient language of Greece;
it denotes at the same time that *the* mountain which bears it is the highest in
Ægina. This mountain was an object of great interest to the ancient inhabitants of the island. On its summit, Æacus, the king of Ægina, was
believed to have prayed to Jupiter, in the name of the whole Hellenic nation,
for a supply of rain, which was then greatly needed, and which was sent by
Jupiter in compliance with his prayer. The summit of this mountain is
believed to be the site of this temple of the Panhellenian Jove, and to have
derived its name from the various circumstances mentioned, upon the following
grounds :

The Panhellenium is placed by Pausanias on a mountain : there is no
elevation in the island which deserves such a title but that under consideration, which bears the express name by which he characterizes the site. The
mountain served, as we know, for a meteorological beacon. If its conical
apex was capped with cloud, then rain was expected. This notion prevails
still. In this respect the crest of the Æginetan Oros is now a beacon to the
Ægæan mariner, and the legend of Æacus is doubtless to be connected with
the observation. This mountain supplied the first prognostic of the coming

shower. Hence Æacus wisely selected this spot as the scene of his supplication to Jove, knowing, as he did, that the mountain would probably give the first intimation of the wished-for rain by its clouded summit. He, perhaps, chose for his prayers a moment when such indications were visible. The shower, however, which followed them was considered by the Hellenic strangers, who were collected in the plain below him, not as a consequence of natural phenomena, but of his entreaties. Thus a coincidence was converted into a cause; and Æacus, the king of Ægina, became the son of Jove.

There is another argument to establish the identity of the summit of Oros with the site of the Temple of the Panhellenian Jove. It is well known to have been the practice of some early Christian Churches to modify the objects of heathen adoration, rather than to destroy them. The stream of Paganism was taught to glide into a Christian channel, with a soft and easy current. On this principle, when temples became churches, and the deities and heroes of mythology gave place to saints and martyrs, there was generally some analogy which regulated the process between the character transformed and that which was required after the transformation. The frequency of such examples argues the identity of Oros and Panhellenium. The Panhellenian Mount was consecrated in the Pagan creed of Ægina by the tradition that Æacus had prayed on its summit, and obtained a shower from heaven in answer to his prayer. The Mountain now called Oros has on its vertex a small chapel, the foundations of which are constructed of huge blocks, in a style of ancient masonry. This chapel is dedicated to the Prophet Elias. A more appropriate successor could not have been devised, to occupy the consecrated fabric standing on this hill.

For while the Pagan might assert, in the words of Pausanias, that Æacus having sacrificed and prayed to the Panhellenian Jove, caused rain to fall upon Greece, the Christian assured him from the graver authority of St. James, "that Elias prayed, and the heavens gave rain, and the earth brought forth her fruit." The foundations, therefore, just noticed of the small chapel of Elias, are, probably, vestiges of the ancient Temple of the Panhellenian Jove.

On the western side of this mountain, at its roots, are some considerable remains of antiquity. Perhaps they are the vestiges of the Peribolus and Temple of Aphæa, the Dictynna of Ægina, which Pausanias saw in his way from the city of Ægina to the Panhellenian Mount. A church now stands upon the site of the temple. It is dedicated to Ai Asostoi. An old column was formerly cased in the walls of this church, and now lies on the western side of the building. Engraved upon this column, in the direction of its length, is an inscription, in an elegiac distich. This inscription affords the

earliest specimen of the Æolo-Doric forms in a monument of this nature, with the single exception of the Elean inscription. The inscription, when translated, runs thus:—

" The man himself, who rear'd this votive stone,
Is called Philostratus; His sire, Damophon "

RUIN OF THE CITY OF ATHENS.

TO describe ATHENS aright, the writer
should be an Athenian. He should
have long looked upon its soil with a feeling
of almost religious reverence. He should
have regarded it as ennobled by the deeds of
illustrious men, and have recognised in them
his own progenitors. The records of its
early history should not be to him a science ;
they should not have been the objects of laborious research, but should have
been familiar to him from his infancy,—have sprung up, as it were, spon-
taneously in his mind, and have grown with his growth. Nor should the
period of its remote antiquity be to him a land of shadows,—a Platonic cave
in which unsubstantial forms flit before his eyes as if he were entranced in
a dream. To him, the language of its Mythology should have been the voice
of Truth. The Temples of Athens should not have been to him mere
Schools of Art. He should not have considered them merely as existing,—
in order that he might examine their details, note down their dimensions,
delineate their forms, copy their mouldings, and trace the vestiges of colouring

still visible upon them. They should not have afforded materials merely for his compass or his pencil, but for his affections and his religion.

This, we gladly confess, is not our case. We commence our description of this City with avowing the fact, that it is impossible at this time to convey or entertain an idea of Athens such as it appeared of old to the eyes of one of its inhabitants. But there is another point of view from which we love to contemplate it,—one which supplies us with reflections of deeper interest, and raises in the heart sublimer emotions than could have been ever suggested in ancient days by the sight of Athens to an Athenian.

We see Athens in ruins. On the central rock of its ACROPOLIS, exist the remains, in a mutilated state, of three temples,—the Temple of VICTORY, the PARTHENON, and the ERECTHEUM. Of the PROPYLÆA, in the same place, at its western entrance, some walls and a few columns are still standing, and its magnificent entrance has recently been cleared. Of its NEW AGORA, the public place where the citizens of Athens met to discuss their affairs, all that is left is the fragment of its gate here represented; while near to it remains the Arch of Hadrian, marking at once the decline of art, and the loss of political power and grandeur of Athens. Of the THEATRE on the south side of the Acropolis, in which the dramas of Æschylus, Sophocles, and Euripides were represented, some stone steps remain, but modern attempts to discover the remainder have not been attended with success. Not a vestige survives of the Courts in which Demosthenes pleaded. There is no trace of the ACADEMIC porches of Plato, or of the LYCEUM of Aristotle. The PŒCILÉ of the Stoics has vanished. Only a few fragments of the LONG WALLS which ran

along the plain, and united Athens with its harbours, are yet visible. Even Nature herself appears to have undergone a change. The source of the fountain CALLIRHOE has almost failed; the bed of the Ilissus is nearly dry; the harbour of the PIRÆUS is narrowed and made shallow by mud.

ATHENS FROM THE VALLEY OF THE ILISSUS.

But while this is so, and while we are forcibly and mournfully reminded by this spectacle, how perishable is the nature of the most beautiful objects which the world has seen,—while we read in the ruin of these Temples of Athens, and in the total extinction of the Religion to which they were dedicated, an Apology in behalf of Christianity and a Refutation of Paganism, more forcible and eloquent than any of those which were composed and presented to the Roman Emperor by Aristides and Quadratus in this place, we are naturally led by it to contrast the permanence and vitality of the *spirit* and *intelligence* which produced these works, of which the vestiges either exist in a condition of ruinous decay, or have entirely disappeared, with the fragility of the *material* elements of which they are composed.

Not at Athens alone are we to look for Athens. The epitaph,—Here is the *heart:* the *spirit* is everywhere,—may be applied to it. From the gates of its Acropolis, as from a mother-city, issued intellectual colonies into every region of the world. These buildings now before us, ruined as they are at present, have served for two thousand years as models for the most admired fabrics in every civilized country of the world. Having perished here they survive there. They live in them, as in their legitimate offspring. They are like aged and decayed trees, the seeds of which have been carried away by birds, or scattered far and wide by winds, and have produced magnificent forests in distant lands. Thus the genius which conceived and executed these noble works is immortal and prolific, while the materials on which it laboured are crumbling to decay. We, therefore, at the present time, having witnessed this fact, have more cogent reasons for admiring the consummate skill which created them, than were possessed by those who saw these structures in their original glory.

Again, not merely in her *material* productions, existing here or elsewhere, does the spirit of Athens survive. Not only is it to be found in her Buildings and her Statues, nor in the imitations of them which are the ornaments of other nations, but also in the purely intellectual creations of her great Minds: it is to be traced in the Writings of her Poets, Historians, Philosophers, and Orators, whose works remain unimpaired by time, and who not merely live in them, but have served as sources of life to others; whose worth could never be estimated till many centuries had elapsed, and who, having now been judged by Posterity to be worthy of immortality, have given an interest to the soil from which they sprung, to the ground which they trod, and to the temples in which they worshipped, which these objects did not, and could not possess, as long as the memory of those was recent from whom they derived it. The city of Miltiades, Themistocles, and Pericles, of Æschylus, Thucydides, Plato, and Demosthenes, could not have been regarded, *as such*, by their contemporaries or immediate successors, with those feelings of veneration which we experience, who know what influence they have exercised, and will never cease to exercise, over the thoughts and deeds of men. In this respect, —and it is a very important one,—the *modern* spectator of Athens enjoys great advantages for a contemplation of this city, which were never known to its ancient inhabitants.

We feel, therefore, a lively sensation of pleasure in tracing, step by step, the vestiges of this place, in examining its topographical details, in exploring the sites of its former buildings, and in studying the character of those which remain; for thus we seem to be brought into the society of men, whose names will never perish; thus we appear to imbibe a portion of that spirit which animated them, and produced the works which have raised their authors from the level of common minds to a loftier elevation of their own.

The Orator Demades, when he was on a visit at the court of Philip of Macedon, and was desired by the King, one day at a banquet, to give him an idea of the dimensions, form, and features of Athens, is said to have sketched a Map of the city upon the table at which he was sitting. We propose now

to attempt an outline of the same kind as far as the existing remains and the
intimations of ancient authors enable us to do so.

In order to obtain a distinct notion of the natural characteristics of the
spot to which we refer, let us consider it, in the *first place*, as abstracted from
all artificial modifications;—let us imagine ourselves as existing in the days of
CECROPS, and looking upon the site of Athens. In a wide plain, which is
inclosed by mountains, except on the south, where it is bounded by the sea,
rises a flat, oblong rock, lying from east to west, about fifty yards high, rather
more than one hundred and sixty broad, and than three hundred in length.
It is inaccessible on all sides but the west, on which it is approached by
a steep slope. This is the future ACROPOLIS, or Citadel of Athens. We
place ourselves upon this eminence, and cast our eyes about us. Immediately
on the west is a second hill, of irregular form, lower than that on which we
stand, and opposite to it. This is the AREOPAGUS. Beneath it, on the south-
west, is a valley, neither deep nor narrow, open both at the north-west and
south-east. Here was the AGORA, or public place of Athens. Above it, to
the south-west, rises another hill, formed, like the two others already
mentioned, of hard and rugged limestone, clothed here and there with
a scanty covering of herbage. On this hill the popular assemblies of the
future citizens of Athens will be held. It will be called the PNYX. To the
south of it is a fourth hill, of similar kind, known in after-ages as the

ATHENAE.

MUSEUM. Thus, a group of four hills is presented to our view, which nearly inclose the space wherein the Athenian Agora existed, as the Forum of Rome lay between the hills of the Capitol and the Palatine.

Beyond the plain, to the south-west, the sea is visible, distant about four miles from this central rock. On the coast are three bays,—the future Harbours of ATHENS,—the PHALERUM, MUNYCHIA, and PIRÆUS; the first being the nearest to us, the last the most distant from our present position. Toward the coast, and in the direction of these Ports, run two small streams, both flowing from the north-east; the one on the south side of us, passing us at a distance of half a mile, the other on the north, and at the distance of two: they do not reach the shore, but are lost in the intermediate plain. The former is the ILISSUS, the latter the CEPHISSUS. To the north of the former, and at a mile's distance to the north-east of the Acropolis, is a rocky conical hill, of considerable height, and one of the most striking features of the scenery of Athens. This is Mount LYCABETTUS. Regarding then the hill of the Acropolis as the centre of the future city of Athens, we have, as its natural frontiers to the north and south, two rivers, while on the east and west it is bounded by hills; its limit on the east being the mountain of Lycabettus, and on the west the lower range which consists of the Pnyx and the Museum. Such is a brief sketch of the physical features which distinguish the site of the Athenian City.

We now quit this period of remote antiquity, when the soil of the future Athens was either untenanted, or occupied only by a few rude and irregular buildings, and pass at once to the time when it had attained that splendour which made it, in Literature and in Art, the Metropolitan City of the World. A more striking contrast than that which is presented by the appearance of this same spot at these two different epochs, cannot well be imagined.

No longer, therefore, as contemporaries of the ancient king of Attica, but existing, in imagination, in the age of PERICLES and of his immediate successors, we now contemplate this City as it then exhibited itself to the eye. First, we direct our attention to the central rock of the Acropolis. And let us here suppose ourselves as joining in that long and splendid procession of Minstrels, Priests, and Victims, of Horsemen and of Chariots, which wound through the agora of the City, and ascended to the Acropolis at the quin-quennial solemnity of the Great Panathenæa. Above the

heads of the train let us imagine the sacred Peplos, raised aloft and stretched like a sail upon a mast, waving in the air: it is variegated with an embroidered tissue of battles, of Giants, and of Gods: it is destined for the Temple of MINERVA POLIAS in the Citadel, whose statue it is intended to adorn. In the bright season of summer, on the twenty-eighth day of the Athenian month Hecatombæon, let us mount with this procession to the western slope of the Acropolis. Toward the termination of its course, we are brought in face of a colossal fabric of white marble, — the Propylæa, — which crowns the brow of the steep, and stretches itself from north to south across the whole western front of the Citadel, which is about one hundred and seventy feet in breadth.

The centre of this fabric consists of a portico sixty feet broad, and formed of six fluted columns of the Doric order, raised upon four steps, and intersected by a road passing through the midst of the columns, which are thirty feet in height, and support a noble pediment. From this portico two wings project about thirty feet to the west, each having three columns on the side nearest the portico in the centre.

The architectural mouldings of the fabric glitter in the sun with brilliant tints of red and blue; in the centre, the coffers of its soffits are spangled with stars, and the antæ of the wings are fringed with an azure embroidery of ivy leaf.

We pass along the avenue open between the two central columns of the portico, and through a corridor leading from it, and formed by three Ionic columns on each hand, and are brought in front of five doors of bronze; the central one, which is the loftiest and broadest, being immediately before us.

The structure which we are describing is the PROPYLÆA, or Vestibule of the Athenian citadel. It is built of Pentelic marble. In the year B.C. 437 it was commenced, and was completed by the architect Mnesicles in five years

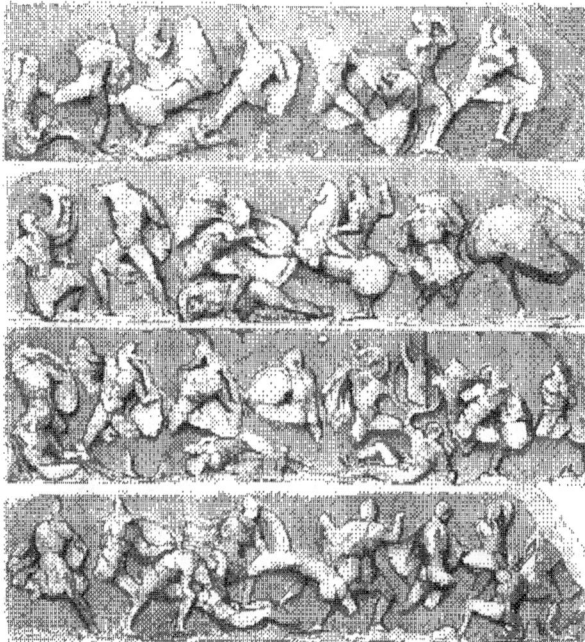

FRAGMENTS FROM ÆSCHYLUS FRIEZE.

from that time. Its termination, therefore, coincides very nearly with the commencement of the Peloponnesian war.

Here we pause, in order to contemplate the objects around us, to explore the Gallery, adorned with the paintings of Polygnotus, in the left wing of the Propylæa, and to visit the TEMPLE OF VICTORY on our right, which possesses four Ionic columns on its western and four at its eastern end, thus being approached by two façades, and whose frieze is sculptured with figures of Persians and of Greeks fighting on the Plain of Marathon. We return to the marble corridor of the Propylæa.

Let us now imagine that the great bronze doors of which we have spoken as standing at the termination of this gallery are suddenly thrown back upon their hinges, to admit the Riders, and Charioteers, and all that long and magnificent train of the Panathenaic Procession, which stretches back from this spot to the area of the Agora at the western foot of the Citadel. The INTERIOR of the ATHENIAN ACROPOLIS now bursts upon our view. We pass under the gateway before us, and enter its precincts, surrounded on all sides by massive walls: we tread the soil on which the greatest men of the ancient World have walked, and behold buildings ever admired and imitated, and never equalled in beauty. We stand on the platform, which is at once the Sanctuary, the Fortress, and the Museum of Athens.

To speak, in the first instance, and very briefly, of minor objects here presented to our notice, which it is impossible to specify in detail. We behold before and around us a grove of statues, raised upon marble pedestals, the works of noble sculptors—Phidias and Polycletus, Alcamenes, Praxiteles, and Myron,—and commemorating the virtues of benefactors of Athens, or representing the objects of her worship: we see innumerable altars dedicated to heroes and Gods; we perceive large erect slabs of white marble inscribed with the records of Athenian history, with civil contracts and articles of peace, with memorials of honours awarded to patriotic citizens or munificent strangers.

Proceeding a little further, we see, on our left, raised on a high base, a huge statue of bronze, the labour of Phidias. It is seventy feet in height, and looks towards the west, upon the Areopagus, the Agora, and the Pnyx, and far away over the Ægean sea. It is armed with a long spear and oval shield, and bears a helmet on its head; the point of the lance, and the crest of the casque, appearing above the loftiest building of the Acropolis, are visible to the sailor approaching Athens from Sunium.

This is MINERVA PROMACHUS, the Champion of Athens, who, looking down from her lofty eminence in the citadel, seems by her attitude and her accoutrements to promise protection to the city beneath her, and to bid defiance to its enemies.

Passing onward to the right, we arrive in front of the great marble Temple, which stands on the most elevated ground of the Acropolis. We see eight Doric columns of huge dimensions elevated on a platform, ascended by three

steps at its western front. It has the same number on the east, and seventeen on each side. At either end, above the eight columns, is a lofty pediment extending to a length of eighty feet, and occupied by nearly twenty figures of superhuman size. The group which we see before us, at the western end, represents the contest of Minerva with Neptune, for the soil of Athens; the other, above the eastern front, exhibits the birth of the Athenian Goddess.

Beneath the cornice which ranges on all sides of the Temple, is the frieze, divided into compartments by an alternating series of triglyphs and of metopes, the latter of which are ninety-two in number,—fourteen on either front, and thirty-two on each flank; they are a little more than four feet square, and are filled by one or more figures in high relief. They represent the actions of the Goddess to whom the Temple is dedicated, and of the Heroes, especially those who were natives of Athens, who fought under her protection, and conquered by her assistance. They are the works of Phidias and his scholars; and, together with the pediments at the two fronts, may be regarded as offering a history in sculpture of the most remarkable subjects contained in the Mythology of Athens. Such was the Parthenon in the age of Pericles, when we imagine ourselves spectators of this Quinquennial Festival.

Attached to the temple, beneath each of the metopes on the eastern front, hangs a circular shield covered with gold; below them are inscribed the names

RUINS OF THE NORTH-EAST END OF THE PARTHENON.

of those who dedicated them as offerings to Minerva, in testimony of their gratitude for the victories they had won: the spoils of which they shared with her, as she partook in the labours which achieved them.

The members of the building above specified are enriched with a profusion of vivid colours, which throw around the fabric a jovial and festive beauty, admirably harmonizing with the brightness and transparency of the atmosphere which encircles it. The cornice of the pediments is decorated with painted ovoli and arrows; coloured meanders twine along its annulets and bands; and honeysuckle ornaments wind beneath them: the pediments are studded with disks of various hues; the triglyphs of the frieze are streaked with tints which terminate in plate-bandes and guttæ of azure dye; gilded festoons hang on the architraves below them. It would, therefore, be a very erroneous idea to regard this Temple which we are describing, merely as the best School of Architecture in the world. It is also a noble museum of Sculpture and a rich Gallery of Painting.

We ascend by three steps, which lead to the door of the Temple at the posticum or west end, and stand beneath the roof of the peristyle. Here, before the end of the cella, and also at the pronaos or eastern front, is a range of six columns, standing upon a level raised above that of the peristyle by two steps. The cella itself is entered by one door at the west and another at the east: it is divided into two apartments of unequal size, by a wall running from north to south; of which the western, or smaller chamber, is called the Opisthodomus, and serves as the Treasury of Athens; the eastern is the Temple, properly so called: it contains the colossal statue of Minerva, the work of Phidias, composed of ivory and gold, and is peculiarly termed, from that circumstance, the

[FRAGMENTS OF THE PARTHENON]

PARTHENON, or Residence of the Virgin Goddess, a name by which the whole building is frequently described.

At the summit of the exterior walls of the cella, and extending along the four sides of it, is a frieze in low relief, representing the Panathenaic Procession: it is moving from west to east, and may be imagined to have just entered the Acropolis by the gate of the Propylœa, to have advanced to the south-west angle of the Temple, and then to have divided itself into two lines, one of which proceeds first along the western end, and then round the north-west corner and along the northern flank of the building; the other by the southern flank, so that when they arrive at the eastern front, they face each other. Here they are separated by twelve seated figures, of size superior to the rest. Six of these figures face the north, and six the south. They form a striking contrast, by their sedate attitudes, to the rapidity of the procession, composed of cars and horsemen chasing each other in quick succession, and increasing in speed as they approach the eastern front of the Temple. The twelve figures which have been mentioned are Deities. To appear in their presence was the object of the Panathenaic Procession; and by the juxtaposition of their dignified

calmness as the goal of its eager rapidity, the train itself seems, as it were, to pass insensibly from the transitory restlessness of earth to the eternal tranquillity of heaven.

Such, then, in its original form, was the PARTHENON of Athens; the work of Ictinus and Callistratus, adorned with sculptures from the hand of Phidias and his scholars, completed under the administration of Pericles, in the year B.C. 439.

Although the Panathenaic procession was sculptured on the Parthenon, yet it was not connected with the Minerva of that Temple. The PEPLUS borne in the Panathenaic solemnity was destined to adorn the statue of MINERVA POLIAS, which stands in the beautiful and singular Temple to the north of the Parthenon. The direction of this fabric is from east to west, its cella is seventy-three feet long and thirty-seven broad, and, like that of the Parthenon, is divided into two apartments; but these two chambers, unlike those of that temple, are dedicated not to one, but to two different deities. This structure, when considered as a whole, is called the ERECHTHEUM, from the ancient king of Attica, who was buried within it. Its eastern division is consecrated to Minerva POLIAS; the western to PANDROSUS: the eastern is faced by an Ionic hexastyle portico, and the level of its floor is eight feet higher than that of the rest of the building. At the north-west angle is another portico, which

consists of six Ionic columns,—of which four are in front, namely, to the north,
and one on each side,—and leads into the western chamber.   A third portico,
at the south-west angle of the Temple, conducting also into the western

chamber, is formed, not of columns, but of
CARYATIDES, or rather, as they should be
described, of Athenian Virgins dressed in their
Panathenaic costume. They are six in number:
four of them standing in front rows towards
the south, and one on each side; they are raised
on a podium, or dwarf wall, about four feet high from the ground.

The western wall of the cella is pierced by three windows, the apertures
of which are narrower at the top than they are at the bottom, and by their
interposition four Ionic columns *engaged* in the wall are separated from each
other. A frieze of grey Eleusinian stone, to which sculptured figures are
attached by metal cramps, surmounts the cella.

This Temple has succeeded in name and site to one of the most ancient
sanctuaries of Athens. On this account it bears the title of the ANCIENT
TEMPLE of Minerva. The present building dates its commencement from the
age of Pericles, although in all probability on account of the death of that
statesman, and the expense incurred by Athens in the Peloponnesian war, and

of a fire which injured the fabric in the year B.C. 406, it was not completed till about thirty years after his decease.

Four different objects of great national interest, contained within the walls of the Erechtheum, give it a sanctity and an importance unequalled by that of any other temple at Athens. We are speaking of the Temple as it existed in the time of Pericles. In its *eastern* chamber is the ancient Statue of Minerva Polias, made of olive-wood, which fell down from heaven. This was the Minerva who had contended with Neptune for the possession of the Athenian soil; she was the original protectress of the Acropolis and of Athens; to her the embroidered Peplos at the festival of the Panathenæa is dedicated; it was to this her Temple that Orestes came as a suppliant from Delphi, when he fled from the Eumenides; before her statue burns the golden lamp both night and day, which is fed with oil only once a-year: the sacred serpent, the guardian of the Acropolis, dwells here: here is the silver-footed throne on which Xerxes sat when he viewed the battle of Salamis,—here the sword of Mardonius, the Persian general at Platæa.

In the *western* chamber, that of Pandrosus, is the salt spring which Neptune evoked from the earth in his contest with Minerva; upon the rock there is the impression of the trident with which he struck it; there, too, is the sacred Olive which Minerva produced from the soil to support *her* claim to its possession. From this tree all the olives of Attica are said to have sprung; and thus the most valuable produce of the Athenian territory is protected and consecrated by its alliance with this sacred plant, which is under the immediate care of the tutelary Goddess of Athens. Such is the ERECHTHEUM.

Let us now turn our attention from the objects within the citadel to those below it. From the central and elevated position of the Acropolis, we enjoy a view of the whole Athenian city lying at our feet. We will imagine it as it existed in ancient times. Looking northward, we have immediately below us, but not visible, hollowed out in the face of the citadel, the Sacred CAVE of AGLAURUS, the daughter of Cecrops, who sacrificed herself in behalf of her country, by leaping in this place from the cliff. It communicates by a subterranean passage with the Erechtheum; by which the Arrhephori, or priestesses of Minerva, descend on the night of the Panathenæa, bearing a basket, in which the mysterious objects of her worship are contained: and by it the Persians scaled the rock of the Acropolis, when they made themselves masters of the citadel and of Athens, a little before the battle of Salamis.

In this spot the *Ephebi*, or youth of Athens, when they have attained the military age, receive their arms from the State, and bind themselves by an oath, in the sanctuary of Aglaurus, to imitate her courage and defend Athens unto death.

To the left, immediately beneath the north-west angle, and the PELASGIC, or northern, wall of the citadel, is a second grotto of similar character to that of Aglaurus. It is sacred to PAN, to whom it was dedicated by the Athenians, in gratitude for the assistance which he rendered them at the battle of Marathon. On its left, or western side, is a flight of steps hewn in the rock, which lead from the Acropolis to the fountain of CLEPSYDRA, and to the city.

The Clepsydra supplies a water-clock which exists in the octagonal TOWER built by Andronicus Cyrrhestes to the north of the cave of Aglaurus. On the eight faces of this fabric are carved in marble the figures and names of the eight WINDS, presented to that quarter of the heavens from which they respectively blow. The building is surmounted by a Triton of bronze, holding out from his hand a pointed wand, and revolving on an axis, so as to rest with the point hanging over the figure of the wind which happens to be blowing at any particular time.

Beneath these eight figures lines are traced on the walls of the tower, which, by the shadow cast upon them by the styles fixed above, indicate the hour of the day, as the Triton's wand does the quarter of the wind. When the sun does not shine, recourse is had to the water-clock *within* the Tower, which thus serves both as a vane and a chronometer.

The quarter of Athens which stretches from this building to the north-east wall of the city is called DIOMEIA ; from it a gate, called the Diomeian, leads

TEMPLE OF THE WINDS, &c.

to CYNOSARGES, where is a gymnasium surrounded by a grove ; this was the school of Antisthenes, the founder of the sect of the Cynics : immediately beyond it, in the same direction, is the lofty mountain of LYCABETTUS, or Hill of Light, over whose pointed top the sun is seen from the west of the Acropolis to rise at the summer solstice, from which circumstance it derives its name.

Diomus was the son of Colyttus ; and in accordance with this relationship, the district of COLYTTUS is contiguous to that of DIOMEIA ; it lies on the west of it : on the west, again, of that of Colyttus, and adjacent to it, is the region of MELITE ; from Colyttus a gate opens through the northern wall on the road

to ACHARNÆ; another from Melite conducts to the suburb of the CERA-
MEICUS, and through the graves of the most
distinguished citizens of Athens, and thence
through a series of magnificent monuments
dedicated to their memory, to the two white
hills of COLONUS, the birth-place of Sophocles,
and to the Olive Grove of the Academy, the
school of Plato.

Constructed of white Pentelic marble, surrounded by a sacred inclosure, and raised upon
steps on a small isolated hill in the
district of Melite, is the TEMPLE OF
THESEUS. Its eastern or principal
front, and its south side, are
visible from our station in the

Acropolis. It has six columns at each end, and thirteen on each side. The
eastern pediment is adorned with sculptures, as are the ten metopes on the
eastern front: the latter relate to the labours of HERCULES; upon the four,
both on the north and south sides, at the east end of the Temple, the exploits
of THESEUS are represented. There is a frieze over both the pronaos and
posticum : the former exhibits a contest of men mixed with Gods, and seems
to refer to the war of Theseus with the Pallantidæ; the latter represents the
battles of the Centaurs and Lapithæ.

The building of this Temple was commenced under the auspices of Cimon
son of Miltiades, in the year B.C. 476, four years after the battle of Salamis,

and may be considered as the first effort of great importance to restore the
consecrated buildings of Athens which were destroyed at its capture by the

Persians before that event. It is a singular circumstance, and worthy of
observation, that one of the first acts of the Athenians, on their return to
Athens after their own temporary banishment to Salamis and Trœzen, was to
restore their national hero, Theseus, who had been exiled by their ancestors,
to his own city. His mortal remains were brought by Cimon from the Island
of Scyros, the scene of his banishment and death, to this place; and, as upon
that occasion the Athenians were beginning to erect for themselves a new and
magnificent city, and to adorn it with public buildings of great splendour, so
they raised for him this noble structure, in which he was buried as a man, and
worshipped as a demigod.

Hercules, as its sculptures show, is associated with his kinsman and companion, Theseus, in the honours of this Temple. It is an agreeable sight to
witness this enduring record of their friendship, and also of the alliance
subsisting between the two nations, Argos and Athens, who are represented,
in the present case, by these two heroes; and who entered into a confederacy
at the period when this fabric was erected, so that this Temple may be
considered as a treaty of peace, consecrated by the sanctions of religion.
Another reminiscence of the same amity is preserved in the tradition, that
Hercules espoused Melite, from whom the district of Athens in which the

Temple of Theseus stands derived its name. Thus the two heroes are locally connected; nor are we surprised to find a temple to Melanippus, the son of the Athenian hero, in the same neighbourhood.

If the eye passes to the south-west from the Theseum, over the small mound of Colonus, not that outside the walls, but the tumulus which stands at the northern entrance of the Agora, it will rest on a low hill sloping down to the north at the western verge of the city, and at a quarter of a mile to the west of the Acropolis. Here is a large semicircular area, of which the southern side, or diameter, is formed by a long line of limestone rock, hewn so as to present the appearance of a vertical wall, in the centre of which, and projecting from it, is a solid pedestal carved out of the living rock, ascended by steps, and based upon seats of the same material. The lowest or most northern part of the semicircular curve is supported by a terrace wall of polygonal blocks.

This area is the PNYX, the place of public assembly for the People of Athens. They do not meet beneath the roof, or within the walls of a closed building, but in this open space, for which Art has done nothing except by hewing the native rock at the south, and raising the wall at the north, which has just been mentioned.

To form an idea of an Athenian assembly in the flourishing times of the Republic, we must imagine this open space, consisting of about twelve thousand square yards, occupied by nearly six thousand citizens seated in groups within it. In the presence of this vast multitude, one Man arises; he ascends the stone steps, and takes his station on the pedestal, which is called the BEMA, at the centre of the perpendicular rock. He has before him not merely these six thousand Athenians, but the city of Athens. Lying at a little distance beneath him, he beholds the Agora, filled with statues and altars and temples, and he is thus brought into the presence of the Great Men of old, the Heroes and the Deities of Athens. Beyond it he sees the AREOPAGUS, the most ancient and venerable tribunal of Greece: above it, on the right, is the ACROPOLIS, presenting to his eyes the wings, the portico, and pediment of the noble Propylæa; towering above them in the air, and looking towards him, is the bronze colossus of MINERVA PROMACHUS, armed with helmet, spear, and shield, appearing from her proud eminence to challenge the world in defence of Athens; rising in severe and stately splendour to the right, is the PARTHENON, exhibiting its front of eight huge marble columns, surmounted with sculptured metopes and pediment filled with marble figures of horses, men, and gods, dazzling the eye with painting and with gold. Visible to the north, beyond the city and its walls, are the plains and villages of Attica, its corn-fields, its olive-grounds, and its vineyards, lying in rural

STONE SEAT ON THE PNYX

quietness, made more peaceful by its contrast with this stirring scene : further
in the distance, are the castellated passes of PHYLE and DECELEA, and in the
horizon, the high mountain ridges of Parnes, Brilessus, and Pentelicus.

Such are the objects which the Athenian Orator sees *before* him from this
pedestal of stone. To his *left* is the road to Eleusis, the SACRED WAY,
which, passing through the beautiful suburb of the Cerameicus, and by the
groves of the Academy, and crossing the stream of the Cephissus, climbs over
the western heights of Mount Ægaleos ; visible in the *rear* are the Two long

PNYX FROM THE PNYX

lines of Wall, which, running along the plain for nearly five miles, unite the City with the Piræus. There are the masts of vessels riding in the harbour, —merchantmen bound for Pontus, Ægypt, or for Sicily: fleets which have gained for Athens empire and glory in distant lands,—in the islands of the Ægean, in the peninsula of Thrace, and on the coast of the Euxine. Further to the left, is the glorious Gulf of Salamis; on one side of it is the hill on which Xerxes sat to view the battle fought beneath him; and on the other is the Cape, where stands the trophy of Themistocles.

Such is the scenery of the Pnyx: such are the objects which surround the Athenian orator as he stands on its Bema. In *their* presence he speaks. In dread, therefore, mixed with delight, inspired by such a spectacle, he proceeds to address his vast audience, like a General going to a battle, when he sees the flags and banners of his country's glory unfurled and streaming before his eyes.

these objects are to the Athenian Statesman and Orator standing on the rostra of the Pnyx, what his brave Epirots were, in after ages, to Pyrrhos upon the plains of Italy. They are the wings which waft him to glory. They are also, if we may so speak, the levers by which he uplifts his audience,—for they stir *their* hearts as well as his own. Let no one, therefore, wonder that in such a soil as this Eloquence flourished with a vigour elsewhere unknown.

Not alone to their natural genius, though in that they stood pre-eminent —nor to rules of Art, though ingeniously contrived and elaborately studied,— nor to frequency of rhetorical exercises, nor to the skill of their teachers, though they were well disciplined by both,—nor yet to the sagacity of their audience, though in that they enjoyed a high privilege, was Athens indebted for the thunders and lightnings that pealed and flashed forth in the oratory of

Pericles, and for the torrents that flowed in the eloquence of Demosthenes, but also, and especially to these objects, which elevated their thoughts, moved their affections, and fired their imagination as they stood upon this spot. The school of Athenian oratory was the Pnyx.

On the north-east side of the Agora, and between the Pnyx and the Acropolis, is the hill of the AREOPAGUS. The ascent to it is by a flight of steps hewn in the limestone rock of which it consists, covered with thin herbage. Above the steps, on the rocky pavement of the hill, are the stone Seats on which the Court of the Areopagus sits. In this spot, distinguished by rude simplicity, is assembled the Council by whose predecessors Heroes and Deities are said to have been judged, and whose authority commands respect and enforces obedience when other means fail, and whose wisdom has saved their country in times of difficulty and danger when there appeared to be no longer any opportunity for deliberation.

Beneath it, at its north-east angle, and near our position on the Acropolis, encircled with a sacred inclosure, fenced with a thick grove, and placed in a dark chasm of high rocks, is the sacred shrine of the Venerable Goddesses, the Eumenides, whose name is not uttered by the mouth of an Athenian without a feeling of awe, and who by order of Minerva were conducted to this spot from the Areopagus after the trial of Orestes there, in which they were the accusers.

By this local and religious connexion of the Tribunal of the Areopagus with the Temple of the Furies, the one partakes in the sanctity and inviolability of the other : and it has thus become not merely a political delinquency, but also an act of sacrilege, to impair the dignity or encroach on the privileges of the Areopagus.

The appearance of this consecrated spot, rendered more awful by antique traditions, and by the peculiar features of its scenery, placed as it is near the Agora, in the heart of the city, must have been very striking, from the contrast it presented by its sacred seclusion to the busy stir by which it was surrounded ; nor could it fail to impress a feeling of sober gravity on the minds of many whose thoughts would otherwise be whirled around in the busy vortex of the city and its concerns.

Between the hills of the Pnyx on the south and the Acropolis on the north lies, as has been said, the Agora. It is a circular or rather an elliptical area, whose greatest length from south-east to north-west is about a third of a mile. It is approached on the north-west from the city gate by an avenue lying between two parallel Colonnades or Stoæ, the one dedicated to JUPITER ELEUTHERIUS, or the Liberator, the other containing the tribunal in which the Second Archon, or Basileus, who takes cognizance of religious suits,

presides : from him it is called the STOA BASILEIOS. Near them, in the Agora,
is a third *Colonnade*,—the POECILÉ STOA, or Painted Porch, so called from the
frescoes, representing the battle of Marathon, which adorn it. From this
porch, frequented by them, the Stoics derive their name.

All the buildings connected with the civil processes employed in the
enactment of laws at Athens are, from its neighbourhood to the Pnyx, fitly
grouped together in this place. Here is the BOULEUTERION, or Council
Chamber, in which the Senate of Five Hundred meet to discuss measures
before they are submitted to the Assembly of the people in the Pnyx. Here
are the statues of the ten Heroes of Athens,—Cecrops, Erectheus, Pandion,
Ægeus, Hippothoon, Acamas, Leon, Œneus, Ajax, Antiochus,—the Eponymi,
as they are called, because they give their names to the ten tribes of Athens.
To these statues the first drafts of laws are affixed, before they are discussed
in the Assembly. Here is the refectory of the PRYTANES, or Presidents of
the Assembly,—a building which may be distinguished from the crowd of
other fabrics in the same place by its hemispherical dome, and in which the
most distinguished citizens of Athens are entertained at the public charge. In
the centre of the area which we are describing stands the altar of the Twelve
Gods, being the point to which all the roads of Attica converge, and from
which distances are measured.

On the south-east verge of the Agora, and at the commencement of the
acclivity by which we ascended the Acropolis, stand the two figures of HAR-
MODIUS and ARISTOGEITON, the liberators of Athens from the tyranny of the
Pisistratidæ, which are treated with such respect by the Athenians, that in

their decrees of honorary statues to be erected to the great men of their own or
other countries, in memory of the benefits which the State has received at their
hands, it is expressly specified that they may be placed in any part of the
Agora which may be most agreeable to the objects of their gratitude, *except*
in the neighbourhood of the statues of Harmodius and Aristogeiton. It is a
pleasing circumstance, and one honourable to the Athenian spirit, that in this
case the Past acts more powerfully upon them than the Present, and that they
cherish the memory of the Dead with warmer affection than they court the
favour of the Living.

Such are the most remarkable objects contained in the Agora of Athens.
We speak of the early times of its glory. The Gate of the New Agora, so
called by some and represented here, is comparatively of recent date.

GATE OF THE SO-CALLED NEW AGORA, CALLED ALSO HADRIAN'S ARCH.

Taking then a general survey of the whole, from the south-west angle of
the Acropolis, we observe at its farthest extremity a vista formed by the two
parallel colonnades, which lead those who come from the north-west gate of
the city into the curved area of which the Agora consists. We behold this
area itself, lying between two hills, which sink gradually into it; we see it
encircled with a zone of stately edifices, shaded by rows of Oriental Plane-
trees, planted by the hand of Cimon son of Miltiades: in its centre is an altar,
the geographical focus of Attica: visible beneath the trees and in front of the
Temples, are statues of marble, bronze, and gold, giving to this spot the

appearance not merely of a great national Atrium, or Hall, whither the People of Athens resort as to their common home, but also of a civic Museum of Architecture, Sculpture, and of Painting, where they learn to admire and love the Arts which give perpetuity to the past; and by exhibiting Men and Things, noble in themselves, as invested with greater nobleness and enduing them with an imaginary grace, borrowed from the ideal world,—and this, too, in an Agora, a place formed for mercantile traffic and mechanical toil,—raise the thoughts of those who frequent it from a consideration of what is, to reflect upon what has been, what ought to be, and what will be hereafter. Therefore we are not surprised, that even among its warehouses and shops, which are separated into compartments and arranged according to their different character, we observe men of a peculiar dress and aspect, who seem to be engaged in deep thought or serious reasoning, who find food for speculation there, and who have come from the walks of Aristotle's Lyceum or the groves of Plato's Academy, to muse or converse in the porches of the Agora.

If we pass to the southern wall of the Acropolis, which is called the CIMONIAN, from the liberal and courageous Athenian above mentioned who erected it, and stand at a little distance from the south-east angle of the Parthenon, and look towards the south, we have a view of the seats, the orchestra, and the stage of the great Theatre of Athens, lying immediately at our feet. The seats are hewn in the living rock of the Acropolis, and descend gradually to the level of the plain, like the marks which are left by a retiring tide on the shelving sand of a semicircular bay. The flat area, half girt by the lowest semicircle, is the Orchestra. Beyond it rises the Stage, which is terminated by a façade fronting the spectator, adorned with statues and supported by tiers of columns. Beyond this, again, he beholds a natural landscape of great variety and beauty: on his left the purple hills of Hymettus; in front of him the sea, the harbour of Athens, and the distant hills of Ægina; and to the right the cliffs of Salamis. Sitting on these semicircular seats of stone,—the steps, as it were, of the great national Temple, the Acropolis,—beneath the Parthenon of Minerva, and the majestic statue of Jupiter;—with such objects before them, at the commencement of the most beautiful season of the year, when the sea is calm and the sky clear, and their dependents come from the Islands of the Ægean to pay their annual tribute, the Athenians listen to those dramatic compositions, which derive much of their freshness and beauty from the place in which they are performed, and can only be duly appreciated when maintained in their natural association with the earth and sea, the air and the light of Athens.

From the combination of artificial and natural scenery which the Athenian Theatre supplied, the imaginary elements of its Drama became real, and the

ACROPOLIS AND INTERIOR OF CORINTH, FROM SOUTH

real were idealized. For example, if the
subject treated by the Poet was the story of
the House of Atreus, the spectator saw in
the distance the hills of the Peloponnesus,
beneath which the hero of the Tragedy dwelt,
and whither the audience could transport
itself by an easy effort of imagination ; if the
adventures of Hippolytus invited their attention, the city and shore of Trœzen, where
he abode, were still nearer to their eyes; if
the acts of Medea, the lofty summit of the Acrocorinth, beneath which they
were performed, gave them a local and historical reality : if the exploits of
their own ancestors at Salamis, the bay itself was before them in which those
deeds were achieved : if the Deities of Heaven or Earth or Sea took part in
the action of the Drama, the Elements themselves were at hand from which

ATHENS, FROM THE NORTH-WEST

They had stepped to visit the dwellings of men. Thus the spectators and the spectacles which they witnessed were blended together in unity.

From the south-east angle of the Theatre, a road winds round the eastern base of the Acropolis. It is called the STREET OF TRIPODS, from the row of small temples which form it, and which bear on their summits the tripods that have been dedicated to Dionysos or Bacchus, the patron Deity of the Athenian drama, by those persons who have defrayed the expense of a chorus to which a prize has been adjudged in the neighbouring theatre for the poetic and musical excellence of the drama to which it belonged.

On the architraves of these temples are inscribed the names of the Victor associated with those of the Poet and the Flute-player of the successful drama, and with that of the Archon in whose year it was performed. From these inscriptions the Didascaliæ, or annals of the Athenian Theatre, are compiled. Its history is written in these fabrics composing the street which conducts to it. The *martial* trophies of Miltiades and Themistocles stand upon the plain of Marathon and the promontory of Salamis, but those of Æschylus, Sophocles, and Euripides are ranged side by side on this spot, and present themselves daily to the eyes of their countrymen, as they pass to and from that place where those peaceful victories were won which these monuments commemorate.

Near the spot where this street communicates with the Theatre, is a building surmounted by a circular roof, and erected by PERICLES: it is designed for musical performances, and is thence called the ODEUM. It was built in imitation of the dome-like pavilion of Xerxes, and its roof is constructed with the yards and masts of the Persian ships which were captured at Salamis. The vault is supported on a circle of columns, which surround the interior of the fabric.

RUINS OF THE TEMPLE OF JUPITER OLYMPIUS.

HREE hundred yards to the south-east of this spot is the vast and elevated platform in the centre of which stands the gigantic Temple of the OLYMPIAN JUPITER, being the largest in the world which was ever erected in honour of that Deity. From the east end of the Acropolis we see its western front, consisting of ten Corinthian columns of Pentelic marble, surmounted by a high pediment adorned with sculpture. This temple was commenced by Peisistratus, and remained unfinished for more than six hundred years.

It thus became a by-word for great intellectual efforts in general, which have experienced a similar fate: it has been employed to describe the productions of literature which have been left in an incomplete condition by their original authors. Thus the portico and peristyle, which, in the lively and fanciful language of Plutarch, were erected by Plato of his great philosophical work, the Atlantis, and to which the cella and roof were never added by that philosopher, are compared by the Chæronean moralist to the structure of the vast and unfinished OLYMPIEUM now before our eyes.

The Temple of Jupiter was one of the first conceived, and last executed, of

the sacred monuments of Athens. The building of this temple went along
with the course of the national existence. Athens ceased to be independent
before the Temple of Jupiter was completed; and it was reserved to a Roman
Emperor, Hadrian, to finish the work. This gigantic building stood, therefore,

TEMPLE OF JUPITER OLYMPUS. FROM THE EAST.

on its vast site as a striking proof of the power of Rome exerted on the
soil of Athens. The remains of this magnificent pile are now reduced to a
few columns, grouped together at the south-east angle of the great platform,
which was once planted, as it were, by its marble grove of pillars; and it
is difficult to conceive when and how the enormous masses have disappeared
of which this temple was built.

The STADIUM of Athens was the most remarkable monument on the south
side of the Ilissus. Here a sloping bank runs parallel to the river; and in
this slope a semi-elliptical hollow, facing the north, has been scooped out of
the soil, of somewhat more than six hundred feet in length, and at right angles
to the river. Its shelving margins were once cased with seats of white marble;
a long and grass-grown hollow retiring into the hill-side is all that now
remains of the Athenian Stadium.

The concave extremity of the Stadium,—which is that farthest from the
Ilissus,—has a somewhat higher level than the others. The racer started
from a point at the lower extremity, and, having completed one course in a
straight line, turned round the point of curvature at the higher end, descending
in his course to the goal, which was a point a little to the east of that from
which he had started. Thus he accomplished a double course of six hundred
and thirteen feet each. The chaplets of victory, and the profusion of flowers
showered on the heads of the successful competitors in the race, by the

spectators in the seats above them, had probably been recently gathered from the blooming banks of the neighbouring Ilissus.

The line of similar fabrics—of which the small circular building of most graceful proportions, called the Choragic Monument of Lysicrates, is the only surviving relic—possessed great interest both from their object and execution. They were a series of temples forming a street. These temples were surmounted by finials, which supported the tripods gained by victorious CHORAGI in the neighbouring Theatre of Dionysus, and were here dedicated by them to that deity, the patron of dramatic representations. Hence the line formed by these temples was called the Street of the Tripods.

Beyond the Temple of Jupiter is the small stream of the ILISSUS. It descends from the slopes of Hymettus, bounds the LYCEUM, which is adorned with porticoes and groves, famed as the school of Aristotle and his successors, and passing between a small Ionic temple dedicated to the Ilissian Muses on the right, and the Panathenaic STADIUM on the left, it skirts the southern wall of the city: near the Temple of Jupiter Olympius it flows in a cascade through several ducts channelled in its rocky bed, and is there joined by the fountain CALLIRRHOE, the only fresh-water spring at Athens. Having irrigated the gardens in the southern suburb of the city, the Ilissus loses itself beneath the rocky soil in the plain, and in the direction of the most southern, the most ancient, and the nearest harbour of Athens,— the PHALERUM.

The mountains Ægaleos, Parnes, Brilessus, Pentelicus, Hymettus and Lycabettus, the stream of the Ilissus, and the harbours of the Piræus and Phalerum, were daily in the eyes of the inhabitants of Athens: they are connected with the most remarkable events of Athenian story; they are the sources whence they derive many of the necessaries and ornaments of life, and a considerable part of their affluence and power, and yet not one of them survives in the extensive remains of the Tragic Poets of Athens, nor have the

Banks of the Ilissus received any favourable notice from the Athenian Poets.
If our knowledge of the geography of Attica were to be gathered only from
the extant works of Æschylus, Sophocles, and Euripides, we should not be
acquainted with the name of a single mountain on the Athenian soil. That
this is not the result of chance is clear, from the nature of the case and from
the fact, that in the less copious writings of the comic Poet of Athens—
Aristophanes—nearly *all* of these appellations occur. This difference, observable in the practice of these two classes of poets, with respect to the great

natural features of Attica, may perhaps be thus explained:—The objects
to which we refer were too familiar to the ear and the eye, and too nearly
associated with the common details of daily life, to be susceptible of that
ideal grace with which Athenian Tragedy required that its materials should be
invested. For this reason, it would appear, the authors to whom we allude
avoided the introduction into their poems of names calculated to excite in the
minds of their audience a train of ideas so different from the thoughts and
recollections which it was the design of the Tragic Muse to produce.

It is unfortunate that we possess none of the dramas which were exhibited
in the Theatres of Argos or of Tanagra, of which the vestiges still remain.
As in the tragedies of the Athenian stage, we meet with frequent mention
of the natural objects in the neighbourhood of those places, and derive much
topographical information about *them*,—as we *there* read of the river Inachus
and the Amelnæan hill, in the neighbourhood of Argos, and of the stream
of the Asopus and of Mount Cithæron in the Tanagræan region, while we learn
nothing of the Athenian streams or mountains,—so, perhaps, might we expect
to have found in the productions of the Argive or the Bœotian Muse, some

reference to the waters of the Athenian Ilissus, and to the mountain ridges of Parnes, Hymettus, and Pentelicus.

We are compelled, in the absence of all early Greek epic, tragic, or lyrical authorities on the subject, to resort to the songs of the Latin Poets, who have not been sparing in their allusions to the objects which we have specified above as forming the most prominent features in the landscape of Athens. It is to be regretted, however, that with few exceptions, their descriptions are so little valuable, from their want of familiarity with the subject, as those of Athenian poets would have been objectionable to Athenian readers from their excess of it.

It was the policy of that great Statesman, who saw that the glory and power of Attica must be buoyed up on the surface of the sea, rather than rest on a fixed and solid foundation of *terra firma*, to endeavour, if we may so say, to make Athens an Island. This was the object to which he directed all his exertions. In the language of the Comic writers of the time, he took the shield and spear from the hands of the Republic, and put into them the rower's cushion and the oar. Having succeeded in rebuilding the walls of the City, notwithstanding the opposition of the Spartans, Themistocles, of whom we speak, turned his eyes to the Piræus. He observed the natural beauty and excellence of that harbour, and devoted his energies to make it worthy of the first maritime people of Greece. He surrounded it with military fortifications, and constituted it, as it were, the stronghold and Acropolis of Athens itself.

But it was not in his power to execute his own plans to their full extent. Themistocles was banished in B.C. 472, six years after he had rebuilt the walls, which he was now forbidden to enter. His father, one day walking with him when a boy on the beach of the Piræus, pointed to an old shattered trireme, no longer sea-worthy, whose gaping planks were left to fall in pieces and rot upon the sea-shore, and—"There," said he, "my son, in that fractured vessel you behold the fate of the statesmen of Athens." He might have added—"There, my son, you see the fate of the great author of the Piræus itself."

Cimon and Pericles carried on the design which Themistocles had begun. About the year B.C. 465, the former commenced the building of the two walls which, starting from the south-west side of the city, ran down, the one to the

northern horn of the harbour of Piræus—the most northern of the three
ports of Athens—the other to the southern side of the port of Phalerum, the
most southern of the same. Thus the Athenian city assumed the form of an
insular triangle, secured by two broad, long, and lofty bulwarks from external
assault, and enjoying, by means of two outlets at its base, an easy communication with the sea. So long as these walls stood alone they bore the name of
the LONG WALLS. But another step remained to be taken, in order to give full
effect to the designs of Themistocles. The Piræus had now become the principal,

and indeed the only harbour of much importance; Phalerum was sinking into
neglect. But if the southern line of fortification, which connected the city
with the latter, were surprised and stormed by an invading enemy, *both* the
harbours became his, and the approach to the city itself was not interrupted by
any further barrier. Besides this, from the largeness of the angle of divergence
of these two walls from the city, the defensive force of Athens was distracted,
and did not easily admit of internal centralization.

For this reason, Pericles, about the year B.C. 444, proposed to the
Athenians in the assembly, that a third wall should be erected, which should
connect the city of Athens with the *southern* horn of the harbour of the
Piræus. Socrates was present in the Pnyx on the occasion; and the speech

which Pericles then made, recommending that measure to his audience, seems to have made a deep impression upon the mind of the future philosopher, who was at that time little more than twenty years of age. The advantages arising both from this restriction of the fortified triangle, and from the more complete consequent insulation of Athens, and also from its closer union with its principal harbour, are too obvious to require any comment or illustration. The city of Athens was now like a large vessel moored by two cables, each of which dropped its anchor in the Piræus.

VIEW OF THE PIRÆUS.

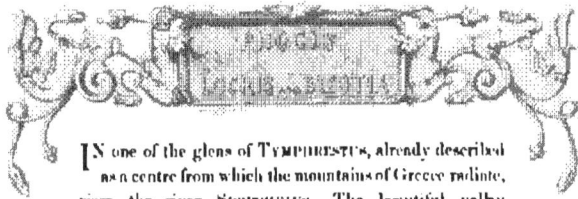

IN one of the glens of TYMPHRESTUS, already described
as a centre from which the mountains of Greece radiate,
rises the river SPERCHEIUS. The beautiful valley
through which it flows is formed by the nearly parallel ranges of Othrys and
Mount Œta, branching from Mount Tymphrestus, and stretching eastward to
the MALIAN Gulf. The length of this valley is sixty miles: it is famed for the

richness of its soil, the luxuriance of its pastures, and the variety and beauty of its woods and groves. To the deity of this river, the most beautiful and most honoured of all the streams which watered his native soil, Achilles, when at Troy, vowed he would pay, if he lived to revisit its banks, an offering of his hair, which, when he despaired of doing so, he placed in the hand of his dear friend and honoured companion, who was born and reared near the same stream, but who was then lying dead upon a funeral pile on the dreary coast of Troy. Near the mouth of the Spercheius, on the left bank of it, is LAMIA, now called ZEITUN, which gave a name to the war kindled by the eloquence of Demosthenes, after the death of Alexander of Macedon, against his Generals Antipater and Craterus, which ended in the total defeat of the Athenians on the Thessalian plain at CRANNON. The Orator survived the calamity of his country but a few months.

At the same distance as Lamia is from that part of the coast where the Spercheius enters the sea, but on the *south* side of it, is the rocky hill of TRACHIS, with its Lacedæmonian colony and suburb of HERACLEA. Trachis is so called from the ruggedness of its soil, from which circumstance the surrounding district derives its name.

The whole TRACHINIAN province was consecrated to HERCULES. To

Trachis he retired, with his wife Deianeira, in quest of an asylum in his exile, after the involuntary homicide which he had committed in the family of his father-in-law Œneus, in Ætolia.

About this little village, as Trachis now is, and around its few cottages and small fields and vineyards, the verses of Sophocles have thrown an interest as lasting as the sea and mountains which surround it, by means of the beautiful recital which he has made of the cares and fears of Deianeira when dwelling on this spot, and counting the tedious days which had elapsed from the time of her husband's departure, and those which were yet to pass away before his return. The female peasants who stand at the doors of the cottages here will be regarded with a feeling of interest as the descendants of the TRACHINIAN WOMEN described by the Athenian Poet.

From Trachis the fatal robe was sent to Hercules, who was sacrificing on the opposite promontory called the CENÆAN, in the island of EUBŒA, beneath which is a small cluster of islands, which recall to mind, by their name, LICHADES, as the promontory itself does by its present appellation, LITHADA, the punishment inflicted by Hercules on LICHAS, the bearer of the poisoned garment,—a subject treated in ancient times by the muse of Sophocles, and in modern by the chisel of Canova.

Across this bay the hero was ferried, when suffering the agonies of approaching death. From the Trachinian shore he was carried to the summit of Œta, which hangs over the site of Trachis. He was then placed on a funeral pile of pines, and oaks, and lentisks,—trees and shrubs which have grown from age to age on this majestic mountain; and here, on its summit, as on an altar, the son of Jove, as Poets feigned, having performed a sacrifice to his father, was himself offered as a victim on his father's mountain; and, having finished his earthly toils, ascended in a cloud of fire to the joys of the Olympian heaven.

As this scene exhibited in the person of Hercules the apotheosis of the heroic character,—in which the strength and dignity of the gods were conceived to be blended with the wants and weaknesses of humanity,—the Greek looked upon it with a feeling of awe which made the mountain not merely an object of admiration to him, but a great moral teacher both of meekness and of courage. The spot was consecrated by the sanctions and solemnities of his religion. It was visited by the Greeks of an early age with the zeal and regularity of an ardent and systematic devotion. It was the scene of processions and of sacrifices; and, in later days, even a Consul of Rome turned aside from the line of his military march to offer his homage to Hercules on the spot from which he was supposed to have passed from earth to heaven.

Such being the reverence with which the summit of Mount Œta was regarded by the inhabitants of the country, and even by those who came there from distant lands, we may well suppose therefore that it exerted a very strong influence upon those who could number the hero, thus deified and adored, among their own progenitors. At no other time would this influence be more deeply felt, than when, like him, they were called upon to undergo toils, meet dangers, and struggle with difficulties, which would lead them to death; and after it, as they hoped, to similar glory and repose.

The Pass of Thermopylæ, like the Plain of Marathon, is connected with the History of Hercules. The warm springs, which flow across the pass from the foot of Mount Œta towards the Malian Gulf on the north, were brought out of the earth, for his use, by the hand of Minerva. They supply a name to the place, and they still flow from the earth, and expand their streams into pools of the clearest blue, as they did in the ages of the Demigod and of the King, while the broad Spercheius has wandered from its course, and it is no longer possible to trace upon the spot the ancient coast-line of the Malian Sea. The Spartan kings also traced their origin to Hercules through the Heraclidæ, Eurysthenes and Procles. On one memorable day, the greatest of them, Leonidas, stood with his three hundred Spartans near this spot, knowing that where he stood both he and his followers must die, and he probably regarded it as a proof of the special favour of the gods towards himself and them, that he and his chosen few were called upon to fight and fall beneath the shade of Mount Œta at THERMOPYLÆ. He felt, we may well believe, no small satisfaction that this spot, above all others, was to be the scene of their glorious struggle and heroic death. The Spartans, while they saw the countless hosts of Persia in their front, and while the Immortals of Xerxes were rushing to the charge in their rear, had above them the summit of Mount Œta; and thence in the last hours of their life they drew courage and hope from the reminiscence which it supplied of their great ancestor,—of the labours which Hercules had undergone, of the death which he had there suffered, and of the glory which he had won.

Thermopylæ was the scene of numerous struggles at various periods of Greek history: it was defended by the Phocians against the Thessalians; subsequently, by Leonidas and his three hundred Spartans against Persia; again, by the Ætolians against Philip; by Antiochus against the Romans, and by the Greeks against Brennus and the Gauls. In the three latter instances, the same manœuvre—namely, the detachment on the part of the aggressors of a force which, having scaled the heights of ANOPÆA or CALLIDROMUS, was to fall on the rear of the defenders of the pass—was resorted to exactly as it had been employed by the Persians, and with the same success. The pass itself was never stormed by main force. Its conqueror, and its only one, has been Time. So great is the change that, in the lapse of ages, has been effected in the character of the place, that it has ceased to be an object of military importance; for, while the river Spercheius has brought down in its channel a copious supply of alluvial deposit to the coast, the waters of the Malian Gulf have retired so far to the north-east as to extend what was once a narrow defile into a broad and swampy plain.

When such a revolution has been wrought in the grander features of this remarkable place,—when the rivers which flowed through the pass of Thermopylæ have formed for themselves new beds,—when fields of rice and salt-pits occupy the space which was once covered by the sea, it is agreeable to observe that the more humble objects which were characteristic of the spot in the time of Leonidas, are still visible here, and recall to the mind of the traveller that he is treading the soil of Thermopylæ. Such is the fidelity and minuteness with which the ancient historian of the battle has described the localities in question, that in spite of the changeful operations of Nature, he has, as it were, fixed the river and the sea in their old positions. Thermopylæ is now no longer Thermopylæ, except in the pages of Herodotus; and there it will remain for ever.

Thermopylæ was the seat of the Congress of the Amphictyonic Council. Its meetings were held near the Temple of Ceres on the Plain of Anthele, which extends itself at a small distance within the pass. The session of a deliberative assembly composed of the chosen Representatives of the confederate powers of Greece, convoked to such a place as Thermopylæ, presents to the imagination a picture of much interest. This spot was, as it were, the Vestibule of Greece. And as in the Homeric Age and in patriarchal times the Councillors of a state or city took their seats before the Towers and Gates of their town, and there held solemn deliberations on matters which concerned their country, so these august Councillors of the great Commonwealth of Greece might thus be regarded as sitting in the vestibule of the Metropolis of which they were all citizens, and for whose interests they were providing by their deliberations in the spot where it might be most necessary to defend them with their arms.

The country to the south of Thermopylæ, as far as the town of Daphnus on the coast, belonged to the tribe of Locrians called Epic-

nemidian, from their neighbourhood to Mount Cnemis, a ridge thrown out by Mount Œta: separated from them by a small portion of Phocis were the Locrians who were termed Opuntian, from their capital city Opus, which was the residence of Ajax Oïleus.

The modern name of this district is TALANTA: it is derived from the little island of Atalanta, which lies at a short distance from the shore, and was once united to it. The town of Opus itself was placed in an open and level country of only a few miles in circumference, which from its fertility was called the Happy Plain. As Ajax was regarded as an object of national pride by this small city, so also were the productions of its prolific soil; it exhibited, there-fore, on its coins a record of both. While on one side of them is a cluster of grapes, the other exhibits the athletic form of the Opuntian Hero.

The Bœotian frontier was at Larymna, a town on the coast a few miles to the south of Opus: the modern village of Puutzomadi, which is near the site of Larymna, seems to preserve in its name a vestige of the former extension of the Opuntian power to this point.

Following the course which we have hitherto pursued, we pass from TYMPHRESTUS along the ridge of Pindus in a southerly direction: at a distance of sixty miles to the south-east of Tymphrestus is the summit of PARNASSUS.

Here we enjoy a panoramic view of PHOCIS, of which province this point is nearly the centre. To the north-west we have the rugged tract of DORIS: a little nearer is the well-fortified City of LILÆA, where the Bœotian river Cephissus arises from the earth: the place is now known by the appropriate name of the MEGALAIS BRYSEIS, or GREAT SOURCES. From this point the

river flows in an easterly direction through a beautiful valley covered with fields of corn and cotton. At a little distance from its left bank, on a declivity sloping to the river, is the village of LEFTA. The walls which crown the summit of this hill belonged to the citadel of ELATEA.

The position of this city gave it so much importance that, among the towns of Phocis, it yielded alone to Delphi in this respect. It commanded the passage from Thermopylæ over the heights of Mount Cnemis into the Cephissian valley, and thence to the plains of Bœotia. It was the key of southern

Greece. Hence the panic and consternation which, as we learn from the great Orator of the time, filled the city of Athens on an evening of the month of June, in the year B. C. 338, when a messenger came to the Prytanes of that city with the news that Elatea had been taken by Philip of Macedon, who had marched by this passage. The capture of this city was followed within a few months by the total defeat of the Athenians on the neighbouring plain of Chæronea.

The river Cephissus flows by the city of Abæ, which stands on its left bank. The place is now called Belisi, and was formerly famed for the sanctity of its oracle. The river there enters the lake, to which it gave the epithet Cephissian, at the foot of the lofty citadel of Orchomenus.

At the same distance from the Cephissus as the city of Abæ, but on the *right* branch of the stream, and immediately below the point at which we now stand,—the eminence of Parnassus,—and in an easterly direction from it, is the city of DAULIS. It still retains its ancient name.

Few of the cities of Greece can be compared with this place in the grandeur of their position, or in the extent and excellent preservation of their remains. The line of the ancient walls of the city can still be traced almost in their entire circuit along the crest of the rocky and isolated hill on which the ancient Daulians dwelt.

What remains of its history is as insignificant as these vestiges of its structures are remarkable. It has derived more renown and has attracted more notice from the writers of antiquity, by the mythological story of Procne, and the story of her sister Philomela, than it has derived from all the achievements in arts and arms of its former occupants. That story itself is one of the indications which survive of the attention that was paid to the habits of animals even by the earliest and rudest inhabitants of Greece, and of the natural humanity of character which such an observation of their customs, and sympathy with their sufferings, may fairly be supposed to produce. To form the character of the naturalist the science of the augur no doubt contributed. Both are united with that of the inventor and promoter of Greek civilization in the ideal person, as described by himself, in the Æschylean drama of Prometheus.

The road from Daulis, to the south-west, leads along a rugged valley to DELPHI, and falls in with another from AMBRYSUS on the south, at a point half-way between the two. This place was called the SPLITTÈ HOUSE, or the DIVIDED WAY; the TRIODOS, or the TRIPLE ROAD.

The rocky and uneven character of the soil over which those roads pass renders it a matter of surprise that they should have been traversed even by the light and small cars which served as conveyances to the ancient Greeks. While we have a proof that this was the case, in the fact that this route was no other than the SACRED WAY, along which a numerous retinue of spectators and worshippers flocked, at stated periods, to the games and religious solemnities of Delphi, we have also an indication of its nature, and of the consequent difficulties by which a journey upon it was attended, in the story of Œdipus, who encountered his father Laius in the Triple Way, as he himself was coming from Delphi. His unfortunate assault upon him was occasioned by the narrowness of the road. The tomb of Laius and of his attendant was seen by Pausanias on the spot where they fell, which is now called ZYMENO.

Beneath us, on the south, is DELPHI. Its site has been well described as a natural Theatre, sloping in a semicircular declivity from the foot of Parnassus. At the highest point of this Theatre stood the Temple of Apollo. Its

SCENERY AT DELPHI.

form may still be recognised on the coins and sculptured marbles which belong to the ancient history of Delphi. An interesting record of the ornaments with which it was decorated is preserved in the Ion of Euripides. In its shrine was the elliptical stone which was regarded as the centre of the earth. Here was the oracular chasm, whence the vapour issued, which swayed the destiny of empires. We cannot contemplate this spot without awe. No one who has considered the history of Heathen Oracles, particularly of this Oracle at Delphi, will deny that the Evil Spirit was permitted to work by their means. Here he vented his influence on the world. But more may be seen on this subject in a fitter place,—in the author's edition of the Acts of the Apostles (Acts xvi. 16).

To the west of the Temple was the Stadium, of which the outline is still visible. To the east of it was the poetic fountain of CASTALIA. It still flows

VIEW OF CASTAL, NEAR DELPHI.

on, while the Temple of Apollo, and the Council Hall of the Amphictyons, the Treasure-house of Crœsus, and the three thousand statues which crowded the buildings and streets of Delphi, even in the time of Pliny, have all vanished as though they had never been. The spring is now dedicated to St. John, in whose honour a small chapel has been erected over the source. It falls from Parnassus down the slope on which Delphi stood, into the river Pleistus, which flows along the valley at the

foot of the city. It
passes, in a westerly di-
rection, through groves
of olives, by the side
of the Delphian Hip-
podrome, and at the
base of the lofty crags
where the Crissa of
Homer stood, which
preserves, in its mo-
dern name of Crisso,
and in the huge poly-
gonal walls of its Acro-
polis, the memorials of
its ancient greatness.
It then receives a tri-
butary stream coming
from the north, and
flowing beneath the
city of Amphissa. Their united waters
glide together through a wide and beautiful
plain, known and reverenced with a feeling of
religious awe in ancient times as the hallowed
Plain of Cirrha, till they fall into the Gulf of
Corinth, in the Crissæan Bay, which is at the
distance of five miles from the site of Delphi, of which
city it was formerly the harbour.

Diogenes, when he had been exiled from Sinope,
migrated into the south of Greece, where he used to
spend his summers at Corinth and his winters at
Athens. Corinth he preferred during the warmer
season of the year as standing upon two seas, and
thus ventilated by a double breeze. But Athens was
recommended as a winter residence by other advantages: it was not overhung by mountains; it was
greatly favoured by soft and pure airs; it was not subject to be deluged by
violent rains, and its dry and light soil speedily absorbed the showers that fell.
Our own experience would lead us to admire the wisdom of this choice.
Returning to Athens from an excursion to Delphi, having passed through
Thebes, Leuctra, and Ambrysus, on our way thither, we found, on our return,

that the overflowings of the Asopus in the plain of Platæa were then covered with ice, as they were at the time of the siege of that city described by Thucydides. On our way back, the cold was excessively severe; it was, in a word, one of Hesiod's Bœotian winters. On Mount Parnassus we were detained by a snow-storm. The snow was drifting with incessant violence as we passed the Triodos already mentioned where Œdipus encountered his father. The hill on which the citadel of Daulis stands, was covered with deep snow. We entered Thebes in a snow-storm, which confined us for exactly a week in a room with no windows. The same cause prevented us from pursuing the ordinary route by the pass of Phyle. That passage was blocked up by snow, and we were compelled to follow the long and circuitous route over the plain north of the Asopus, which brought us out on the sea-coast, a little to the south of the Euripus.

Of the beauty of this scene in summer, and of the peculiar features which distinguish it, no better or more accurate description can be given than that which is contained in the following lines of Milton, to whose imagination a landscape presented itself similar to that which the traveller beholds from the ruins of the citadel of Crissa:—

> " It was a mountain at whose verdant feet
> A spacious plain, outstretch'd in circuit wide,
> Lay pleasant; from his side two rivers flow'd,
> The one winding, the other straight, and left between
> Fair champaign with less rivers intervein'd,
> Then meeting joined their tribute to the sea.
> Fertile of corn the glebe, of oil and wine;
> With herds the pastures throng'd, with flocks the hills;
> Huge cities and high-tower'd, that well might seem
> The seats of mightiest monarchs ."

MOUNT HELICON is to BŒOTIA what Parnassus is to Phocis. The principal cities of that country are grouped about its sides, as the Phocian towns are connected with those of their own mountain; and as the mountain of Phocis could show upon its summit the CORYCIAN CAVE, which was dedicated to the Parnassian nymphs, so upon the heights of the Bœotian hill were the favourite haunts of its own deities. Here flourished the grove of the Muses, whose statues stood beneath the shady recesses of these mountain glades; here flowed the sacred spring of Aganippe, round which the Muses danced; here was the clear source of Hippocrene, in which they bathed. The whole mountain was celebrated for its fresh rills, and cool groves, and flowery slopes; and while the legends connected with the other mountains of Greece were sometimes of a terrific and often of a stern and savage character, those which were produced by the soil and scenery of HELICON, partook of the

softness and amenity which distinguish the mountain from which they sprung.
Helicon had no Œdipus nor Pentheus.

It is remarkable that many of the names which characterize the natural
objects of this mountain are of Macedonian origin. They afford historical
evidence of the extraction of its ancient colonists. The regard which the
early settlers upon the ridges of Helicon still cherished for the land from
which they came, is expressed in the appellations of LIBETHRA, PIMPLEA, and
PIERIDES, which they brought with them from Macedonia, and transferred to
analogous objects in their adopted country, when they had found, after their
migration, a resting-place in the glens of Helicon.

The nearest city to the summit of Helicon, on the north of it, is LEBADEA.

CAVE OF TROPHONIUS—ACROPOLIS OF LEBADEA.

The stream which flows by the eastern foot of its
Acropolis takes its rise in one of the dells of this
mountain. It was called HERCYNA. Before it
arrives at the city of Lebadea, it passes through
a dark ravine, which seems to recommend itself
by its gloominess and the frowning height of the
crags which overshadow it, as a place peculiarly favourable for the exercise of
the influence of a mysterious and awful mythology. As such it was chosen
for the seat of the oracle of the Bœotian hero, Trophonius. He delivered his

responses to the inquirer in the hall of a dark subterranean cave, which was on
the left side of this stream, and beneath those lofty rocks. Thither the worshipper descended after having undergone a rigid discipline of religious
preparation, under circumstances well fitted to inspire him with that devotional
dread which was necessary to render him a fit recipient of the oracular
influence supplied to his imagination by the strange sights, and mysterious
voices, and unearthly terrors of this dark place.

The Hercyna flows from Lebadea to the east; it then enters the rich plain
of the Cephissus, and falls into the same lake which receives the waters of
that river, and which was formerly called the CEPHISSIAN or COPAIC, and now
the lake of TOPOLIAS. In this plain is the city of CHÆRONEA; it stands on
the southern margin of the north side of a rocky hill, on which the walls of
the citadel and the remains of its ancient Theatre are yet visible; below it is
the field on which was fought the celebrated battle which laid the city of
Athens at the feet of Philip of Macedon,—on which was won what Milton
calls

> "———— that dishonest victory
> At Chæronea, fatal to liberty,
> Whose tidings killed that old man eloquent."

At the entrance of the Cephissus into the Copaic Lake stands the city of
ORCHOMENUS. Its situation at the mouth of the river, and at the end of
the valley through which the Cephissus flows, and its vicinity to the lake

whose fertilizing waters gave to the land about them an Ægyptian fatness,
afforded to Orchomenus advantages which were not lost by the early inhabitants of this city.

Even in the time of Homer, it rivalled in wealth and splendour the hundred-gated Thebes. Its opulence was amassed under the princes of the family of Minyas, who have left behind them a monument of their power and affluence in the huge ruins of a marble THEASURY, which exhibits a very significant and striking evidence of the former richness and greatness of this magnificent city, and which the Asiatic topographer, who saw it in the times of the Antonines, does not hesitate to compare with the pyramids of the Ægyptian Kings.

Pursuing the road from LEBADEA to THEBES, which runs in an easterly direction along the plains at the northern foot of Mount Helicon, the traveller will pass a succession of sites which have obtained considerable celebrity in the mythology and history of Greece. CORONEA will remind him of the battle fought beneath its walls between the armies of Bœotia and Athens, in which the Athenian general fell; near ALALCOMENÆ he will be presented with evidence of the Thessalian origin of the tribes which once dwelt in its neighbourhood in the name of the ITONIAN PALLAS, whose worship they brought

CITY OF THEBES.

from a river CURALIUS in that country to this Bœotian stream, on whose banks they erected a temple to the same goddess, and which they endeared to themselves by the familiar name, Curalius, transferred to it from the river of their native Thessaly. Passing the fount of TILPHOSA, at which the ancient seer Teiresias died, and the extensive ruins of HALIARTUS, be will arrive, after a journey of about thirty miles from Lebadea, at the capital of Bœotia, Thebes.

What Thucydides says of Sparta as contrasted with Athens, and the inferences which, after the destruction of both, would be drawn with respect to the relative power of each from a comparison of their remains, may be with equal justice applied to the city of Thebes, as opposed to its Athenian rival. While the vestiges of Athens are such as to leave no doubt in the mind of the spectator with regard to the truth of the tradition he has received of its pristine glory, he is scarcely able at this day to recognise any trace of the ancient Thebes in its modern successor and representative, except in its physical features and in its name.

The circular and isolated hill upon which the present town stands will recall to his mind the ancient features of the Cadmean citadel: and the brooks which flow at its feet bring with them the recollections of those streams which, under the illustrious names of DIRCE and ISMENUS, appear in the records of history at a time when all the mighty rivers of Europe and America were nameless. The name of Thebes is still the same as it was in the age of Cadmus.

PLAIN OF THEBES.

From Thebes to Platæa is a distance of about six miles. The road lies across the rich pasture-lands and corn-fields which, unbroken by any divisions of hedges, and diversified with very few variations of wood, stretch to the east along the banks of the Asopus, in a wide and fertile valley, from the north-eastern foot of CITHÆRON, by the sites of TANAGRA and OROPUS, to the shore of the Ægean Sea. From Ompus to Tanagra, the distance may be estimated at ten miles. It is still shaded by shrubs, but the olives are now not so common as when seen by Dicæarchus. The site of Tanagra is a large hill nearly circular in form, neither abrupt nor high, rising from the north bank of the Asopus, and communicating by a bridge with the south side of the stream. The circuit of the walls of the citadel can be traced; there is, however, little left of them but their foundations. The north-west corner of this citadel commands an extensive view. Looking eastward, the plain of the Asopus stretches beneath us from east to west. To the south is a range of mountains, of which Mount Cithæron is the western, and Mount Parnes the eastern extremity.

Notwithstanding the successful enmity with which the citizens of the Bœotian capital exerted their power against their rival and dependent city Platæa, in the treatment which it has received from the hand of Time it has been more favoured than its more powerful neighbour. While scarcely a fragment remains of the city which wielded the sway of the whole province of Bœotia, the walls of Platæa remain in nearly the same state as they were two thousand years ago. At that time it had indeed lost all its political power, and, in the language of the comic poet Posidippus, all that it could then boast were "two temples, a portico, and its GLORY."

The passage from Platæa into ATTICA lies over the heights of Cithæron, which, together with the ridges on Parnes, a continuation of that mountain, serves as a line of demarcation between that country and Bœotia. The road from Platæa passed by ŒNOE and ELEUTHERÆ, and then fell into the SACRED WAY, which led from Eleusis to Athens, and was also the road to MEGARA.

It then skirted the northern coast of the bay of Eleusis, and brought the traveller in sight of the full beauty of the Acropolis of Athens as he stood in the gap of the pass which climbs over the hill of Ægaleos.

Another route from the Vale of the Asopus, to the east of that which has been just noticed, passed through the gorge of Phyle, between Mount Cithæron and Parnes, and descended into the Athenian plain near the largest of the one hundred and seventy-three boroughs of Attica, Acharnæ.

A third, still further to the east, commenced at the frontier town of Oropus, and traversing the ridges of Parnes, touched, in its course towards Athens, the important fortress of Decelea and the ancient city of Aphidnæ.

The other mountain pass which deserves particular notice was that which led from the bay and temples of Rhamnus, on the north-eastern coast of Attica, crossed the plain of Marathon, mounted the height of Pentelicus, and, having visited the marble quarries of that mountain, fell into the plain near the towns of CEPHISSIA and PALLENE.

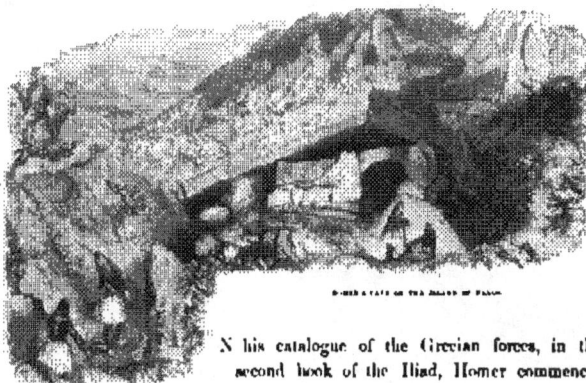

In his catalogue of the Grecian forces, in the second book of the Iliad, Homer commences with a description of the vessels supplied by Bœotia. He enumerates thirty cities in that country which furnished men and ships to Agamemnon. It is a remarkable circumstance, that while he refers to so many towns as already existing in his age in the Bœotian territory, he specifies only a single city in the neighbouring district of Attica. The sole place in the latter province which he mentions as having augmented the numbers of the Greek army, is Athens. But it is observable, that the contribution of this single city amounted to precisely the same sum as that which was supplied by the thirty towns of Bœotia. Each of these two parties furnished fifty ships.

We hence conclude, that while Bœotia was much more thickly peopled than Attica when that catalogue was written, the natives of that state had already attained a degree of maritime skill which placed it as far above its rival in that respect, as it was inferior to it in numerical strength.

Both these circumstances are in strict accordance with the physical

qualities and features of the two countries to which they relate. Of the causes
which tended to produce the nautical and commercial celebrity and affluence
of Attica, we have already spoken. Both negatively and positively they existed
there in the highest degree. The same may be said of the natural endowments
which conduced to give Bœotia a superiority over its neighbour in the number
of cities which covered its soil, and in the aggregate amount of its population.

If we take our station on the summit of the lofty citadel of Orchomenus,
at the north-west angle of the Cephissian or Copaic lake, and cast our eyes
westward, we have below us the principal river of Bœotia,—the Cephissus.

It takes its rise at LILÆA in the mountain district of DORIS, at a distance
of thirty miles to the north-west of this point, and flows down a rich and beautiful valley near the walls of ancient towns of great importance and renown in
the early days of Greek history. It leaves AMPHICLEA, TITHOREA, DAULIS,
and PANOPEUS on its right bank, and ELATEA, HYAMPOLIS, and ABÆ on its

PLAIN OF LADOPEIA, FROM THE WALLS OF PANOPEA

left. It then crosses the boundary of Phocis, and soon after discharges itself
into the lake at the south-eastern foot of the Acropolis of Orchomenus.

This valley is the avenue by which the inhabitants of DORIS, MALIS, and
THESSALY communicate with those of Bœotia, and with the south-eastern
parts of the continent and peninsula of Greece. A little before its arrival
at Orchomenus, it expands itself into a wide plain, on the eastern side of

which is the Copaic Lake, while the western is bounded by the cliffs of
Parnassus, and the southern by the slopes of Helicon.

This plain is the largest in Bœotia; situated as it is on the margin of an

extensive lake, and watered by a river which is fed by numerous tributary
streams flowing into it from Mount Cnemis on the left bank, and Parnassus
on the right, and intersected by various other brooks which descend from the
glens of Helicon on the south; placed also at the termination of the defile

which leads from the north-eastern provinces of Greece into the rich pastures of Brotia, it became naturally the seat of affluent and powerful cities, which derived their principal revenues from the productions of its soil.

Of these towns, five may be mentioned as the most eminent. They lie in a semicircular curve, and at nearly equal intervals from each other. The series of mountain heights on which they stand, taken together with the western boundary of the lake, girds the plain of which we have been speaking.

The first of these five cities, which stands at the north-eastern verge of

the plain, is Orchomenus: to the west of it, at the distance of five miles, separated from it by the river Cephissus, and placed upon a steep rock of grey granite, is the elevated fortress of CHÆRONEA. To the south of Chæronea, at a similar distance on a northern declivity of Helicon, and on the left bank of the river Hercyna, is the citadel of LEBADEA, rising from a precipitous cliff, on the eastern foot of which lies the town. Passing from this place to the south-east for the same number of miles, and along the roots of Helicon, one of which bears the name of the Laphystian hill, we arrive at the base of the crested summit of CORONEA.

If we pursue our course to the east of this spot, we cross several rills which flow from the heights of Helicon on our right, one of which bears the name, sacred to the Muses, of the LIBETHRIAN, and which enter the Copaic Lake at some distance from the road.

After a journey of a little more than five miles in the same direction, we find ourselves at the western gate of HALIARTUS. As we commenced at Orchomenus, with the shore of the Copaic Lake at its north-west angle, so here at Haliartus we are brought once more upon its brink at its south-eastern extremity.

Those who treat of the geographical divisions of particular countries on the face of the terrestrial globe, feel, we apprehend, sometimes tempted to

envy the privilege which is conceded to the topographer of the heavens, who is permitted to group the objects of his science into certain forms and combinations; thus increasing the facility with which his speculations are comprehended by those to whom they are presented, and enduing the objects themselves with the qualities of a living and social existence.

But to earthly topography such licence is rarely and reluctantly allowed. In *geography*, properly so called, are no *constellations*. Each object is contemplated individually and in detail. This circumstance is partly a misfortune, arising from the nature of the subject itself, and partly a defect proceeding from the traditional practice of Geographers, who are wont to look rather at the natural and artificial features of the individual object before their eyes, than to regard the relations which may subsist between it and others united with it by physical and local connexion.

We are inclined, however, to suppose that, without being guilty of any violation of the laws of strict and literal accuracy, and without running the risk of depreciating the particular objects described, either in importance or in interest, the Geographer might safely claim to himself more liberty in this respect than he has usually enjoyed.

We confess that we envy the Astronomer the possession of his Orion, his Lyra, his Pleiads, and his Boötes; and we are inclined to demand for ourselves, in fit proportion, and with due deference to his sublimer occupation, a share in that privilege which allows him to associate the objects of his science in such combinations.

This remark has been suggested by a consideration of the form presented by the five different cities of which we have spoken, when contemplated both with respect to each other, and to the principal features of nature with which they are placed in immediate juxtaposition. Situated in a semicircular curve, at equal distances from each other, and mounted on the crests of a range of hills which slope down into the plain between them and the Copaic Lake, they suggest the name of a natural THEATRE, as the most appropriate designation by which they may be described. The semicircular line which connects these cities together, may be regarded, in technical language, as its PRÆCINCTION, or semi-zone: the sloping lines which descend from the heights on which they are placed, into the level area between them and the lake, form the CAVEA, or shell of this Theatre; the roads which lead in the same direction from their summits, and converge, as it were, to the centre of the circle, are its VIÆ; the semicircular area itself may be considered as the ORCHESTRA of the Theatre: nor is it unworthy of observation, that this is the precise title which was given to it by ancient geographers, who, on account of its having been the field of so many battles, called it,—in the Greek though not in the more modern acceptation of the term,—the ORCHESTRA OF MARS. In the same manner, the western line of the Copaic Lake may be called its PULPITUM, or Stage. On the grounds, therefore, which we have stated, we speak of this district, which from its great importance in the annals of Greek history deserves especial regard, as the natural Theatre of Bœotia.

We have referred in general terms to the conflicts which gave celebrity, and communicated a peculiar appellation, to the plain which lies at the feet of these five cities. From its position at the mouth of the valley of the Cephissus, and from its other local advantages, as well as from the richness of the soil, the plain of Orchomenus was frequently, from the earliest ages of Greek history, the scene of military operations, especially in the struggles of that city with its neighbour and rival, THEBES.

The name of CHÆRONEA is connected with that last and fatal effort which the City of Athens, at the instigation of Demosthenes, made in conjunction with Thebes, in the summer of the year B.C. 338, to defend the liberties of

Greece against the aggressions of Philip of Macedon ; and with the brilliant and decisive victory which was achieved in the same place by the Roman army under Sylla, over Archelaus, the general of Mithridates.

At the foot of the hill of CORONEA, the gallant and courageous leader of the Athenians, Tolmides, fell in a skirmish in the year B.C. 447. He was on his way homeward, after the bold attempt, made with the aid of only a thousand volunteers, to strengthen the Athenian party which the victory of

BATTLE OF CHÆRONEA.

Myronides, ten years before at ŒNOPHYTA, had established in all the cities of Bœotia, but whose power was destroyed by this disaster.

In the year B.C. 392, the same place was distinguished by the victory which was gained there by the Spartan leader, AGESILAUS, and the inhabitants of Orchomenus, over the combined forces of Argos and Thebes; on which occasion the victor spared the fugitives who took shelter in the neighbouring Temple of the ITONIAN MINERVA, and after which he proceeded on a religious pilgrimage to the Oracle of Delphi, in order to offer a tithe of the spoil that he had taken in his Asiatic campaign,—an oblation which amounted to one

hundred talents. The neighbouring city of HALIARTUS was as fatal to another
general of Sparta, as Coronea was honourable to Agesilaus. In the year
B.C. 395, Lysander—having previously dispatched a letter, which was intercepted by the Thebans—marched from Lebadea to Haliartus, where he hoped
to be joined by the army of Pausanias. This commander being unacquainted
with that movement, was unable to appear in its support, and Lysander found
himself suddenly surrounded, near the fountain CISSUSSA, which flows into
the lake by the western wall of Haliartus, on the one hand by the main body

OFFERING AT THE TEMPLE OF DELPHI.

of the Theban troops coming from Thebes, and on the other by a detachment
of the garrison which sallied forth from Haliartus itself. The Spartan general
fell in the skirmish; and the Thebans, strengthened by a powerful reinforce-
ment of Athenians, eager to avenge themselves on the destroyers of their city,
and to regain their own pre-eminence in Greece, and aided by the military
force of Haliartus, pursued the Spartans, who fled to the high grounds of
Helicon which rise to the south of the city, and made much havoc among
them ; by rashly venturing upon the steeps of the mountain, from which the
fugitives assailed them with missiles and fragments of rock, they themselves
lost two hundred men, and were driven back into the plain. This battle
was fatal to the Spartan influence in Bœotia : Pausanias was compelled to
evacuate that country under circumstances of great ignominy and loss.

We have spoken of the mountain cliffs which rise on every side, except
the eastern, of the basin of Orchomenus, and of the neighbouring cities

specified above. The description may also be correctly applied to the *whole*
country of which this district forms a *part.* Bœotia is girt with a belt of
mountains forming an elliptical ring, whose *length* extends from the south-east

to the north-west. Beginning at the point where the eastern coast approaches
and almost touches the island of Eubœa, namely, at the bay of AULIS, immediately to the north of which it is connected with that island by a bridge, we
have the grey limestone summits of MYCALESSUS, and the precipitous rocks of
MESSAPIUS, which leave between them and the sea a narrow slip, in which
stand the remains of SALGANEUS, and of the fishing town of ANTHEDON.

Proceeding further to the north-west, we observe the bare ridges of Mount Ptoum, which rears three lofty peaks into the air, whose sides were formerly covered with thick woods frequented by wild boars, and through whose hard and rugged calcareous rock the waters of the Copaic Lake have pierced for themselves a subterranean channel into the sea.

The Cnemidian hills, which stretch along the coast above the pass of

Thermopylæ and the waves of the Malian Gulf, take their rise from the slopes of Mount Ptoum, and unite it with the long ridge of Œta, which falls into the chain of Pindus at the hill of Tymphrestus, a point noticed above, as the centre to which the mountain radii of the southern part of the Greek continent converge.

On the western side of Mount Ptoum rises the hill of ACONTIUM, which is the eastern barrier of the vale of Cephissus. On it are the remains of the ancient cities of ABÆ and HYAMPOLIS. Beneath its western foot the river Cephissus runs through rich and beautiful pastures, corn-fields, and olive-yards, into the Cephissian Lake. Over the other, or western, side of the stream hang the steep eminences of LYCOREIA, consisting of dark marble cliffs capped with snow, which are the eastern projections of Mount Parnassus. Beneath them is the craggy hill of Daulis, lying in the fork between two streams which water the vine-clad slopes of the valley below it, and then, having united their waters at its eastern foot, flow together into the channel of the Cephissus.

From this point commences the long range of Helicon, which stretches onwards till it sinks down in a declivity near the city of THESPIÆ and the Plain of Leuctra. Through this valley a river flows to the south-west into the Corinthian Gulf, being the only stream of Bœotia which discharges its waters there. After the interval of this plain, the ground again rises in the stern and rugged cliffs of Cithæron, which are separated from Mount Parnes on the east by the gorge of Phyle. A series of low undulating hills stretching along the coast and interrupted by narrow plains,—such as that of Oropus, through

which the river Asopus flows into the Euboic Sea, and the low level of DELIUM, famed for the battle in which Socrates saved the life of his young pupil, and for its Temple of Apollo,—connect the north-east extremity of Parnes with the heights of Aulis and Mycalessus at the narrowest part of the channel of the Euripus, and thus conclude the circuit which we have traced of the natural frontiers of Bœotia.

The greater axis of the elliptical curve which has been just described measures a little more than sixty miles,—the lesser nearly amounts to forty. The curve itself contains an area of more than one thousand square miles, being more than three hundred above the number of which Attica consists.

The narrow Bridge, of which we have spoken as connecting Eubœa with Aulis, has influenced the fortunes, altered the name, and changed the character of that island, now called NEGRO-PONTE. It was the policy of Bœotia, contrived with more than Bœotian shrewdness, to make " Eubœa an island to every one else but themselves." By its means the Bœotians blockaded against their southern enemies, the Athenians, these Dardanelles of Greece. They locked the door of Athenian commerce, and kept themselves the key. This was the channel by which the gold of Thasus, the horses of Thessaly, the timber of Macedonia, the corn of Thrace, were carried to the Pirœus. Nor must we forget the importance of Eubœa itself, which, from its position and its produce, its quarries, its timber, and its corn, was of inestimable value to Athens. The bridge was built over the Euripus by the Bœotians, B.C. 410, and from that time the communication of Athens with the northern markets was either dependent on the fear or amity of Bœotia, or it was exposed to the dangers of the open sea, the perils of the treacherous Cœla and the "vengeful Caphareus."

Plutarch, in his Treatise of Rivers and Mountains, cites from Hermesianax, the historian of Cyprus, the following legend descriptive of the character of the two principal mountains which belong to the chain which encircles Bœotia :—" HELICON and CITHÆRON were two brothers; but very different from each other in temper and character. The former was mild and courteous, and dutiful to his parents, whom he supported in their old age. Cithæron, on the other hand, was covetous and avaricious. He wished to obtain all the property of the family for himself. To gain this object, he destroyed his father, and afterwards threw his brother by treachery down a precipice : but he himself, also, was carried over the cliff at the same time from the thrust with which he impelled his brother. After their death, by the will of the Gods, these two brothers were changed into the two Mountains which bore their name. Cithæron, by reason of his impiety, became the abode of the Furies; but Helicon, on account of his gentle and affectionate disposition, was chosen by the Muses as their favourite haunt."

The natural features of these two mountains are, as might be expected, in harmony with this mythological narrative. The dales and slopes of Helicon are clothed with groves of olive, walnut, and almond trees; clusters of ilex and arbutus deck its higher plains; and the oleander and myrtle fringe the banks of the numerous rills which gush from its soil, and stream in shining cascades down its declivities into the plain between it and the Copaic Lake.

One of the heights of Helicon is the Libethrian hill, where stood, in ancient times, a consecrated grove intersected by two fountains; beneath its shade were the statues of the Goddesses to whom it was dedicated. Here also was the hallowed grotto of the Libethrian Nymphs. The site is now occupied by a Monastery about three miles to the south-west of Mazi, the modern village, which stands very nearly upon the site of the ancient Haliartus.

On Helicon, according to the ancient belief, no noxious herb was found. Here, also, the first narcissus bloomed. The ground is luxuriantly decked with flowers, which diffuse around a delightful fragrance. It resounds with the industrious murmur of bees, and with the music of pastoral flutes and

the noise of waterfalls. Two of the sources which rise from its soil have acquired a celebrity unequalled by that of larger rivers. Not far from the site of the village of Ascra, the residence of Hesiod, which is five miles to the south of Haliartus, gushes forth the spring of Aganippe; the river of Permessus takes its rise at the same spot. Still further to the south is the fountain of Hippocrene, which springs from the earth above the valley of Marandali, shaded by pine trees, planes, and hazels. Near this fountain Pausanias saw a very ancient copy of the Works and Days of the Bard of

Ascra, written upon lead, which poem the inhabitants of Helicon, who showed it, maintained to be the only genuine production of that author.

At a Monastery of St. Nicolas, a little to the north-east of Marandali, was recently found an inscription containing a catalogue of the Victors in the Musia, or Games in honour of the Muses, which seems to prove that the grove consecrated to them, in which these games were celebrated, stood near that spot.

Pausanias enumerates the works of Art existing in the place at the time in which he visited it, namely, in the age of the Antonines. Here, at that period, were the statues of the nine Muses, sculptured by three different artists: here stood a group consisting of Apollo, Mercury, and Bacchus, contending for the lyre; near them was an erect figure of Bacchus, one of the finest works of Myron; here was a portrait of EUPHEME, the nurse of the Muses. The statues of great Poets adorned the same place: here stood the ancient minstrel Linus; near him was Thamyris, already blind, striking a broken lyre; Arion was there, riding his dolphin; Hesiod with his harp upon his knees; Orpheus surrounded with animals attracted by the melody of his song, at that time stood under the shade of these trees; but they have all now disappeared; while the trees wave, the flowers bloom, and the streams flow as they did of yore.

Connected with Mount Helicon, and hanging upon its eastern slopes, is the ancient city of THESPIÆ. The character of its early inhabitants forms an agreeable and an appropriate feature in the natural scenery which has just been described. The Thespians were regarded as the most refined and intellectual among the ancient tenants of Bœotia. Here stood the famous statue of Love, from the chisel of PRAXITELES, which induced so many strangers to visit Thespiæ, as his Venus attracted them to the island of Cnidos. At the present day a broken inscription remaining on the spot exhibits the name of Praxiteles, which was probably attached to one of the productions of that sculptor. Here also were works of Lysippus and other masters of renown.

The EROTIDIA, or Games in honour of the Deity of Love, drew also a large concourse of foreigners to Thespiæ. The story of Amphion and Zethus, who were natives of this place, is of Thespian origin, though they are both intimately connected with the history of Thebes. The character of Amphion, indeed, as contrasted with that of his brother Zethus,—the yielding and humane disposition of the one, and his intellectual refinements, compared with the inflexible austerity and the illiterate rudeness of the other,—might well be considered as fit representatives of the two different tempers which distinguished the inhabitants of this city from those of its rival, Thebes.

It redounds much to the honour of the Thespians that their successful cultivation and patronage of the imitative arts seems to have given them refinement without fastidiousness, and delicacy without effeminateness. Seven hundred Thespians alone were found among all the inhabitants of Continental Greece to join the army of Leonidas at the pass of Thermopylæ. At the conflict on the neighbouring plain of Platæa, this city sent eighteen hundred men, who contributed their energies to win the glory of that day, while the soldiers of Thebes fought against them in the ranks of the Barbarians.

A little before the battle fought on the field of Leuctra, which lies on the way between this place and Platæa, the walls of Thespiæ were destroyed by the hostile Thebans. But it is probable that, at a subsequent period, when their city had been restored, it owed its preservation to this very hatred and revenge of the Thebans, which won for the Thespians the favour of the Romans, who, exasperated with their Theban foes, were on that account more amicably inclined toward the inhabitants of Thespiæ. In the time of Strabo, —that is, in the Augustan age,—there remained but two Bœotian towns which had not fallen into decay. One of these was THESPIÆ, the other TANAGRA.

There is a road which leads through the gap of Helicon and Cithæron from

Thespiæ to the Bay of Crèusis in the Corinthian Gulf, which was the
EPISEION, or maritime station, of that city, and the only Bœotian port upon
that sea. From Crèusis a road conducts to ÆGOSTHENÆ by the coast
round the western foot of Cithæron, which leaves a narrow ledge between it
and the shore. This is the route by which the armies of the Peloponnesus
usually penetrated into Bœotia.

The aspect of Cithæron is, as has been observed, the reverse of that of
Helicon; it is savage, cold, gloomy, and inhospitable. Helicon was consecrated to the Muses; but Cithæron was the mountain of the Erinnyes, and
rang with the frantic yells of the wild nocturnal orgies of Bacchanalian
revelry. All the mythological traditions which are connected with it partake
of the physical sternness which characterises the mountain itself. The dark
forests of pine trees and silver firs which crown the precipitous cliffs, and the
caves which are hollowed in their craggy sides, were, according to the songs of
Greek poets, the witnesses of inhuman and sanguinary deeds. Here Pentheus,

the Theban King, was pursued by the infuriate troop of women, led on by his
mother and sisters, and torn in pieces by their hands. Here Actæon, the son
of Aristæus and of Antonoe, the daughter of Cadmus, having, on a sultry day
when he was hunting, ascended from the Gargaphian fount in the plain below,
where Diana, when bathing, was seen by him, was mangled by his own dogs,
which were set upon him by that Goddess. Here the luckless Œdipus was
exposed by order of his father. Here, a little more than a mile to the south
of the loftiest summits of the mountain, which is upwards of four thousand
feet in height, and overhangs the site of the ancient Platæa, was the altar of
the Cithæronian Jupiter, to which the fourteen cities composing the Bœotian
Confederacy brought, at the feast of the Dædalia, every sixty years, fourteen
statues of oak, and burnt them upon an altar of wood on the summit of the
mountain. Here is a grotto formerly dedicated to the SPHRAGITIAN Nymphs,

who inspired men with the frenzy known to the Greeks of old by the name
of Nympholepsy. The whole mountain was associated in their minds with
the wildest and darkest passions which distract and agonize the heart. It
was dedicated to Tragedy, while the mountain on the western side of the
valley was sacred to the genius of Pastoral Poetry. Cithæron and Helicon
were, if we may venture to use the comparison, the Mount EBAL and the
Mount GERIZIM of Greek geography.

From Thespiæ to Platæa is a distance of seven miles : the road lies to the
south-east, across the valley which we have described as severing Helicon

from Cithæron, and as the only outlet leading from the interior of Bœotia to
the Corinthian Gulf.

The ruins of the city of Platæa are on the steep and rugged slopes which
fall from the heights of Cithæron into the valley on the north. In this lower
ground, and near the walls of the city, two small rivers take their rise, and
flow in opposite directions. They are both fed by small brooks falling from
the sides of Cithæron. The one is the ancient OEROE, which rises to the east
of Platæa, runs along the valley in a westerly course, and discharges itself
into the harbour of Creusia. The other is the ASOPUS, which, in the language
of Bœotian mythology, was described as the Father of Oëröe. It springs
from the plain between Leuctra and Platæa, and flows on the north of the

latter towards the east. It passes by the sites of HYSIÆ and ERYTHRÆ on its
right bank, leaves Tanagra on its left, and falls into the Euboic Sea a little
to the north-east of the town of Oropus.

The tract of country watered by these two streams is the great southern
vale of Bœotia; it measures in length nearly forty miles.

Between the sources of these two rivers the road from Thebes to Platæa
passes, and then, after entering the latter city, it climbs the heights of
Cithæron, and, at a spot formerly known by the name of the OAKHEADS, or
DRYOSCEPHALÆ, divides itself into two branches. That to the south-east passes
by the defile of ŒNOE and the city of Eleutheræ, to Megara on the right, and
to Eleusis and Athens on the left. The other leads to the south-west, by the
mountains of GERANEIA, to the isthmus of Corinth and the Peloponnesus.

DESCRIPTION OF THE ARRANGEMENT OF MARDONIUS.

In the autumn of the year B.C. 479, Mardonius, the Persian General, who
had been left in Greece by Xerxes, with three hundred thousand of his best
men, marched from Athens, which he had destroyed, over the heights of
Parnes, by the pass of Decelea. He proceeded by Oropus, and having crossed
the river Asopus there, marched along its left bank till he came to the city of
Tanagra. Here he halted for one night. He then proceeded in the same
direction till he arrived, on the next day, at SCOLUS, the frontier town of the
Theban territory. There he laid waste a part of the meadow land, not for the

sake of injuring the Thebans, who were his friends, but in order to form an encampment for his large force, and to provide himself with a place of refuge in case of emergency. With this view, he surrounded with military fortifications of planks and palisades an area of a square mile. This fort was on the left bank of the stream; its southern face was parallel to, and nearly coincided with, the interval between the cities of Erythræ and Hysiæ on the other side of the stream. The line of the army not only exceeded this interval, but also extended westward, so as to face a part of the Platæan territory.

Such was the position of Mardonius and his army before the battle of Platæa. His force consisted not merely of Persians and Medes, Bactrians, Indians, and Sacæ, but was strengthened by auxiliaries from the Greek cities who had espoused the cause of the invader. Macedonia, Thessaly, Phocis, and the greater part of Bœotia, were now in his power, and augmented his numbers. Besides these, a mixed multitude of different nations, Phrygians, Mysians, Thracians, Pæonians, and Ægyptians, swelled the ranks of Mardonius. His army is said to have amounted to three hundred and fifty thousand men, exclusive of cavalry. It nearly doubled the number of that which had fought eleven years before in the same cause on the field of Marathon.

In order to understand clearly the circumstances of the battle of Platæa, we must remember that the Greek force occupied *three* wholly distinct positions, at three different periods; while, with the exception of temporary advances for the purpose of attacking their antagonists, the Persians remained, during the whole interval, from the time of their first appearance in the Platæan territory to the day upon which they left it, in the same square encampment which has been described above.

The Athenians, having joined the Lacedæmonians at Eleusis, marched over Mount Cithæron at the pass of Dryoscephalæ, and took up their station on the rugged declivities of the mountain, at Erythræ, on the south side of the Asopus. This was their *first* position. Here they stood in face of the Persian encampment, which was on the other side of the river. While occupying this post, they were attacked by a detachment of the Persian cavalry, commanded by Masistius, the next in dignity to Mardonius in the hostile army. It was met by the Megarians and Athenians, who formed the Greek van. Masistius himself fell in the encounter, and the Persians fled to their camp.

The result of this skirmish encouraged the Greeks; being also in want of water, they determined to descend lower into the plain, and advanced a little to the westward, towards Platæa: they then encamped near the fountain

GARGAPHIA, not far from the sacred inclosure of the hero Andocrates, on the right of the road from Platæa to Thebes, and about a mile to the east of the former. This spot was well supplied with water, being irrigated by several streamlets flowing from Cithæron into the Asopus. Such was the second position of the Greeks.

The Lacedæmonians held the right wing, or that nearest to the mountain, according to the received practice in such cases at that time. But a question arose, who should occupy the left. There were two competitors for this honour,—the Athenians and the Tegeæans of Arcadia. The matter was referred by common consent to the Lacedæmonians, who decided in favour of the Athenians. The latter accordingly posted themselves in a lower part of the valley, near the banks of the river, and almost at right angles to it. The Greek force, beginning from the right wing, consisted of Tegeæans, Corinthians, Potidæans, Orchomenians of Arcadia, Sicyonians, and of troops from different cities of Argolis, Eubœa, and Epirus, from Leucas, Cephallenia, and Ægina, and towards the left wing from Megara, Platæa, and Athens. The greatest number from any one city was ten thousand: this was furnished by Sparta : the next was eight thousand, and was supplied by Athens. The entire force amounted to one hundred and ten thousand men; it possessed no cavalry.

The Lacedæmonian King, Pausanias, had the command of the whole. The *right* wing of the Greeks was confronted by the Persians : next in order in the Barbarian force stood the Medians, Bactrians, Indians, and Sacæ : the Bœotians, Locrians, Malians, Thessalians, and Phocians were stationed in the right wing, opposite to the Athenians in the Greek left.

In this state, the armies remained in sight of each other for ten days. Both parties were indisposed to commence the attack. The Greek soothsayers who were retained in the camp of Mardonius, promised him the victory, provided he remained on the defensive ; and Tisamenus, the son of Antiochus, a native of Elis, who was the most renowned among the augurs of that age, predicted to the Lacedæmonians, that if they abstained from crossing the Asopus, their cause would be successful. A change in the disposition of the Greek force, by which the Lacedæmonians were transferred to the left wing and the Athenians to the right,—although it was a mere temporary manœuvre, and the two parties resumed in a short time their former positions,—induced Mardonius to believe that a panic had seized the camp of his antagonists, and inspired him with that confidence which proved the cause of destruction to him, and of success to the enemy.

He despatched a herald to insult the Lacedæmonians in consequence of this supposed avowal of inferiority and fear, and to challenge them to send a detachment into the plain to meet an equal number of Persians, in order that the fate of the two armies might be decided by the issue of that contest.

Pausanias, unmoved by this contumelious defiance, and having held a council of the Greek generals, gave orders for a retreat further to the west. The point to which the troops were commanded to retire was called the ISLAND,—more correctly speaking, it was a *peninsula*,—formed by the confluence of some small tributary streams, falling from the slopes of Cithæron into the river Oëröe.

The Greek centre, not content with this retrograde movement, fell behind the city of Platæa, two miles in the rear of their former position. The decision of the generals was but partially executed by the rest of the army. The right wing retreated only for a mile, and took up its station about a thousand yards to the east of Platæa, upon the rugged declivities of the mountain, by which it was protected from the incursions of the enemy's cavalry. The Athenians on the left wing fell back from their former position in the direction of the Island, and posted themselves in the plain between some low hills and the city of Platæa. Such was the *third* and last position of the Greeks.

By the reluctance which they had shown to obey the orders of their commander, and by the consequent separation of its different members, the destruction of the Greek army would have been inevitable, had not the presumption of the Barbarians been greater than the insubordination of the Greeks.

Mardonius, having observed the movements of the enemy, and relying upon the persuasion which he had before felt that they were attempting to escape from him, led forth the Persians from his encampment, and rapidly crossed the Asopus, as if in pursuit of the Lacedæmonians. He did not perceive the Athenians in the plain, on account of the low hills which intercepted his view. The rest of his army, observing the advance of their general, rushed with one accord, in great confusion, with loud shouts, and at their utmost speed, from the same place, in full confidence of making their foe an easy prey. Pausanias, in great distress, sent to the Athenians for aid. As they were advancing to the right in order to relieve him, they were themselves met by the auxiliaries on the Persian right, and checked in their march. Thus the Lacedæmonian king was left alone to face, with only fifty-three thousand men, the main body of the host of Mardonius. The victims were unfavourable, his army unwilling to move, and exposed to a shower of missiles shot by the Persians from behind a breastwork of shields. At this moment the presence of mind of Pausanias rescued his army, and saved Greece. He turned his eyes to the Temple of Juno behind him in the city of

Platæa, and in the midst of the conflict invoked the compassion and aid of
that Goddess. Immediately the sacrifices became propitious. The courage of
his troops was restored; they burst through the breastwork of the Persians,
who flung away their bows and grappled with their adversaries in close fight.
The Persians displayed great courage: they seized the javelins of the Greeks,
while the latter were in the act of discharging them, and snapped them
asunder. Mardonius, mounted on a white horse, and surrounded by his
chosen cavalry, consisting of a thousand men, appeared where the conflict was
hottest, and turned the tide of battle by his presence. But, having exposed
himself by his bravery, he receives a wound from a noble Spartan, Aeimnestus,
and falls. The flower of his army—his chosen cavalry—die near him; and
the rest of the force being unprotected, on account of the looseness of their
garments, and fighting, as it were, unarmed, against heavy-armed men, betake
themselves to flight, and rush to their encampment on the other side of the
Asopus. This, having been assaulted in vain for some time by the Lacedæmonians, was at last stormed by the Athenians, who arrived soon after the
former had commenced the attack.

The Persians made no longer any resistance: they stood still, stupefied by
fear, and were mowed down by the enemy. Of three hundred thousand men,
only forty-three thousand survived the battle of Platæa.

Having traced the outline of mountains by which Bœotia is surrounded, we
proceed to consider some of the physical, political, moral, and social consequences arising from the particular position and natural qualities of the country.

We observe, in the first place, that this mountain circle touches *three*
different seas: on the north-east side it is bounded by the north Eubœan
channel, by which Bœotia is brought into connexion with Thessaly, and
Macedonia, and the Euxine Sea. On the east, the south Eubœan Gulf opened
to it a way to the Archipelago, and to the Asiatic shore; and on the west
side, the Crissæan and Corinthian bays afforded it the means of communicating
with Africa, Italy and Sicily, and the other parts of the west of Europe. The
advantage of thus possessing a triple sea was enjoyed by no other country in
Greece; and though this privilege was in some degree impaired by the
mediocrity of the harbours and the difficulties which obstructed the access to
them, on account of the mountain barriers which intercepted them from the
interior, yet, if the character of its inhabitants had been such as to profit by
the benefits conferred upon them by Nature, Bœotia would have become one
of the first among the commercial nations of ancient Europe.

Another result of the physical formation of this country exhibited itself
within the horizon of mountains of which we have spoken.

The numerous Rivers which flow down from the rocky sides of Mounts Messapius, Ptöum, Parnassus, Helicon, Cithæron, and Parnes, into the circular basin which they form, have, with only one exception, no natural outlet by any defile or valley into the sea. The Asopus alone, of all the Bœotian streams, pursues its course along its channel, and discharges itself into a small bay in the Euripus without any interruption.

To compare great things with small, the Basin of Bœotia resembles the ATRIUM of an ancient house, such as we see at Pompeii and Herculaneum, into the centre of which the water falls from the roofs, sloping inward, of its four sides. To adopt the technical term, applied to the reservoir formed by this confluence of water,—the *impluvium* of Bœotia is the Copaic Lake.

This collection of streams is the largest inland sea in Greece. Its circumference was estimated by Strabo at forty miles; since his time it has increased to sixty.

This lake has exerted great influence upon the fortunes of Bœotia and on the character of its inhabitants. Much of the fertility of the surrounding country is due to it. It was to that part of Bœotia which bordered upon it, what the Nile is to Ægypt. The wealth and splendour of the ancient Orchomenus were mainly derived from it.

On the other hand, the encroachment of its waters has deprived the Bœotian agriculturist of some of his richest soil. The cold and humid fogs, which added to the inclemency of the climate of this country, and were prejudicial to the health and intelligence of its inhabitants, proceeded from the same source.

Nature has exerted herself to diminish these evils. The formation of the mountain interval which divides the eastern end of the lake from the sea is calcareous. The fissures opening in its strata admitted the water of the lake, which gradually wore itself a passage through the rock. It mined a subterranean passage through a mountain barrier of four miles in length. By this communication the streams of the Copaic Lake discharge themselves into the sea.

At the north-east corner of the lake are three of these channels : they are called KATABOTHRA, or Subterranean Gorges, in the language of the country. By these chasms the water passes from the lake, and pursues its course in a north-eastern direction, till it issues from the ground in the vale of LARMES, the LARYMNA of Strabo, and flows down into the bay which served as the harbour of that ancient city. Having, as the river Alphëus was said to have done, dived under the water, the Cephissus reappears, at the mouth of the sluice, in this stream, which bore its name.

These subterranean emissaries were in ancient times not unfrequently closed by an accumulation of alluvial soil, which caused the lake to inundate the neighbouring country. To obviate this evil, numerous vertical shafts have been sunk through the rock into the channel of the river, by means of which

it was freed from the obstructions that impeded it. These shafts exhibit some
of the most interesting and wonderful specimens which exist in Greece of the

skill and power of the civil engineers of antiquity. They were probably the
means by which the princes of Orchomenus, Agamedes and Trophonius, who
were famed for their mechanical genius, obtained from their fellow-countrymen the honour of an apotheosis. In later times, these pits were repaired and
cleared by Crates of Chaleis, who presented to his employer, Alexander the
Great, a report, which was afterwards seen by Strabo, of the success he had
achieved in draining by their means the surrounding plain, and bringing
again to light some ancient cities, which had been submerged by the deluges
consequent upon this obstruction.

In considering the different ways in which the Copaic Lake exercised an
influence over the population of Bœotia, we must not forget one of its natural
productions, which, though humble in appearance, was by no means unim-
portant in the effects it produced. This is the reed which shoots from the
lake, and whose tufted top waves in the wind over the surface of the water.
It did much to affect the natural character of Bœotia.

It has been said, and not without some ground of truth, that what the
Pentelic marble was to Athens, that the Copaic Reed was to Bœotia. Both,

through the exercise of very different arts, supplied the natural means of expressing their thoughts and feelings to the inhabitants of these two countries. The reed furnished instruments for the periodical contests of flute-players in the Games in honour of the Graces at Orchomenus, where it grew in the greatest perfection, in the musical festivals of Love at Thespiæ, and in those of the Muses at Libethra; it produced a class of minstrels peculiar to Bœotia; it aided the muse of Hesiod, of Pindar, and of Corinna; it gave a melodious charm to the songs of the shepherds in the pastures of Helicon and on the banks of the Asopus; and it was welcomed even to the Theatre of Athens, where it gave life to the songs and dance of the tragic chorus. It indeed excited the jealousy of the Athenian, who loved to disparage the minstrelsy of Bœotia on the comic stage, and who feigned that his own Goddess, Minerva, had been the first to play upon the flute, but that having observed, while so doing, the distorted reflection of her face in a brook, she threw away in disdain the instrument which disfigured her divine countenance.

It has been observed, that a great part of the ancient affluence of Orchomenus, under its Princes of the house of Minyas, was due to its contiguity to the lake of Copaë. That city stood at the confluence of the MELAS and Cephissus; the former flowing beneath its northern, the latter by its southern wall; and between Mount Acontium on the west, and the Copaic Lake on its

eastern side. It was, therefore, fortified by natural defences. It occupied the
north-east angle of the plain, the largest in Bœotia, which was under its sway,
and from which it drew much of its power. It exhibited a perfect specimen of
an ancient city. Its walls inclosed an irregular triangle, of which the apex
and highest part was at the west, whence the two sides diverged, so as to
follow the lines of two mountain ridges, commencing from that point, and
sloping down toward the plain and the lake; and many vestiges of it still
remain. Below the eastern side, which subtended the angle at the vertex, are
the huge remains of the Treasury, and of the Temple of the Graces, which
carry back the thoughts of the beholder from the present day to times which
preceded the siege of Troy.

On the vertex of the hill just described was the citadel; it is approached
by two flights of nearly one hundred steps cut in the rock. It commands a
magnificent view of the lake and the plain.

The basin of Orchomenus is separated from that of Thebes by a mountain
ridge at the south-east angle of the Copaic Lake. It resulted from the natural

PLAIN AND CITY OF THEBES

formation of the country, that the political government of Bœotia was vested
in the two principal cities of these two plains. In the earliest times, indeed,
of Greek History, Orchomenus was not a part of Bœotia, which, strictly
speaking, was confined to the Theban region, while that of Orchomenus formed
an independent province. It seems also to have arisen from similar causes,

that, after a long struggle for the pre-eminence, Thebes eclipsed her rival in
affluence and power. Her soil was celebrated for its produce of corn and
wine; its fertility is further shown by the crops of tobacco, cotton, and Indian
corn, which cover it. Thebes had also the advantage of a ready export for
her productions, by her convenient position in the vicinity of three seas.

The character of her inhabitants appears to have been affected in a remarkable manner by the physical properties of the place. The seven-gated citadel
of Thebes stood on a small circular hill, about one hundred and fifty feet above
the level of the surrounding plain. The base of the hill on the eastern and
western sides is bounded by two small streams, which take their rise in the
plain on the south, and flow in parallel courses to the north: further to the
east, and running in a similar direction, is a third stream: this is the
ISMENUS; that to the east is DIRCE; between them is CNOPUS.

Though at present the aspect of the place is bare and dreary, the suburbs
of the city are described by ancient writers as having been verdant and picturesque, delighting the eye by the luxuriance of the gardens interspersed with
the houses. The coolness of the climate, and the freshness of perennial streams,
rendered it a delicious abode in the heat of summer; but a Theban winter
was a cheerless one. There were no woods in the neighbourhood to supply

fuel, or to afford a shelter to the town from the keen winds and the drifting
snow, which often blocked up the roads and streets of the city. The writer
of these pages has reason to remember this from his own experience of a winter
at Thebes. Frequent hurricanes swept down from the cliffs of Cithaeron, and
the water torrents deluged the plain. A proud, stubborn, presumptuous, and
savage temper, and an insolent confidence in their own bodily strength and
physical resources, were the peculiar characteristics of the ancient inhabitants
of Thebes; and these national peculiarities seem to have been engendered and
strengthened, in a considerable degree, by exposure to the inclemency of such
seasons,—as the elegance and refinement of the Athenians was partly due to
the light air, the dry soil, and the genial climate of Attica.

ERXES, in his march from Asia to Greece, visited in a Sidonian vessel the spot where the river PENEUS discharges itself into the sea. He expressed much surprise when he contemplated the termination of its course, and inquired whether it were not possible to divert the stream by some other channel into the Thermaic Gulf. The guides who conducted him to the place informed him that there was no other practicable issue for the stream, because the whole of Thessaly, within whose limits it takes its rise, was girt by a belt of mountains.

Herodotus, who records this fact, adds that there existed an ancient tradition that Thessaly was formerly a Lake, inclosed on all sides by lofty hills. It is confined on the east by Pelion and Ossa; on the north Olympus, and Pindus on the west, form a natural frontier; while, on the south, the range of Othrys closes the outlet to the lower provinces of Continental Greece. The basin of Thessaly lies within these boundaries.

It is observed by the same author, that five large rivers descend from the sides of these mountains; the PENEUS, APIDANUS, ONOCHONUS, ENIPEUS, and

Pamisus; and that the four latter discharge their streams into the first, and that they all flow in a single channel, that of the Penēus, through one narrow outlet into the sea.

In the earlier ages of Greek Mythology, when this defile, through which the Penēus passes into the ocean, did not exist, the confluence of these streams, together with contributions from the Bœbean Lake, inundated the country with a deluge of water, which, as poets say, first found a free egress when Neptune, with the stroke of his trident, severed Olympus from Ossa, and made a channel for the river through the beautiful vale of TEMPE.

The legends of Thessaly all speak of the peculiar character of the country with which they are connected. They refer to the two physical elements which constituted the most remarkable features of this region. We have extensive views or distant glimpses of Sea and Mountains in them all. We

PLAIN OF GREEXVA

have already noticed the origin assigned to the long and narrow ravine of Tempe, which affords the only means of communication between the plains of northern Thessaly and the sea. We have also contrasted with this tradition, which derives its origin from a time when the country was agitated by some great natural convulsion, the picture which has been drawn by ancient Poets of the more quiet and joyful scene exhibited in the palace of the old city of

Pharsalia, when the hero of the land, Peleus, espoused Thetis, the goddess of
the sea. In that hymeneal festivity, to which the Deities of the neighbouring
Olympus brought contributions, at which the Muses sang, the Nereids danced,
and Ganymede poured forth nectar, we seem to recognise an imaginative
expression of the calmer and happier state of Nature that succeeded the violent
shock which had disturbed the foundations and altered the aspect of the wide
district of Thessaly.

The pleasure which the inhabitants of this country experienced,—which
the Shepherd or the Huntsman felt,—when, from the lofty cliffs of Olympus
or of Ossa, or from the more cultivated declivities of Pelion, he looked down
upon the wide expanse of sea below him, and beheld its swelling waves
subside after a storm, and the hills of numerous islands in the distance
gradually emerging from the mists as the dark clouds broke, and the white
sails of many small vessels which had now ventured forth upon the sunny sea
—are indescribable. The impression thus conveyed received form and expression in the fable of CEYX and HALCYONE, the Thessalian princess. Ceyx was
wrecked on his return from a voyage undertaken to consult the oracle at
Claros. His wife, on finding her husband's corpse upon the shore, was about
to throw herself into the sea; but both were changed into birds, which give

their name to those seven halcyon days of winter which succeed the tempestuous
weather of that season, and are undisturbed by storms, during which the
female sits upon her eggs on the smooth surface of the waves.

It is not a matter of surprise, in the particular circumstances of the case,
that Thessaly among all the nations of Greece was the first to distinguish

itself in the history of maritime enterprise. Jason, the prince of Iolcus, proclaimed the preparations which he had made for the voyage he was about to undertake, and princes and heroes flocked to him from the different capitals of the Grecian soil, eager to join in the first attempt to cross the solitary sea, and to explore a land which no vessel had ever visited. In the woods of Mount Pelion, which hangs over Iolcus, the pine-tree was felled which furnished timber for the ship in which the band of heroes sailed, and a town in the MAGNESIAN peninsula beneath the south-western roots of that mountain was called APHETÆ, or the *launching-place*, as being the spot from which their vessel, the Argo, commenced its voyage to the shores of the Euxine.

The contrast between Plain and Mountain, which is strikingly exhibited in the landscapes of Thessaly, appears to have assumed a sensible shape in the mythological narratives of the struggles for superiority which occurred between the two tribes into which the population of Thessaly was anciently divided. I refer to the celebrated contests between the LAPITHÆ and the CENTAURS, which are often described in Greek poetry and represented in Greek sculpture. One of these tribes stands forth, if we may so speak, as the representative of the plain and of the manners and interests of its inhabitants; while the other displays all the characteristics, both natural and social, which distinguish the dwellers in the wild forests and on the steep rocks of the mountainous districts of Thessaly. It is worthy of remark that to the former of these, namely, the Lapithæ, is attributed the honour of having first tamed the horse, and taught him, by the use of the rein, to perform the evolutions of the stadium and of the field, and of having thus laid the foundation of that glory which was afterwards the peculiar distinction of the Thessalian Cavalry. At the present day the traveller is reminded of the physical properties of this region, which conduced to the superiority of its earliest occupants in this respect, by the sight of the wide and level road in the neighbourhood of LARISSA, upon which the carriages of the modern Scopadæ and Aleuadæ of the country are sometimes seen to roll, and by the appearance of those large wooden wains, supported by solid wheels, which are drawn by slow teams of oxen across the broad fields, undivided by hedges, that stretch from the southern side of the Penëus to the hills of Pharsalia. The bridge over the Penëus at Larissa, represented in the preceding page, offers a further confirmation of this view. It consists of nine arches, and is three hundred feet in length, faced with large squared stones; the piers which terminate below in spurs, are fenced with Saracenic arches, curved and pointed. The roadway is wide enough for two carriages to pass. This Bridge is one of the most considerable works of the kind in Greece.

The wilder character of the Centaurs, who dwelt on the lofty regions of the mountains which surrounded the lowlands of Thessaly, was expressed in the origin from which they were said to have been derived. In the mythological traditions of their birth, their ancestor, Centaurus, was reported to have sprung from a cloud which dropped him on the earth in its course over the summit of Mount Pelion. The semi-ferine form, under which the Centaurs were represented by the poets and sculptors of Greece, is comparatively of recent date. Nor, indeed, is it consistent with the hypothesis which regards them as the original inhabitants of the *hills*, in contradistinction to the Lapithæ, the dwellers in the *plain*. To Homer the Centaurs were nothing but men of a rude and savage character. Of their equine form he knew nothing. It has been well observed that by Hesiod, or rather by the unknown Author of the "Shield of Hercules," they are distinguished from the Lapithæ only by the greater rudeness of their warlike weapons. The measure of their relative civilization is supplied by the circumstance recorded by him, that while the latter attack their antagonists with javelins, the Centaurs repel them with pine-trees uprooted from their native mountains. In the lyric verses of Pindar, and on the marble walls of the Temple of Theseus, they first appear in the horse-like shape which was generally assigned to them by subsequent poets and sculptors; a fact which may be attributed partly to their extraction from Thessaly, the land, among all the countries of Greece, in which the horse seems to have been first used, and which was distinguished from the rest by the equestrian superiority of its inhabitants. But in the plastic representations of the Centaurs to which we refer, the same character of wild ferocity is preserved; they are exhibited as hurling on their foes huge fragments of rock torn from the hills on which they dwell, while the Lapithæ are equipped with the usual weapons of Greek warfare. The Hellenic Heroes, Theseus and Pirithous, appear also in the ranks of the latter. The conflict, therefore, may be regarded as a general representation of the struggle, which is of so common occurrence in the earlier ages of Greek history, of rude physical force against courage disciplined by intelligence.

So much for the evidence with respect to the natural properties of the soil of Thessaly and the character of its earliest inhabitants, which is supplied by the mythological traditions of the country. If we turn to a cabinet of ancient medals, and examine the compartment assigned to the numismatic productions of this region, we recognise similar expressions of the same thing. In some of the coins of that collection we observe the figure of a horse reined; in others we see the steed ranging at will and grazing in his pasture; in those of Larissa the fertility of the arable land as well as the richness of its meadows is indicated by an ear of corn combined with the form of the same animal; while the ancient pre-eminence of Thessaly in the naval history of Greece is announced by the representation of the ship Argo bearing the figure of Apollo on its prow, and accompanied by the maritime emblems of a Dolphin and a Star, the harbingers of a prosperous voyage, which appear on the coins of the Magnesian Peninsula.

The circumstance to which the stamped symbols last specified refer, namely, the ancient distinction which this country obtained from its connexion with the SEA, and perhaps also the fact of its having once been, as is supposed with great show of probability, covered by water, seems to receive some illustration from the denomination which it bears.

The name of THESSALY, as assigned to the region bounded on the north by the Cambunian hills, by Mount Pindus on the west, the Ægean on the east, and Mount Othrys on the south, is not of high antiquity. It does not occur in Homer. The Thessalians, as a confederate body, were unknown to him, while he speaks of the different individual tribes who occupied that district to which this title was subsequently applied.

The Thessalians themselves, indeed, did not hesitate to derive their origin from a king of the heroic age who bore the name of Thessalus: but the practice of creating from their own imagination not merely one, but a series of

ancestors, in order to account for their own national designations by means
of such flattering etymologies, was too prevalent among the Greeks to allow
of our placing much reliance on such genealogical deductions, unless supported
by authentic and independent evidence. With respect to the princely person
mentioned above, those who claimed to be his descendants were not agreed
among themselves concerning his origin. At one time Thessalus was the son
of Jason: at another he became the son of Hæmon, from whom this country
had before been called Hæmonia; while another tradition made him a member
of the family of Pelasgus. The historical account of the fact is this—that
a party of Pelasgians from Thesprotia, in Epirus, crossed the Pindus and
descended into the plain then called ÆOLIA, to which they gave the name of
Thessaly. The invaders are said to have derived their origin from the Pelasgians, who had been themselves expelled by the HELLENES from the same
region, and had carried with them the worship of the DODONÆAN Jupiter, and
the sanctity of his Oracle, from the banks of the Peneüs to the foot of Mount
Tomarus on the Molossian and Thesprotian frontier. Their descent upon
Thessaly was therefore rather a return to an old, than an occupation of a new
settlement. We are inclined to conjecture, from the early maritime character

THE LAKE AND CITY OF JANNINA

and history of this country, that the original appellation was THALASSIA, or
the land of the SEA: this name, by a very common transposition of letters, and
for adaptation to the metre of epic poetry, became Thessalia, and for the sake
of harmony, and to avoid the repetition of the same letter, THESSALIA.

Let us imagine ourselves as issuing forth from the gates of JANNINA, on
the eastern frontier of Epirus, to survey this country. A good road conveys

us along the western brink of the lake of that city, whence we wind round its southern extremity, and pursue our course to the north-east. At about twelve miles from the town we stand on the summit of the hill of Daisko, where is a kiosk, a fountain shaded by a plane tree, and a magnificent view. From one of its slopes the city of Jannina is seen, with its shining domes and minarets and white castle rising out of the bosom of the placid lake: in front of us is a grand ridge of mountains, running parallel to the great Pindus chain.

THE JANNINA, AND BANK OF THE PINDUS

At the eastern foot of the hill of Drisko is the valley of BALDUMA, where is a bridge over the stream which winds along it: it is the work of the renowned Ali Pasha, as indeed are most of the bridges and the khans upon this route to Thessaly; but now the grass grows over the paved road, the bridges are broken down, and the khans deserted. The most melancholy objects in this country are the improvements which were once made in it. They are effected, and then fall into decay, for there is no continuity of action in the governing power. The redeeming element of most other despotisms—hereditary succession—is here wanting. An Ali Pasha dies, and the roads of his Pashalic become impassable.

It is well for the traveller who pursues his journey in the summer, when the stony bed of the Arachthus and the Peneus—which in the winter season are swollen into formidable streams—serves him as a road. In a few miles from the valley above mentioned the ascent becomes steep. The scenery is wild. Wood grows in abundance, but there are no marks of cultivation except a few starved vines, and some patches of Indian corn. Now the valley becomes a ravine, and the river a torrent. Soon we leave the latter, and ascend a steep to the left: this brings us on one of the crests of Mount Ztoo, which falls down to the right in an abrupt and deep chasm, parallel to the road. To one who passes along the edge of this chasm, in the gloom of a dark evening, the effect of the gulf beneath is very grand. Having passed onward, he is surprised by the sight of many lights far beneath him on the right, closely glittering together on the opposite side of this deep valley. There is the town of MEZZOVO.

Let not the traveller who enters the khan of this place at night—and we may consider it as a fair specimen of those which occur in his road through this part of the Turkish empire—dream of enjoying the comforts of an European inn. He mounts the external stone staircase, which leads up to the open wooden gallery, or balcony of the building, from which doors open into dark and bare cells, the planks of whose floors gape into crevices, through which he sees and hears what takes place in the stable below. The walls are begrimed with smoke, and a wooden window admits the light and wind. The rooms possess no ceiling; but the common roof of the khan serves equally for all. An attendant appears, and sweeps the dusty floor with a fan-like brush, which serves also to ventilate a wood-fire when it is kindled. He then brings in and strews on the floor a mat or two, and leaves the pilgrim to his resources. It is no doubt agreeable to reflect that, as the invention of alphabetical characters enfeebled the memories of men, and the excellence and frequency of inns have checked the domestic welcome and entertainment of strangers, so the amount of private hospitality must needs be great in a country where the public accommodations are restricted to a roof, a mat, and a fire.

In the ancient language of Greece, the term MESAVO was applied to the central part of the yoke which is placed on the necks of oxen, and thus unites the pair together. We are inclined to believe that this town derived the name which it now bears from its position in the centre of the mountain range which, let it be observed, is known at the present day by the appellation of Ztoo, a term which signifies a YOKE both in the ancient and modern dialect of this country. We would go further, and hazard a conjecture that the Mesapian chain, on the gulf of the Euripus, received its name from a similar circumstance; and perhaps Mesapus, the yoker of horses, in the work of the Latin Bard, may have borrowed his name from that of the instrument of his art.

MEZZOVO contains about seven thousand inhabitants. It is one of the

principal stations for merchants engaged in the carrying trade from western
Greece to Salonica and Constantinople. A proof of its prosperity is seen in
its large school, supported by the town, on the walls of which are hung the
maps of the famous Riga, which seem to show that when they were made
little was known of Greek geography by Greeks. Near the school is a church
and a churchyard. On the graves in the latter a small square wooden box is
placed, which opens at the top, and contains a skull and a small funeral lamp.
Three times a-year these lamps are lighted, and incense burnt on the spot.
At a funeral the body is brought into the church on a bier, and loaves are
distributed to the congregation. The marriage ceremony is called by the
ancient Greek term *Stephanos*, or the crowning. The chaplet is carried in a
basket, the sacred *canistrum* of old; and the kinsmen of the bridegroom
still faithfully preserve their primitive appellation of *sympeatheri*, slightly
modified.

The road over the Pindus dips down into the vale of Mezzovo, and then
rises upwards towards the east. From this point to the summit of Zygo the
ascent is steep and difficult. The rocky soil is sprinkled with trees and shrubs,
of which the most numerous are the pine and box. Near the summit is a
noble grove of beeches. This spot is about two hours distant from Mezzovo.
The prospect from this point is bounded on the east by the snowy peaks of

OLYMPUS, distant from it about fifty miles. The sight of the plain of Thessaly
is intercepted by the projections of the eastern ridges of the mountain : on these
we behold the villages of MOKARA and MALACARA. This position is the most
important and remarkable in the geography of Continental Greece. As such
it has been selected (in the early part of this work) as the first central station
from which a general survey should be taken of the most prominent features
of that country. Near it, as we have seen, the five principal rivers of
Greece take their rise, and by their means we communicate from this place
with all the Hellenic provinces and seas. By the Achelous we send our
thoughts into Ætolia ; with the stream of the Arcethus we visit the pleasant
plains of Ambracia ; the channel of the Aöus conducts us back to the shores
of the Adriatic and of Italy ; the Penëus wafts us on to the plains of Thessaly
and through the vale of Tempe ; and the Haliacmon, rising from the same hill,
bears us to the same coast, that of the Thermaic Gulf.

GENERAL VIEW OF METEORA.

Our course lies from the source of the Penëus almost entirely upon the
broad stony bed of that stream. On the right and left are parallel ranges of

woody hills, rising from the river's edge, shading it by the thick foliage of plane-trees. In the dusk of a summer's evening the traveller who has started from Mezzovo at early dawn, will perceive in the distance the dark and lofty rocks of METEORA, standing before him like massive obelisks in the plain.

Simeon Stylites placed himself on the capital of his pillar, where he led the life of a hermit in solitude and self-mortification. Here we see the abode

" Of the monastic brotherhood upon rock
Aërial,"—

who dwell, like Stylitæ, some hundreds of feet from the plain below, on the summit of the cliffs of Meteora.

OUTER OF METEORA.

The road leads from the khan of KASTRAKI through a plain covered with fields of cotton and groves of mulberries, winding to the left through the straits made in the vale by the huge rocks seemingly flung in confusion over the soil upon which these monasteries stand. A mythologist might imagine that these piles had been raised here by the ancient Giants, when they block-aded heaven with Olympus and Ossa, and the other mountains of Thessaly, and that they were abandoned as part of their artillery when the Belligerents of earth were discomfited and routed by the Powers of heaven.

While the traveller is standing beneath the principal Monastery of Meteora, he sees a rope dangling from the cornice of the lofty rock above him; he

beholds it descend gradually, and at last drop at his feet. Attached to the
rope by an iron hook is a small net. The hook is unclasped, the net spread
upon the ground, and he takes his seat within it. The net is then closed
around him and fastened again to the rope by the hook, and he begins his
aërial ascent. He passes about four minutes and a half swinging in the air,
and is then lodged on the landing-place of the Monastery.

In this singular manner do the Monks of Meteora communicate with the
earth three hundred feet beneath them. They cast their net into the world
below; sometimes these monastic fishermen draw up an inquisitive traveller,
sometimes a brother Coenobite from Mount Athos, sometimes a Neophyte,
yearning for ascetic solitude: once they received in this manner an Emperor,
who came here, as is said, to exchange the purple of Constantine for the cowl
of St. Basil. The Monks show in their cloisters a tomb which they assert
contains the ashes of that Emperor, John Cantacuzene. If their information
is correct, or rather if the writer's recollection of it is accurate, the name of
their Monastery—commemorative of the transfiguration on Mount Tabor—as
well as that dedicated to Barlaam, which stands on the rock opposite, are
curious mementos of the religious controversy concerning the nature of the
divine light upon the Galilean Mountain, in which the Emperor, who thus
abdicated his royal dignities to assume the character of Monk and Historian,
took so active a part against the Calabrian Monk to whom the opposite
Monastery is inscribed.

The interior of the church is as handsome as painting and decoration can
make it. Having passed through the narthex, or ante-chapel, we enter the
body of the building, which is panelled with stalls; on the right is the
episcopal throne and the Prior's crozier. On a horizontal tablet in the nave
is a picture of the Virgin, inviting the devotion of her worshippers. In the
library of the Convent is a large collection of ecclesiastical authors, among
which are manuscripts of St. Chrysostom and St. Basil; the Codex of
Sophocles, which is said to have been there, has now disappeared.

It is remarkable that no notice of the singular rocks upon which these
monasteries stand should survive in the records of antiquity; the Hellenic
name, Meteora, which they bear, belongs to the present language of the
country. It is true there is an ancient town, described by a Roman Historian
as impregnable, which seems to have derived that character from its vicinity
to these towering rocks. The city to which we refer is ÆGINIUM, and this
supposition is confirmed by an ancient inscription which exists on the eastern
wall of the Church of St. John the Baptist at KALABAKA, a large village at
the southern foot of the cliffs of Meteora. The purport of this marble is to
commemorate certain honorary distinctions paid by that city to the Emperor

Lucius Septimius Severus, and his son Marcus Aurelius Antoninus Caracalla.
Addison, in his agreeable work on Medals, reminds us of *their* uses to
Geography and History. This stone furnishes an instance of the illustration
afforded by ancient INSCRIPTIONS to Topography. From it alone we are
enabled to determine the site of Æginium, a place of nearly the same
importance to those who entered Thessaly on the west, as the defile of Tempe
to an army marching into it from the east. From a knowledge of the position
of Æginium, that of other places before unknown may be determined. The

river ION flowed by Æginium : it is therefore the stream of Meteora. That
river was also the eastern boundary of the Tymphæan territory : hence the
limits of that district are ascertained. The city of OXYNIÆ, again, stood on
the banks of the Ion : its position therefore may be defined with a very near
approximation to the truth. Thus a fragment of stone, inscribed with only a
few words, may serve the same purpose as a chapter of Strabo or Pausanias.

Julius Cæsar, when he marched into Thessaly to meet Pompey, thought it indispensable to possess the fortresses of Æginium and Gomphi. By the first he kept open the communication with Dyrrhachium and Italy; through the second he corresponded with Athamania and the Ambracian Gulf. The former was the first object which he sought to gain on entering Thessaly; the latter was his next conquest when he penetrated further into that country. Æginium, we have seen, corresponds with the modern Kalabaka. The site of the latter was on one of the mountain ridges on the opposite or south side of the Penéus.

The ancient towns in this district are so numerous, that the traveller has neither time nor strength to examine them all. We are tempted to envy the lot of the Athenian General, for whom, while he was sleeping, Fortune, according to the picture, caught cities in a net. Few tourists have been able to climb all these hills in person, and explore the ruins upon them.

Passing along the left bank of the Penéus, and leaving on the right the castle of Tricca and the Cemetery, which contains many ancient columns, now used as tomb-stones, some of which perhaps once adorned the far-famed temple of Æsculapius in that city, we arrive at the small village of Glokoto. On the hill to the east of it are the walls of an Hellenic fortress in good preservation, and of four different eras, presenting specimens of the rough unhewn style of masonry, of the polygonal, the horizontal, and, lastly, of Roman brick-work. It is an agreeable surprise on mounting to the summit of this hill to find, not merely the ruins of one Greek citadel, but also to descry from them the walls of two others, on two eminences called Kortiki and Bloko, upon the opposite side of the stream. There exists another ruined fortress at Gritzano, about six miles to the north of our present situation.

The ancient walls of Bloko are seen from the plain, running up the hill in a zigzag line like a mountain road. The reader of modern Greek will recognise in its name the Εὔλοχος of the royal Byzantine Historian to whom we have alluded above, and it has perhaps succeeded the ancient city of Metropolis, which was formerly so important a station in this district of Thessaly, as leading from it into Ætolia. The same reason which induced the Athamanian King, Amynander, to aim at the conquest of Gomphi, led his Ætolian confederates to wish for the possession of Metropolis. Hence arose their dissensions. These places were the keys which unlocked the granaries of Thessaly to their respective countries, Gomphi to Athamania, Metropolis to Ætolia. From a consideration of their positions, the reason is evident why Cæsar in his Thessalian campaign passed immediately from the conquest of the one to the siege of the other.

In about four miles from Glokoto, we leave the town of Zarco on a hill nearly two miles to our left. This place is supposed, with much show of

probability, to coincide with the ancient PHARCALION. Here ends the district
of Thessaly, formerly called HISTIAEOTIS, and here we cross the river Penéus
by a ford to the right bank, shortly afterwards coming in sight of the white
minarets of the town of LARISSA.

The walls of this place exhibit that singular combination of fading
antiquity and tawdry novelty, which is generally seen in the productions of
Turkish art. They consist of fragments of old columns and architectural
mouldings, promiscuously stuck together in a coarse crust of mud. The city
gates are formed of gaping planks; their clumsy wooden cornice is surmounted by a marble slab, bedizened with a lunar crescent shining from a
dark cloud of straw and mortar. The Mosques are remarkable for their
number and magnificence: there are said to be twenty-four, while there exists
at Larissa but one Christian Church. The character of the population corresponds with these appearances. Nowhere will the traveller, who has come
from the west or the south of Greece, see so many grave figures, attired in
rich dresses, sitting quietly before their doors, as here. Nowhere will he meet
so many of those spectral female forms stealing along the streets in their long
white stoles, whose only visual communication with the world is by means of
the two orifices for their eyes, cut in their linen shrouds. Such is the

appearance of these Turkish Women, who recall to the memory the funeral-processions of the Florentine or Roman Fraternities, when engaged in their solemn functions of chanting a dirge, and following the bier of one of their brethren to the grave.

It is a peculiarity of the city of Larissa that carriages are occasionally seen passing to and fro through its gates; but the heavy creaking carts, which swing slowly over the wide plains of the neighbourhood on the opaque disks of their spokeless wheels, are more agreeable memorials of the past, and supply more significant expressions of the natural qualities which rendered the political and social character of the Thessalians what, in ancient times, it actually was.

This spacious, fruitful, and level region was the base on which that character was reared; it produced most of the excellences which distinguished it, and was abused to foster most of its vices. As upon it we see, for the first time, these tardy wains which, in the other parts of Greece, with few exceptions, would be useless; so in early times equestrian figures were first descried by the Greeks in the same plain, and grew here in their fancy into Centaurs.

In war, the Bow would prove a weapon of the most service in an open country similar to the present, and therefore Thessaly was famed in the military history of Greece for the skill and efficiency of its archers. Contrasting the bleak limestone cliffs, on the crests of which the towns of the other provinces of Greece are generally placed, with these level areas shaded by branching plane-trees, and watered by copious streams, you seem to perceive a reason why the inhabitants of Thessaly were distinguished from those of the other Hellenic tribes by their luxury and refinement, and especially by their passion for the dance. From the same cause it arose that this country was the arena of so many military struggles, and the theatre of so many campaigns, from the earliest period of Greek history to the days of Cæsar; and such being the case, it is not to be wondered that there was little of independence or integrity in the Thessalian character, which resembled that of men who proffered the loan of an Amphitheatre to any two rival *families* of gladiators who applied to them for its use, and, *after* the contest had terminated, professed a devoted attachment to the cause of the victors.

Some of the more generous and enthusiastic spirit of the former inhabitants of this country seems to have descended to their posterity. "What have we done," said the Primate of Larissa to the author of this volume, while at a window of his mansion looking over the waters of the Peneus, "of what have we been guilty, that we should be excluded by the last general treaty from the limits of free Greece? Have we not striven side by side with our fellow-countrymen for the liberty which they now enjoy? Have we not

UNIT BY OLYMPUS, FROM THE PLAINS OF THESSALY.

resisted year by year the cruel violence of our present masters, and struggled to shake their yoke from off our necks? We, the inhabitants of the ancient Hellas,—the cradle of Greece,—are banished from our own country! Olympus is excluded, and with it the Gods of Greece are exiled from Greece by your treaties! Look,"—pointing from the window as he spoke, to the stream which flows beneath it, which was then very low, and to the mountains capped with snow beyond it,—"the Peneüs has wept itself almost dry for grief, and Mount Olympus has grown old and hoary, for they are both exiles from their own land!"

The remains of the ancient city of Larissa are very inconsiderable; some fragments of the walls of the Hellenic citadel are said to be enclosed by the buildings of the Turkish bazaar. The modern name of the town is identical with the ancient. In the walls of the palace of the Greek Archbishop are many early inscriptions, which principally refer to contracts for the manumission of slaves, and call attention to the well-known fact, which reflects little honour upon the Thessalian character, that the traffic in slaves was here carried on with great activity, and that a considerable portion of the wealth of its former inhabitants was derived from this source. Other ancient inscriptions are supplied by the tombstones, which have been perverted from their original purpose, and now stand over the graves in the Turkish cemeteries of Larissa. One or two of them which we find there are not unworthy of a place in the Greek Anthology. The burying-grounds in which they are found present a singular appearance. They cover a considerable space; their columnar grave-stones of white marble, which are thickly crowded together, generally terminate in a crest or head-dress, which indicates the rank or profession of the person whose monument it is; the Bey, the Mollah, the Cadhi, and the Imam, each has his own badge in this funereal heraldry; the rank of one is expressed by the device of a mural crown, that of another by a conical apex, and of a third by a spherical tiara. The aid of colours is also called in to lend their eloquence to the silent epitaphs. We leave Larissa and proceed eastward:—

" Passing from Italy to Greece, the tales
Which Poets of an elder time have feigned
To glorify their Tempe, bred in me
Desire of visiting that Paradise.
To Thessaly I came, and, living private,
I, day by day, frequented silent groves
And solitary walks."

The character of the celebrated place thus referred to by Ford in his " Lover's Melancholy," is best illustrated by a reference to the inscription cut in the

rock on the right side of the vale,—" LUCIUS
CASSIUS LONGINUS, the PROCONSUL, made the
road through TEMPE."

The entrance of the Peneus into the narrow
defile of TEMPE, between the mountains of Olympus and Ossa, a few miles before its entrance into
the sea, suggested to Xerxes the reflection that
Thessaly might easily be flooded by damming up

this only outlet of the stream ; and the opinion that Thessaly was actually
covered by the Sea in more ancient times, appears not only probable in itself,

VALE OF TEMPE.

from a consideration of its physical form (and, as has
been suggested, from its name), but is confirmed by
the ancient traditions, which have assumed the form
of mythological legends, with respect to that country.
NEPTUNE, in these legends, strikes the rock with his
trident, and opens a passage for the imprisoned water
by the fissure, which received, from this circumstance,
the name of TEMPE, or THE CUTS. The war of the
GIANTS with the Gods, and the uprooting, by their
hands, of one of the mountains which flanked the
aperture in question, and its super-position on the
other, refer to a similar convulsion ; and the celebration of the nuptials, on a third and neighbouring
mountain (PELION, which was upheaved by the
belligerents' force), of the hero of the land, PELEUS,
with the goddess of the sea, THETIS, seems to refer
to the calm and peace of nature, and the reconcilia-
tion of the elements which ensued, when the tumult
of physical rebellion had subsided.

Tempe is a strong and important military pass.
To compare small things with great, Longinus did
for it what the Conqueror of Italy has done for the
Simplon. Tempe is a narrow rocky defile five miles
long, in which there is sometimes room only for the Peneus and a caravan to
travel side by side. The ledge of rock between the inscription specified
above, and the level of the stream, is only four feet in breadth, and the steps
hewn in its surface, which is furrowed by the wheels of military waggons, are
the result of the pioneering labour which that inscription is meant to commemorate. It was a suitable work for a general of Julius Cæsar to facilitate
the communication from Thessaly to Macedonia,—from Greece to the world
beyond it. The vale is, as its name indicates, a gorge or chasm ; a deep natural
canal, as its history records, through which an inland Lake once rolled away
from the plains of Thessaly into the waters of the Ægean Sea.

The prominent features of Tempe have a stern and severe aspect. The
rocks which wall in the valley on either side are lofty in size, abrupt in form,
in colour grey and sombre. The amenity of this celebrated glen does not
consist, if we may so say, in the *walls* of this natural Corridor, but in its
pavement. Let us pursue this comparison: it cannot boast of possessing any

mural arabesques or frescoes, but it is inlaid with flowers, and adorned as it were with a tesselated floor.　In this mosaic, more beautiful than that which

may be seen representing the Nile and its living and inanimate scenery in the Temple of Fortune at Praeneste, the river Peneus runs in a gentle stream, stimulated here and there by eager springs, bubbling from the earth by its side.　One such spring will be seen, close to the inscription to which we have before adverted, of the brightest and clearest green.　Growing in the river, and spreading their broad branches and thick foliage over its waters, are shady plane-trees, around whose boughs twine clusters of ivy and tendrils of the wild vine.　The banks are fringed with the low lentisk, the pliant Agnus Castus, and the sacred Bay from which Apollo culled the shoot which he transplanted to the borders of the Castalian rill.　The stream is said to abound with fish.　The solitary wood-pigeon haunts the trees.

Such are the beauties of Tempe; but it possesses other charms from its proximity to objects contrasted with it.　The traveller who has toiled through long and sultry days across the dusty plains of Thessaly, without a tree to shade or a breeze to refresh him, and with little variety of hill or dale to relieve the dull monotony of the landscape, will gladly and gratefully turn his steps into this valley, and will tread with delight the green turf by the water-side, beneath the shadow of these branching plane-trees, and of the grand and picturesque cliffs above him; and he will not then inquire too scrupulously what portion of the pleasure which he enjoys is derived from the presence of some agreeable qualities of the scene, and how much of it is due to the *contrast* it presents with others of a different description through which he has passed.

Pompey, after his defeat at PHARSALIA, rode rapidly from the field of battle to Larissa, and thence hastened to Tempe. That valley was the only outlet by which he could escape from Thessaly. He checked his horse upon the banks of the river in this glen, and quenched his thirst with some of the fresh water of the Peneus. It was then the height of summer, and he had ridden more than forty miles. . . . He never drank again of the rivers of Greece.

We are now tracing his course in an inverted direction. There are few objects of interest between Tempe and Pharsalia; the road lies over a wide vacant plain, with a few groups of huts here and there scattered about it, swelling occasionally in low undulations, but without trees or hedge-rows to vary and cheer its interminable expanse. The traveller seems to make little progress: he appears as it were to be becalmed in a sea of plain. At about twenty-five miles' distance from Larissa, and a little more than one before entering Pharsalia, or, as it is now called, Phersala, we cross a bridge over the wide bed of a river which in the summer season is nearly dry. Here is a fine view of Pherrala ; above the town, to the south-west of it, rises a craggy limestone hill, the site of the ancient Acropolis. With it commences the brink of the great basin of Thessaly. Beneath its declivity is a low range of white houses, irregularly built, and set off to advantage by the contrast of the dark groups of cypresses spiring upward among them, and seeming to multiply, by their natural tall minarets, those of the mosques which are near them. At the entrance of the town during the summer are fields of tobacco, with their tall flowering stalks ; on the rugged hill above the town we trace a long line of wall climbing upwards, which, from its massive rudeness, seems to have been contemporary with the heroic ages of Greece. Above these enormous masses are occasionally courses of the later polygonal style: at the crest of the hill this range of fortification abuts on a keep, from which another wall descends into the plain, so that the area of the Acropolis, contained by these two diverging lines and a third at their base, resembled that of a triangle, which was the usual form of ancient Greek citadels.

From the Acropolis we have a view of the plain lying at our feet, on which Cæsar gained the decisive victory which made him master of the Roman world. The field where the battle of Pharsalia was fought is situated between this hill and the river of which we have above spoken, formerly known by the name of Enipeus. Pompey drew up his forces so that his right wing might be protected by the rugged banks of that stream. The battle took place in August ; and whatever defence was afforded by them, little could then have been derived from the river itself. This part of his army consisted of the Cilician legion and the cohorts of Spain, which Pompey considered as his best troops. In the centre was Scipio, at the head of the legions from Syria. Pompey himself commanded the left wing, formed of the first and third legions, which had been transferred by the Senate from Cæsar to him at the commencement of the war. His camp was in the rear, on the south-east. Opposite to Pompey was Cæsar, at the head of the tenth legion, which he placed, as was his custom, in the right wing. As Pompey had strengthened his left with the whole force of his cavalry, amounting to about seven thousand men, and also with a numerous body of slingers and archers, Cæsar drew off from his own rear six cohorts, and posted them in opposition to these on his own right. His centre was led by Cneius Domitius Calvinus, and his left, which was the nearest to the Enipeus, by Mark Antony. The force of Pompey is said to have amounted to forty-five thousand, and that of Cæsar to about half the number. Pompey gave orders to his troops not to move from their position, in order that their enemies might be exhausted by a rapid charge through the whole interval which separated the contending armies. Cæsar's men having perceived this, slackened their pace of their own accord till they

came within a short distance of their antagonists, who received them with
firmness and intrepidity.   After the first onset, when both parties had discharged their javelins, and betaken themselves to their swords, the Pompeian
cavalry upon the left wing, together with the slingers and archers, succeeded
in turning their opponents, and were driving them from the field, when the six
cohorts which Cæsar had purposely stationed against them in anticipation of
such an event, made an attack upon them with so much vigour that they
completely routed and drove them immediately, as Cæsar himself relates, to
the loftiest mountains in their rear.   Pompey, seeing that the day was now
lost, rode to his camp, whither he was soon followed by the victor.   It was
now noon-day, and the weather was sultry, but the spirit of the pursuers
was not to be abated by heat or by fatigue.   The camp, after a strenuous

defence on the part of the cohorts, and especially of the Thracian auxiliaries
who had been left to guard it, was at last taken: in it were found bowers
twined with ivy, and furnished with tables loaded with plate, and all the
apparatus of a splendid banquet.   Such was the assurance with which the
adherents of Pompey looked forward to the result of the battle of Pharsalia!
He himself having entered the camp by the Prætorian Gate, or that nearest
the enemy, escaped from it by the Decuman, on the opposite side, and did not
check his horse till he arrived at the gates of Larissa.

It is a singular circumstance that the Conqueror on the plain of Pharsalia,

in the brief and modest narrative of a battle by which he became the master of
the civilized world, has omitted to mention the name of the place on which that
exploit was achieved. In the Commentaries of JULIUS CÆSAR we search in
vain for PHARSALIA. One would be almost tempted to believe that his
relation of that great victory was designed by him to be rather a private
memorial to himself, than the means, as it has proved, of extending the
fame of his military courage and skill to all countries and through all ages of
the world. How different from this is the treatment of the same subject by
the Poet, who has made the campaign of Pharsalia the theme of an Epic
Decad, and has put an eloquent speech, framed to deter Pompey from the
engagement, into the mouth of the great Orator of the time, who, at the period
of which Lucan speaks, was at a distance of more than two hundred miles
from the Pharsalian field!

After crossing, on our way eastward toward PHERÆ, the bridge of the
Enipeus, we arrive at the small hamlet of Magoula. The remains of ancient
Thessalian cities are said to exist at Dirilé, Kaslar, Zanglé, and Inilé, all of
which, in the above order, are on the right side of the road from Pharsalia to
Pheræ. Hills low and broken now begin to rise on both sides of us, and the
road to wind among the fibres of the roots of Mount Othrys; amid those on

the left, the armies of Philip and Flamininus were entangled, till at length the
former found his adversary and conqueror at CYNOSCEPHALÆ.

The natural beauty of Pheræ—the modern Belestina—was perhaps one
of the reasons why it was chosen as the scene in which a wife is represented as
consenting to die for her husband. The sacrifice of herself by ALCESTIS,
marvellous as it appears when we consider the notions generally entertained
in Greece of the female character and the conjugal relations, derives fresh
interest from the features of the place with which it is connected. The
Thessalian Queen resigned all the pleasures and bade adieu to all the charms
with which human life is adorned in a beautiful country; and even now, when
that country is as it were extinct, and there is no Alcides at hand to revive it,
as he restored her—

"Rescued from death by force, tho' pale and faint,"—

to its former life and grace, yet Pheræ is still remarkable for its fairness among
the cities of Greece. The old walls of the city skirt the lower town on the
south; on the outside of them, in the southern valley is the cemetery, glittering
with white tombstones; within the walls are houses scattered in picturesque
groups, and intermingled with trees,—elms, planes, poplars, and cypresses,—
almost concealing the city from itself, so that the place presents the appearance
of a cluster of houses in a woody dell. Proceeding a little further to the north,
we cross a stream expanding itself into a wide basin of clear water overhung
by Oriental planes. The white kiosks which stand upon its brink prove the
pleasantness of a place to which we may be allowed to imagine Alcestis
addressing the words of her tenderest and most affectionate farewell. This
lake was to her what the flowers of Paradise were to Eve :—

"Farewell, Phœraœn land! and thou, my own
Fount HYPEREA, most beloved by Gods!"

The site of the ancient Acropolis is further to the north, on a ridge of
hills in shape like large tumuli running from east to west. Here the lake of
BŒBE is distinctly seen lying a few miles to the north, on the right of the
road to Larissa. To the west of the Acropolis are the foundations of a temple
on which a church now stands, and with which walls of polygonal masonry—
perhaps those of the sacred inclosure—are connected.

The approach from Pheræ to VOLO from the north is remarkable for its
beauty. The road slopes gradually down a gentle declivity between two
ranges of undulating hills; in front is the wide plain, and beyond it the Gulf
of Volo. The town stands at the centre of the bay. On the left is Mount
PELION rising aloft, and stretching down the length of the MAGNESIAN peninsula; its crest even in the summer is capped with snow, and its shelving sides

are starred with a rich profusion of white villages, hanging, one above the other, on the sides of the grassy mountain. Within them are luxuriant gardens, in which the vines weave themselves into trellis-work, or cluster round the branches of trees. Beneath the plane-trees which abound there glistens the bright leaf of the pomegranate bursting with its red fruit. By the garden hedges numerous springs gush from the earth, and run downwards into the vale of Volo.

The traveller who walks from Volo to the south will arrive in an hour's time at the summit of an isolated hill, which is as it were one of the last struggles of Mount Pelion before it loses itself in the PAGASÆAN Gulf. It is called GORITZA. On it are considerable remains of an ancient city: it juts into the sea, so as almost to form a peninsula, a circumstance which added much to the strength of the place. The masonry is for the most part of the style called *emplecton*, being composed of loose stones thrown into the interval between the two external faces of the wall, and is not therefore of a very early age. The city whose area we are now treading was one of much importance. If we regard its general position, it is on the brink of the Gulf of Pagasæ : if the peculiarity of its site, it stands on a strong peninsula. In extent it occupies a wide space ; in form it is elevated on a rugged hill, and, in its external relations, it is far superior to any other site in its neighbourhood.

These circumstances afford strong evidence that this city was one of the three *Fetters of Greece*,—that these walls are, in a word, the remains of the ancient DEMETRIAS.

This conviction is strengthened by a visit to the conical hill about a mile to the north-west of Goritza. We pass through vineyards and across a brook

in our way thither. On its summit is a venerable church of the mediæval style, called Panaghia Episcopi : in it are many marbles, fragments of a more early structure ; and in its walls is inserted a slab inscribed with the name of Demetrias, which is the title now given by the villagers in the neighbourhood to the whole district, and which it undoubtedly derived from the city whose ruins we have just visited, which was the capital of the circumjacent province.

Having determined the position of Demetrias, we are furnished with a clue for the discovery of some of its lost dependencies. We know from Livy and Strabo that the city of JASON was about a mile to the north of Demetrias : is, therefore, this conical hill, with its venerable church, the site of the citadel of Iolcus ? The mountain stream of the Anaurus flowed between Iolcus and Demetrias : is the clear rivulet which we crossed in our way hither, and are the vineyards through which we passed, the same as those of which Simonides sang when he recited the praises of the hero who conquered all the youth of Thessaly, by hurling his spear from the vineyards of Iolcus over the eddying stream of the Anaurus?

On the summit of Mount Pelion was the cave of Cheiron. With him, the "*justest of Centaurs*," was associated the idea entertained by the Greeks of early Hellenic education. This grotto was the School from which their national heroes went forth into the world. The hero of Pharsalia, for instance, was brought from the plains of Thessaly to the summit of Mount Pelion. Here, as in a natural Observatory, he was taught to contemplate, by night, the motions of the stars; by day he was led over the mountain sides, and instructed in the nature and properties of the plants with which they abound; and within the cave he learnt to touch the lyre.

The *form* of Cheiron, the ideal instructor of the heroic age, presents an evidence that the animal and intellectual were blended together in the instruction of that period; the intellectual element, however, bearing the same ratio to the animal, that the human *head* of the instructor did to his equine *body*.

His name seems to be derived from his *manual* accomplishments, and furnishes proof of the value attached, in the earliest times,—a fact well known from the special testimony of Homer,—to skill in the medical and surgical arts. Indeed, it is not improbable that the *botanical* fertility by which Mount Pelion is distinguished among the mountains of Greece, may have recommended it for the site of the Greek heroic School, in whose course of instruction a knowledge of Pharmacy,—to which those sciences were then chiefly

restricted.—held so prominent a part, and which was peculiarly necessary to
the warriors of that age.   It is sufficient to refer to the *name* of IASON, who
was educated here, and who sailed from Aphetæ, on which now stands the
castle of THIKERI, at the south-western foot of this hill, as a confirmation of
this.   It is a noticeable fact, that at the present day the country of Cheiron
has produced very many of the medical practitioners of Greece.

EPIRUS
ACARNANIA
ETOLIA

WE cast anchor at the mouth of the
Ambracian Bay, or, as it is now called, the
Gulf of Arta. On the right of us is a low
headland;—on the left the modern town of Prevyza. The Roman Poet, Propertius, invites the
traveller to be mindful of Augustus Cæsar in his
voyages over the whole of the Ionian Sea. Here, upon
this coast, stood that Emperor when he had just conquered
the world.

Let us contemplate the appearance which this spot now
presents. At the entrance of the bay of Actium are two mud-built forts,
one on each side of it; on their battlements are mounted some rusty cannon,
in whose mouths are fixed certain dingy implements employed to sweep the

cobwebs from these crazy pieces of Turkish artillery; above them floats a standard displaying gilded stars, and a tinsel crescent. You may see children playing in the rotten hulk of a ship of war; and the waters themselves seem weary, as if sinking into a languid lethargy on the shallow shore.

On the southern promontory of which we have spoken, stood the Temple of the ACTIAN APOLLO. On the second of September, the famous fourth of the Nones of that month, in the year B.C. 31, the whole of the strait between this point and the opposite coast, as well as the basin to which they form the entrance, and which is as it were the outer court of the large area of the Ambracian Gulf, was filled with the vessels of Mark Antony. These vessels were distinguished by their enormous size and the variety of their equipments. Bactria, India, and Armenia furnished contributions to that vast armament. In the rear was Cleopatra in her gilded ship, spreading to the wind its purple sail, and attended by an Ægyptian fleet bearing the standard and the Gods of that country. At this spectacle the Galatian troops of Antony, consisting of two thousand horse, deserted to Cæsar, while some of his vessels retreated stern foremost to the harbour on their left upon the Acarnanian Coast.

The fleet of Augustus stretched from north to south, facing the entrance of the Bay. He at first attempted to draw Antony from his position in the straits into the open sea; but, having failed in this endeavour, he advanced toward the east, with the view of inclosing the enemy by expanding and subsequently contracting his own wings. To prevent this, Antony moved forward, and the engagement commenced. He was superior in the magnitude of his vessels, bearing a resemblance to moving castles or fortresses, and which the Poet compares to Cyclades riven from their foundations; and even the sober language of History describes them "as groups of islands resisting the assault of the foe like Cities under a siege."

The fleet of Augustus was composed mainly of triremes, whose excellence consisted in their lightness and celerity. Several of them at once surrounded the large ships of Antony, whose soldiers defended themselves by hurling missiles from the wooden towers which they bore. The battle lasted for several hours, and, in the language of Shakspeare's Soldier of Antony,

" — Vantage like a pair of twins appear'd
Both as the same, or rather ours the elder ; "

when a breeze from the land sprung up, as is not unusual upon this coast in the day-time, and Cleopatra, taking advantage of the favourable gale, as represented by Virgil on the shield of Æneas, was seen unfolding her canvas, and sweeping along with her sixty ships at full sail through the forces of the enemy into the main sea, and thence along the western coast of the Peloponnesus. Antony forthwith abandoned his fleet, and followed her. But notwithstanding his absence, the battle lasted till evening, when the wind changed, and a heavy surf from the sea broke upon the large vessels, rendering it impossible for them to resist any longer the attack of their assailants, who set them on fire by torches, while flaming javelins and combustibles were discharged from their engines; five thousand men were slain, and three hundred ships taken by the victorious army.

IN the angle at the southern side of the entrance of the Bay is a promontory now called PUNTA, and formerly ACTIUM. Here, as was before noticed, stood the temple of the Actian Apollo. From this point that Deity was pictured by the Poet as aiming his shafts against the foes of Augustus; and here games were afterwards celebrated in honour of Apollo, and in gratitude for the victory obtained by his aid.

To the north and west of this point lie the ancient countries of Acarmania and Ætolia, their northern frontier being formed by a continuation of the Ctuan chain, under the name of the AGRÆAN Hills, terminating on the shores of the Ambracian Gulf, the Ionian Sea with its islands forming the western boundary. Towards the entrance to the Gulf of Corinth the coast-line retires, leaving the narrow passage between the mainland and the island of Zante

WESTERN COAST OF GREECE, FROM THE INDIAN SEA.

occupied by the group of low islands, lying opposite to the mouth of the
Achelous, which are known as the ECHINADES. The island of Cephalonia
on the north forms, with Zante on the south, the passage into the gulf known
as the Canal of Patras. From the mouth of the Achelous and Cape Artemita,
the northern shore of the Corinthian Gulf forms the southern boundary of
Ætolia, passing the bay and town of Missolonghi, rendered famous for its
obstinate defence during the war of Greek independence. From Patras the
coast of Ætolia appears as represented in the accompanying view. On the
opposite shore Mount Chalcis rises bold and precipitous from the water to the
height of several hundred feet. More to the left the bay of Missolonghi and
the Echinades are visible.

COAST OF ÆTOLIA, FROM PATRAS

A little higher up the gulf, the eastern boundary of Ætolia is reached at
Naupactus. This promontory may be considered as the termination of the
range of Mount Pindus, which forms the eastern boundary of the countries
now under consideration.

The straits of Lepanto are formed by the ancient promontory of Antirrhium on the north and Rhium on the south side of the gulf; beyond it
towers the lofty Mount Rigaro, rising four thousand feet above the level of the

sea.   On a ridge of this mountain stands the ancient castle of Naupactus, now Lepanto, at the height of four hundred and eighty feet above the sea.

The principal rivers which water these countries are—the Achelous, now the Aspropotamo, (separating Acarnania on the east from Locris and afterwards from Ætolia, it flows in a south-west direction into the Ionian Sea at Cape Artemita,) and the Evenus, flowing through Ætolia into the Gulf of Corinth between the bay of Missolonghi and the ancient Naupactus. Numerous lakes also occur, of which the largest is Lake Cynia, whose circumference is about twenty miles.

Returning to the Gulf of Arta, we proceed to the south across the straits to the town of Prevyza, on the opposite coast. The streets of this town are narrow and roughly paved; no carriages, and few women are to be seen there. In the summer season the shops ex-hibit supplies of tobacco, peaches, and figs, and other natural produce, but very little display of manu-

CASTLE OF PREVYZA.

factured goods.   A woolen awning projects over their windows, under which their tenants sit in cross-legged indolence.

The Pasha's Serail is on the north side of the entrance of the gulf.   If the traveller should wish to pay his respects to his Highness, he will enter a courtyard, where he may see his horses ranged side by side, and will thence ascend by a staircase to the apartment of the Vizier.   The floor is matted: a divan or sofa, covered with red embroidered Albanian cloth, runs round the walls.   There is a whitewashed fire-place, and the panels of the room are unpainted.   He will probably find the Pasha reclining on the divan near the window which looks towards the ruins of Actium and the Temple of Apollo. Several Turks stand before him with shoeless feet, and among them a drago-man wearing a dark-red tunic and light-coloured sandals, who, when the

Pasha, or Most Sublime Vizier, as he is called, has finished a sentence, puts
his right hand to his heart and then to his lips, in order to intimate that the
words of his lord and master have entered the one and will soon issue from
the other. He then translates them to the party for whom they are intended.
The visitors are invited to sit on the divan, and are presented with long
cherry-stick pipes with amber mouth-pieces and brown clay bowls by the
attendants, who then kneel and put small brass basins on the floor under the
pipes for the reception of their ashes. This practice, devised for the sake of
cleanliness and for the protection of his carpet, indicates that the Turk is not
destitute of prudential principles in household economy, and that he has not
carried his doctrine of fatalism into the smallest details—even into the pipe
bowls and brass basins of daily life.

At the close of the day, the traveller returns to his night's lodging in the
town of Prevyza. The Greek mistress of the house lights the small lamps
which hang before the pictures of the saints upon her wall; the voice of the
Turkish Muezzin has ceased to call from the Minaret to evening prayer, and
nothing is heard but the dismal howl of the jackal, which becomes more
distinct as the darkness steals on.

On our route to NICOPOLIS, we pass through the northern gate of Prevyza.

A few muskets of different fashions are ranged under its archway; some Albanian guards in motley attire doze or smoke on the drawbridge. Immediately beyond is the Turkish cemetery. The white tombs are overgrown with thistles, and the sentences of the Koran inscribed upon them are becoming illegible. The road crosses a wide sandy plain covered with low clumps of myrtle, fern, and bramble. In three quarters of an hour we arrive at the remains of Nicopolis.

The words of Mamertinus, addressed to the Emperor Julian, which refer to this city, are very descriptive of its present appearance. " The town of Nicopolis," he says, " which the deified Augustus erected as a Trophy in memorial of his Victory at Actium, has almost fallen into lamentable decay. The palaces of the Nobles are rent; the Forums are roofless; the Aqueducts crushed ; everything is smothered with dust and rubbish."

The grandeur of the impression produced by these ruins arises from their solitude and extent. A long lofty wall spans a desolate plain. To the north of it rises on a distant hill the shattered Scene of a Theatre, and to the west the extended though broken line of an aqueduct connects the distant mountains from which it tends with the main subject of the picture, the city itself. The very spacious area bounded by these objects is filled by an irregular group of mouldering red-coloured ruins of houses, baths, tombs, and temples. The external appearance of these remains probably conveys a tolerably correct idea of the ancient city in its political, social, and moral character. It was built principally of Roman brickwork: and the details of its architecture indicate but little skill, strength, or refinement of execution. It was erected to commemorate a victory gained on a Grecian sea by a Roman conqueror; and was intended by him to prove and consolidate his power over the inhabitants of the Hellenic soil ; it was, if we may be allowed the comparison, a great Zoological Garden, into which Greeks of the different tribes of Epirus, Acarnania, and Ætolia, were brought from their native hills, in order to be trained in the arts of civilisation and caged like prisoners by Imperial Rome.

We cannot forbear from sympathizing with these wild mountaineers when, uprooted from their own free villages, they quitted the massive walls and castellated gates by which those villages were defended, and came to live under the protection of the red brick ramparts which surrounded this City of Victory. They descended from their healthy hills into this low and swampy plain, and exchanged the clear native fountains which gushed from beneath the rocks of their own citadels, for water drawn from lead pipes and a stuccoed aqueduct,—they sacrificed the natural pleasures of the field and of the chase in order to come and sit through their long days under an awning on the seats of one of these Theatres, filled with courtly gentlemen and Romans. It is said that the festival of St. Peter ad Vincula has superseded that which commemorated the battle of Actium; and we would fain indulge a hope that in lieu of all these enjoyments and blessings, of which they were then deprived, the Greek colonists of Nicopolis were consoled with one greater than them all,—that they saw, heard, and talked with the Apostle St. Paul, who was debtor to the Greeks, when he spent a winter at Nicopolis.

We have imagined the Spectators in this Theatre as sitting under a Velarium; and this we do on the authority of the stone grooves which still remain inserted in the external wall of the Cavea, and in which the vertical props for this awning were fixed. When the awning was outstretched, the Theatre would not have been darkened by its expansion, for there are windows in the wall of the Cavea. Between them are niches, in which

statues were placed. There do not appear to have been more than two Praecinctions: the Viae were ten. The Pulpitum is raised to a considerable height above the area of the Orchestra. In the provisions for its Velarium, as well as in its general arrangement, the larger Theatre at Nicopolis, of which we are speaking, bore a strong resemblance to the greater one at Pompeii, and to that of Taurominium in Sicily. Augustus does not seem to have so far Romanized the character of his subjects in this city, as to invite them to the sanguinary exhibitions in which his own countrymen sought relaxation and delight. There is no Amphitheatre at Nicopolis; but the pleasures of the Circus were more congenial to the taste of its inhabitants,—and with good reason; for their country, Epirus, was celebrated for its breed of horses. We have therefore a Stadium here, a little to the west of the Theatre. It measures two hundred and sixty paces in length, and twenty-five in level breadth.

The wall of the city, along which we pass from the Stadium to the minor Theatre or Odeum, is of varied masonry. On three horizontal courses of stone rise six of brick, surmounted by a large stage of *opus incertum*, which is again overlaid by a heavy pile of brick, and the whole crowned with a coping of rubble. A fit emblem this of the miscellaneous population with which the city was filled! The Greek stone at the foundation, then the Roman brick, then the *opus incertum* of the Barbarian and Oriental elements, all conglomerated together!—How different from the one solid mass into which the heavy blocks of Greek masonry are wedged by their own pressure, or even from that regular and systematic network into which a genuine Roman wall is woven with equal symmetry and strength !

CYCLOPEAN WALLS AT EPIDAURUS

Toward the southern extremity of this wall and to the north-west of the Odeum, is a large oblong building whose sides are indented with niches, in each of which are the outlets of small pipes, which communicate by canals along the wall of the fabric with two stuccoed *castella*, or reservoirs of water, one at each end, which are still encrusted with a calcareous deposit, and which were fed by the aqueduct of the city. We are to conceive now, that each of these niches was adorned with a marble statue of a Naiad or a Nereid, holding before them lavers or shells of marble; we are also to imagine liquid streams spouting from every outlet into these lavers, and then flowing over their brims into a large clear Frigidarium of the same material. Such a picture, especially in the heat of a summer's day, will give us an idea of the arts by which the wild inhabitants of the neighbouring hills were seduced into civility and servitude by the Imperial Conqueror at Actium.

The road from Nicopolis to Arta follows the direction of the Aqueduct

mentioned above along the eastern inclination of Mount ZALONGO, till it
arrives at the village of LURO, which consists of twenty-five huts; it passes
in its way through gardens of melons and gourds, and through hedges shaded
with plum-trees hung with the tendrils and clusters of the wild vine. At a
little distance from Luro we arrive at the river of the same name, which is
crossed in a ferry-boat. No remarkable object occurs in the road, which
passes over a series of low hills, till it comes to the brink of a second river,
that of ARTA.

Arta stands upon the site of the ancient AMBRACIA. The proof of this,
derived from classical authorities, is much strengthened by a personal in-
spection of the place. The general character of the site corresponds with that
which is ascribed to Ambracia. It lies in a wide fertile plain surrounded by
hills; which circumstance, a remarkable one in this region, seems to have
suggested the name of the city, and to have attracted the attention of the
Corinthians, who selected it as a desirable place for planting a colony. In
after times, it also induced the enterprising Pyrrhus to make Ambracia the
seat of the government of Epirus.

The river of Arta, flowing from the north-east, bends itself into a bow, in
the interior of which, on the eastern side of it, the city stands. Just within
the north-eastern horn of this curve stands a castle of the Greek empire,
distinguishable by the painted minaret of its mosque. It is on a gentle
declivity about a mile in circuit, and built upon ancient foundations formed
of massive blocks in horizontal courses. This is not the oldest remnant of
Ambracia. To the south of it, separated by a narrow valley, in which is the
church of St. Theodore, rises a craggy hill, more than two miles round,
surmounted by walls of polygonal style, the vestiges of the ancient Acropolis.
On the north-east of this hill one of the gates of the citadel is still visible,
now called Megale Porta, or the Great Gate. Near it is the church of the
Madonna Phaneromené,—so called from a miraculous image formerly hidden
and then suddenly brought to light,—which is built on ancient foundations,
perhaps those of the Temple of Minerva, which seems to have stood on an
eminence like this. The hill itself appears to have been called PERRHANTUE.
In the beautiful plain beneath it the town of Ambracia extended northward
and westward from its roots to the curve of the river. The modern city
occupies part of the same space, and presents a pleasing sight to the spectator
from this hill, with its domed churches and tall black cypresses and white
mosques grouped together amid fruitful gardens of great luxuriance. Looking
in the opposite direction from the highest point of this hill, we have a view of
the gulf to which Arta gives a name now as Ambracia did of old.

The population of Arta is now estimated at six thousand. The town suffered severely in the plague of 1815, as its buildings did in the campaign of 1821, which decided the fate of Ali Pasha. It is a place of considerable importance, as being the key of the commerce between the towns of the Epirot provinces, such as ARGYRO-KASTRO and BERAT, and those of Acarnania and Ætolia. The principal articles of this trade are exhibited to the eyes of the traveller as he passes down the bazaar, a long street covered over with an awning of fern and reeds, which fence off the heat and sun, and admit a dim light. The shops which line this avenue are of wood; the windows are unglazed; from them projects a low wooden platform covered with a mat, upon which the occupant of the shop sits, with his rich stuffs and other wares hanging behind him. On some of these wooden platforms are piled large brown heaps, almost like haycocks, of tobacco; others present an array of red sandals; here hang embroidered belts; there lie pistols and dirks with silver classed handles; here sit money-changers with wire-cases before them, containing varieties of coinage from many quarters of the world; silk shawls of the gayest hues, vests richly braided with gold, sparkling phials of rosolio, and, at the furthest extremity of the vista, a profusion of melons and grapes: these objects together present a beautiful picture of the resources of Arta, even under its present governors. It is, indeed, very agreeable to pass from the open sky and the glare of the hot sun into this shaded avenue, whose gloom is enlivened by many cheerful colours, while its tranquillity is not disturbed by the sound of wheels or the noise of its inhabitants, who sit in grave postures, and generally in profound silence.

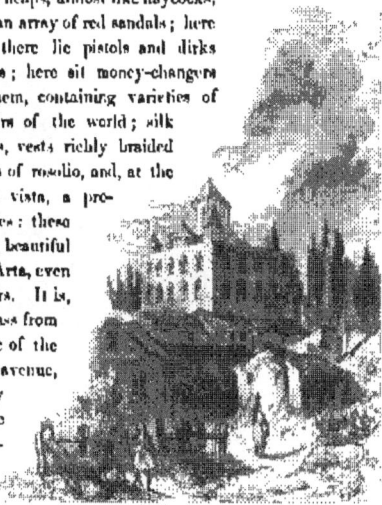

The churches of Arta are remarkable for their size and beauty; that of the Madonna Paregoritza, or of Consolation, is one of the oldest and most magnificent among them: the interior of its principal dome is inlaid with gilded and painted mosaic in the Byzantine style, from the centre of which hangs a tall branching chandelier. In its pavement is an inscription of the early times of Ambracia, too mutilated to be transcribed, and containing only a few

syllables of proper names, which, like those of greater men, who have been
deprived of immortality by some evil chance, have been broken off from after
ages by a few inches.

Another church of some interest is that of St. Theodora: it contains
the tomb of that saint, who is described as one of the Comnenian family,
and foundress of a monastery dedicated to the Virgin. On the paneling
between the nave and the chancel, and above the three doors which lead to the
latter, are whole-length portraits inlaid with gilding in a gaudy style, as is
usually the case in Greek churches of large dimensions: the figures are
thirteen in number, and placed as follows:—At each of the two extremities
are two apostles; nearer to the centre, on each side, are two evangelists;

RUINS OF THE ACROPOLIS.

corresponding to each other, are St. Peter and St. Paul; next to the former
is the Virgin, and to the latter St. John the Baptist; and in the centre of
them all, is our Blessed Saviour. The order in which they are arranged is
that which is usually adopted for such paintings by the Greek Church. On
the walls of the Triforium are portraits of male and female saints. It is remarkable that while the former *face* the spectator, the latter are seen only in *profile*.
This method of representation seems to have derived its origin from the
opinion, that while the faith of a Christian man should exhibit itself with a

bold full face fronting the world, the religion which usually best becomes women is that of meekness and modesty, gentleness and retirement.

Perseus was detained for several days on the banks of the Arethon, or Aracthus, the river which flows by the town of Arta, and from which it derives its name; and the traveller who remembers this circumstance will be thankful for the facility now provided for crossing it by a handsome stone bridge over the stream. On the other or western side of this bridge, the paved road lies through a rich and well-cultivated plain, which received from its ancient Monarchs a pleasing acknowledgment of its fertility, in the emblems engraved upon the coins which recorded their own honours. Thus on those of Pyrrhus, the Epirot king, Ceres appears holding ears of corn in her right hand. Ancient money, in this respect, possessed this advantage over modern, that in presenting to the eye the principal characteristics of the soil and country to which it belonged, it indicated and inspired a feeling of patriotism, which was thus made, as it were, a part of the national currency.

Passing the small village of Roca, perhaps so called from the large quantity of Indian corn, known here by that name, which is cultivated near it, we arrive, in an hour and a quarter from Arta, at the river of Luro, which is the western limit of the Ambracian plain. The stream is crossed in a canoe; and in a quarter of an hour, going westward, we arrive at the foot of the hill on which stand the Hellenic ruins, now called Rogus.

The site of this ancient city is a very fortunate one. It commands the western entrance to the basin of Ambracia, and is defended on three sides by a navigable river. The ruins themselves are not of a very early date; the plan of the Acropolis is regular, and proves that, at the time of its erection, the science of military architecture was far advanced. In the surrounding wall, rectangular towers occur at regular intervals, and built in horizontal courses of masonry. The structure of the wall itself is beautifully symmetrical, and partakes almost of the precision and compactness of mosaic.

This city is rendered very interesting by the excellent preservation of its remains. In a few weeks it might be made ready for the reception of a colony from Corinth or Ambracia, and put in a condition to stand a siege. The restorations of its walls, both of Roman and Gothic times, prove that it was considered of importance in both. In the centre of the citadel are the ruins of a monastic church, containing some frescoes which might have furnished materials to Dante for sketches in his Inferno. At the southern angle of the Acropolis is a pleasing view of the river winding at the foot of the city, and of the broad expanse of the Ambracian Gulf in the distance.

Proceeding among the woods on the right or western bank of the river, we bear to the north-west, among the low hills which lead into the plain of

Lelovo. At a few miles to the north-east of that village is the woody, steep, and conical hill of Kastri, on which are the ruins of an ancient Greek citadel. Beneath the hill, on the east, is seen a beautiful valley, with a lake. The remains of Kastri appear to be of the same date as those before described of Rogús; but there is this difference in the character of the two places, that the former seems to have been built almost exclusively for the purpose of attack and defence, and not for habitation; while the latter was well adapted for both. The one was a citadel, the other a city.

But, in the meantime, who were the inhabitants of these two places, which we have just visited?—by what achievements were they distinguished?—to what nations did they belong?—what were the fortunes, what were even the names of the cities themselves? The evidence which is afforded for replying to these questions is very scanty, and can only conduct to a conjectural result. Philip, the son of Demetrius, King of Macedon, was induced by the urgent entreaties of the Epirots to besiege Ambracus, which was favourably situated for furthering the designs of an enemy desirous, as the Epirots were, of hovering over the territory of Ambracia. Ambracus is described by the historian Polybius, in his narrative of Philip's campaign, as situated among marshes, and having only one approach from the Ambracian country by a narrow artificial causeway through the morass. Supposing, as seems most natural, that Ambracus was on the frontier line between Epirus and Ambracia, this marsh must have lain between Ambracus and the plain of Ambracia; that is, on the south-east of the former. It was of no great extent, but was well fortified by a wall and towers. After a siege Philip took it, and delivered it to the Epirots. He then marched rapidly by a city called Charadra, aiming at the narrowest part, that is, the mouth of the Ambracian Gulf, which he was eager to cross in his route into Acarnania. It appears from this circumstance, that Charadra was in a direct line between Ambracus and Actium. These details are, we think, sufficient to warrant the surmise, that the Ambracus coincided in site with Kastri. The Epirots, from their situation and from their want of strength, would neither have desired, nor have been able, to maintain a fortress hanging over the Ambracian frontier had it not been in their own neighbourhood, and therefore on the north-west side of the enemy's country. Again, we hear of no opposition made by the city of Ambracia to the besiegers of Ambracus; which, had Ambracus been on the Gulf of Ambracia, and thus the door of the commerce of that city, would surely have been the case. The site of the lake and morass on the south-east of the hill of Kastri, confirms the above conclusion.

Allowing its correctness, we have little difficulty in ascertaining the ancient name of the city above described, which stood upon the site of Rogús. Philip, after the siege of Ambracus, hastened towards Actium, and passed Charadra in his way, which was therefore in a direct line between these two points. The only site which satisfies this condition, and where there are any remains of an Hellenic age, is Rogús. The name, too, of Charadra supposes a river in its vicinity, which is there the case. The term Charadrus, by which the river of Charadra was known, indicates a soil broken into ravines and gullies; and, in a similar manner, the word Rogús seems to be derived from the appellation given to abrupt chasms and gorges in the ancient language of Greece.

The Lake of Xero-Limnó bears some resemblance to that of Ulleswater, in Westmoreland. It lies among high limestone rocks, which are covered by many varieties of dark green shrubs and trees hanging over the water, and deepening the shade cast on it by its steep banks. Here and there some water-flowers bloom upon the surface, and throw a little light upon its gloomy colour. The only sounds near it are those of the wild-fowl startled from its weeds by the footsteps of the traveller. The road lies on the eastern brink; it is skirted by a forest of oak, beech, and maple, which thickens on both sides as we proceed. The river is heard dashing along its rocky bed, at no great distance to our right, but is not seen from the route till we cross a path which passes over it by the bridge of the "Pasha's Lady." The views here are magnificent,—such as Salvator Rosa would have exulted in. The river tosses itself in cascades; shattered plane-trees torn up by its violence are lying over the stream; along their trunks some speckled goats may be seen climbing, while on the other side of the water the goat-herd appears with his scarlet cap shining through the trees. We continue our track on the right bank of the stream. The traveller who diverges from his course here will perhaps be driven back to it by wolves, which are not uncommonly met with in this solitary wood. Ascending to the right over some grand castellated rocks of grey limestone, we enter a more open country; but there is no appearance in it of living creature or human habitation. After proceeding a little further to the north, we again approach the river, and enter a small village by its side.

In the summer and autumnal months, CHARADZO—for that is its name—is deserted; the inhabitants close their windows, lock up their doors, and quit their houses, which they surrender at this season to the mosquitoes that infest the place, and drive them from their homes. Apollo Apomuios might do good service here. The luxuriant fields of rice, as well as an abundance of marshy plants in the neighbourhood, present infallible indications of the prevalence of malaria, which operates as another cause for their emigration.

The road from Charadzo lies along the wide and pebbly bed of the ancient Charadrus, a name which seems to be connected with that of the village above mentioned: it leads through long thickets of thorny paliurus, and occasionally deviates into swampy fields of Indian corn. The valley contracts itself into a defile, on both sides of which are very lofty rocks: those on the left are clothed to their summit with trees; the shrubs which wave in the wind at the top are scarcely visible, on account of their height; the cultivated patches of the valley are filled with granone, and the soil is everywhere irrigated with limpid streams. An ancient fortress rises on the rocks to the right, to guard the entrance of the gorge; it is called TEBAVO: a second, named MESITITZA, is at two miles' distance from it on the left; in the valley beneath is a water-mill, pleasantly sheltered by trees. The ridge of mountains to the north is called TOMARITZA, that to the north-west OLITZA. Following the valley, we leave on our right the narrow pass of ZAGATORO, where, it is asserted by the peasantry, are ruins of an ancient citadel on the north side of the defile. Similar remains are said to exist between Mules and Kopáni, at THEMAKEN.

The present route offers a prospect of many geographical and antiquarian discoveries to the traveller; and, even should his success in these respects be below his anticipations, it will more than repay him for his labour by the singular beauty of its natural scenery. After a ride of twelve hours from Charadzo, we arrive at the gates of JANNINA.

Of Jannina much has been said and written. Its site and surrounding objects are as familiar to all as descriptions and sketches can make them. Its history, society, and government have all received due notice; antiquities it has none. The city certainly, perhaps even its lake, is but a few centuries old. The place now possesses less interest than was recently the case, and has fallen into comparative decay with the fortunes of Ali Pasha, its late extraordinary master.

A few steps lead us from the palace of Ali to his grave. It is a simple tomb of white stone, shrouded over with some wild plants growing above it. It affords a striking evidence of the vanity and emptiness of all the eulogies which have been lavished upon the political prudence and sagacity of this Napoleon of Greece. They would indeed have been worth something, could he, while domineering far and wide from this his citadel, have foreseen this one event, which most concerned himself,—that this would be the result and end of the system he was then pursuing with all his ingenuity and power, that his headless body would in a few years lie under a plain plastered slab, in his own court-yard!

There is a Mosque near the tomb, which commands a fine view of the lake over which it stands. The traveller is permitted to enter it when he has taken off his shoes. It is a plain square room, daubed over with paint. Sentences—probably from the Koran—are inscribed in vermilion upon the walls. A narrow pulpit is attached to the east end. Inserted in the wall near this rostrum is what may be called the cynosure of a Turkish mosque, namely, the Kebla, or window through which the eye of the Faithful is directed toward the holy city. In the centre of the interior is a lustre of glass lamps, from which some ears of corn are hanging. Above the passage at the entrance is a gallery.

than that of the late Pasha. It is carefully inclosed with palisades, through which the bystanders look, some in attitudes of devotion. It contains the body of a Turkish saint of high reputation, and has therefore the privilege of being painted green, which is, as is well known, the sacred colour of the Turks, and suggests the question, whether this may not be one of the many indications discoverable in that religion, that Mahometanism is partial in its origin and application; that, as it was born in, so it was adapted particularly to, a parched, sandy, and arid country, where verdure would be refreshing to the eye, and a green surface would be looked upon with a feeling of delight.

From Jannina to Tepeleni,—the ancient Antigoncia,—the road leads through the village of Zitza and through the district of Argyro Castro. At the base of the lofty mountains Trebushin and Khórmova the river Dandja

joins the Aöus, forming together a noble river; and on the promontory formed
by their junction stands the town of Tepeleni, whose ruined palace and
shattered walls give an air of solitude to a scene one of the grandest in Epirus.
From the steep sides of the mountain overlooking the Bandja, the town with
its rocky peninsula seems an insignificant spot in comparison with the magnificent mountain scenery by which it is surrounded.

To the northward of Tepeleni, the road follows the banks of the river
Aöus, now a formidable stream rolling along its white rocky bed. The cliffs
rise in several places, almost perpendicularly, to a great height above the
stream, and in some places the path presents a descent,—difficult and even
dangerous,—through gorges so dark and so narrow, as to seem at a short
distance altogether impassable. Pursuing its tumultuous course, the Aöus
rushes through its many channels, and discharges its waters into the Gulf of
Avlona to the northward of the town of that name. At the bottom of the gulf
formed by this promontory are the ruins of the fortress of Cannia, placed on a
projecting rock, and also the small port of Oricum. The Chimeriote mountains
extend in a narrow strip along the coast as far as Buthrinto on the south; they
are bounded on the north-east by the hills of Argyro Castro, and terminate in
a rocky headland which sinks into the sea opposite to the town of Avlona, forming the Acroceraunian promontory, whose lofty crests, rising to a great height
above the sea, were objects of dread to the ancient mariner in those seas.

Horace speaks of them as " infames scopulos Acroceraunia." They are bare and barren, except towards the base, where they are feathered with brushwood. An English traveller, who encountered a dreadful tempest in this sea, says, " the night was unusually black, but at intervals the lightning streamed across

BAY AT VLOMINA, FROM THE COAST OF AVLONA.

the firmament and set it in a blaze. The brightest sunshine could not have cast a more vivid glare over the Acroceraunian crags." The most projecting part of the Acroceraunian rocks is a tongue of land called, from its form, Linguetta. It was on this dangerous sea that Cæsar, disguised as a slave, when caught in a storm, in an open boat in which he was sailing to join his army in Italy, re-animated the courage of the pilot—"Fear not, thou bearest the fortunes of Cæsar."

To ascertain the site of DODONA would seem now to require a response from the ORACLE itself. The former dwelling of the spirit, which once guided half the world, is lost. For many generations, kings, generals, and statesmen came from the extreme coasts of Greece, from all the countries stretching between AMPHIPOLIS on the east, and APOLLONIA on the west, and from the shores of Asia and Italy, to consult the Oracle; but now none can

point to its place. Still even the uncertainty of its site is not without its
interest, and we do not believe that the search for it is hopeless. There must
be something peculiar and distinct in the remains of so remarkable a place.
The ruins of a large capital are easily distinguished from those of a dependent
city ; the ruins of a city, again, from those of a mere fortress ; but the ruins
of an oracular city will have something very different from both.

What has perplexed the investigation of this question is, as it appears
to us, not the paucity of identifying data, but their multitude and variety.
There are so many and conflicting conditions to be satisfied, that it is impossible to satisfy them all. A lake, a high mountain, a hundred springs,
a miraculous fountain which extinguishes lights and then rekindles them ;
a forest of oaks and beeches, a wide plain of excellent pasturage: these
characteristics are all put together, as in the hue-and-cry description of a
military deserter ; these are the attributes and features by which Dodona is

to be recognised and brought back to the post which it has deserted in the maps of Greece.

But has not this varied description been sketched without due discrimination? Regarding Dodona as a *city* only, and not as a country, we may observe that it was the most remarkable in this district; indeed, it was the only one of any consideration within a circuit of many miles. Its importance also, from its *sacred* character, is not to be neglected. Now, supposing a traveller in this part of Greece, but not in the *immediate* neighbourhood of the Oracle itself, to have met with a phosphoric fountain, for instance, which he found to extinguish and then to ignite any inflammable substance, if he were asked, on his return home, where this spring was to be found, what answer would he have made but this,—" he had seen it near Dodona!" and thus a cluster of wonders would soon group themselves about that place, as the best and almost the only point for their adhesion and support; and so these phenomena, though really detached, but connected with it by association, would soon be assumed to be the features of the Oracle itself.

But Dodona was not a *city* merely; it was, we believe, a *country* also.

SOURCE OF THE PEITINO

Its dimensions may be presumed to have been of sufficient extent to comprise within their general range all those characteristic features which are now crowded into the immediate neighbourhood, and almost into the sacred precincts of the oracular shrine.

It has been alleged that, because some authors place Dodona in MOLOSSIA,

and others in THESPROTIA, it must, therefore, have been upon the borders of
both.   But this inference must be received with certain limitations.   In
earlier times Dodona was in Thesprotia; in later ages it was in Molossia;
simply because the greater part of Thesprotia itself became Molossian by the
southward encroachments of the latter power, which, in the Peloponnesian
war, reached nearly to the shores of the Ambracian gulf.   Again, in that
important datum for determining the position of Dodona, namely, its distance
of four days' journey from BUTHROTUM, at the mouth of the modern DELVINO,
and of two from Ambracia, the present Arta, it must be remembered that
the latter journey would be *with*, and the former *against*, the grain of the hard
mountain ranges which stretch from north to south, between the Pindus and
the Ionian sea.

These considerations are suggested by the ruins of an ancient city, which
have deservedly attracted much attention.   In our way towards them we
proceed from Jannina in a south-westerly direction, and in an hour's time
from that place pass by the village of Grapsista on our left, then turn to the
right up a mountain pass, whence we descend, having a church called ECCLESIA
BONIATA on the left, into an extensive plain, which lies below the eastern
slopes of Mount Olitza.   The ruins, which are situated in the middle of this
plain, are about eleven miles to the south-west of Jannina.   They are known
by the name of the Kastro, or ancient citadel, of DRAMISUS.

The first thing which strikes the spectator in looking at these remains is
their situation.   They stand in a *plain*.   The selection of such a spot shows
a remarkable confidence in the inherent resources of the city; for if there is
one particular attribute of an ordinary Hellenic town, it is this—that its
citadel is placed upon a *hill*.   A Greek city was always full of suspicions:
the exception furnished by the example of Nicopolis, a *Roman* Greek city,
which is placed in the middle of the plain, is an exception which illustrates
the rule.   These ruins, which we are now viewing, are exclusively Greek,
and in a similar situation; and that, too, in the heart of one of the most
mountainous districts of Greece.   There was no want of localities admirably
suited for the erection of a fortress upon them, in a country where there are
pointed hills shooting up their heads on every side, vying, as it were, with one
another to be encircled with the mural crown of an Hellenic city.   The
choice, therefore, of a level site in such a region as this was, we conceive,
made deliberately, and for some especial reason.

This peculiarity is made more remarkable by the smallness of the city
itself.   The strength of its population could never have compensated for the
weakness of its position.   The whole circuit of the walls of its upper and
lower divisions does not amount to two English miles.   The consideration of

these two facts, the lowness of the situation, and the small extent of the city, seem conclusive objections against the opinion which has ascribed these ruins to Passaron, the metropolitan seat of the house of Pyrrhus.

But, though the place which we are now viewing could have possessed no military power, still, in a social respect, it seems to have been of considerable importance. Attached to the Acropolis, on the south-east, is the shell of a magnificent Theatre, one of the largest now existing in Greece. It is scooped in the declivity of the hill, with a southern aspect. Now, the existence of a theatre at all, especially in this district, is a very singular circumstance; but the existence of so grand a theatre, in so insignificant a place, is without a parallel in the whole of Greece.

Proceeding eastward from the theatre, we observe another object, very unusual in the remains of Epirot cities. On the north of the theatre, between it and the gate of the lower city, are vestiges of two temples; of the most distant of the two, fourteen columns, or at least the fragments of them, are still standing. There are not, we believe, fourteen other columns remaining together in the whole of Epirus.

Considering these circumstances, and the inferences to be deduced from them, we feel disposed to inquire whether, when contemplating these ruins, we are not treading the soil once hallowed by the presence of Dodona? Does not this supposition explain the peculiarities above noticed? The oracular city needed no extrinsic defence of a strong natural position; it was protected by its own sanctity. Being situated in a plain, it was easy of access for the inquirers who came to it from every side. Hence, too, we may account for the disproportion between the city and the buildings with which it was adorned. The theatre was not designed for the entertainment of citizens only; it served as an attraction for strangers, and provided gratification for those who were brought there by the celebrity of the oracle. Whether the temples of which we have spoken were connected with the worship of the Dodonæan Jupiter, and whether they were contained in a Temenos, or sacred inclosure, in which the theatre probably stood, as was the case with that at Epidaurus, will be better determined by those who may be enabled to make excavations among their ruins.

For the reasons adduced above, it is not wonderful that we do not discover here all the natural phenomena usually associated with Dodona. In order to reconcile the modern picture with the ancient original, the other features of Dodona must be collected by the topographer from various places in the neighbourhood, as the limbs of his son, scattered about the country, were by Æetes. We may be compelled to go eight miles to Jannina for the Dodonæan lake; its phosphoric spring may, perhaps, be found near the sulphuric mines

worked by Ali Pasha, near Djerovini; the mountain of Tomarus will be
represented by Olitzka, with its hundred sources in its glens, and this fertile
plain at its roots.

Another vestige of the oracle deserves notice. There are records of a
Bishop of Dodona existing in the fifth century, and the name which the place
bears in the imperial documents of that period, is Bonditza. This appellation

ISLAND AND CASTLE OF JANINA.

is perhaps to be recognised in that of the small church of Bodista, which we
passed, as above noticed, at a short distance from this spot. It seems worth
an inquiry, whether the same name, in an abbreviated form, is not preserved
in the compound Xero Boutza, a village a little to the north-west of these
ruins.

We leave the remains of Dramisus, and take the road towards SULI. In
about two hours' time we arrive at a spring, and a little further, on an

CHURCH OF THE ACHERON

eminence, there is a noble view of the valley which lies between the Suliot mountains on the west, and those of Olitzka on the east. At twelve miles to the south-west of Dramisus, we enter the solitary hamlet of Bourrelleska, consisting of ten cottages and a church. We now follow the course of a branch of the Acheron, and then, as we proceed to the westward, at a turn in the road the long and wide plain of PARAMYTHIA bursts upon our view. The appearance of the place from this eminence is very picturesque. A castle stands on a rocky hill to the left of the town, the site of an ancient citadel. The town itself is beautiful at a distance. Cypresses and plane-trees grouped with mosques and houses, give it a pleasant and refreshing aspect, which, however, almost vanishes when you enter its narrow street.

The scenery of Suli is singularly fine. The river, after descending in a south-western course from Jannina, makes a rapid bend towards the north, and enters this wild and magnificent region by a narrow chasm.

The sudden change in the scenery is striking; the waters pass through a valley eight miles in breadth, meeting in one channel shortly before it turns off to the north. The chasm into which it now enters rises precipitously from its bank to the height of several hundred feet above the stream. The only path by which an entrance can be gained, lies along the higher ledges of the mountains, and the access is both difficult and dangerous. The ascent attained, however, the chasm is suddenly exposed to view. Vast and almost

perpendicular precipices conduct the eye downwards to the dark line where the river foams beneath in unsurpassed grandeur. At one point, the course of the river may be traced for six or seven miles flowing between these mountains, some of which rise upwards of three thousand feet,—their precipitous ledges beginning to rise even from the water's edge, the projecting cliffs covered with small oaks, and brushwood. Higher up, where they recede further from the perpendicular line, they receive the same sombre character from the dark thickets of pines which rise at intervals among the rocks.

Following this rugged path, which winds among the rocks for about four miles within the pass, the traveller reaches a spot where further progress seems impossible. The path turns suddenly off to the right, and nothing but

pine-covered precipices meet his eye on every side. A second turn to the right
presents an ascending zig-zag path, steep, rugged, and nearly inaccessible.
From the lofty point now attained the scenery opens out in a most magnificent view. The insulated mountain on which the fortress of Suli stands,
hitherto only visible at intervals through the deep pass, is now directly in
front of the landscape. The river, flowing in its profound channel underneath,
is here entirely concealed from the eye.

We pass onward along the plain to the south, and mount one of the
summits of its eastern barrier of mountains. This eminence is called Kastro
Logeioda, from the fortress upon it. The view here is very extensive: the
island of Santa Maura,—the ancient Leucas,—and the grand outline of the
Acarnanian hills, form the southern horizon. At our feet lies the whole plain
of Paramythia: rising from its western edge, the range of the mountains of
PARGA, scattered over with white villages, are seen standing in array against
those of Suli, on one of which we are. A river, the ancient COCYTUS, flows
from Paramythia along the plain into the ACHERON.

ISLAND OF SANTA MAURA.

Pausanias expresses his belief that Homer drew his description of the Lower World from this part of Thesprotia. The character of the Homeric Inferno is very simple. Two rivers, a rock, some tall poplars and barren willows, are all its scenery. Very different indeed from subsequent representations of the same regions. This rocky glen, through which the Acheron tumbles, over steep and dark cliffs, into the Paramythian plain, what a contrast does it present to those later, and especially Roman, representations of the subterranean world, in which a splendid vestibule leads through massive walls and a peristyle of adamant into lengthening corridors, and thence into groves of myrtle and fragrant laurels,—into the Inferno, in short, of an age and nation which introduced a Baian luxury even into its dreariest abodes, and dressed up the gloomy mansion of Pluto with the pomp and splendour of a palace of the Cæsars. Very different, too, the principles which suggested these later descriptions, from the melancholy language in which the Achilles of Homer declares upon this spot that he had rather cultivate these swampy fields as a day-labourer than enjoy the honours of the royal state among the dead: and very different the influence of this diversity of belief on the character of the nations by which it was entertained.

Three or four cottages, a ruined church, and a ruinous fortress, are all the artificial adjuncts of this spot. They stand on the verge of a plain, on the right bank of the Acheron. The place is called ALA GLYKY. Above them, to the north-east, rise the lofty mountains of Suli, one crowning the other, and some bearing on their summits those proud castles which nothing but famine and avarice could storm. The Acheron falls from these hills through a deep and rocky gorge: leaving these cottages to the right, it expands into a turbid and eddying stream, and then winds quietly through a flat, marshy country, in which it forms the Acherusian Lake, and, uniting itself with the Cocytus, falls into the Ionian Sea.

VALLEY OF THE ACHERON

The port of GLYKY, into which the Acheron discharges itself, seems to have communicated its name to the place where we now are. Its adoption may also have been suggested by a desire to merge all the former sadness of the spot in such an agreeable euphemism. The feeling which in other cases appeased the most awful Deities, and beguiled the most painful diseases, by the charm of a Name, might also hope to *sweeten* the river of woe: the name, too, it is evident, was conferred at a time when Christianity gave an additional reason for the choice, as well as another meaning to it when made.

The ruined church at Ais Glyky stands on the site of an ancient temple. The fragments of eight or nine granite columns of the former structure still remain. We are inclined to believe that this was the oracular shrine where the spirits of the dead were consulted. It was natural to inquire of the departed in the place where they were supposed to have passed into another state of being. The banks of the Acheron, therefore, were the favourite resort of Necromancy. There was also high authority for this practice: Homer no

sooner places here the souls of his Seers and Heroes, than he begins to consult them on the spot. We see no willows at present, such as are placed by him on the banks of the Acheron. There are, indeed, few trees of any kind in the plain, and none of any size: a few Oriental plane-trees, and some low tamarisks, skirt the water's edge, two or three wild fig-trees, and some bright-leaved pomegranates: a somewhat melancholy group, but not inappropriate. A plucked fruit of the latter tree, bursting with the crimson grains which give it its name, and placed, as it was in ancient times, in the hands of a sculptured figure of a deceased person reclining on a sarcophagus containing his ashes, served as a pleasing symbol to express the assurance that, though his life was now plucked from its tree, yet that it was not gathered too early, but ripely teeming with many seeds of rich fruit. The price of a few grains of the same fruit gained also a Queen for the nether world.

In our way up the dark chasm of the Acheron, the River is on our right. We mount the hill of ZABRUCHO, whence there is a magnificent view of three fortresses crowning the crests of three lofty rocks, the citadels of Suli; that on our left is KUNGHI, in front is KIAFFA, to the right is AVARIKO. Descending eastward from this hill, we arrive at the junction of the Acheron and a river falling from the left, which we cross by a bridge at a ruined mill. The

ANCIENT SARCOPHAGUS.

valley is clothed with a luxuriant profusion of shrubs, among which may be seen the myrtle, the lentisk, the prinári, the arbutus, and the broom. How little have the appellations of the most lowly natural objects been changed in Greece! These humble plants are known by the same words which they bore of old, whilst the ancient titles of her Cities and Nations are heard no more. The name of Epirus has vanished, while the names of its shrubs and herbs are in the mouth of every shepherd.

Mounting along this woody glen, we pass between the Suliot castles of Kunghi and Kiaffa, seated, as it were, on their rocky thrones, from which they once domineered over the plain below. At SAMONIBA, in the intermediate valley, are some ragged uninhabited huts, shaded by wild fig-trees; but the most desolate object is the village of KAKO-SULI, lying a little beyond, once the capital of the mountain Republic. The skeletons of the houses are still standing; the hearths are yet black with their former fires; the staircases still lead to the upper chambers; but no one now dwells in the house, or sits by

the hearth, or mounts the staircase. Over the doors hang the boughs of figs
and pear-trees, which seem to have grown wild. Once, it is said, there were
three hundred houses in this village: and there are still more than a hundred
cisterns lying close together in the rocky soil. One hut upon the spot still
lodges a few goat-herds. The former inhabitants of Suli have in their misfortunes one consolation; their courage and their fate have raised them in the
eyes of the world from bandits into heroes, and given to their country an
interest and a name equal to that of an ancient republic of Greece.

Let us retrace our steps from Suli in a southerly direction.

The ancient geography of the interior of Ætolia now claims attention. For
the elucidation of this subject we possess very scanty materials. A passage
of Polybius is here our only guide; and we confess that, after an examination
of it, and a comparison of its details with the features of the country itself,
we have been led to no satisfactory result.

Let us follow the march of Philip in our modern maps of Acarnania and
Ætolia. We pursue his course from Cephalonia to Santa Maura, thence, by
the sites of Actium and ANACTORIUM, we arrive at Limnæa, near ARGOS
AMPHILOCHICUM, at the south-east angle of the gulf; we accompany him
through the Agræan territory till we reach the banks of the Aspropotamo,—
the ancient ACHELOUS,—which we cross at the ford of LEPENU, near the ruins
of STRATUS, the ancient Acarnanian capital. Here we enter the district now
called BRAKO, the northern division of Ætolia, which consists of a wide and
fruitful lowland called the "Great Ætolian plain" by early geographers. On
the south of this plain are two lakes separated from each other by a narrow
causeway: one of them, perhaps both,—for their waters are frequently united,—
was formerly called the Trichonian. Philip, we are told by Polybius, had this

lake upon his *left* during three miles of his march towards Thermus, to which
he was advancing in a direct line from the point where he had passed the
Achelous, and at full speed. We know not, therefore, how to avoid the
conclusion that the capital of Ætolia stood on one of the *northern* crests
of Aracynthus, the modern Zygo, at a distance of three miles to the south of
the lakes above mentioned.

The ancient road-book of central Ætolia is reduced to a single passage of
one historian, and our geographical conclusions with respect to that province
must stand or fall with the position which we assign to Thermus.

Under these circumstances we do not feel disposed to pronounce with any
degree of confidence, on a point concerning which the evidence is so scanty
and inconclusive, especially as an error, committed in this particular, would
affect the whole of the topographical results in this district. We therefore
content ourselves with commending the subject to the investigation of future

geographers, in the belief that a spot of so much interest and importance as
Thermus cannot but preserve some still-surviving vestiges of that splendour
by which it was formerly distinguished, and that it will thus furnish encouragement to their researches before they are commenced, and incontrovertible
evidence of their success when those researches are completed.

The other two cities in Ætolia of the greatest celebrity in ancient times
were PLEURON and CALYDON. The older town of Pleuron stood at the south-
east foot of the Aracynthus, on a site now called Gyphto Kastro : the newer
was on a hill farther to the west, on a summit which bears the name of the
Kastro of Iréné, about three miles to the north of the modern town of
Missolonghi. The remains here are considerable ; they consist of walls, gates,
and an ancient theatre.

Calydon, the city of Meleager, and distinguished by the description of its

siege by the Curetes, given in the Iliad of Homer, stood on a gentle declivity
sloping down to the banks of the river Evenus, which flows by its foot into
the sea. Some of the walls contemporary with the great Epic Poet still
remain. In the plain below them were the vineyards and cornfields which the
Ætolian inhabitants of Calydon offered to Meleager as an inducement for him
to join them in repelling their assailants. The spot is now known by the
name of Kurt Aga. A little above it to the north is the point in the river
Evenus at which the Centaur Nessus bore Deianira from the western to the
eastern shore, when she was accompanying her husband, Hercules, for the first
time on his expedition from Ætolia. The stream is now called Fidaro, probably from its winding course : the word seems to be formed from the
modern Greek terms Fidi and Fidari, a snake, and may properly be rendered
Serpentine.

The name of Missolonghi, a small Greek town opposite to Patras, belongs
to modern History ; the heroic resistance of its garrison in the war of Greek
independence made the name famous throughout Europe. For ten months,

with feeble and insignificant ramparts, its small garrison defied the efforts of
the whole Turkish army under one of its greatest leaders.   Seeing all their
hopes destroyed, they determined to cut their way through the besieging army.
Two divisions succeeded in the attempt; the third, encumbered by the women
and children, was driven back into the town and cut to pieces.

On the morning of Sunday the seventh of October, A.D. 1571, the Armadas
of the Sultan of Constantinople, and of the Christian States of Europe which
were opposed to him, found themselves in sight of each other on the waters at
the entrance of the Gulf of Corinth, to the west of the town of Naupactus.

The King of Spain, Philip the Second, had dispatched thither his fleet of
more than a hundred sail, under the command of his brother John of Austria.
John Andrew Doria, the descendant of the great admiral of that name, led on
the galleys of Genoa to the battle; they were joined by twelve vessels of the
Pope, Pius the Fifth, and more than a hundred from Venice.   The Princes of
Parma and Urbino were present.   Twelve thousand Italians, five thousand
Spaniards, and more than six thousand of other nations, took part in the
engagement.   The Turkish fleet, which was much superior in number to that
of the Christians, had set sail from Naupactus, where it had been stationed,

and came in front of the enemy at the small islands—now before us as we sail from Ætolia—of Kruzolari, on the south-eastern side of the mouths of the Achelous. Each of the armaments formed itself on the spot into three ranks, drawn up in the form of a crescent. It is said that John of Austria, the admiral of the allied forces, embarked in his frigate and went along the lines exhorting each individual to combat boldly for the defence and honour of the Christian Faith, assuring them all of the protection of God, in whose cause they were about to fight. It is added, that the soldiers were so much affected by his words that they shed tears of joy, and replied only with loud acclamations of Victory! Victory! In the meantime, as they well knew would be the case, all Christian nations, both far and near, were offering up prayers with one heart for the success of the arms which they were wielding. The conflict lasted four hours without producing any decisive result; but when the wind veered to the southward, the attack of the Christians became more impetuous, and their foes, who were not able to resist the force of the wind and sea, began to give way: the death of their admiral added to their consternation; their rout soon became general. Upwards of fifteen thousand Turks fell in the battle. More than twelve thousand Christian slaves, who were found in the Turkish vessels, were set at liberty. Sixty-two Ottoman ships were sunk, and more than a hundred and twenty were taken. So ended the battle of Naupactus, or Lepanto.[*] The arrival of the news of this great victory at Rome revived the memory of her ancient triumphs. The General of the Papal arms was received with the utmost splendour by the Senate and Magistrates, and escorted to the Capitol and into the presence of the Pope at the Church which stands on the lofty site of the Temple of Jupiter Capitolinus.

We pass over the waters on which this engagement took place, and cross the narrow strait at the entrance of the Corinthian Gulf. The passage is a little more than a mile broad, and lies between two promontories, that to the south being the Rhium, and the northern the Antirrhium, of ancient geography. On each of these capes stands a castle, where formerly was a Temple of Neptune. The depth of the water between them is about thirty fathoms.

THE IONIAN ISLANDS

WEST VIEW OF THE CITADEL AT CORFU

E take leave, for the present, of the continent, and pass
from the coast of Epirus to the ISLANDS of the IONIAN Sea.
We commence with the principal and most northern of them,
that of KORFOU, the ancient CORCYRA.

The modern town of Korfou, which lies in the centre of the eastern coast
of the island, is, in its appearance, neither Greek nor Italian, but partakes of

both characters. On entering its low gateway, from the interior of the island,
we are reminded a little of the ancient dwellings of Pompeii by the uniform
smallness of the houses, and the narrowness and regularity of the streets. It
may be called a geographical mosaic, to which many countries of Europe have
contributed a stone and a colour. Thus the streets are Italian, at least in their
style and names: the arcades by which they are flanked, might have come

from Padua, or Bologna; the winged lion of St. Mark is seen marching, in
stone, along the Venetian walls of its fortress; beneath them you find rusty
pieces of cannon stamped with the words Liberté and Egalité, which carry you
back to the time when the island was held under French rule; and if you walk
to the other end of the Strada Reale, you will there hear, in the market, more
than one Ionian vendor debating with an Irish or English soldier, how much
he is to receive for his wares in certain Greek oboli, which bear the Venetian
Lion on one side, and a Britannia with her Ægis on the other, and present

an epitome of the modern history of the island, and make an interesting
addition to the series of brass and silver records of the same kind which
tell what Korfou was in former ages. A Triton striking with his trident;
a prow of a ship, a galley in full sail, the gardens of Alcinous, and a
Bacchus crowned with ivy; these are some of the monetary memorials of the
former power, commerce, and productions of Corcyra.

On the east of the same street is the Spianata, or esplanade, one side of
which is bounded by the palace of the Lord High Commissioner, a handsome
building of Maltese stone; on the east is the citadel and the two conical
crests,—the "aërial summits of the Phæacians" in Virgil,—from which the
Island is said to derive its name; though the word Gurfo, by which it is
designated in Boccaccio, as well as the modern Greek term Korfou, would lead
us to seek its origin in a Romaic corruption of the ancient word for Kolpo,
Gulf, or Bay, which might be well applied to the harbour beneath the
summits above-mentioned.

The esplanade is enli-
vened by reviews of three
or four thousand English
troops, and, toward even-
ing, is the resort of the
Greek Priests of the neighbouring university. There
is something very pictur-
esque in the appearance
of these persons, with their
black caps, resembling the
modius seen on the heads
of the ancient statues of
Serapis and Osiris, their

long beards and pale complexions, and their black flowing cloak—a relic,
no doubt, of the old ecclesiastical garment of which Tertullian wrote—as

they sit upon the benches, or pace beneath the acacias and lime-trees of the place.

There is a work on Korfou, written by one of its patricians, which gives some interesting details with respect to the island and its inhabitants: the author asserts that, among other superstitions, the common people have a strong objection to go on the left side of a mill-stream, or near the house of a dead miser, to be married on a Wednesday, or in the month of February. Some of these antipathies are, probably, as old as the time of Hesiod, who prescribes certain days for marriage and other ceremonies. The wind which sighs through the leaves of a forest in a dark winter's night, is said by them to be made up of the souls of bad men. At LEUCIMNA, the modern Capo Bianco, where the Corcyræans erected a trophy after their naval struggle with the Corinthians, at the southern extremity of the island, is an eminence which is the favourite resort of the Nereids, who are supposed to have great influence over the health and fortunes of their neighbours, and which is called from them Nereido Kastro.

It is worth while to observe how these mythological playthings are thrown away on more trying and solemn occasions. At the deathbed, when the nearest relative has closed the eyes of the deceased, and when the windows of his chamber have been thrown open to give his soul a free passage to heaven; when the Mœrologists, or professional mourners, have ceased their doleful exclamations, the simple words are uttered by those present, "He is now before his Maker, who judges,—and may He pardon him!" The corpse is then washed, dressed in its best attire, wrapped in the winding-sheet, and laid out for twenty-four hours. The last embrace is concluded with a chant of the solemn and melodious hymn attributed to Damascene:—"Seeing me speechless and breathless, oh! weep over me, all my brothers, friends, kindred, and acquaintance; for yesterday I was talking to you. Give me the last embrace, for I shall not walk or speak with you again. I go away to the Judge, with whom there is no respect of persons; I go where servants and masters stand together; kings and soldiers, rich and poor, in equal dignity, for every one will be either glorified or condemned according to his own works."

It is difficult to draw a map of the Homeric Phæacia which shall coincide in its details with the localities of Korfou. Nor will the topographer find it an easy task to discover the natural objects connected in the Odyssey with the city of Alcinous. Where are the two fountains which flowed near it?—where is the stream of the River God whom Ulysses invokes in his prayers? Is it to be found at the beautiful village of Potamo, or not far from Cape Sideri, to suit the hypothesis,—the most prevalent one among the Phæacian antiquaries

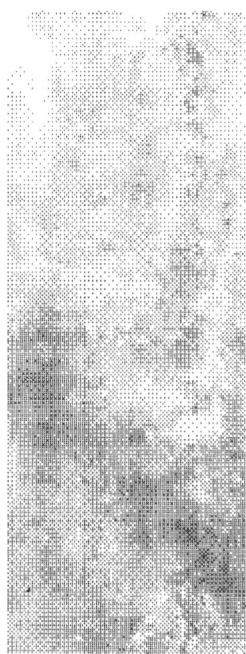

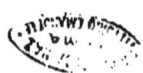

of the present day,—which lands Ulysses in the north-west extremity of the island, because he is brought to it by a northerly wind, and which places the city of Alcinous at Aphiona in that district?

It is to be regretted that proofs are wanting to show the identity of the Phæacian town with that of the Liburnians who were dispossessed by the Corinthian colony, which settled in the island; for we have conclusive evidence in the name of Palæopolis, in its existing remains, and in the general correspondence of its features with the descriptions of the ancient

capital of Corcyra, that the hill to the south of the modern town is the site of the colonized city. Wherever the Phæacian town of Homer may have been, there can be no doubt that this was the Corcyra of Thucydides.

On visiting Palæopolis we feel some compensation in reflecting, that although we may not be permitted confidently to indulge the belief that the hero of Ithaca ran and wrestled with the flower of the Phæacian youth beneath this woody hill, yet that we are beholding a scene invested with a painful interest by the memorable contests of Corcyra with Corinth, her mother

country. This hill was the Coreyræan Acropolis; but which of the two
harbours that lie, one on the north, the other on the south of it, was the
HYLLAIC? That, as well
as the Acropolis, was in
the hands of the popular
party, while their antagonists were in possession of
the Agora, and of the harbour near it. We find in
the narrative of Thucy-
dides that the nobles set
fire to the Agora in self-
defence, and that the whole
town would have been con-
sumed had not the wind
been contrary. Which way
was the wind? This ques-
tion is answered by the
arrival, the next morning,
of the Athenian fleet from
a point to the south as far distant as Naupactus. Thence we may infer that
the Hyllaic harbour was to the *south* of the site of the Acropolis, and that it
is to be identified with the lagune of CALICHIOPOULO, and that the Agora and
its adjacent harbour lie to the north of the peninsula of Palæopolis, and
toward the modern KASTRADES. It also follows, that the temple of Juno to
which the nobles fled, stood near the place now occupied by an English
cannon,—thence called the One-gun Battery; that they were carried to the
rocky islet opposite the temple, now called PERAMA, or the Ferry of the
Hyllaic harbour; and these olive-trees remind us of the voluntary death by
which, on being brought back to the temple, they rescued themselves from the
hands of their fellow-citizens.

Of one of the temples which adorned the ancient town the remains are
still visible. They are prettily situated among trees on the high cliffs
upon the coast at the north-east side of the Acropolis. From its neighbourhood to the sea, and from the circumstance of the small chapel which once
stood upon its ruins having been dedicated to Saint Nicolas,—the sailor saint
of the Greek Church,—we might conjecture that these remains belonged
to some modern form of the temple of Neptune, the "beautiful POSIDEIUM"
of Nausicaa.

Of Nausicaa herself we should be very glad to find here some trace or

reminiscence. There is no character in the whole history of this island of so much interest as hers. We turn away with pleasure from the savage scenes of the Peloponnesian war, when this land was the victim of civil feuds, to the peaceful occupations of the Homeric time, and among all the objects which the contemplation of that period brings before us in this place, none is so attractive as the daughter of Alcinous; we feel emotions of affectionate respect towards the author of the Odyssey for having conceived and delineated a character like hers. That age could not be barbarous when the descriptions of such delicate refinement, gentleness, and kindness as are there portrayed, could be acceptable to the audience of the poet.

In the absence of any special objects with which her memory may be connected, we look at the natural features of the island as the remaining witnesses of the age and state of society in which she passed her days. These are remarkable for their beauty. In every part of Korfou we have glimpses of the sea, which is so interlaced with the land as to give it the appearance of a group of islands. From the absence of all hedges, and of almost all show of division of property in the island, through which the road seems to wind with the freedom of a river, there is a unity in it which is very pleasing to the eye. The surface is broken into hill and valley, and sprinkled over with olives, the principal produce of the soil, which would fatigue the sight with their monotony, were not their pale and quivering foliage agreeably relieved by dark groups of tall cypresses, looking in the distance like the spires of some venerable minster. By the side of one of the clear streams which flow from the rocks beneath their shade, the pencil of Poussin or of Claude would have placed, as in an appropriate spot, the nymph-like Nausicaa and her maidens, to enhance the beauty of the scene.

In our voyage from Korfou southward we sail near the SYBOTA Islets, and the deserted harbour which is described in Thucydides as the roadstead of the Corinthian fleet. We next pass near the island of PAXO. " HERE," in the words of the old annotator on Spenser's Pastoral in May, " about the time that our Lord suffered his most bitter Passion, certayne persons sailing from Italie to Cyprus at night heard a voyce calling aloud, Thamus, Thamus! who giving care to the cry, was bidden, (for he was pilot of the ship,) when he came near to Palodas, to tell that the great God Pan was dead; which he doubting to do, yet for that when he came to Palodas there was such a calme of wind that the ship stood still in the sea unmoored, he was forced to cry aloud that Pan was dead; wherewithal there was such piteous outcries and dreadful shrieking as hath not been the like. By which Pan of some is understood the great Sathanas, whose kingdom was at that time by Christ conquered, and the gates of hell broken up; for at that time all Oracles surceased, and enchanted Spirits that were wont to delude the people henceforth held their peace."

SANTA MAURA, FROM THE COAST OF EPIRUS.

The words in which Milton refers to this incident in his Ode on the Nativity
will recur to the memory of the English traveller, as he sails over this spot,
particularly if it be in the darkness of night by the island of Paxo,—

> "The Oracles are dumb;
> No voice or hideous hum
> Runs through the arched roof in words deceiving, &c.
>
> "The lonely mountains o'er,
> And the resounding shore,
> A voice of weeping heard, and loud lament."

Passing along the west coast of Santa Maura, the ancient Leucas, we are
brought to the southern extremity of the island, on which the temple of the
Leucadian Apollo formerly stood. The promontory was then called LEUCATES,
and now by a common change corrupted into Ducato, and is known to the

modern Greek sailor as the Lady's Cape. The latter appellation may be
derived from its connexion with the history of Sappho, who is said to have
thrown herself from its summit into the sea. Since her time it has been
generally called the LOVERS' LEAP. Whether she was the first who made trial
is doubtful. Ovid indeed tells us that the virtues of a plunge into the waters
beneath it were known at an earlier date, even in the age of Deucalion:
while Menander affirms, that no one had preceded the Æolian maid in the
experiment.

Toward the extremity of the cape the cliffs decrease in height, gently
shelving into the sea, till at the low white promontory itself the surface of
the rock coincides with that of the water. It was, probably, the tendency of
this rocky point to run into a reef that rendered it proverbially dangerous to
ships. Above it stood, visible from afar, the "Apollo dreaded by sailors," who
was regarded with peculiar veneration by the mariner of the Ionian Sea.

It is remarkable, that the uses for which this rock was originally employed
were religious and judicial. In critical times, slaves and criminals were thrown
from its summit as an expiatory sacrifice: it seems also to have served as an
ordeal by which the guilt or innocence of an accused party might be determined. In some instances, the priests of Apollo's temple above it offered
themselves as victims; though upon those occasions it is said that care was
taken to buoy them up by live birds and artificial pinions in their descent,

which was thus broken and made easy, and that so they were enabled to
repeat the experiment at different times, and to increase the number of similar
attempts by their own example. They assured those who had fruitlessly
wandered in search of their parents, that they would find them after a dive
in this vision-clearing sea; and they persuaded others that Apollo, the God of
Medicine, had prescribed a leap from his own rock as a cure for ill-requited love.

On the slope above the base of the promontory
we observe the remains of an ancient building, among
which lie the fragments of a column, which perhaps belonged to the Temple of Apollo. The soil
above it is overgrown with myrtles and other aro-
matic plants. From this point, in the calm which precedes the dawn of
a summer's day, the traveller may behold the smoke mounting from the hills
of Ithaca, the sight which, as Homer says, Ulysses longed to see.

But here arises a question. Is the modern THIAKI, at which we have now
arrived, the ITHACA of the Odyssey or not? On the one hand, we are assured
by some, that we need not be under any anxiety on this point; that it is
perfectly easy for us to see to-day the view which Minerva showed to Ulysses,
when he landed here from the island of Alcinous on his return home some
three thousand years ago; that in our rambles through the island we may
visit the harbour of the venerable PHORCYS, and see the votive niches in the
Grotto of the NYMPHS; that when oppressed by the heat of a mid-day sun,
after having quenched our thirst under the shade of the "RAVEN'S ROCK,"

with the "black water" of the fountain of Arethusa, we may regale our
appetites with fruits gathered in the gardens once tilled by the hand of Laertes,
and refresh ourselves by the coolness of the sea-breeze playing over the rocks
and among the walls of the lofty palace of the Hero of the Odyssey himself.

There is something, it is true, very fascinating in thus being brought into
immediate contact with Homeric scenery and characters, and in reading with
our own eyes the original of which his poem is a transcript.

But we are not allowed to migrate, unmolested, to this Island of the
Happy, or to remain in the peaceful enjoyment of this Heroic society. We
are presented by a German topographer with a map of this and the neighbouring islands as they are thought by him to have existed in the mind of the
Poet; and we are warned that, without availing ourselves of any licence for the
purpose of reconciling the geography of Homer with that of actual observation,
we must confine ourselves simply to the latitudes and longitudes which are
drawn by the hand of the bard on the surface of his own poem. The result
of this investigation, we are informed, is no other than that the author of the
Odyssey has been at the pains of composing more than twelve thousand lines,
more or less concerning the history and geography of a place which he not only
could never have seen, but of which no sailor who had seen the place, could, by
tracing for him a map upon the sand of the sea-shore, have ever given him
an idea. In order, therefore, to delineate for ourselves the Homeric chart of
the kingdom of Ulysses, we are called upon to treat the modern Ithaca with
the same contemptuous usage with which it is said the Sublime Porte once
menaced some refractory islanders, when they were told that, if they did not
obey the edict which had been sent them, they and their country should be
swamped in the sea: if Thiaki is permitted to survive any longer, it is

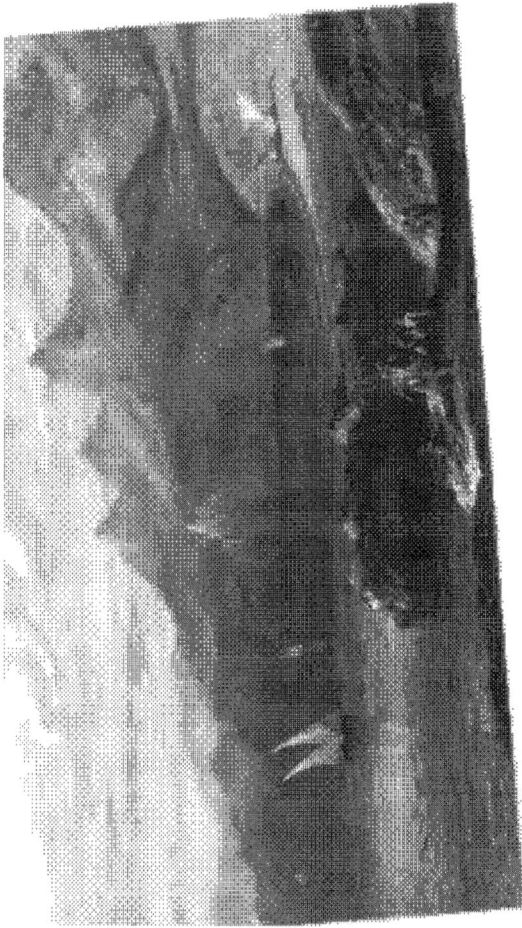

ordered to sail from its present position, and, after a short cruise in the Ionian sea, to cast anchor on the *western*, instead of the *eastern*, side of the island of CEPHALLONIA.

We are assured that, however we may lament the fact, the sentence of transportation has been passed upon Ithaca, in the lines of the Odyssey in which Ulysses gives a history of himself to Alcinous. They occur near the commencement of the ninth book.

> " I dwell in sunny ITHACA, where waves
> With woods the hill of Neritos; around,
> Close to each other, many Islands lie,
> Dulichium, Samè, woody Zacynthus—
> It steadfast stands, highest above the wave,
> Westward ; the rest apart, to eastern sun.
> Rugged, but kindly, nurse of youth : and I
> A land more dear than this shall never see."

It is alleged that, in these verses, Ithaca is placed to the *west* of the other islands, whereas, in fact, it is to the *east* of them ; nor can it be denied that we are here met by a difficulty, in our attempt to identify the geography of Homer with that of our own maps.

But neither, in the first place, can it be asserted that *one* stubborn passage in a long poem is sufficient ground for a theory which contradicts the universal principles and practice of human nature.

It is clear that the author of the Odyssey was a traveller, not so much from the geographical knowledge of countries far removed from one another which he displays, but from the leading idea and moral of his poem, namely, the paramount attachment and love which a man feels for his own country, be it but a rugged rock,—a love which neither Læstrygons, nor Anthropophagi, nor even the witcheries of fairy islands, can eradicate from his breast. This is a feeling of which no one would be deeply sensible, much less is it a principle which any one would work into a poem, who had not himself been a wanderer.

Granting, then, what it seems impossible to doubt, that the poet had personal acquaintance with different parts of the globe, is it probable that he would lay the scene of a long poem in a country of which he had no distinct information, in preference to fixing it in one which he had himself visited ? Was there anything in the country, thus selected, to justify that preference ?

And, not only who would care to write, but who, it may be asked, would care to hear, a long tale about a country with which the Poet was wholly unacquainted ? When the recital is one which enters into the minute details of real life, and,—as is the case with that part of the Odyssey which refers to

Ithaca,—is not embellished by fabulous imagery, the existence of an audience at all seems to suppose some pre-existing sympathy in their minds with the physical and social relations of the country described. But with what incredulity and derision would they have turned from the narrative of a Prince who begins his account of himself with a geographical blunder about his own dominions!

Were it, therefore, necessary to reject the passage, above cited, as interpolated or corrupt, we should have little difficulty in doing so; but the truth seems to be, that it does not require so much to be expunged as explained. In it, we may observe, the islands are grouped *about* Ithaca. Ithaca, therefore, itself is not placed at the western extremity of them all. It seems, also, very natural that, after enumerating the islands collectively, the narrator should digress to particularize their individual positions, that he should assume ZACYNTHUS, the last mentioned, as the point to which the rest should be referred, and that he should add, in conclusion, that Zacynthus (and *not* Ithaca) lay to the west, and the other islands in an easterly direction from it. To Zacynthus, therefore, and not to Ithaca, we refer the lines:—

> " It steadfast stands, highest above the wave,
> Westward; the rest apart, to eastern sun."

And so, we believe, did Virgil long ago, when he wrote:—

> " Woody Zacynthus o'er mid wave appears."

Thus the Homeric geography of the Odyssey becomes clear.

One more remark on the general question. In the Odyssey, the Region of *Fable* begins at the Leucadian rock, and stretches from that point, in a northerly direction. That rock is on the road by which the Shades of the Suitors are conducted by Mercury from Ithaca to Hades. No one can pass from the description of Phæacia to that of Ithaca without feeling that he has exchanged " the meadow of asphodel," and the "land of dreams," for real and practical life. And whence this difference? Not from any objective dissimilarity, as we believe, in the things described, but in their relations to the describer and his hearers. Plutarch tells us that, in his time, the framers of geographical charts betrayed their ignorance of portions of the countries which they undertook to delineate, by the sort of vague compensation which they offered for them. In the unexplored outskirts of their maps they placed sandy deserts destitute of water, peopled with beasts and monsters,—what Swift calls "elephants instead of towns;" in other parts, of which they also knew nothing, they laid down insuperable bogs, Scythian snows, or a frozen ocean. Their comparative knowledge, however, of the more central districts was proved by well-marked coasts, distinct headlands, capes, and rivers, cities, and villages, specified with minute accuracy. Such a chart the Odyssey of Homer seems to be; and the same inference may be drawn from the different manner in which its central and extreme regions are treated. The Cyclops and Lotophagi are its bogs and deserts, but its meridian passes through ITHACA.

It seems probable that the Poet has sketched his own character in that of the minstrel Phemius; and that one of his designs was, to recover for the house of Ulysses, the political influence which it appears to have lost by the vengeance inflicted by him on the suitors, and to regain for it the royal prerogative and precedence among the rival families of the island. The Odyssey was a poetical Apology for the person and dynasty of Ulysses. It did for them what was done by the Æneid of Virgil for the house and throne of Augustus.

LOVERS LEAP.

But what is to be said of the reputed PALACE and CITY of Ulysses? We leave BATHY, the modern capital, for a walk thither. We pass along the barren and rocky shore, by patches of corn, groups of olives, and under hills topped with windmills, and, after a walk of more than three miles, arrive at the foot of the mountain on which the ruins stand. It is called ÆTO, and is the narrow central isthmus which connects the northern with the southern half of the island. As we climb the rough and rugged paths, and follow the line of these huge unshapen walls, which stretch down from the summit of the hill, we might imagine them to belong rather to a city whose walls have been stratified by nature, than to a work fashioned and elaborated by the hand

of man. With these gigantic masses before us, indicative of great physical
force simultaneously applied, we feel it easier to pronounce an opinion as
to what age they can not, than to what age they can, be attributed. They do
not appear to belong to that of the Odyssey. They could hardly have been
produced in the state of society portrayed in that poem. The Ulysses of
Homer is a prince of some power and name, but he is also represented by the
Poet as a mechanic, who shows his ingenuity in the construction of his
own bed, and builds his own chamber with his royal hands; his father,
Laertes, is found in his orchard, among his olives and pear-trees, with a

pruning-knife in his hand, and wearing thick gloves to defend himself from
the briars and thorns. Although the existence of a public assembly, convoked
for national purposes, may be thought to evince some popular concert among
the inhabitants of Ithaca, yet the personal influence of those Princes could
not be great who were left by their subjects to perform menial duties for
themselves. Of the Public itself executing any national work for its own
good, there is no example in the whole poem. The Fountain of the *village*
(for such the capital of Ulysses seems to have been) required the successive
exertions of three heroes, Ithacus, Neritus, and Polyctor, for its construction.

There is no mention of walls to the city, though we hear a good deal about the wooden palisades which protected the stalls of Eumæus.

Half an hour of laborious ascent brings us to the top of this rocky hill, which is, as we have mentioned, called Aëto, or the EAGLE, because from this point, as a centre, the two wings of the island appear extended from north to south like those of an eagle, somewhat in the same manner as the appearance of the spread pinions of that bird gave the same name, among the ancient Greeks, to the tympanum or pediment of a temple. Here, on the narrow level of the summit, is the Acropolis of the city. The peculiarity of its form, and

CYCLOPEAN WALLS OF ITHACA.

the loftiness of its situation, seem to have been the causes which procured for it the title of the palace of Ulysses,—a title which it has retained longer, from the celebrity of the English geographer, Sir W. GELL, who first conferred it. We consult the plan founded on his observations of this so-called palace, and endeavour to compare it with the original. On the bed of these ruins, by a sort of Procrustean topography, the Odyssean palace, as described in Homer, has been stretched and fitted. Here, in this ruined bulwark, is a curved projection: the plan converts it into an heroic *tholus*. We pass by a fragment of wall, and find that we have intruded into the GYNÆCEUM of Penelope; the apartment to the right is the HYPERONM; an OROTHURE, or secret door, conveys us from the vestibule to the street, where we come directly upon the corn-mills of Ulysses!

There is a reflection which suggests itself to every one who contrasts the two opposite theories of the geography of Ithaca which have now been noticed,—that the one has produced the other. The traveller who discovers everything, leads all the world to suspect that he has, in reality, found nothing. And by such a process as this, the modern Ithaca, from being proposed as too accurate a resemblance of the Ithaca of the Odyssey, has ceased, in the minds of some, to be any resemblance at all.

But a distinction must be drawn between the identification of existing remains, with monuments of a perishable character, and others of a more permanent description:—between the identification of works of *art*, and those of *nature*. The traveller may still see what, there seems little reason to doubt, was the Homeric GROTTO OF THE NYMPHS, in which the sleeping Ulysses was deposited by the Phœacian sailors. Homer felt himself unequal to the task of describing the raptures of Ulysses in approaching his native land, and therefore he very wisely landed him asleep. This is quite consistent with human nature, which sometimes sinks from exhaustion, even in times of the greatest excitement.—In this cave,—thanks to the permanence of Nature,—we believe the Author of the Odyssey to have been. A mountain, a valley, a harbour, or a lake, may exist anywhere, and can hardly furnish any characteristic by which one country may be discriminated from another; but a Grotto such as this to which we refer is so remarkable an object, that, if Ithaca were set afloat like a second Delos in the sea, or exposed to be tossed upon the ocean like the Perseus of Danae, with such a badge of cognisance as this, the description of the Grotto of the Nymphs, as it exists in the Odyssey, would be the best guarantee to secure its being discovered and brought again to its own home.

Of the Cave itself, after Homer's description of it, there remains little to be said. It is situated on Mount SAINT STEPHEN, and is called the cave of Tronpos. Its only entrance is at the north-west. At the southern extremity there is a natural ledge descending into the cave, but more practicable for Nymphs than for Men. The northern entrance is narrow, and admits but little day: the interior, and particularly the vault of the subterranean crypt, is lighted up by delicate gleams of a bluish hue, and, though of a paler tinge, yet not unlike that blue sky of stone which hangs over the Grotta d'Azzurro in the island of Caprea. The vault itself is hung with stalactites, some of which expand into what Homer calls webs of stone, where the Nymphs might be supposed to have woven their threads whose colour was like the sea.

We are tempted by the name of a village on the north-west coast of the island to pay it a visit. It is called POLIS. Opposite to it is the islet of DASCAGLIO, perhaps so called from having been the abode of a *diduscalos*, or monk. This is the only rock in the channel of CEPHALLONIA, and ought therefore to be the ASTERIS, where the Suitors lay in ambush for Telemachus, on his return from Pylos to Ithaca. Dascaglio contains no harbours such as Homer attributes to Asteris, but this seems no valid objection to this supposition; for every one knows what Homer's vessels were,—that anchors were no part of their equipment,—and that harbours, therefore, were simply places to disembark in. Besides, the name of Asteris sufficiently proves that the Homeric island was a mere *starlike* rock, which Dascaglio is; and lastly, we would observe here, what is applicable to the poem in general, that it is not the part of sound criticism to fetter the imagination of the poet with rigid material restrictions. The Odyssey is to be regarded as an *ideal* structure, erected upon geographical and historical foundations. If now, Dascaglio be Asteris, the Homeric city should be near, and cannot be to the south of it. Was it therefore at Polis? Thus much may be said in its favour: the ruins on the woody hill rising to the north of Polis are of much ruder and more ancient style, though considerably less in extent than those of Aeto. The stones are rough and unhewn, and not closely fitted to each other. The principal remains are on the western side of the summit, and are piled on a very steep rock.

A harbour generally supposes the existence of ancient remains in its neighbourhood. Hence, on our arrival at the port of SANTA EUPHEMIA, on the eastern coast of Cephallonia, we are not surprised to hear that there are vestiges of Hellenic buildings at no great distance from the water. A quarter

3 A

of an hour's walk to the west brings us to the PALATIA, or Palace, as these ruins are called. Here is an ancient fort, consisting of two apartments, and built of polygonal masonry. The south wall remains entire, and is pierced with three embrasures for observation and the discharge of missiles. Coasting the island in a southerly direction, we arrive at POROS, probably so called as being the passage into the fertile vale of RAKLI, a corruption of the ancient Heraclea. The valley of Poros, which runs from north to south, is walled in on all sides but the north by high mountains: on the east it is hidden from the sea by ATROS: on the west it is divided from the interior by the ÆNESIAN range; the southern extremity is blocked up by the gable of Mount KORONUS,

CYCLOPEAN WALLS OF CEPHALONIA.

on the cliffs of which stood the strong fortress of PRONI, whose ruins still remain.

We enter at the north, and proceed down this romantic valley: the torrent-bed along which we pass is overhung with gay oleanders: in the freshness of a summer evening, after confinement on the sea in a small vessel, the transition to this valley is very delightful. Goats are browsing on the lentisk and arbutus upon the woody cliffs above us; and some, more bold, are climbing on the branches of the taller shrubs; the shepherd's flute is heard from the mountains, and the peasants are gathering in their harvest of uva passa. We proceed on till we arrive at a cottage, pleasantly situated near a stream and a mill: it is sheltered by walnuts and carroubas of luxuriant foliage; behind it is a small garden, in which are almonds, gourds, asparagus, and lavender. Here is a noble view of the Black Mountain, the ancient Ænus, the outline of which is boldly marked against the golden hues of the sun setting behind it. Here we spend the night.

The ruins of Proni stretch from north to south on a high rocky ridge, which hangs over the ravine of Poros. The fall of the rock into this gulley is almost perpendicular. At this eminence stood the Northern Acropolis: at the southern extremity of the ridge is another citadel, connected with the northern by parallel walls. The coins of Proni bear upon them the club of HERAKLES or HERCULES; and the name of RAKLÉ, by which the vale beneath it is known, is another indication of the Hero's connexion with this place. Perhaps this connexion arose from a belief that Herakles had opened with his club—for such actions were usually ascribed to him—the passage of Poros, that the waters which before inundated it might empty themselves into the sea, and had thus bestowed the fruitful valley of Raklé upon the grateful cultivator.

The SAMÆANS were probably right in thinking that the site of their town was too favourable not to be an object of ambition and envy to the Romans, who regarded the command of the channel of Cephallonia as essential to the conquest of Greece. These Roman ruins on the margin of the Bay of Samé, in the central point of the eastern coast of Cephallonia, prove that the city was inhabited by its conquerors. In proceeding toward the valley which divides the two citadels of Samé, so well described by Livy in his account of the siege conducted by the Roman Consul, we are reminded by the successive terraces of wall, which were perhaps erected on that occasion, of the device by which the besiegers for a long time baffled the enemy.

In the intermediate valley mentioned above, are many Tombs dug in the rock. These must have been contained within the range of the city walls. A Greek city, when besieged, supplied to the inhabitants an incentive to courage, from which, by a law of the Ten Tables, the Roman citizen was debarred. They had, within the walls of their cities, the tombs of their ancestors. We have several specimens before us, at Samé, of these graves, which are hollowed in the living stone. Proceeding upwards to the Northern Acropolis, we meet with a magnificent specimen of ancient masonry. On the highest of these courses of massive stone is a block of fourteen feet in length hanging obliquely, and, as it were, still trembling from the shock of the Roman engines. The Acropolis is remarkable for the varieties of architectural style which it exhibits: there are specimens in it of the polygonal and the horizontal, of emplecton, and of Roman brick-work. We observe a sally-port in the eastern wall, and a subterranean mine in the centre of the citadel,

apparently communicating with the western. The Southern Acropolis was the
point first gained by the Romans; it was called CYATHIS, probably from its
cup-like form.

We cross the island to ARGOSTOLI, on the western coast, the principal
town and harbour of Cephallonia. It is a walk of forty minutes from this
place to the foot of the hill upon which the ancient city of Cranii stood. Its
ruins are similar in character to those of the other cities of the island. Its
Acropolis, like theirs, is not fortified with towers; but in the plain to the
westward of the citadel is a long series of rectangular turrets, built with
horizontal courses. Following the valley to the south-east, we arrive at a line
of rocks which have been excavated for tombs. We enter a sepulchral

chamber containing a sarcophagus, near which is an inscription cut in the
living stone. The last of the four ancient cities of Cephallonia is PALÉ,
which lies to the north-west of Cranii, separated from it by the Gulf of
Lixuri.

The town of ZANTE, the ancient ZACYNTHUS, is beautifully situated on
the margin of its semicircular bay. It is flanked by two high hills; on one
is the castle; that to the south is called, from its extensive view, Mount
Scopo; probably it is the same as the ancient ELATUS, or mountain of silver
firs, which formerly, as may be presumed from its name, gave a reason, no
longer existing, for the woody Zacynthus of Homer. Much has been said con-

cerning the origin of the name of Zacynthus itself, and, as is usually the case, heroes have been created at will, from whom that appellation has been derived. But names of places are generally assigned in consequence of some peculiarity existing in the sites themselves. Mount Cynthus in Delos, and Ara-cynthus the mountain of Ætolia, and Bere-cynthia the name of the Earth, seem to show, that Cynthus in the early Greek language was a general term for a Hill. Cynthia was the goddess of Hills. Looking at these two mountains

before us, and the town placed between them, we prefer to go no further than the immediate neighbourhood of Za-cynthus for what it so well supplies, namely, the reason for its designation, which we may compare with that of a woody mountain of Epirus, called Za-longus, of which word the latter part (longus) is the general Romaic term for a forest. Za is only the Æolic form of the ancient preposition Dia, and denotes size or intensity.

The interior of the town of Zante has not much to recommend it. The streets have Venetian names, and dark, dwarfish arcades: in the houses are latticed windows, and in the shops none at all.

We pass through pretty lanes and hedges of pomegranates, quinces, smilax, and aloes, toward the south-west district: in the distance are long lines of cypresses. We observe on the left of the road a wine-vat similar to those in which Bacchus is represented treading out the grapes in ancient monuments. It consists of two compartments, about three feet deep, and covered over with stucco: after the fruit is trodden out with the feet in these receptacles, the grape-juice is drained off by funnels in the side of the vat.

It is certainly a curious sight to see pitch and rushes produced together, as is the case at the tar-wells of KIERI, which are the object of our next excursion. It is pleasant to watch the bituminous bubbles floating on their clear water, and to extract a myrtle branch, dripping with genuine pitch, from the viscous slime beneath; but it is more interesting to picture to ourselves the feelings with which, more than two thousand years ago, a party of Greek emigrants looked upon this spot in their way from the old capital of Greece to a new settlement in Italy: we are delighted to remember the interest which this same well excited in the mind of the most eminent of that party; we seem here to behold him inquiring into the nature of the phenomenon, measuring its dimensions, sounding its depth, and registering in his note-book all its particularities with the greatest equanimity and cheerfulness, although he was then an exile from his own country, and did not possess a foot of land in any other. Such a mind was that of him to whom we here allude—HERODOTUS. It must have been quite as profitable a source to its possessor as this singular well, which enables its possessor to carry on a lucrative trade.

In the year B.C. 211, Philip of Macedon, the son of Demetrius, raised the siege of Pale in Cephallonia, and sailed to Leucadia, whence he commenced an expedition through Acarnania into the heart of ÆTOLIA. He was invited to do so by the inhabitants at that particular season, because half of the Ætolian army was then absent in Thessaly, under its general Dorimachus. Philip, as we are told by Polybius, proceeded from Limnæa, which appears to have been on the south-eastern shore of the Ambracian Gulf, and thence marched to the river Achelous, which he crossed near STRATUS, the Acarnanian capital, and thus passed into Ætolia. He directed his course with all speed to THERMUS, the principal city. In his way thither he had Stratus, Agrinium, and Thestienses on the left hand; and on the right, Conope, Trichonium, and Phœteum. He then arrived at a city called Metapa, which lay at the entrance of the defile on the borders of the TRICHONIAN Lake, and about six miles from Thermus. Having taken the necessary precautions to render the route secure,

he entered this defile. His right wing was protected by Thracian auxiliaries and light-armed troops, and his left by the lake, along the side of which he marched for about three miles. The road from Pamphia, at the termination of the defile, to the walls of Thermus, was a steep ascent, having ragged precipices on both sides for the same distance of three miles.

On his arrival there he met with no opposition; such had been the rapidity of his march, and such was the confidence of the Ætolians in the natural strength of the place.

Thermus was the Acropolis of Ætolia. It was the spot in which the national assemblies were held,—the citadel where arms and provisions were stored,—the treasury which contained the wealth both of individuals and of the state,—the Sacred Inclosure in which the great national Temple stood,—and the Museum which comprised within it the most beautiful objects of art which Ætolia could boast. All these fell into the hands of Philip, who used his victory in a manner which has drawn forth an expression of well-merited censure from the grave and philosophic historian.

To the other islands of Greece we can only very briefly allude. The Ionian seas, as we have seen, are studded with important and picturesque islands, full of classical interest. The bold and rocky headland of the southern coast, with the Island of Cythera, are the first objects which meet the tourist on his approach to the shores of Greece from the south, and the mountains of Laconia, overtopped by the Taigeton range, is the loftiest group which presents itself. To the eastward, in the Argolic Gulf and the Sea of Ægina, coasts and islands of the most beautiful and varied form multiply on the eye, but, on approaching them, unmitigated sterility prevails. More to the eastward, in the Grecian Archipelago, are the Islands of the Cyclades. The most distant of these is the isle of Scio, represented on the preceding page, which stands at the entrance to the Sea of Marmora. The Island of Syra is in the centre of this group, and its capital is now one of the most important emporiums in Greece. The island is barren but picturesque. The town is built on a conical hill covered to the summit with white-washed houses, and crowned at the top by a monastery. Below this it spreads down even to the water's edge, where numbers of boats unloading, and crowds of sailors, attest the rising prosperity of the place. The town has a noble appearance from the harbour as well as from the heights above. Other islands, which are too numerous to mention here, are scattered round the islet of DELOS,—the cynosure of Ancient Greece—the bright polestar in the insular constellation, which once shone so fairly in the lucid and liquid heaven of the Ægean Sea.

THE PELOPONNESUS

WE now propose to describe the country lying to the south of the Corinthian Gulf, and known as the PELOPONNESUS. The form of this country is nearly insular, being only connected with Northern Greece by the narrow slip of land, known as the Isthmus of Corinth, at its north-eastern extremity. It thus presents a considerable extent of sea-coast, indented with

3 B

inland Gulfs, Bays, and Seas, broken by headlands, inclosed by mountains, and studded with islands.

The land which stretches along the southern coast of the Corinthian Gulf, from Patras to the citadel of Corinth, is about sixty miles in length and ten in breadth, and is backed to the south by another chain of mountains from six to seven thousand feet in height, decreasing in altitude towards the eastern termination of their range. The principal of these, commencing at the west, are OLONOS, ERYMANTHUS, and CYLLENE: they separate this strip of land, formerly called ACHAIA, from the inland province of Arcadia.

Nothing can be more marked than the contrast presented by the aspect of these two neighbouring countries: the latter, surrounded as it were by a circular wall of lofty mountains, four of which—namely, Erymanthus and Cyllené at the north, and Lycæus and Mænalus at the south—stand aloft like the castellated Towers of this mural circumvallation, and having no outlet but one on its western verge, seems as it were imprisoned within itself. Numerous streams fall down into its vales from the mountains around it, but are unable to find any exit for their pent-up waters except by mining for themselves a channel through the limestone rock of which these mountains are composed. The country was isolated; for hundreds of years its population underwent

little change: it had no commerce with nations without, and little with strangers within. Such was the constancy of its inhabitants and the permanence of their society, that they did not compare their national existence to any other objects of *earth*, but elevated their State, if we may so say, to a *heavenly* rank, and claimed for it an antiquity equal to that of the first-created Powers of the Universe. The Arcadians, according to their own mythology, existed before the Moon, and they called themselves by a name indicating that belief.

Let us now turn to the northern side of the mountain chain which we have just noticed. Everything here bears the appearance of openness and liberty. Numerous rills flow down its declivities, all running parallel to each other in a northerly direction, and, after a short and uninterrupted course over the plain or along hollow valleys, fall into the waters of the Corinthian Gulf. Unfortunately for the commercial qualifications of the country, the distance traversed by these streams is so insignificant, that they have not time to swell into navigable rivers, nor force sufficient to form in the coast-line projections which might have supplied a want very remarkable in so extensive a shore,—

that of a commodious harbour. No good port exists in the whole of Achaia.
What might have been the result if the contrary had been the case, is evident
from the commercial importance attained by the cities of Patræ and Sicyon
in ancient times, although possessed of inconsiderable advantages in this
respect.

The traveller feels pleasure in considering some of the moral, social,
and political results which arose from the physical character of the territory
of ACHAIA, especially when contemplated in juxtaposition with that of its
neighbour on the south. In the earliest times of Greek history' it bore the
name of ÆGIALUS, or the Coast-land, a designation derived from its position :
it was then inhabited by Ionians of Attica, who built twelve cities upon its
soil. The facility of communication between one part of this district and

PLAIN OF ÆGIRA, AND ONE SIDE OF ITS RAVINES.

another seems to have favoured the organi-
zation of that federal system of state policy
which existed at a very early period in this
province, and which made its institutions
the model of popular legislation, not merely in Greece, but among the Asiatic
and Italian Colonies from that country. Eighty years after the Trojan war,
the ACHÆANS, who derived their origin from Thessaly, were driven by the
descendants of Hercules from the territory of Laconia and Argolis, in which
they had settled. They emigrated in a northerly direction, and at last fixed
their abode in Ægialus, whence they expelled the Ionian population, which
having returned to Attica, and there put itself under the direction of the sons
of Codrus, crossed the Ægean Sea, and settled themselves on that beautiful
strip of land which extends along the western coast of Asia, and was called,
from the name of its new colonists, Ionia. Between this country and that

which they had left, many points of resemblance may be noticed. Ionia was the Asiatic Achaia, and Achaia was the European Ionia. There was much in the country they had quitted to prepare the Ionians for their new habitation, and much in Ionia to remind them of, and to console them for, the home which they had lost. It is interesting and agreeable to trace their love and regret for their ancient seats, which shows itself in the similarity of names between the towns, rivers, and promontories of Ægialus and Ionia, just in the same manner as English names reappear in our own day in America.

. It is also not less pleasing to reflect that some part of the commercial and maritime distinction of the latter might have been derived from the habits and feelings which its colonists brought with them from the coasts of Greece: and, as in the federal union of the twelve cities of Ionia, we recognise the vestiges of that which combined the twelve cities of Ægialus,— as in the Panionian assembly held in the Temple of the Heliconian Neptune, upon the Asiatic promontory of Mycale, we perceive the revival of that which had been convened in former times in a temple of the same Deity upon the cape of the Greek Helicé,—so, in the wealth and splendour of Smyrna, of Ephesus, and of Miletus, upon the shores of the Ægæan, we see a development of that spirit which received its first impulse in the humbler cities of Patræ, Pellené, and Ægium, on the shores of the Corinthian Gulf.

The Achæans, having dispossessed the Ionians, changed the name of the country which they had invaded from Ægialus to Achaia. This latter designation too, has, we are inclined to think, some reference as well as the former

to its position and character. The names of Acheron and Achelous assigned
to rivers suggest the conjecture that the title of Achaia was conferred upon
that country, as Apulia was upon a district similarly situated in Italy, on
account of its *aqueous* character, as peculiarly the marine land,—the land
of waters among the different provinces of the Greek peninsula.

In the Homeric catalogue of the Grecian fleet at Troy, the ships of
Pellené, Ægium, and Helicé, and of the rest of Ægialus, are ranged with
those of Mycenæ, Corinth, and Sicyon, under the command of Agamemnon.
At that period the Achæans were in possession of Lacedæmon and Argos, and
exerted the greatest influence over the rest of the Peloponnesus. After that
time for many centuries the inhabitants of the cities first named took little
part in the general concerns of Greece. During the Persian invasion, the
Achæans, says Pausanias, neither joined Leonidas at Thermopylæ, nor aided
Themistocles at Salamis: they were absent from the engagement at Platæa,
being unwilling to submit to the authority of the Lacedæmonian General,
to whom as a Dorian they felt a strong national antipathy, looking back
with pride, as they did, to the pre-eminence which they had themselves
enjoyed in the heroic times of Greece, when they possessed the territory now
governed by Lacedæmon. The state of neutrality and inactivity in which the
Achæans remained during the most stirring part of Greek history may be
explained by the consideration, that they entertained no feelings of attachment
to either of the two great rival parties of that period. With the Athenians,
the representatives of the Ionian family, the Achæans were not connected by
the bonds of friendship and sympathy, for the Athenians were in possession of
the soil from which the Ionians had been driven by their ancestors; much less
did they look on the Lacedæmonians, the leaders of the Doric race, with a
friendly eye, having been themselves expelled from their hereditary seats in
Argos and Laconia, by the progenitors of those who now dwelt at Sparta.
Hence it arose, that while their neighbours were engaged in long and
violent contests, the Achæans enjoyed a state of tranquillity and repose,
which harmonized with the natural character of their open and even soil,
compared with the stern and savage features of those lands which bordered
upon theirs. In this condition they remained for a considerable time; and
it was not till the glories of other Greek states had faded away, that Achaia
began to display that power which afterwards gained such distinguished
renown. It seems as if Achaia had deliberately delayed its own progress
until the other nations of Hellas were wearied with their exertions in the
pursuit of fame, in order that it might advance and claim the prize which
they resigned, as the last in the Lampadephoria of the Greek Nations, to receive
the torch which had been transmitted in succession from the hand of one City to

another. The splendour of Athens had been some time on the wane; Sparta was sinking by the weight of pressure from without and the undermining of corruptions from within; Thebes—having shown what she was capable of effecting, when guided by the counsels, and animated by the example, of two wise and intrepid leaders—had fallen with them, never more to rise. Now, therefore, that these cities were reduced to this humiliating condition, it was a glorious opportunity for Achaia to show what results might be attained by arts and virtues of such rare growth in Grecian soil, namely, civil harmony and concord.

RUINS OF ALBANA.

The twelve cities of Achaia, whose names are preserved by Herodotus and Strabo, being united in a compact body among themselves, and enjoying a form of civil polity wisely tempered by an admixture of popular and aristocratic elements, subsisted, as has been said, during a long period in a state of happy and undisturbed prosperity. The political storm from Macedonia which broke upon Greece shattered for a time the League which bound them together. But when that had passed, some of the fragments coalesced, and the effects of their dissolution began to disappear. In the year B.C. 280, when the attention of the Macedonian princes was engaged at home by domestic discords, four of the Achæan cities, DYME, PATRÆ, TRITÆA, and PHARÆ, took advantage of the opportunity thus afforded them for reviving the independence of their country; when five years had elapsed, they were joined by ÆGIUM,

CERYNEA, and BURA, which had ejected their tyrants, or expelled their Macedonian garrisons. To these, four others shortly afterwards attached themselves; the twelfth, HELICE, had been swallowed up by an inundation of the sea. Annually in the spring and summer, assemblies were convoked of deputies from these states, for the purpose of consulting concerning war and peace, the framing of alliances, the creation of magistrates, and the enactment of laws. The place of their convention was the sacred grove of Jupiter Homagyrius, near the temple of the Panachæan Ceres at Ægium. Every citizen from any of the confederate states who had passed his thirtieth year was at liberty to be present, and to propose measures to the Assembly for their adoption. The session was limited by law to three days. A common system of weights and measures was employed by the cities of Achaia; so that they were all, as it were, members of the same state.

PELLA.

The cities of this province, having combined themselves together in a federal union, proceeded to increase their power by foreign conquest. They wrested Corinth from the hands of the Macedonians, and attached that city to their own body. To strengthen themselves in this conquest, they allied themselves with Rome, and thus for a temporary gain, they authorised the introduction of a principle which afterwards proved the cause of their dissolution. They discovered too late that the real victory thus gained was not a triumph of one Greek over another, but of Rome over Greece. Still, however, they pursued the infatuated course: they joined the Romans in their expeditions into Macedonia against Philip, and fought under the Roman standard against their neighbours in Ætolia. Their resources, thus increased, tempted them to gratify their ancient enmity against Lacedæmon, which they succeeded in reducing to dependence upon themselves for a time, and alienating from them for ever. By so doing they paved the way for their own degradation, and for the ultimate loss of the liberties of their common country. The appeal of the Lacedæmonians against the overbearing conduct of the Achæans towards themselves, was joyfully welcomed by Rome as affording an occasion for her own interference in the internal affairs of Greece. The exiles of

Sparta were recalled by her orders, and its walls, which had been destroyed by the Achæans, were rebuilt. On the false accusation of the traitor Callicrates, more than a thousand of the principal citizens of Achaia were summoned to Italy under suspicion of collusion with Perseus, when he was at war with Rome; and it was only when seventeen years had elapsed, that, having been detained as prisoners in different parts of Etruria, three hundred of the number, among whom was the historian POLYBIUS, returned to their own land. Instructed and exasperated by this treatment, the Achæans resorted to defensive measures against the encroachments of Rome. But it was too late. The Achæans had been instrumental in reducing to bondage those by whose aid they might have been able now to preserve the liberties of Greece. As a retribution for this act, they were now to become the slaves of Rome. For a short time they survived after the independence of the rest of Greece was extinct. It was a poor consolation for their folly, that when Greece was politically defunct, the Romans inscribed upon its tomb the name of ACHAIA.

At the north-west extremity of Achaia stands the town of Patras, the ancient PATRÆ. It overlooks a fertile plain, which is now principally devoted to the cultivation of the small grape which flourishes here in much greater abundance than at Corinth, whence it derives its name. The city enjoys great advantages, arising from its position at the southern entrance of the Corinthian Gulf, and from thus possessing ready means of communication with western Greece, the Islands of the Ionian Sea, and the shores of Italy and Sicily. After the battle of Actium, Patræ was to the Peloponnesus what Nicopolis, as described above, was to continental Greece. On account of its local qualifications, it was chosen by Augustus as the spot to which he might transplant colonists from different cities which were not so favourably placed for commerce. Here in later times were seen some of the ancient statues of the Deities, brought from those dismantled towns; here was an Odeum, the second in beauty and magnificence in Greece, where the rude inhabitants of

ODEUM AT PATRAS

those old mountain towns learnt to forget their rustic habits; here, near the sea-side, was a grove containing temples of Apollo and Venus, and intersected with walks which served as a delightful place of resort in the summer season. There are now but few remains of this ancient maritime capital of Achaia. The spring which is described as gushing from the earth near the two temples above mentioned, is still visible on the sea-shore, about a mile's distance from the town. Some vestiges of the walls of the ancient Acropolis may be traced in the substructions of the modern castle, which stands on an eminence at the northern extremity of Patras; some remains of an aqueduct of Roman brick, like that of Nicopolis, which brought water from the hills on the east of the citadel, are still visible; but the most interesting memorial which survives of the former history of Patræ is the tradition which here prevails, that this was the spot which witnessed the evidence given to the cause of Christian truth by the glorious death of its Apostle and Martyr, Saint Andrew.

Passing by Rhium, the port of the ancient Panormus, and proceeding onward in an easterly direction, we arrive, after a journey of rather more than twenty miles along the sea-coast, at the foot of a hill, beneath which are plentiful sources of water shaded by an umbrageous plane-tree. This is the site of the ancient Ægium, which, after the destruction of Helicé by an inundation of the sea, was chosen as the place of assembly for the members of the Achæan league. It is now called Vostitza; and from the goodness of its harbour, compared with any other upon this coast, from the excellence of its water, and from its position at the centre of the southern shore of the Corinthian Gulf, it still preserves some of its ancient importance, being the only town of any note which occurs in the voyage from the port of Patræ to that of Corinth.

At a little more than the same distance to the east of Ægium, than Ægium is to the east of Patræ, stands a circular hill with a tabular summit, about two miles from the sea-shore, and between two rivers which flow past it into the Corinthian Gulf. Towards the northern extremity of the hill is the modern village of BASILICA: this was the site of the ancient city of SICYON, the date of whose foundation is prior to all records of Greek history. The situation combines all the advantages which were generally looked for as the requisite qualifications for the erection of a Greek city. The Acropolis stood upon the spot now occupied by the modern village. The walls of the town followed the crest of the tabular hill mentioned above, and communicated with the harbour by means of lines of fortification stretching from their circuit to the sea-shore.

The principal remains of Sicyon which now survive, are found on the
south-west side of this mountain platform. We there find a Theatre facing
the sea, of which the foundations and some of the seats are hewn in the living
rock. By its side, and running parallel to it, is a Stadium, of which the
southern end is excavated in the soil, while its two northern extremities are
formed of massive walls in the polygonal style. The Theatre is the only one
of the numerous buildings existing at Sicyon in the time of Pausanias, and
described by that topographer.

It is a melancholy thing to read on this spot the catalogues which
Pausanias has left of the many temples, statues, and pictures, which once
adorned this desolate place. Here stood a painted portico, which vied with
the Pœcilé at Athens; here was the Senate-house erected by the hand of
Cleisthenes; here, bronze statues of Hercules and Jupiter, the works of the
illustrious Lysippus, a native of this place; here, a figure of Pan in ivory and
gold, the production of Calamis; near it was a marble statue of Hercules,
from the chisel of Scopas; here were numberless compositions by Crato,
Telephanes, Cleœtas, and Canachus, and by other artists of Sicyon, who made
this City the most famous among the ancient schools of painting and of
sculpture from the earliest times to the days of Alexander the Great, and of
that distinguished Sicyonian citizen, ARATUS, who, to his endowments and
distinctions as a Statesman and a Warrior, added the graceful accomplishments
of a skilful judge and liberal patron of the Arts. His statue adorned the
theatre whose ruins we see before us: his ashes repose upon this hill, where
his obsequies were celebrated with great pomp, and where a monument,
surpassing in magnificence all that the age could boast, was erected to his
memory by his grateful countrymen. He died, not without suspicion of
having been poisoned by Philip the Third of Macedon, in the year B.C. 213.
His country did not long survive him: for a few years the gallant Philopœmen sustained the cause of the Achæan league; he, when seventy years of
age, having reduced the city of Lacedæmon, and fighting before the walls
of Messene, was, in B.C. 183, taken prisoner and put to death. His funeral
urn was borne by the son of Lycortas, his successor in the dignity of chief
magistrate of the Achæan confederacy, the youthful Polybius, the future
historian of the war. Thirty-seven years afterwards, the city of Corinth was
taken by Mummius, the Roman consul, and with the fall of that city fell the
fortunes and glories of its neighbour, Sicyon.

Greece triumphed over her Roman victors by the peaceful influence of her
Arts. Exiled, as it were, from her own soil, she took refuge in the asylum
afforded to her by them; as Orestes, banished from Argos, did in the temple
of Pallas—the Deity of Wisdom—at Athens. The destruction of Corinth was,

in a certain sense, the source of glory and victory to a conquered nation. The soldiers of Mummius robbed the temples of Corinth of their statues and pictures; they even tore from its theatre the bronze vessels which made it more sonorous; they were guilty of acts of rapine and excess in a manner to extort from Polybius, the Greek panegyrist of Rome, the strongest expressions of reprobation. But these hardy warriors soon gave way to the gentle influences exercised by the objects which they carried in triumph to their own country; and the spirit of Greece, when the body was extinct, was worshipped in the palaces and forums of the Roman capital, like a divinized being which had passed from earth to heaven.

The route from Ægium to Megaspelion is full of interest. The Corinthian Gulf affords here its noblest views, and, although twenty miles across at this point, the mountains beyond it seem to tower into the skies. In descending towards the shore, the magnitude of the rocks of Megaspelion strike the beholder with surprise. In the course of the journey several copious streams are passed, which descend from Mount Chelmus, shaded with trees and bounded by fine precipices. Shortly after leaving Ægium, the road strikes into the opposite mountains, the summits of which are attained in about thirty minutes. Descending from this elevation, in about half-an-hour more the insulated rock of Palaio-Kalavrita is attained. From this spot the monastery of Megaspelion is visible at the opposite extremity of a deep and uneven valley.

A journey of two hours brings the traveller to the monastery. It is erected upon a steep and narrow ridge, and against the mouth of a large natural cavern, most of the interior being a portion of the cave itself. Externally it is a large white building, of a picturesque and irregular form, facing the west, and having twenty-three windows in front. A magnificent precipice of from four to five hundred feet in height rises from the cave and overhangs the building. Around the monastery the country is rich in picturesque grandeur; trees of aged growth are seen on the mountains, and the rocks are bold and precipitous.

To the south-east of the monastery rises the lofty chain of Mount Chelmos, and issuing from its rocky bed, tumbling and tossing, descends the fabled stream of the Styx. It has its source, according to Herodotus, near to the Arcadian town of Nonacris, and the ravine by which the river descends through

masses of rock, of ice, and of snow, is one of
the most striking in nature. The grand and
the picturesque are here happily blended. Cliffs,
cascades, and rocky chasms strewn with wood
torn from its precipitous sides, fill up the picture.
The valley as seen from below, backed by the
loftiest ridge of Mount Chelmos, is a striking subject for a picture; the
great valley of the Styx appears in full view on the descent amidst huge
and fantastic assemblages of rock.

If we retrace our steps from Sicyon to the west, and mount along the side
of one of the streams which fall into the Gulf of Corinth near the site of the
ancient Ægium, pursuing the upward track in a southerly direction, we shall
arrive on one of the woody summits of Erymanthus, from which, if we look
westward, we command a view of the territory of Elis lying beneath us. Two
rivers, which water that plain, take their rise here. The one is the river
Peneus, which leaves the site of the ancient city of Elis on its left, and waters
the country, once called THE HOLLOW ELIS from its form, and inhabited in
the Homeric age by the Epeians; the other stream bears the same name as
the mountain from which it descends: having flowed to the south for a considerable distance, it falls into the river Alphéus, which continuing its course

to the west, passes to the left of the spots occupied formerly by the magnificent buildings of Pisa and Olympia. This country was anciently called the
PISATIS. In the time of Homer it was possessed by the PYLIANS, whose
dominions extended from the slopes of Taygetus over the country subsequently
called Messenia, and reached to the Epeian frontier, on the southern side of
the Penéus.

VALLEY OF THE PENEUS, NEAR GASTOUNIA.

The proportion of the Power of the Epeians to that of the Pylians is
expressed in Homer, by the contributions made by each to the fleet of
Agamemnon. Ninety ships were furnished by the Epeians, whereas the
Pylians supplied forty only. There are many points of resemblance in the
geography and history of Elis and Achaia. Looking in a cursory manner at
their great physical characteristics, we observe that they both consist of flat
lowlands stretching along the sea, broken, indeed, occasionally, by declivities
of mountains waving down from the lofty ridges in the interior, and by mountain streams running in deep woody ravines from the same rocky eminences,

which thus dispense fertility to the plains beneath them. Both the provinces present a favourable appearance in variety and richness of produce when contrasted with the other divisions of the peninsula.

It is a consequence of those natural properties which conduced to its fertility that so few remains at present survive of the former splendour of Elis. The soil consists of a rich alluvial loam, deposited, in the lower grounds, by the rivers of which we have spoken; and the stone of the country is of a more porous description than the limestone and marble supplied by the

THE ALPHEUS IN ELIS.

quarries in the other parts of Greece. Consequently the remains of the buildings have disappeared more rapidly beneath the covering of soil brought down by the streams from the mountain slopes. The same observation may be applied generally to the other provinces of the Grecian continent and peninsula, upon which Nature has bestowed a larger share of her endowments; the remains of Antiquity are generally in the inverse ratio of the fertility of their soil. Scarcely a sculptured group or fragment of a frieze is to be seen at the present time within the limits of those districts of Hellas most distinguished' for their fruitfulness: namely, Thessaly and Bœotia on the continent, and Achaia and Elis in the Peloponnesus.

We have observed the pacific character of Achaia as compared with that of other states in the peninsula. A similar remark may be applied to Elis. The possession within their frontier of the national sanctuary of the Olympian Jove invested it with a hallowed dignity, which was a more powerful protection to them than the force of arms. We accordingly hear of many of the Eleans passing their time as country gentlemen in the quiet enjoyments of rural life on their own estates, which they rarely quitted to visit the larger towns even in their own neighbourhood; and thus the security, which they derived from their peculiar national privilege, rendered works of fortification, and military architecture in general, matters of less necessity than they would otherwise have been. The search, therefore, for the vestiges of walled towns will here be attended with little success.

"Many objects," says Pausanias, "may a man see in Greece, and many things may he hear that are worthy of admiration, but, above them all, the doings at Eleusis, and the sights at Olympia, have somewhat in them of a soul divine."

In descending the slopes, which fall to the south-west of Mount Erymanthus, we come in sight of a valley, about three miles in length and one in breadth, lying from east to west below the hill on which we stand, and bounded on the south by a broad river, running over a gravelly bed, and studded with small islands. Its banks are shaded with plane-trees, and rich fields of pasture and arable land are watered by its stream. The valley is OLYMPIA, the hill is Mount CRONIUS, the river the ALPHEUS. The eastern and western boundaries of the plain are formed by two other streams, both flowing into the Alphêus. Beginning at Mount Cronius, and following the western of these two brooks, formerly called the CLADEUS, among clusters of pines and olives, to the point where it falls into the Alphêus, and tracing our course eastward along the Alphêus for about a mile, till we arrive at a ridge which falls downward to the east, and pursuing this ridge, which runs to the north, till we come to Mount Cronius, from which it descends, we have made the circuit or traced the limits of the peribolus of the ancient ALTIS, or sacred grove of Jupiter, which was formerly the seat of the most glorious and holy objects of Olympia. On the south and east it was bounded by a wall, on the north by the mountain which we have mentioned, and on the west by the Cladeus.

Looking downward towards the river Alphêus from the southern slopes of Mount Cronius, we have immediately on our right the positions of the

ancient Gymnasium and Prytaneum. Beneath us stood the row of ten
TREASURIES from west to east, which were raised by different Greek States,
and contained statues and other offerings of great value and exquisite workmanship. Below them, on a basement of stone steps, were six statues of
Jupiter, called Zanes, made from the fines levied upon athletes who had trans-
gressed the laws by which the Olympic contests were regulated. Further to

PLAIN OF OLYMPIA

the left, in a wood of wild olives in a declivity of Mount Cronius, and
running from north to south, was the STADIUM. It was approached by the
Hellanodicæ, or judges of the course, by a secret entrance. The starting-
place, or aphesis, was at the northern extremity, near which was the tomb
of Endymion.

Beyond the Stadium and the eastern limit of the Altis, still further to the left, was the HIPPODROME, which stretched from west to east: its western façade was formed by a portico built by the architect Agnaptus. Passing through it, the spectator arrived at a triangular area, of which the base coincided with the back of the portico; in each of the two sides, which were more than four hundred feet in length, was a series of stalls or barriers, in which the chariots and horses stood, parallel to each other; all looking straight towards the course. A rope was stretched in front of these barriers. At the apex of the triangle, or the point nearest the course, stood a bronze dolphin raised upon a style. In the middle of the triangle was an altar of unbaked brick, which was whitened at every successive Olympiad; raised above it was a bronze eagle, stretching its wings at full length. When the proper time had arrived, the officer of the course touched the spring concealed within the altar, and the eagle began to soar aloft, an impulse being thus given to it, so that it became visible to all the spectators. At the same time the bronze dolphin fell to the ground. Then the rope was withdrawn, first from the barriers on each side nearest to the base of the triangle, so as to allow the horses in them to start: when they had arrived in a line with those in the second barriers, these latter were let out, and thus the next in order, till, gradually, they were all liberated, so that at the moment when the last pair were released, they were all side by side in a line drawn through the apex, parallel to the base.

An isolated longitudinal ridge, or spine, commencing at some distance from the apex, divided the Hippodrome into two parts; around this the course lay, beginning on the right or southern side of it.

Nearly in the centre of the Altis, or consecrated ground, stood the temple of the Olympian Jove. It was erected from the spoils taken by the Eleans, in their contests with the inhabitants of Pisa. It was a Doric edifice, hypæthral and peripteral, ninety-five feet in breadth, two hundred and thirty in length, and sixty-eight to the summit of the pediment in height. The interior was divided into three compartments, by two rows of columns, each in double tiers. The stone of which it was constructed was the poros of the country; its architect, Libon of Elis.

A golden vase adorned both ends of the roof. In the centre of both the pediments was a golden statue of Victory, and under the Victory a shield of gold, having a figure of Medusa upon it. In later times, one-and-twenty gilded bucklers hung upon the architrave over the columns, the offering of Mummius after the destruction of Corinth. In both the pediments were groups of sculpture: the eastern exhibited the contest between Pelops and Œnomäus; this was the work of Pæonius, a native of Menda in Thrace: that on the western front represented the contest of the Centaurs and Lapithæ, and was the work of Alcamenes, a contemporary of Phidias. In the metopes were scenes from the history of Hercules.

But the most glorious ornament of this magnificent fabric, and one which, in the language of the ancient critic, added dignity to religion, was the statue of Jupiter within the temple. It was the work of Phidias, and formed of ivory and gold. This combination, as a great English sculptor, Flaxman, observes, "equally splendid and harmonious, in such a colossal form, produced a dazzling glory, like electric fluid, running over the surface of the figure, and thus gave it the appearance of an immortal vision in the eyes of the votary." No wonder, therefore, if it was commonly believed that Jupiter himself had lighted up the statue by a flash of lightning from heaven, and so had kindled in its aspect a blaze of divinity. The ivory, with which the greater part of the figure was overlaid, had a tint of flesh, which communicated to it the appearance of a living and intelligent object; while the gold, the precious stones, and painting with which its accessories were decorated, together with the stupendous size of the whole work, sixty feet in height, produced an effect which awed the beholder into a belief that he was looking on the face of Jupiter himself. Nor let it be forgotten, that the whole work was imbued by a spirit within, breathed from the lips of Homer; for it was his description of the King of Gods and Men which filled the mind of Phidias, as he himself confessed, when he executed this statue.

The god sat upon his throne, wearing a crown like an olive wreath upon his head. In his right hand he supported a statue of Victory, which he seemed to offer to the combatants who came hither to adore him; it was made of ivory and gold, and bore a chaplet. In his left hand was his staff or sceptre, inlaid with metals of every description, and having an eagle perched upon its summit. The sandals of the deity were of gold, as also was his robe, which was embroidered with figures and lilies. The throne on which he sat was adorned with gold and precious stones, with ebony, and with ivory, with painted figures and others in relief. Embossed on each of the four feet of the throne were four dancing Victories, and beside them two statues of Victory standing near each foot. In addition to this, on the two front feet were represented the children of the Thebans seized by the Sphinges; and below the Sphinges, Apollo and Diana were transfixing with their arrows the sons of Niobe.

Between the feet were single horizontal bars: on that towards the entrance were seven figures in relief, and on the others the contests of Hercules and his comrades with the Amazons. Each of the bars was bisected by an upright column, which, together with the feet, served to support the statue. Other decorations of a minuter character were scattered near it in rich profusion. Such was the appearance which the Olympian JUPITER presented to the view

when the purple embroidered veil which hung before him fell to the ground
and exhibited the Father of Gods and Men in all the glories of which the
greatest spirits of antiquity could conceive and execute the idea.

The Olympic Games were celebrated once in four years. They lasted for
five days, and terminated on the full moon which succeeded the summer
solstice. Contrasted with the particular æras which served for the chronological arrangement of events in distinct provinces of Greece, the epoch
supplied by their celebration to all the inhabitants of the Hellenic soil deserves
peculiar attention. While the succession of Priestesses of Juno at Argos,—
and the Ephors at Sparta, and the Archons at Athens, furnished to those
States respectively the bases of their chronological systems, it was not a
Personage invested with a civil or sacerdotal character who gave his name
to the four-yearly periods observed as measures of time by the whole of
Greece; it was he who was proclaimed Victor, not in the chariot-race of
the Hippodrome, but as having outrun his rivals in the stadium at Olympia.
A reflection on the rapid course of Time, that great Racer in the Stadium of
the World, might well have suggested such a practice; and it is very remarkable as illustrating the regard paid, by the unanimous consent of the States
of Greece, to those exercises of physical force that preserved them so long
from the corruptions of luxury and effeminacy, into which, through their
growing opulence and familiarity with Oriental habits, they would very soon
otherwise have fallen. Olympia was the Palæstra of Greece. The simplicity
of the prizes, the antiquity of their institution, the sacred ceremonies with
which they were connected; the glory which attached not merely to the victor,
but to his parents, his friends and country; his canonization in the Greek
calendar; the concourse of rival tribes from every quarter of the Greek continent and peninsula, to behold the contests and to applaud the conqueror; the
lyric songs of Pindar or Simonides; the garlands showered upon his head by
the hands of friends, of strangers, and of Greece herself; the statue erected to
him in the precincts of the consecrated grove, by the side of Princes, of
Heroes, and of Gods; the very rareness of the celebration, and the glories of
the season of the year at which it took place, when all the charms of summer
were poured upon the earth by day, and the full orb of the moon streamed
upon the olive groves and the broad flood of the Alphëus by night; these were
influences which, while they seemed to raise the individual to an elevation
more than human, produced a far more noble and useful result than this—
that of maintaining in the nation a general respect for a manly and intrepid
character, and of supporting that moral dignity and independence which so
long resisted the aggressions of force from without, and were proof against the
contagion of weak and licentious principles within.

OLYM...

...the...
...at...
...wards...

...during four years. They held...
full moon which succeeded...
...order area which served for...
...in most positions of Greece...it was...
...the observance of the Hellenic festivals...
...in of Priests exclusive at the...

Archons at Athens, formed the...
...or chronological systems, it was...
...superficial character who gave to...
...as measured time by the work...
...dated. We...not in the character...
...events private in the nations of Ohio...
...That first Race at the Stadium...
...which practice as it is very...
...by the numerous races of the Sta...
...physical force that preserved them so...
...and seminaries into which Greece was...
...ty with Oriental habits, they would very...
...n was the Palestra of Greece. The multitude...
...of their production, the sacred ceremonies...
...by which attached most nearly to the rac...
...the entry; his consecration in the Gre...
...throughout every quarter of the Greek con...
...to all the events and temple at the conquerors the...
...Sta...it the lands showered upon his head...
...cause of Greece he... If, the same exalted...
...consecrated power, to the side of Priscus...
...ness of the conquerors, and the glorious...
...which they achieved the chase of an hon...
...a..., and the full orb of the moon announced...
...festival of the Apollo...yet his...There were...
...and to raise the medal which we celebrated...
...which is so noble and useful is not that hon...
...the real essence of a penny, and in rep...
...and the joys of...rising exchange which is...
...trace were eventually a great accession to...
...possible...

Without interruption, for upwards of a thousand years, the full moon after the summer solstice every fourth year witnessed the celebration of these Games. The first Olympiad coincides with the year B.C. 776, the last with A.D. 394, or the sixteenth of the Emperor Theodosius, when the calculation by indictions was adopted in its stead. According to the assertion of Polybius, Timæus, the Sicilian historian, who flourished B.C. 300, was the first annalist who introduced the regular practice of comparing chronologically the Archons of Athens, the Priestesses of Argos, and the Ephors and Kings of Sparta, with the contemporary victors at Olympia. He was thus the founder of the

THE [illegible] OF ELIS

Olympic era as applied to history, without which no records for the general use of Greece could have existed.

There is now no habitation on the site of Olympia. On the north of it are rocky heights crowned with wood; some pines are seen on the hills to the west, and Oriental plane-trees hang over the wide gravelly bed of the river Alphĕus on the south. A few ruins of brick are scattered over the soil of what was once the Altis, or consecrated inclosure, but hardly a vestige remains of the foundations of the Temple of the Olympian Jove, and all the altars and statues which once crowded its precincts have passed away, like those countless multitudes who came here and departed hence in successive generations during

a fifth part of the long period of time which has elapsed from the Creation of
the world to the present day.

On the opposite side of the Alpheus, at a little more than two miles
distant to the south of Olympia, is the site of the small village of SCILLUS.
It stood in a woody valley, watered by the river SELINUS. In this picturesque
and solitary glen, the friend of Socrates, of Agesilaus, and of Cyrus,—the
Athenian General, Philosopher, and Historian, XENOPHON, an exile from his
country,—spent the latter part of his days. By the side of this stream and
among these woods he composed the greater part of his works. In one of them
he has left a description, forming a pleasing contrast to the stirring narratives
of marches and battles which succeed and follow it, of this peaceful place and
of his own occupations here. Perhaps a more agreeable specimen of simple
and unaffected piety in a heathen can nowhere be found, than in his account
of the small temple of Diana erected here by himself; of its cypress statue;
of its sacred grove of beautiful shrubs planted by his own hand, and of the
annual tithe set apart by him for its maintenance from his estate. What a
beautiful character is his! and how beautiful would it have been, if he had
lived when heathenism had given place to the milder light of a purer faith!

The Arcadian country, as we have seen, commences on the southern side
of the woody Erymanthus, which forms its northern boundary; running in a
north-easterly direction towards the more central eminence of Mount Cyllene,
it continues its course in the same direction till it joins the hill of Mænalus,
separating Arcadia on the east from the Argolic peninsula. A line drawn
from this point westward separates Arcadia from the Messenian territory on
the south. Arcadia is a picturesque and richly-wooded country, with well-
watered valleys, abounding in rugged and rocky mountain scenery. The cities
have most of them the remarkable castellated appearance represented in the
engraving, which represents the citadel of Arcadia near to the mouth of the
Neda, in the Arcadian Gulf.

The south-western portion of Arcadia, which borders upon the territory of
Olympia, contains within it two objects of interest: one of them is the oldest,
the other the youngest city of Greece; the former, LYCOSURA, whose ruins are
seen on the south-eastern side of Mount Lycæum, the modern Diophorti;
the latter near it, but on the other or eastern side of the Alpheus, MEGALO-
POLIS, founded by Epaminondas, in a beautiful valley clothed with noble
forests and irrigated with fresh streams, and still preserving in its vast Theatre
the signs of its ancient magnificence, nor less deserving attention as the birth-
place of Philopoemen and Polybius.

The city of Megalopolis is nearly in the centre of Arcadia; its valley
abounds in beautiful scenery. The sides of its mountains are covered with

oaks, chestnuts, and other trees; while the valley itself presents an undulating surface, the Alpheus flowing through it with its numerous tributary mountain rivulets. The northern approach to this city from Heræa proceeds along the valley of the Alpheus, crossing the river Buphagus, which forms the boundary between Heræa and Megalopolis; shortly after, at the point where the Marathα joins the Alpheus, the road passes over to the left bank. Near to this spot, at a place called Rhætea, is the confluence of the river Gortynius with the Alpheus. This river, near to its source, is named Lusius, because, as Pausanias tells us, Jupiter was washed in its stream shortly after he was born. After passing the village of Gortys, it becomes the Gortynius. The Grecian traveller adds, that this is said to be the coldest of rivers, especially in summer. On this road also the ruins of the ancient city of Derenthe occur. As the traveller proceeds towards Megalopolis, the valley is suddenly closed up at its northern extremity by the rock of Karitena, on the high and craggy summit of which stands the citadel, while on the opposite side of the river are the ruins of the city of Trapezus. It is probable that the modern town of Karitena is the ancient Derenthé, whose lofty citadel is represented in the

accompanying view. Through this country the Alphēus flows in a broad
stream, amid mountain villages, woods, and cultivated grounds. The path
lies along the right bank of the river till within a short distance of the ruins
of the temples of Æsculapius and Apollo at Gortys, where a long mountain
valley conducts to the lower district of the river, which at Heræum makes
a gentle inclination towards the west, and passes into the picturesque plains of
Olympia. A few miles from Gortys a curious phenomenon presents itself,—
a whole river, fifty or sixty feet wide, rushes at once into existence as it were
from under a low ledge of limestone rock, and at a short distance from its
source hastens to join the Alphēus.

There is a relic of antiquity in this region, which, from its position, its purpose, and its beauty, has powerful attractions for the traveller. The noble edict wherewith the Senate of Florence gave orders for the erection of their Cathedral,—by which the mind of Brunelleschi inspired the genius of Michael Angelo,—expressed the conviction of that celebrated Republic, that, having obtained renown in war, and wealth in peace, it became the inhabitants of their illustrious City to erect a Christian Temple worthy of a powerful and prosperous State. In the beautiful structure of BASSAE, on one of the ridges of Mount COTYLIUM, three miles to the west of Diophorti, we have an evidence of the operation of a somewhat similar feeling, attended by circumstances more striking than those to which we have alluded. *This edifice was erected*, not by a large and wealthy metropolis like Florence, but by a small *village* of Arcadia, the neighbouring community of PHIGALEIA.

THE MOUNTAINS, WITH SCENERY AND TEMPLES

This village, which is distant about a day's journey from Arcadia, is reached after passing through a variety of hill, dale, mountain, and woodland scenery. Ascending Mount Cotylium—a branch of Lycaeum—and passing through rich pasture-lands for two hours, a forest of oaks which covers the summit of these mountains is reached. The surrounding scenery is bold, varied, and romantic. Mountains rise over mountains till they are lost in

the distance to the right. Mount Ithome forms the centre of the picture, and on the eastern side of the glen are the summits of Mount Lycæum.

The Temple was not founded in a spot to which the materials for building could readily be brought, or where it might display to the passing crowd an evidence of the affluence and skill of those by whom it was erected; on the contrary, it stood alone, exposed to winds and storms, on a bleak and rugged mountain, difficult of access, and seeming, by its seclusion and solitude, to ask for no other notice than that of the Deity to whom it was consecrated. The first Theatre which was constructed at Rome was designed to appease the wrath of the Gods during a pestilence. This Temple of Bassæ was an offering of a more pleasing kind; it was raised, not during the ravages of a plague, but as a grateful record of deliverance from them. It was inscribed to APOLLO EPICURIUS, or the HELPER. It suggests the question to those Nations who boast a more enlightened faith—*What* public religious buildings have *they* erected as thank-offerings for their rescue from the scourges of a pestilence?

TEMPLE OF APOLLO AT BASSAE, RESTORED

The Temple stands, not from east to west,—the usual direction of Greek temples,—but from north to south. Another peculiarity is observable in the number of its columns: for while it is usual for the pillars on each flank to exceed by one the double of those at each end, here are six at each end, and fifteen upon each side. The building was a hundred and twenty-five feet in length by forty-seven in breadth. It was in the Doric style, peripteral and hypæthral, and raised upon three steps. It was built by the Architect of the Parthenon at Athens, Ictinus.

Pausanias speaks of this Temple of Bassae as eclipsing all the fabrics of the same kind in the Peloponnesus by the beauty of its stone and the harmony of its construction. The principal entrance was on the north. Having mounted the steps, passed through the columns of the portico and of the pronaos, we arrive in the cella. Here, on each side, and attached to the wall, were arranged five Ionic columns of white marble, for the purpose of supporting the roof, which stretched from the walls of the cella so as to

cover the greater part of its interior, leaving only an aperture in the centre, like that in the vault of the Pantheon at Rome, for the admission of light and air. Between the two most southern Ionic columns stood one of the Corinthian order, also of white marble, which supported the architrave over the southern entrance into the cella. The frieze which once adorned the interior—in all probability, the work of the scholars of Phidias—requires no description for those who have access to it in the national Museum of England. Suffice it to say, that as the architects and sculptors employed in the erection and decoration of this temple were of Athenian extraction, many of the subjects represented in this frieze are connected with Athenian history. They refer to the struggles of Theseus with the Centaurs and Amazons.

Such is the seclusion in which the Temple of Bassae stands, that for many ages its very existence was either unknown or forgotten. Like the temples at Paestum in this respect, it was not till after the middle of the eighteenth century that this, the most beautiful and most perfect of all the remains of Greek architecture in the Peloponnesus, was discovered in nearly the same state as when visited more than a thousand years before by Pausanias.

The country of MESSENIA was endowed much more liberally by Nature than the neighbouring territory. It is described by Pausanias as the most

the being only an approximate measure of
of the ancient Rome, for the advances of I
the two most southern Doric columns and some of
of which the whole supported the architrave
into the order. The frieze which once adorne
work of the sculptor of Phidias is pre
to it in the national Museum of Eng
the artists and sculptors employed in the erec
were of Athenian extraction, many of the subj
connected with Athenian history. They rep
of the Centaur and Amazon.

on which the Temple of Bassae stands, that it
was rather unknown or forgotten. Base to
Temple, it was not till after the middle of
the most beautiful and most perfect of all
in the Peloponnesus, who dressed about
a thousand years before by

fertile province of the Peloponnesus in his day; while Euripides speaks of it as a land well watered and very fertile, with beautiful pastures for cattle, possessing a climate neither too cold in winter nor too hot in summer. It is separated from Laconia by the mountain chain of Taygetus on the east, and from Elis and Arcadia by the river Neda and the high grounds in which it has its source. On the south and west the country is bounded by the deep gulfs and bays of the Ionian Sea.

The River Neda, which forms the northern boundary of Messenia, takes its rise in one of the ridges of Mount Lycæum, flows westward in a winding course through a beautiful valley by the walls of IRA—the fortress of Aristomenes,—passes the valleys of Phigaleia, and falls into the Ionian Sea a few miles north of the town of Arcadia.

The road through the country drained by the Neda, passes along the rocky defiles of the mountains which separate the maritime districts of Elis and Arcadia from Messenia. Sometimes winding along the sides of the mountains, the path is scarcely distinguishable from the sheep tracks; at others, crossing the more elevated ridges which separate the neighbouring valleys where all is wild and savage, but from whose summits distant glimpses are occasionally obtained of smiling and cultivated plains, whose apparent softness and fertility contrast strangely with the naked barrenness immediately around. Again the track lies through deep and thickly-wooded glens, where the path is cut out of the hill-side, and where the only natural passage is that occupied by the bed of the river, which has forced its way through its rocky strata, now foaming and roaring as if in fury at the obstacles obstructing its passage—now rushing rapidly along its smoother bed, and occasionally extending itself into small lakes. After leaving Phigaleia and entering the level country, the Neda—joined by several smaller streams—now flows a broad and rapid river, through woods of the ilex, myrtles, and bays, and discharges its waters into the gulf.

— SEE OF THE NEDA

On the southern slopes of the same ridge of hills, in which the Neda has its source, several smaller streams issue, and unite their waters in a deep and rapid channel to the north-east of Mount Ithomé in the Stenyclerian plain. This river, which is the Balyra, inclines to the south-east, and, skirting the eastern foot of Mount Ithomé and Mount Evan, joins another river opposite to Andrusa. This is the Pamisus, which has its source on the southern slopes of the Skala ridge, at the foot of which a large marsh and several ponds have been formed by the streams from the heights. Having received the waters of the Balyra and other tributary streams, and drained the northern parts of Messenia and Laconia, it empties itself into the gulf which separates these two countries. It is described as the largest stream of the Peloponnesus.

Watered by these rivers, and possessing besides many woody valleys and wide plains through which they flowed, Messenia was famed for the number and beauty of its herds and flocks, and for the variety of its shrubs and fruit-trees. In addition to this, the mountains here were not of sufficient height to render its climate inclement, as was the case in Laconia, by retaining the snow for the greater part of the year, or by screening the lands beneath them from the sun.

THE PYBALI.

It was not wonderful, therefore, that the Lacedæmonians were covetous of a neighbouring land so superior to their own. In the year B.C. 724, Ithome, the Acropolis and capital of Messenia, was taken by the Spartans. In 685, the war was renewed against Aristomenes, who fortified himself in Ira, in the fastnesses of Mount Lycæum. Here he remained for many years, and performed those wonderful feats of courage, and was saved by those marvellous escapes, which made him the national hero of Messenia. But, in 668, Ira fell into the hands of Sparta, as Ithome had done before. Nothing remained for the conquered Messenians but to become Helots or Exiles. Many of them fled beyond the sea, and settled in Sicily, Italy, and Africa;

3 r

but enough remained behind to render Sparta the mistress of two hundred
thousand slaves.

After a long banishment, during which they preserved their language and
manners unaltered, the Messenians returned, in the year B.C. 370, to their
ancient abodes, from which they had been driven by the Spartans. Having
been recalled by the Theban general and statesman Epaminondas, who had
just laid low the power of Sparta on the field of Leuctra, they proceeded, with
the sound of flutes and pipes and vocal melodies, and with the sacred pomp
of procession and of sacrifice, to rebuild on the ridges of Mount Ithome
their city which had so long lain desolate. That day was the return to
them from a Captivity of near three centuries. The responses of the
Augurs, who were consulted whether the new city would prosper, were

favourable. The victims were propitious. Everything bore the aspect of
hope and joy. Artificers of every kind were present, materials flowing in
from all quarters, temples rising, and streets stretching along the vacant
space; a new MESSENE grew up on the site of the old, like a fabled city
charmed into life by the sound of the Orphean Lyre. In order to connect
themselves with their Progenitors, and with the Powers of Heaven, they
invited to come and dwell among them, by special invocations, their own
Heroes of ancient time—Eurytus, Aphareus, Cresphontes, Æpytus, and above
all, with the unanimous voice of the whole city, the great ARISTOMENES.
Those deities were also invited, who were believed to wish well to the
Messenian State. The work of building was carried on, as it had begun,
with the sound of the Argive and Bœotian flute.

The present aspect of MESSENE is not surpassed in interest and beauty by
that of any ancient city in the Peloponnesus. The scene is grand and solitary.

On the north and east of it rise the magnificent cliffs of Mounts ITHOME and EVAN. Towards the west stretch fine plains of arable and pasture land, varied with coppices of shrubs in rich profusion. This level site was selected by Epaminondas, on account of the water with which it was well supplied.

In the forum of Messene, as we learn from Pausanias, there was a statue of Jupiter the Saviour, and a fountain called Arsinoë, from the daughter of Leucippus. Water flowed into this fountain from that of Clepsydra, which is seen on ascending to the summit of Mount Ithomé—the tower of Messene. The Messenians lay claim to the honour of Jupiter having been born among them, and in this fountain the nymphs Ithomé and Neda are said to have washed him at his birth, after receiving him from the Curetes. In

the time of the Greek traveller, the inhabitants of the city carried water daily from it to the temple of Jupiter Ithomatis. The fountain still remains. It is now in the centre of a small village of some twenty huts, which stands at the foot of Ithomé. A copious stream flows through this cluster of huts in a south-westerly direction. This is the ancient Clepsydra.

The Walls of the city, which, together with the public buildings originally existing at Messene, although not less than four miles in circumference, were erected in the course of eighty-five days, present one of the most remarkable specimens of military architecture to be found upon the soil of Greece. We look upon them with a feeling of deeper interest in consequence of the fact, that they were raised from the plans and under the direction of

Epaminondas. They make us as it were his contemporaries, by exhibiting to us a model of the system of fortification adopted in his age. The walls are built in horizontal courses, and generally with rectangular stones. They consist of an exterior and interior facing of such masonry, the space between the facings being filled with rubble. At distances, varying from seven to ten feet, the two faces are tied together by transverse courses of stone. This method of construction corresponds to the Roman Emplecton. Projecting from the walls at different intervals, are Towers of stone: their ground-plan is generally rectangular. But on the north-east of the city are two towers with circular fronts. They seem to have been surmounted by flat roofs, from which

COTTAGE OF CLEFTY...

missiles might be discharged on the besieger. One of these, which remains in nearly a perfect state, was divided into two stories, in each of which are windows and embrasures; those in the lower story being splayed, to admit more light and to afford a freer range for the emission of projectiles from within. At certain distances are flights of stone steps, ascending from the interior of the city nearly to the battlements of the walls, so as to afford an opportunity of assailing the besieger beneath them; and thence similar flights lead into the towers which have been described.

One of the most remarkable features in the fortifications of Messene is the Gate in the north-west part of the walls through which the road passed that led to Megalopolis. It consisted of an outer area, thirty-one feet in

breadth, and flanked by two massy projections. Within this was an outer door, which led into a circular court sixty-three feet in diameter, and through this court to an inner door, which opened into the city itself. A paved Road, formed of parallel slabs lying transversely, succeeds to the gate, and descends rapidly towards the interior of the town. The marks of ancient wheels are still visible in the court-yard, and the road itself is one of the very few specimens of ancient paving which remain in Greece; it shows a method of road-making very different from that adopted by the Romans, of which we have still many examples in the closely-wedged strata of polygonal blocks in the Appian, Præncstine, and Latin Ways.

Toward the southern part of the city are the remains of a small THEATRE, looking to the south, and also of a STADIUM with a similar aspect, which was environed on three sides by a colonnade.

For some time after their restoration, the Messenians maintained an alliance with their neighbours the Arcadians, according to the advice of Epaminondas: they afterwards joined the Achæan League, but seem in a short time to have been alienated from that confederacy by the encroachments of their allies. In the year B.C. 183, the Achæan General, Philopœmen, fought before these walls, and was taken prisoner and cast into a dungeon, where he died. The city was soon afterwards stormed and taken by Lycortas, the successor of Philopœmen, and Messene was again united to the Achæan Confederacy, with which it maintained its connexion till the dissolution of the League. Thus the second existence of Messene lasted for two hundred and twenty-four years. It still retained the evidence of its former power in

the third century of the Christian era; and Pausanias, who then visited it,
asserts that he could not compare these fortifications, of which the vestiges
still remain, with the walls of Babylon or the Memnonian bulwarks of Susa,
for these he had never seen; but cities such as Ambrysus, Byzantium, and
Rhodes, which in his judgment were more strongly defended than any others,
could not bear a comparison with Messene.

There is but one harbour of any excellence on the western coast of the
Peloponnesus. This is the port of Pylos in Messenia, which has enjoyed a
celebrity superior to that of any other place in the peninsula, with the exception of Corinth, from the time of the Trojan War to our own days. As might
have been presupposed from such a circumstance, it is a spot connected with
many interesting recollections. Let us imagine a semicircular bay of two miles
and a half in diameter, lying from north-east to south-west. Let us place a
castle on each of its two horns,—that on the northern being on a lofty ground
and in ruins; let us suppose a large lagoon stretching along the coast to the
east of the latter, and fields of maize covering the lowlands near it; let us add
two small streams flowing down from the limestone hills on the east, and
emptying themselves into the bay; let us next plant some small churches here
and there on the eminence of these hills, and trace some mountain paths

winding in an inland direction upon their surface ; on the southern horn of the bay let us plant a large fortress of a pentagonal form ; a number of small houses and a cemetery, and near it, further to the east, a small creek filled with Greek boats ; let us stretch across the harbour a long, narrow island, leaving a passage between itself and the southern castle of rather more than half a mile, and one of about five hundred feet between its northern point and the other promontory of the bay,—the latter being shallow and fordable, the former having an average of twenty-seven fathoms of water ;—we have then a picture of the ancient harbour of Pylos, and, as it is termed from the names of the castles we have mentioned, the modern bay of NAVARINO, famed in modern times for the battle which has led to recovery of liberty to Greece. The island of which we have spoken was called SPHACTERIA.

HARBOUR OF PYLOS.

Notwithstanding the objections that have been made, both in ancient and modern times, against the supposition, we need not hesitate to recognise, in the northern fortress and the plain now occupied by the lagoon beneath it, the site of the sandy Pylos, the well-built city of the Neleian Nestor. With this spot we may connect the scene described by Homer in the third book of the Odyssey. Here we may suppose Telemachus, attended by Minerva in Mentor's shape, landing with his companions. Here they found nine companies of Pylians, with five hundred persons in each, engaged in offering a sacrifice to Neptune on the sea-shore. Here sat Nestor with his sons. Here that intercourse took place between Telemachus and Minerva which presents so fair a specimen of youthful modesty supported and encouraged by Divine aid. Here

SPHACTERIA AND PYLOS, FROM THE SOUTH.

Minerva rejoiced, as the Poet says, in the piety of the young Pisistratus, Nestor's son, who had requested her to pray and make libations to Neptune, and then to give the cup for the same purpose to her companion; "*for all men*," he said, "*stand in need of the gods.*" Here the old Nestor was approached with reverential awe by the youthful son of his fellow-warrior, Ulysses. Here commenced the acquaintance between Telemachus and Pisistratus, who was nearly of the same age with himself, which was soon ripened into intimacy by their journey together in the same car from Pylos, the city of Nestor, to that of Menelaus, Lacedæmon.

We should be loth to be without some local habitation for such scenes as these. We confess that we would willingly surrender the site of a field of battle in exchange for a fixed spot wherewith to combine those beautiful representations of the manners and feelings of the heroic times in Greece, which the poetry of Homer has associated for ever with the name of Pylos. Nor do we suppose that any one, who has examined the details he has given of the voyage of Telemachus from Ithaca and his subsequent journey to Sparta, will entertain a doubt that the bay now before us is that in which the youthful son of Ulysses landed, when he came to inquire of Nestor concerning his father.

The reader will contrast, in his own mind, with these scenes, the other events of a different nature and character, with which in more recent times the harbour of Pylos was connected. In the year B.C. 425, the island of Sphacteria, which lies in its front, was witness to the calamity so degrading and injurious to Sparta, which has been described with such elaborate minuteness

by the historian of the Peloponnesian war, Thucydides. Twenty-one years after that event, Athens, which then won so splendid a victory, was destroyed. More than two thousand years after that time, Athens has again become the Capital of Greece, by a victory gained in 1827 upon the same spot. May the consequences of Navarino be more durable and more glorious to her than those of Sphacteria!

Besides the harbour of Pylos, two other bays of Messenia deserve notice—those of Methone and Coloniues,—one the modern bay of Modon, the other that of Coron in the Messenian Gulf. They occupy in the Messenian peninsula the same position that the small bays of Anaphlystus and Thoricus do in that of Attica. From Messene to Modon the road traverses an undulating country with low eminences covered with wood, and but little cultivated. These heights are the roots of Mount Kondovana, and are intersected with narrow valleys watered by streams from that mountain. After continuing in a southerly course for some time, and crossing several streams of considerable magnitude, the road turns suddenly off to the west, leaving Mount Temathia on the left, and passes through a forest of short and stunted oaks. Here are the

Town of Modon, from the sea.

highest ridges of the undulating country which we have described; and the rivers flowing into the Messenian Gulf are here separated from those tending towards the western coast. Descending into a valley at the foot of Mount Temathia, on its northern side, the traveller enters the district of Modon, which is four miles to the south of Pylos, being separated from it by a rocky ridge, on which stands the church of St. Nicolas. On the south of these heights is the town of Modon, built on a slip of coast jutting into the sea, occupying the extreme point of a ridge of rocks stretching southward along the coast from the foot of Mount St. Nicolas. It is now occupied by a tower and lantern, and is connected by a bridge with the fortifications of Mothoni, the latter being a small insulated rock off the most southerly part of the town, which forms a narrow entrance to the bay. A wall which branches from it runs parallel to the eastern wall of the town, and forms a port which is used as a harbour for small vessels.

The climate of Mothoni, standing upon a promontory, open to the sea in the direction of the prevailing breeze, is temperate and salubrious. Upon it is a lighthouse, placed on the southern slip of land which projects from it towards the island of Sapienza, which covers the bay of Modon on the south, as Sphacteria does Pylos on the west. The bay is an unsafe anchorage, being exposed on the west side, and but little protected on the east.

BAY AND CASTLE OF CORON

CORON is the first port in the Messenian Gulf after doubling Cape GALLO,—the ancient promontory of Acritas. From Modon the road passes through a succession of olive-gardens and corn-fields, which adorn its immediate neighbourhood. Emerging from these, the traveller ascends the hill on the eastern side of the valley, and the olive plantations gradually give place to a range of barren hills, formed by the southern extremity of Mount Temathia. As he crosses the southern slopes of this mountain, by a rugged and rocky path, the town of Coron becomes visible, in the midst of groves of cypresses, of olives, and fields of corn, by which it is surrounded for several miles. He descends the eastern side of the mountain, and after a short journey gains the town. It stands upon a promontory, or tongue of land, which extends eastward for about half a league into the sea. A fertile plain of considerable extent forms its western suburb, which is sheltered by the lower ranges of hills which join Mount Temathia. Its roadstead is much exposed, except on the south-west, where a sandy beach extends for about two miles, affording every means of landing, except when the wind is from the south. The castle-hill is very steep on all sides, and was probably the Acropolis of the ancient city of

Colonides, which is supposed to have occupied this site. Its principal
recommendation as a place of commerce arises from the great productiveness
of its neighbourhood, and from its being well supplied with wood and water.
In general, the western or Messenian side of this gulf, called either the Gulf
of Coron or of Kalamáta, presents in its open plains, its rich fields and olive
grounds, a striking contrast to the rugged barrenness of its eastern or
Laconian coast. The mountain range of the Taygetus, which we have traced
from its junction with the mountains of Arcadia and Achaia, continue their
course and retain their bold and rugged character till they are finally lost
in the Tænarian promontory at Cape Matapan.

From the Laconian shores of the gulf the view is rich and imposing. The
district of Coron contains upwards of seventy villages, more or less populous,
skirting the bay or dispersed among the olive groves. Towards the head of the
gulf is the fertile plain of Palisus, and more to the north rises the mountain
range of Temathia, Evan and Ithomé, now nearly united into one.

The town of Kalamáta is at the head of this semicircular bay, formed by
the projecting headland of Cape Matapan—the most southerly point of the
Laconian territory,—and Capo Gallo—the most southerly point of the Mes-

senian country on the western shore. From the mountain pass above this town a view of great extent and beauty is obtained, which embraces the whole of the bay, with the mountains stretching to the most southerly point of the Peloponnesus on the one hand, and the distant mountains of the Arcadian Gulf on the other. Kalamáta, the ancient maritime city of Pharæ, occupies a prominent point in the picture. This city stands about a mile from the sea on a delta formed by the waters of the Nedon,—a broad and rapid river, which has its source in the mountains a mile to the north. Shortly before it reaches the town its waters divide, and the river enters the sea by its two mouths.

To the south of Kalamáta, nearly opposite to Coron, and at a short distance from the sea, stands the ancient city of CARDAMYLE, mentioned by Homer as one of the gifts of Agamemnon to Achilles, to induce him to return to the war. Although claimed by the Messenians, it was subject to Sparta; but this claim seems to have led to an adjudication by which Philip, the son of Amyntas, supported by the Congress of Corinth, compelled the Lacedæmonians to cede the district to the Messenians. Augustus Cæsar reversed this decision, and wrested it from the Messenians, in consequence of their having taken part with Mark Antony in the struggle for power between the Roman chiefs. The city lies in the bosom of a range of hills which

descend in a westerly direction from the Taygetan range. A castle of the middle ages crowns the rounded central hill,—once its Acropolis. A cluster of houses occupies the slopes at its foot, and the lofty peak of Taygetus, towering its majestic pinnacle in the distance, closes the view.

Let us follow Telemachus in his journey from Pylos, and direct our course to the eastward along a level country for about thirty-five miles, and we shall arrive at Pharæ, not far from the Messenian Gulf. Here he and his friend unyoked their horses, and reposed for the night. The next day they drove to Sparta, which is a distance of not quite thirty miles. The approach to Sparta lies through masses of broken walls, the ruins of the Acropolis being supposed to occupy the hill on the right, and the tomb of Leonidas being seen in front on entering the town. The great plain lies at a level of about fifty feet below the site of the ancient city. Mount Taygetus presents a barrier to the whole district, and a back-ground to the picture.

Homer describes Lacedæmon, by which he seems to mean the Valley of the Eurotas, and not the town of Sparta, by an epithet derived from the ravines into which it is broken. He calls it "*the hollow.*" The site of the town itself,—bearing some resemblance to Olympia, as being placed between two small streams flowing parallel to each other into a third, the Eurotas,—may, on account of the low hills upon which it stands, be compared rather with that of Rome than with any other important city on the soil of Greece. It is singular also that the principal remains which Sparta now exhibits are not of Greek but of Roman age and character. On entering the city from the modern village of Mistra, which is about four miles to the west of Sparta, we have

on the left, in the plain, the ruins of Roman baths, and before us, further to the east, a hill surrounded with Roman walls of a recent Imperial age. Upon the hill are the vestiges of a Roman temple, and below it, to the east, those of a Roman circus. To the north of the hill is an aqueduct of a similar character. The only Hellenic ruin of any note that survives at Sparta is a spacious Theatre. The prophecy, therefore of Thucydides, with respect to the probable remains of Athens and of its rival city, has been fully verified. No one who looks upon these fragments would suppose that the city to which they belong had ever held the sway of Greece.

The vale of Sparta was justly celebrated for its picturesque character. Being also sheltered on three sides from the severity of cold winds, and open on the south to the soft and refreshing breezes which were wafted upon it from the southern sea, and being watered by the streams of the Eurotas, which vied in size—to adopt the ancient belief with respect to their common origin— with its twin river the Alpheus, the largest of the Peninsula, it enjoyed natural advantages, which, if its soil had corresponded in excellence with its other qualifications, would have rendered the Laconian valley the most productive province of the Peloponnesus.

Its low grounds, indeed, are remarkable for their fertility, and for the variety of their productions, and exhibit a beautiful luxuriance of shrubs and fruit trees. Here are figs and oranges, pomegranates and myrtles. The acclivities which rise above the plains are clad with Olives, for the cultivation of which the soil of the Taygetus is so favourable that it may justly seem to demand an apology from the Athenian bard, who rejects all the pretensions of the " Dorian Isle " to share in the production of that tree.

These Olive plantations are succeeded by forests of firs, which cover the loftier heights of the mountains, whose sides are ploughed into deep gullies by torrents that flow from the summit of Taygetus into the vale, where they mix their waters with the Eurotas. At this stage of the ascent, the mountain assumes a different character. It becomes bleak and savage: it is broken into deep gorges and abrupt precipices. It then shoots up its lofty and jagged peaks, which are covered with snow during the greater portion of the year.

The long and majestic range of these mountain piles, contrasted with the green banks and the flowing stream, the blooming gardens and the rich corn-fields, that fringe the river, and gild the vale beneath them, presents a beautiful picture, which might well have excited the admiration and inspired the love of the ancient inhabitants of Laconia, rejoicing in the bodily exercises for which a beautiful country and a fine climate supply motives and means in abundance.

To impart additional beauty to this scene, we may imagine it, as in ancient days, peopled with living objects,—choruses, for instance, of Helen's country-women,—such as Theocritus describes in her Epithalamium—dancing on the slopes of the mountain, along the banks of the stream, or beneath the shadows of the grove. We may listen, in fancy, to the shrill echoes with which the mountain rang of old at early dawn, when the fellow-countrymen of her twin brothers followed the dogs of Sparta to the chase, through the glades and glens of Taygetus.

There is one important characteristic of her internal policy, in which Sparta presents a remarkable contrast to that of the capital of Attica, and which is forcibly suggested by the aspect of the physical objects about us, compared with those which we surveyed at Athens. Sparta seems by nature to be excluded from all communication from without. She was placed at the distance of many miles from the sea. She was hemmed in on all sides by lofty mountains. She lay secure and unmolested in her own nest-like valley. She possessed a plain sufficient to supply her frugal wants. During many ages she owned the rich neighbouring territory of Messenia on the west, productive of corn and abundant in cattle. She was therefore possessed of all the necessaries of life in great abundance within herself. But it was far otherwise with Athens. Everything there was free and open; the sea was near, and the earth barren. It was on her efficiency abroad, not upon her self-sufficiency at home, that Athens was led by nature to depend. Hence the two different systems of Education adopted by these States,—systems which seem to have been produced by the physical forms of the two countries themselves. At Sparta, the distance of her position from the coast, the lofty hills within

which her valley was pent, her situation at the extremity of Greece, so that no
stranger would pass through her territory in his way to any other land,—all
these her natural properties spoke of restraint and control, of abstinence and
self-denial. They prepared the way for the establishment and reception of
a system founded upon the single principle of unhesitating and implicit
obedience to the Law.

In the objects about us at Lacedæmon we appear to recognise the elements
that led to the creation of the spirit which is nowhere more truly or more

emphatically described than in the epitaph
engraved upon the tomb of the Spartan heroes
who fell at Thermopylæ,—" O stranger, go and tell the Lacedæmonians
that we lie here in obedience to their commands." Not for personal
glory, not even for public aggrandisement, not for the sake of national
revenge, much less from private animosity, but because he was animated by a
sense of duty, did the Spartan march to the field. He trod the path of duty,
and that led him to glory. Here was the same spirit that afterwards produced
the Conqueror at Waterloo.

At Athens a different system of Education prevailed. Morally and politically she was the antipodes of Sparta. Everything about her struggled
against restraint; everything was eager for the freest development of which
it was capable; all things in nature,—her air, her soil, her wide plain—her
earth barren in corn and in pasture, but fertile in marble and in silver—the
sea flowing before her—her excellent ports, formed by the hand of Nature—
the islands not far beyond them, tempting her across the deep to the Asiatic

coast and to the regions of the East—her facilities for communicating with
strangers of all countries both at home and abroad,—these, and other circumstances of a similar kind, led to the adoption of a system of Education,
which produced the greatest possible development and exercise of individual
energy and personal enterprise in quest of glory.

The southern portion of the Laconian territory possesses the same rugged
and mountainous features which we have traced from the junction of the
Taÿgetus with the mountains of Arcadia and Achaia. Pausanias, in his

BAY OF LACONIA.

survey of this coast, describes many cities and towns as existing in his time,
inhabited by the Eleuthero-Lacones, and adorned with temples and statues,
some of these cities being the scenes of events described in the Homeric
Poems. The promontory Tænarum extends itself into the sea at a short
distance from the ancient town of Teuthrone, having beneath it the ports of
Achilleus and Psamathus. In the days of Pausanias there was a temple
resembling a cavern, on the promontory, with a statue of Neptune, which was
a sanctuary in the time of Thucydides, and held in peculiar veneration by
all the Greeks. Tænarum itself is a peninsula of circular form, about seven

miles in circumference, and is the terminating point of the great Taygetan range of mountains, which is here lost in an isthmus of about half a mile in width. The Laconian coast, commencing at Cape Thyrides, bends so much to the east as to conceal the promontory from all parts of the Messenian gulf, except the opposite promontory of Gallo.

The bays and creeks of the Laconian gulf, are, like the country itself, bold and rocky—towering high overhead, and surrounded by deep water to their base. The inhabitants, boastful of their presumed descent from the ancient Spartans, are a bold and tameless race, placing all their pride in imitating the sterner actions of their ancestors, which has displayed itself in all ages by their habits of pillage by land and piracy by sea. Their sea-girt territory, with its numerous and nearly inaccessible headlands and rocky bays, has nourished this habit, and rendered the neighbourhood of Cape Matapan almost as much dreaded by the mariner as storm or shipwreck. On the western side of the bay is the port and town of Marathonisi, near to the ruins of the ancient Gythium. On its eastern shore is Cape Xylo, a high rocky peninsula terminating in a low tongue of land, which projects into the sea on the south. On the summit of the hill stands one of a line of towers that once served to protect the coast, which is here lofty and precipitous.

The road by which we proceed from Sparta, the city of Menelaus, to Mycenae, the city of his brother Agamemnon, leads, as we have seen, through Tripolitza, a modern town which stands on the site of Pallantium, one of the oldest and most venerable of the cities of Arcadia,—the city of Pallas and Evander. It is celebrated for the horrors it witnessed in the wars of Greek Independence.

From Tripolitza to Argos, the road passes along a narrow defile between the hills of Artemisium on the north and Mount Parthenium on the south. That from Nauplia thither lies through the Argolic plain, which is confined by a curved barrier of hills on all sides but the south, where it is bounded by the waters of the Argolic sea. Mycenae lies in the northern apex of this curve of hills, on the northern margin of the plain, at a distance of nine miles from the head of the gulf. No more appropriate designation could be devised than that which describes Argos—by which we mean the province and not the city—as *hollow*, and Mycenæ as lying in the corner or *recess* of Argos. It seems not improbable that Mycenæ derived its name from the word in the ancient language signifying "recess." The description of Pausanias shows that Mycenæ has undergone less change since his time than any other town in Greece.

The plain over which we pass in our way thither is dry and dusty, and has few objects to relieve its bare level. It is not intersected by hedges, and the few modern villages which are scattered over its surface are small and nearly deserted. They consist, in general, of a low church, of a well, whose stone edges are deeply furrowed by the ropes which draw up the buckets of water, of heaps of large hewn blocks of stone near them, and of a few mud cottages, on the walls of which, at the close of the summer season, stalks of Indian corn and tobacco are hung to dry. On the northern margin of the Argolic plain stands the city of Mycenæ. Its site is visible from the Acropolis of Argos. It still remains in nearly the same state as it appeared in the days of the Athenian historian, Thucydides, who deduced, from the extent and condition of its remains, as they then were, an argument with respect to the magnitude of the power of the house of its sovereigns, the ATRIDÆ, compared with that of more recent dynasties.

We look with a feeling of awe on a city which was in ruins in the time of Thucydides. Nor is it without a sensation of delight that we contemplate the same venerable monument of antique sculpture which was seen here in later times by the traveller Pausanias, and which still stands in our days as he describes it standing in his own, over the principal, and, indeed, the only gate, with the exception of a small postern, of the city of Mycenæ.

In exploring the site of this town, and in contemplating the structure and ornaments of this, the GATE OF LIONS, at the north-west angle of the city, we seem to become the companions of those two Authors, who saw what we now see. Nay, more,—carried on, as it were, down the stream of *their* faith, and resigning ourselves to the current of feelings by which *they* were impelled,—we appear to recognise here the same objects with which, in their imagination, this place was peopled in earlier times.

Thus, for instance, while halting before the principal portal of the city of Mycenæ, to which we have just alluded, and which is still flanked by the

walls and tower of its massive and heroic masonry, and surmounted by the
architectural and sculptural ornaments of its earliest days, we picture to ourselves AGAMEMNON, the king of men, arriving before it in his car, on his
return from his expedition to Troy; we behold him resigning the reins to his
attendant, and descending from his chariot, and planting his foot on the
tapestried road, which, in the description of the dramatic poet, Æschylus,
conducts him to his ancestral palace in the citadel, which he is now about to
revisit, after an absence of ten years. Or again, we seem to behold Orestes,
the son of Agamemnon, arriving at day-break with his friend Pylades, as
described in the Choephoroe of the same author, and in the Electra of

PLAIN OF ARGOS, FROM THE GATE OF LIONS.

Sophocles, and visiting the tomb of his dead father, which was seen here by
the Grecian traveller of whom we have just spoken, and to whose diligent
researches all who feel an interest in the geography and antiquities of Greece
are deeply indebted. Again, we may then behold, as in a vision, the
procession of the Virgins passing through the same gate, and bearing their
libations and garlands to the same tomb, amidst the lamentations of the
sorrowful Electra, and we are present at her recognition of her brother,
Orestes, which changes her sadness into joy. In the subterranean chamber, or
TREASURY, which is outside the city, and not far from the same gate, whose
doorway is supported by columns of green basalt, with fantastic, perhaps

Oriental, zig-zag ornaments, and whose remarkable structure and symmetry
attracted the attention of Pausanias, and is described by him, we see the
mysterious depository of some of the wealth of its early kings, which gained
for this city the title of the GOLDEN MYCENÆ.

We may imagine this vaulted apartment as it probably existed in the
remote age of Atreus the king of Mycenæ, to whom Pausanias assigns it.
We may picture to ourselves ears of excellent workmanship, whose sides are
embossed with figures in curious relief, hanging on the walls, which were then
sheathed with metallic plates; we may imagine vases and tripods of bronze
and gold, the gifts of Greek or Asiatic sovereigns, piled upon the floor;
helmets and bucklers, swords and lances, hauberks and greaves, golden bits
and ivory frontlets, dyed by women of Mæonia, and once worn by richly-

caparisoned horses, with other insignia
and weapons of ancient heroes, suspended upon nails, or ranged along the
walls,—some of them believed, it may
be, to be the works of Vulcan, or the
gifts of Minerva. In the chests beneath,
lie embroidered tunics and cloaks,
bright with purple and with gold;
webs woven by honourable women
and noble princesses of the house of
PELOPS, of PERSEUS, and of ATREUS.
Such are some of the pictures which
will exhibit themselves to the imagination of the traveller, as he stands before
the Treasury, treads the soil, and contemplates the monuments, of Mycenæ.

The ruins of Mycenæ are in some respects unequalled in interest by any

object in Greece. Their position is fortunate ; there is no habitation near
them. The traveller ascends from an open plain to the deserted hill upon
which they stand. The citadel occupied an eminence stretching from east
to west, and supplying a platform of about a thousand feet in length, and half
that distance in breadth. Two mountain-torrents, coming from the hills on
the east, flowed in their rocky beds, one on the north, the other on the south,
along the foot of the Acropolis, and thence were carried into the general
receptacle of the neighbouring mountain-streams, the Argolic
plain. The walls of the citadel may still be traced in their
entire circuit, and on the western side they rise to a considerable
height. The interior of their inclosure, or area of the
citadel, is covered with the common turf and moun-
tain-plants of the country. Only a few foundations of

THE CITADEL GATE NEAR THE STREETS.

ancient buildings remain, and one or two cisterns hewn in the rocky soil and
lined with cement. Such is the present state of the Acropolis of Mycenæ.

It was entered by two gates, and by two only,—one on the north-east, the
other on the north-west of the city. In an ancient city, gates seem to have
been regarded as necessary evils, which it was unsafe to multiply, and a large
number of them was honourable, as proving the confidence of the citizens in

their own strength and courage to defend them. Hence the epithets applied to Thebes and other similar cities. Nor was the line of the walls of the citadel of Mycenæ even varied by projecting *towers;* only two approximations to a tower-like structure occur in their whole circuit. These are placed to guard the two entrances just mentioned, and project in such a manner on the right-hand side of each gate that the sword-arm of an assailant was exposed to missiles hurled upon him by the besieged from the tower.

Both these points are worthy of notice; the connexion of the gate and the tower, and the projection of the latter with a view to defence; and in both these respects the construction of the citadel before us supplies an interesting commentary upon the military architecture presented to our notice in the Iliad of Homer. That poem and the walls of Mycenæ seem to belong to the same age. In the Iliad, when a tower is mentioned,

a gate is always to be supposed as contiguous to it. Helen, for instance, is conducted to a tower, that she may view from its flat summit the Grecian leaders on the plain of Troy. She is welcomed there by Priam and the Trojan Elders, who are described as sitting at the Scæan Gate. Andromache, in another passage, ascends a tower for a similar purpose; Hector goes in quest of her, and they meet, we learn, at the Scæan Gate. The usual contiguity of gate and tower is assumed to be well known to the hearers of the poem, in these and in other places. But in cities less ancient than Mycenæ, and in poems more recent than those

of Homer, although the gate never exists without a tower, yet a tower does not necessarily involve the presence of a gate near it.

The principal of the two gates, described in a former page, exhibits above its lintel the most ancient monument of Sculpture in Greece. These two lions, carved in low relief, are the only survivors of their age. This single block of green basalt on which they are graven contains the most interesting remains of the Greek sculpture of that remote period. What was the object of this work it would seem unnecessary to inquire, after the elaborate disquisitions that have been produced upon it. It has been conjectured from the column which divides the two lions, and from its probable termination in a spiry flame—for the capital and epistyle are mutilated—that this device was a symbol of the solar worship, which Mycenæ is supposed to have derived from its connexion with Persia. This supposition is a bold one, and rests upon insecure foundations. Pausanias, sensitive as he was upon such subjects, and prone to find a mystical meaning, does not seem to have considered these animals as affording any grounds for the application of a process by which sculptural representations are converted into scrolls of religious hieroglyphics. To him they are mere lions. Standing as they do over the principal gate of Mycenæ, through which the citadel was entered by all who had ascended from the plain of Argos

GATE OF LIONS, AT MYCENÆ

below it, they seem to suggest a more simple conjecture,—that they were devised and placed there as significant intimations to the stranger, of the strength and " courage leonine " of that city which he was about to enter by the gate upon which they stood. They were heraldic badges upon the national scutcheon of Mycenæ. The sculptured dogs placed at the entrance of the Palace of Alcinous, according to the description of Homer, indicated the vigilance with which it was guarded. The lions of Mycenæ, in a similar position, declared the bolder spirit which animated the inhabitants of that city. The King of Mycenæ also, as we are told by Pausanias, bore a figure of Fear, with a lion's head, emblazoned upon his shield : that animal, therefore, was probably not merely an appropriate characteristic, but also a national emblem of the Mycenæan power, as it is of the British sway.

To complete the picture which is presented to the eye and imagination of the spectator, on the summit of the citadel of Argos, let us look northward. We there see, at a distance of four miles, and on the slope of the hills which gradually sink from the east into the Argolic plain, the site of the HERÆUM, or Temple of Juno, the tutelar goddess of Argos. The hewn masses of its substructions still remain.

It is worthy of observation that a spot so distant from the capital city itself should have been selected for the position of the edifice consecrated to its patron deity. Thus removed, however, as the temple of Juno was from the haunts of men, placed upon a quiet and solitary hill, visited by shepherds and their flocks, surrounded by groves of trees, watered on each side by a mountain stream, with a long ridge of lofty hills rising at its back, and with the wide Argolic plain stretching itself at its feet, this sacred building inspired more of that feeling of awe and veneration which was due to the stately dignity of the Dorian goddess, the wife of Jove, and the queen of the heathen deities than if it had stood on a less sequestered spot, or had been exposed to the daily gaze of men amid the noise of streets, or in the crowd of the agora of the Argolic capital itself.

The road which leads from Argos to this temple, and which we can trace with the eye, from the spot where we suppose ourselves now placed, has gained a lasting interest—an interest similar to that possessed by the PLAIN OF THE PIOUS, on the sides of Mount Ætna—from the act of filial affection of two brothers, who, as Herodotus tells us, drew along it with their own hands, from the gates of Argos to the door of the temple, a distance of forty-five stadia, the car of their mother, to join, in due state on the festal day, the joyful concourse of her countrywomen, who had then assembled in that place. Having been crowned as victors in the gymnastic contests, the two youths were welcomed on their arrival at the Heræum, by the congregated people, who congratulated the mother on her sons, and the sons on their strength and virtue. The mother rejoicing in her own happiness, and in her children's love, repaired to the shrine of Juno, and standing before the statue, prayed for her sons that they might have the greatest blessing which the goddess could give, and they receive. After their mother's prayer, and when they had offered their own sacrifices, the two brothers, overcome with fatigue, reclined in the temple, and were found entranced in a sound sleep, from which they never awoke. A much envied euthanasia : their statues were erected at Delphi, by the hands of their admiring countrymen ; and their lot was declared by the wise Solon to the wealthy Crœsus, to be only inferior in happiness to that of the Athenian Tellus.

South of the Herræum, or Temple of Juno, and at the north-east corner of the Argolic gulf, placed on a low oblong rock, is the ante-Homeric city of TIRYNS. The road from Nauplia to Mycenæ passes under the lofty rock on the south-east of Nauplia, on which stands the ancient citadel of PALAMEDI, and leaves the Cyclopean walls of Tiryns, the city of Hercules, at about a

mile on the north from Nauplia, on the right hand. Exhibiting, as it does, the most ancient remains of the military architecture of Greece, and exciting the wonder of the beholder, by the hugeness of the rude blocks with which its walls and galleries are constructed, and which called forth an epithet expressive of admiration, even from the mouth of Homer himself—it survives as a striking monument of the power of men concerning whom all written history is silent. It arose, and flourished, in times antecedent to history, and seems to exist to make mythology credible. We are acquainted with TIRYNS only as built by the CYCLOPES, and as the early residence of HERCULES.

CASTLE OF TIRYNS.

From Tiryns to Nauplia is about an hour's ride. The history of Nauplia and its fortress, which guards the entrance to the Argolic gulf on the south-west, belongs to the period of the Byzantine empire and the middle ages, and it seems to have been only used in ancient times as the naval depôt of Argos. In the time of Pausanias the town was desolate, the ruins of the walls and a temple to Neptune only remaining. The modern town stands on the north-eastern side of a height which projects from a steep ridge at the south-eastern angle of the bay of Argos, and which was formed into an island by cutting through the neck of the small peninsula when the wet ditch was formed. The ruins of the ancient wall still remain, and seem to be of the same date with those of Argos.

One of the most ancient cities in Argolis is Trœzen, said by Pausanias to have been built by Orus, an Egyptian. It is situated on an eminence on the eastern coast, about two miles from the sea, and its ruins are still seen in and about the modern village of Damala. Trœzen was a sovereign city, with considerable territory and several small townships. In the Persian wars the Trœzenians joined their countrymen with an army of one thousand men and five ships. Pausanias describes its temples and public buildings as numerous, and mostly filled with costly works of art.

The city of Argos is three miles to the north of the gulf, and to the west of the gravelly bed of the Inachus, and at an equal distance from Lerna and Nauplia, namely, six miles. Its Acropolis was a conical hill, nearly a thousand feet above the level of the sea, and connected by a neck of land with a lower platform on the north-east. The former was the old citadel of Phoroneus, and was called by the Pelasgic term for a fortress, Larissa, and also Aspis, or Shield, from its circular form. The latter, from the connexion above mentioned, was termed Deiras, or Neck. The principal remains of antiquity at Argos are seen in the substructions of this citadel, which are blended with works of modern date; the three lines of ramparts and the three several castles of which the fortress consists being for the most part of Venetian architecture.

Beneath the citadel, looking nearly to the south-east towards Tiryns, is a well-preserved specimen of an ancient Theatre, whose seats are hewn in the rocky soil; they were divided into three separate tiers by two precinctions. In the lowest portion of the caves there seem to have been thirty-six seats, sixteen in the second division, and upwards of fourteen in the highest. " They were formed into cunei by three viæ. Such being the state of preservation in which this theatre exists, it is a very agreeable and not very difficult task to re-people it with the spectators which once thronged these now deserted seats, and to contemplate in fancy the actors who moved on the stage before them; to indulge, in short, in that pleasing fancy which afforded so much delight to the Argive nobleman of olden time, who, as Horace tells us, was wont to come to these seats, while empty as they now are, and there dream away his time in listening to imaginary tragedies, " a joyful sitter and applauder in a vacant theatre."

But though the former glories of Argos have faded so as to have left such scanty traces behind them, yet from her ancient conquests she has been able to borrow and to appropriate to herself honours which do not strictly belong to her. In the year B.C. 468 the neighbouring city of Mycenæ was taken and destroyed by the Argives. From that time the history of that ancient seat of the house of Atreus became merged in that of Argos, and thence it happens that events which took place at Mycenæ are transferred by the dramatic poets of Athens to Argos; and so the gods and heroes, as well as the walls and inhabitants of Mycenæ, may be said to have come into the possession of the victorious city, of whose history and mythology they have now become a part.

Consistently with this notion, Æschylus, in his tragedies connected with Mycenæ, has never once mentioned the name of Mycenæ, but always substitutes that of Argos in its stead; while the other two tragedians use both the names Mycenæ and Argos concerning the same subject.

A road issues from the Argolic plain on the south-west, which leads to the modern town of Tripolitza. The Argolic plain extends from north to south to the distance of about ten miles, commencing at the head of the gulf, and terminating in the mountain passes

which lead northward to the Isthmus of Corinth. Its breadth is equal to
about half its length. The higher or more northern parts of this plain suffer
from the want of water: whence the epithet applied to it by Homer, indicative
of the thirstiness of the soil. The lower district of it, on the contrary, is
covered by swamps during the greater portion of the year, and is intersected
by the copious stream of the river Erasinus, which issues from a picturesque
cave, formerly dedicated to Bacchus and Pan, beneath the rocks of Mount
Chaon, through which it has worked its way from the Arcadian lake of
Stymphalus. A little beyond it to the south, on the sea-shore, are the
Lernæan Marsh and the unfathomable pool of Halcyone, from which a large

volume of water issues, and after a short course falls into the gulf. The river
Inachus, which flows from the higher part of the plain, rarely finds its way
into the sea except when it has been swollen by a recent fall of rain: it then
becomes a broad and impetuous torrent.

There are three routes from Argos to Corinth: the one the most circuitous, but also the most easy, issues from the Argolic plain at its north-
west angle, passes over some low hills and through a valley clothed with
vineyards, then turns to the right, and arrives at NEMEA; thence bearing to
the north-east, it leaves CLEONÆ on the right, and arrives at its destination,
after traversing a distance of about thirty miles.

The other two roads are to the east of this, the one nearest to it following two narrow defiles after its exit from the plain, which were formerly known by the name of TRETUS, or the *perforated* road, where the cave of the Nemean Lion was anciently shown, and which are now called the Dervenakia; the other to the east of this, skirts the rugged mountains to the north of Mycenæ, and was termed of old the CONTOPOREIA, or the Pedestrian track. These two latter routes, which are both shorter but more difficult than the first, were rendered memorable in the autumn of the

year 1822, by the havoc which the Greeks made in the Turkish army when it was endeavouring to escape by those defiles from the plain of Argos, into which it had rashly thrown itself without securing its retreat, and where it could no longer subsist, from the failure of provisions, from the drought of the plain, and from the prevalence of sickness. The Turks

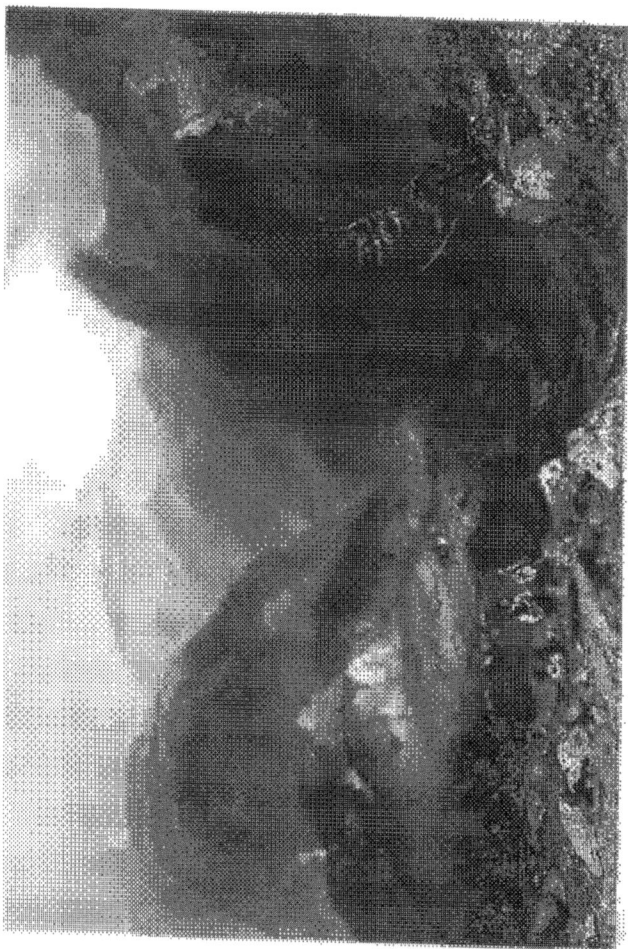

plunged into these Caudine Forks of Argolis in the hope of reaching Corinth,
which was in the hands of their friends, and of finding supplies there.
On two several occasions, and in each of the routes we have mentioned, they
were encountered by a destructive fire from the enemy above them;
thousands of them fell beneath the volleys discharged from the rocks, without
the power of making any resistance or return; horses, mules, and camels
fell into the hands of their foes in immense numbers; all the baggage and
treasure of the army was taken, and for several weeks afterwards all the
towns of the Morea, in the words of the Author of the History of the
Greek Revolution, who has vividly described these events, resembled so many

RUINS OF THE TEMPLE OF JUPITER AT NEMEA

auction marts,—rich dresses and arms being offered for sale about the streets
from morning to night.

There are but few remains at NEMEA. Three columns alone survive to
tell where the temple of the Nemean Jupiter stood. It was once surrounded
by a sacred inclosure, and embosomed in a cypress grove. Now there is
but one solitary wild pear-tree upon the spot. As at Olympia, the place
set apart for the celebration of the Nemean Games was a level plain; it
stretched from north to south,—was nearly three miles in length and one in
breadth,—but it had not, like Olympia, an Alpheus to adorn it, and was
watered only by several rills which flow down from the mountains that

encircle it. The Stadium or race-course still exists; it measures six hundred feet,—the ordinary length of the places in Greece designed for such purpose. It was hollowed in the slope of the hill to the south of the temple, and was entered from the north.

Corinth has been called in modern times the Gibraltar of Greece. The town stands at half a league's distance to the south of the gulf. Further to the south is that magnificent hill, nearly nineteen hundred feet in height, which has served as the citadel of this place for three thousand years, and was called by its ancient inhabitants the Acrocorinthus. In former time, two long walls stretched from those of the city to the sea-shore, and con-

CORINTH AND THE ACROCORINTHUS.

nected it with its harbour in the Corinthian Gulf; the port there was called the LECHÆUM. A road led from Corinth to the south-east, which terminated, after a distance of about five miles, in its other harbour,—that of CENCHREÆ, on the Saronic Gulf. The traveller by land, who was going from the Peloponnesus to visit any of the cities of Northern Greece, passed beneath the walls of Corinth; and all who came into the Peloponnesus from those cities entered it by the same route. By its two ports, therefore, Corinth communicated at once with the eastern and western world; while by the Isthmian road it had intercourse with the north and south. No wonder, therefore, that it was called "The wealthy."

There are few remains of antiquity now surviving at Corinth. The traveller who arrives in the modern village from Nemea, perceives on his right hand five fluted columns of a very ancient date, which once formed part of a temple. What the name of that temple was, is a subject for conjecture alone. The ascent to the hill of the Acrocorinth is steep and difficult. The first gate, which is approached by a drawbridge, is flanked by an impregnable

ACROCORINTH, FROM THE NORTH-WEST.

wall of rock on the right, and by artificial outworks on the left. From this gate a road leads to a hill on the south-west, in form like a truncated cone, upon which is a fortress: it is called Pente Skouphia. Proceeding upwards towards the summit of the Acrocorinth, we enter a semicircular battery, and after seventy paces another gate, defended by artillery. Within this gate is the steep rocky fortress on the southern crest of the Acrocorinth.

The eastern wall of this inclosure is strengthened by four square towers, and the angles are formed with ancient polygonal masonry. After a little more than a hundred paces we enter a third gate, on the right of which is a square tower of Pelasgic architecture, by which we pass into the large inclosure, which comprehends in its circuit the two northern crests of the Acrocorinth. On the eastern or higher of these crests are the remains of the ancient temple of Venus, on the site of which a mosque now stands. This larger inclosure seems to be comparatively easy of access, and has been entered by a besieging force along a path leading between the two crests, of which we have spoken. By a well-concerted attack at different

THE SUMMIT OF CORINTH, FROM THE W.

points it might, perhaps, be surprised, and could not easily be defended, on account of its vast extent. If the eastern crest, which commands the whole citadel, were walled into a separate inclosure, it would seem almost impregnable. The large inclosure resembles a town; it contains many houses, cisterns, churches, and mosques,—all of which are now in ruins. There is a fountain in this inclosure, to the east of the southern crest of it, which is approached by a descent on a subterranean slope, which is nine feet broad, and seems to have been covered with marble steps. The water is contained in a rectangular basin, at the termination of the slope: above the water the rock is hewn into an architectural form, resembling the façade of a small temple; it consists of a tympanum supported by a architrave resting upon two antæ, and a pilaster in the centre of them: above the tympanum there is an arched vault. On the rock, near the water, are inscribed commemorations of vows offered in ancient times in this place, which was probably known in the earliest days of Corinth as the Fountain of PEIRÉNÉ.

There are two other fountains in the lower part of the city, one at the foot of the citadel, the other in the modern town. The former was believed to be supplied from the source in the Acrocorinth, and is now called the Fountain of Mustapha; that in the town is named Paliko. From the descriptions of Strabo and Pausanias, it is not easy to collect which of these three sources bore the name of Peiréné; but the probability is, that this was a title applied at different times to them all, or at least to the two first of the three, which were supposed to have a subterranean communication with each other.

We prefer to imagine that the Peiréné, at which PEGASUS was caught while he was drinking, by Bellerophon, was that source which springs from the rock on the summit of the Acrocorinth, and that it was from this high point that he soared aloft into the air. It is remarkable that the winged Pegasus appears upon most of the coins of Corinth and her colonies. The mythological analogy between the Horse and the element of Water,—an analogy which shows itself in the name of Pegasus, and which appears in the activity of both the animal and the element, each in its own manner, struggling to burst from its confinement, foaming with restless fury, and, as it were, "pawing to get free," and at other times bridled, whether by reins of steel or stone, and in the circumstance that they both are to man the means of conquering distance and of conversing with things remote,—may have led to the adoption of this device; and the symbol upon these coins was, perhaps, intended to express the national sense entertained by Corinth of the advantage which she enjoyed in the excellence and superabundance of her fresh water,— an advantage not possessed in the same degree by any other maritime city of Greece.

The summit of the rock affords an extensive view—sufficient to give a faint idea of its magnificence under more favourable circumstances. Beneath is the isthmus dividing the two celebrated seas, which we could trace from Parnassus on the one extremity to Cape Sunium at the other, with the islands of Salamis and Ægina in the distance; while behind lie the mountains of the Morea, like the waves of a troubled sea, extending in interminable succession as far as the eye can reach. Immediately below is a barren marshy desert; and at the foot of the hill is the town, reduced to an insignificant cluster of houses surrounded with heaps of ruins. How different the Corinth of ancient times! Thus writes Hieron of the same spot: "There was hardly a stronger fortress in all Greece, and perhaps no spot afforded a more splendid view than the Acrocorinthus. Beneath it might be seen the busy city and its territory, with its temples, its theatres, and its aqueducts; its two harbours, Lechæum on the western bay, Cenchrææ on the eastern, filled with ships, and the two bays themselves, with the isthmus between them, all in sight." The scene is now changed. Corinth and its territory, and its two harbours, are still to be seen, but its bays and its ports are no longer frequented as of old.

A road which commences at the foot of the citadel, and winds towards the east among low shrubs and stone quarries, arrives, after a distance of about eight miles, at the ancient port of Schœnus. At about a mile short of that place is the site of the Sacred Grove, in which the Isthmian Games were celebrated. The only vestiges which survive of its ancient buildings, are those of the STADIUM in the southern part of the inclosure, the shell of a THEATRE nearly three hundred yards to the north of it, and the foundations of the sacred precinct, which contained the temples of Neptune and Palæmon. Immediately to the east of the inclosure are the substructions of the long line of Wall which stretched from the Saronic Gulf on the east to the Corinthian on the west, and defended the Isthmus; and a little beyond, upon the western shore, are the excavations for the Canal, of three miles and a half, by which Nero designed to unite the waters of these two Gulfs, and to make the Peloponnesus an Island. Returning towards Corinth from this part of the coast of the Corinthian Gulf, we pass, at a quarter of a mile from the eastern entrance of the modern town, the remains of an ancient AMPHI-THEATRE. It lies from north to south, and measures about a hundred yards from one end of its length to the other, while its breadth is half that distance. Several of the seats and rice, hewn in the rocky soil, are still visible.

We have thus had before our eyes three objects which exercised a powerful influence upon the tastes and manners of the Corinthians of old,—their

.

Theatre, their Stadium, and their Amphitheatre. While, brought together as they now are by being almost the only survivors among the public monuments of ancient Corinth, they remind us of the spectacles once exhibited within them; they at the same time recall to our recollection, in the most forcible manner, the circumstance, that the Apostle, who spent nearly two years in this city, refers, in the Epistle which he addressed to

its inhabitants, to all these three objects, or to circumstances connected with them. Familiar as they were both to him and to them, they supplied the most vivid illustration of the expressions he used, and of the emotions he both felt and wished to inspire. The Amphitheatre, for instance, afforded to the readers of the Epistle a specimen of what he had endured, who for the sake of the truth, as he there tells them, had fought with beasts at Ephesus. His words, again,—"We are become a Theatre to the world, to angels, and to men,"—came home with double force to the minds of those who saw how the mere actors of fictitious dramas were exposed in the eye of day to the gaze and censure of innumerable spectators in this Theatre upon their own shore; and nothing could give a more vivid picture of the Christian's duty, difficulties, and reward, than the question,—"Know ye not that they who run in the STADIUM run all, but one receiveth the prize? and every one who contendeth is temperate in all things? they indeed that they may receive a corruptible crown (a pine-tree wreath or parsley chaplet), but we an incorruptible,"—coupled with the allusion which follows to the gymnastic and athletic exercises practised before their eyes near the same spot. The traveller in Greece feels a lively pleasure in reading ancient historical descriptions of sieges, of battles, of civil assemblies, of harangues, and of social conversations, upon the spots and amid the scenes where they took place; but the delight will be more exquisite which he will enjoy in tracing, at Corinth, the reference to the objects before him which he finds in the language of Inspiration; and while he sees remains of *buildings* which St. Paul saw, he will also look with more delight upon the *natural* objects around him,—upon the sea, the isthmus, the winds, the fountains of Corinth, and all the beauties of the wide plain about him, varying with all the successive seasons of the year,—when he reflects that these objects were probably in the mind of St. Clement of Rome, the fellow-labourer of St. Paul, when he thus wrote in *his* Epistle to the Corinthians:—" The teeming EARTH brings forth at its appointed seasons overflowing nourishment to man and beast, not gainsaying nor altering any of God's decrees; the hollow of the immeasurable SEA, collected together in heaps by His workmanship, passes not out of the barriers thrown around it; the Ocean not lightly crossed by men, and the worlds beyond it, are ruled by the same ordinances; the seasons of Spring, Summer, and Autumn, give way to each other in peace; the Posts of the WINDS perform their duty in their proper seasons, and trip not; and the perennial FOUNTAINS, shaped for delight and health, give their breasts of life to man, and never fail."

INDEX.

A.

Aa se, city of, now called Belitzi, 137, 218.

Academy, of Athens, Plato's Olive Grove, 162; view from the gardens, 162.

Acamas, statue of, at Athens, 212.

Acarnania, general account of, 307—342.

Achæan League, formation and political results of, 113.

Achaia, comprised of, 108; mumismatic symbols of, 114; contrasted with Arcadia, 271, 272; her high antiquity, 271; change of name, 273; powerful state of, ib.; early history of, 274; the twelve cities of, 277; democratic and foreign policy of, 276, 277; her political extinction, 318.

Acharæ, victory of Thrasybulus at, 149; the subject of Aristophanes' comic muse, 149; description of, 149, 750.

Achelous, a river of Ætolia, 91, 126; the synonyme of water, 91; its course, ib.

Acheron, course of the, 331; the river of Homer's Inferno, 331; delta of the, 331; valley of the, ib.; its scenery, 331; its exit, ib.; ascent up the gorge of, 331.

Acherusian lake, 331.

Achilles at Scyros, sculptures of, 124, 125 (pl.)

Achilles and the river Spercheius, 331.

Acontium, mountain view of, 216.

Acroceraunian rocks and promontory, 96, 329.

Acrocorinthian citadel, 193.

Acrocorinthus of Corinth, 276, 449, 636, 637.

Acrolithi, statues so called, 20.

Acropolis of Athens, 136, 137, 162; numerous ruins remaining, 136; contemplative view from its summit of the ancient glories of Athens, 202 et seq.; its Propylæa, 201, 207; its southern wall, 209.

Actium, battle of, 91, 296, 299; bay of, 297; its present appearance, 211, 212; temple of Actian Apollo, 299.

Adriatic, the sea of Fiume, 172.

Æacus, king of Ægina, legend of, 191, 192.

Æanfe, tribe of, 162.

Ægæon fort, view of the, 111.

Ægaleos, Mount, 129, 141, 142; slope of, occupied by Xerxes at the battle of Salamis, 141.

Ægeus, statue of, at Athens, 212.

Ægina, temple of Minerva at, 14 (pl.); island of, 191, 192, 193; city of, 194; marble sculptures of, ib.; its maritime greatness attributable to its harbour, 187; ruins of an ancient temple at, 192, 193; curious inscription, 193; volcanic appearance of, 193.

Æginetan school of art, marbles of the, 44—50.

Ænianes, ancient city of, 290; its site, 148.

Æolium, town of, in Achaia, 113; now called Vostitza, 273.

Ægosthena, town of, 262.

Ælion, route from, to Megalopolis, 261.

Æsun, flight of, gained by Polyperon, 88.

Ætna, mount, 363.

Æschylus, engaged in the battle of Salamis, 141; a native of Eleusis, 141; recommended before the Areopagus, 141; its battle of Salamis immortalized by, 171.

Æsc, ruins of, 312.

Ætolia, general account of, 307—342; coast of, 311; rivers of, 311; curious geography of, 312, 440, 786; probable site of its capital, 309; cities of, ib.; mountains of, 340; passage from to Achaia, 341; Philip III.'s campaign in, 344.

Agamemnon, the king of Mycenæ, 422.

Agnalippe, sacred spring of, 241, 242.

Aglaurus, sacred cave of, at Athens, 210.

Agora, at Athens, ruins of the, 165, 772, 216; description of the, 215, 216; gate of the, 215.

Agrotas Hill, a branch of the Pindus, 199, 200.

Agriculture, early development of in Attica, 126.

Agrigentum, inscription of, 26.

Ain Gisby, village of, 235, 236.

Ajax, tomb of, 141; statue of, at Athens, 212.

Ajax and Cassandra, painted by Polygnotus, 48.

Alalcomenæ, site of, 286.

Alban Lake, in Italy, stupendous works connected with the, 113.

Akrotis, self-sacrifice of, 362.

[illegible] Hymettus, [illegible]; described by Milton, [illegible]; her language and arts, [illegible]; protected by her mountain bulwarks, [illegible]; Sacred Way of, 144—146; her early history, [illegible]; Acropolis of, [illegible]; Minerva the tutelary deity of, [illegible]; her early history under Theseus, [illegible]—[illegible]; places from which she obtained her marble, [illegible]; her silver mines, [illegible], [illegible]; general account of, [illegible]—[illegible]; requisites necessary for describing, [illegible]; her Acropolis, her temples, and her [illegible], [illegible] et seq.; physical changes of, [illegible]; the city of Miltiades, of Themistocles, and Pericles; of Sophocles, Thucydides, Plato, and Demosthenes; of poets, historians, philosophers, and orators, [illegible]; her spirit and intellect everywhere manifested, [illegible]; physical and topographical sketch of, [illegible] et seq.; her principal buildings and monuments, [illegible]; walls of, [illegible]; restoration of, [illegible]; her glorious works of art, [illegible]—[illegible]; temple of Victory, [illegible]; the Acropolis, [illegible]; the Parthenon, [illegible]—[illegible]; the treasury of, [illegible]; the Erechtheum, [illegible], [illegible]; grottoes of Aglauros and of Pan, [illegible]; temple of the Winds, [illegible]; temple of Theseus, [illegible]—[illegible]; the Pnyx, [illegible], [illegible]; the Areopagus, [illegible]; temple of the Furies, [illegible]; statues of Harmodius and Aristogeiton, [illegible]; the Agora, [illegible]; the theatre and the Athenian drama, [illegible], [illegible]; the street of Tripods, [illegible]; the Odeum, [illegible]; temple of Jupiter Olympius, [illegible]; the Stadium, [illegible]; choragic monument of Lysicrates, [illegible]; [illegible]; Latin writers on, [illegible]; the Piraeus, the ports, and Long Walls of, [illegible], [illegible]; again the capital of Greece, [illegible]; compared with Sparta, [illegible]; education at, [illegible].
[illegible], treasury of at Mycenae, [illegible].
Atreus, the sovereigns of Mycenae, [illegible].
[illegible], the son of Cranaus, [illegible].
Attica, different views of, [illegible], [illegible], [illegible], [illegible], [illegible]; general account of, [illegible]—[illegible]; extent and influence of, [illegible]—[illegible]; diffusion of its language and arts, [illegible]; position, climate, and geography of, [illegible], [illegible], [illegible]; geological formation of, [illegible]; rivers and plains of, [illegible]; [illegible] to which its sterility led, [illegible]; her first inhabitants [illegible] to be indigenous, [illegible]; northern boundary of, [illegible]; mountain walls of, [illegible], [illegible]; Mount Parnes the northern range, [illegible]; comparison of, with Boeotia, [illegible]; her early history, from Cecrops to Theseus, [illegible] et seq.; historical scenes of her ancient traditions, [illegible], [illegible]; mines and mineral wealth of, [illegible]; [illegible] of, [illegible]; notices of, by Latin poets, [illegible]; maritime force of, [illegible].
Augustus, Apollonia the youthful retreat of, [illegible]; his subsequent [illegible], [illegible].
Auletic reed of the Copaic lake, importance of, [illegible].
Aulis, bay of, [illegible].

B.

BACCHANTE, from the Townley collection, [illegible] (pl.)
Bacchus, religious ceremonies in honour of, [illegible]; early traditions of his visiting Attica, [illegible].
Baldama, valley of, [illegible].
Balyra, the river, [illegible].
Bari, cave of, [illegible].
Basilica, the site of the ancient Sicyon, [illegible].
Basreliefs, early history of, [illegible].
Bassae, temples at, [illegible], [illegible], [illegible]; architecture at, [illegible].
[illegible], the modern capital of [illegible], [illegible].
Beck of Hymettus, [illegible].
[illegible], the ancient [illegible], [illegible].
Bema of the Pnyx, at Athens, [illegible].
[illegible], tales of, [illegible].
[illegible], ancient city of, [illegible].
[illegible], ancient walls of, [illegible]; district of, [illegible].
[illegible], lake of, [illegible].
Boeotia, temperature and soil of, [illegible]; valley of, [illegible]; intellectually inferior to Attica, [illegible]; general account of, [illegible]—[illegible]; [illegible] of, [illegible]; maritime force of, [illegible]; plains of, [illegible]; natural theatre of, [illegible], [illegible]; mountains of, [illegible], [illegible], [illegible]; geographical extent of, [illegible]; her physical position, [illegible] et seq.; [illegible] of, [illegible]; [illegible] of her [illegible], [illegible]; [illegible] of, [illegible].
[illegible], Bishop of [illegible], [illegible].
Bouleuterion, the Council Chamber at Athens, [illegible].
[illegible], hamlet of, [illegible].
Boustrophedon, system of writing, [illegible], [illegible].
[illegible], in Arcadia, city of, [illegible].
Bridge at [illegible], [illegible]; over the [illegible], [illegible].
[illegible], a mountain chain of the Pindus, [illegible].
Bronze, early figures cast in, [illegible], [illegible].
——— early workers in, [illegible].
[illegible] vase, specimen of the, [illegible].

C.

CALAMIS, the Greek sculptor, [illegible].
Calauria, island of, [illegible].
Callistratus, engaged in the battle of Marathon, [illegible].
Callimachus, the inventor of the Corinthian order, [illegible].
Callirrhoe, fountain of, [illegible], [illegible], [illegible], [illegible].
Calydon, city of, [illegible], [illegible]; now called Kurt Aga, [illegible].
Cambunian mountains, the barrier of Greece, [illegible].
[illegible], view of, [illegible].
Caryatides, at Athens, [illegible], [illegible].
Carpathus, the lofty summits of, [illegible], [illegible].
[illegible], fountain of, described, [illegible].
[illegible], early art of, [illegible].
Cecrops, the first king of Attica, [illegible], [illegible]; **statue of, [illegible].**
Cenchreae, gulf of, [illegible].
Centaurs, bas-reliefs of, [illegible], [illegible]; their combats with the Lapithae, [illegible] (pl.), [illegible]—[illegible]; mythologically appropriated to Thessaly, [illegible].
[illegible], cliffs of, [illegible].
Cephallenia, island of, [illegible], [illegible]; Cyclopean walls of, [illegible].
Cephisia, village of, [illegible], [illegible].
Cephissus, vale of the, [illegible], [illegible]; the river, [illegible], [illegible], [illegible], [illegible]; the grotto at its source, [illegible].
Ceramicus, a suburb of Athens, [illegible], [illegible].
Ceres, temple of, at Eleusis, [illegible], [illegible]; early traditions of her visiting Attica, [illegible].
[illegible] and [illegible], fable of, [illegible].
Chaeronea, city of, [illegible]; battle of, [illegible], [illegible], [illegible]; [illegible] of, [illegible], [illegible].
[illegible], mount, [illegible].
[illegible], a mountain in Arcadia, [illegible], [illegible].
[illegible], Mount, view of, [illegible].
[illegible], identified with [illegible], [illegible].
Chiron, cave of, on Mount Pelion, [illegible].
[illegible], Mount, [illegible], [illegible].
Choragic monument of Lysicrates, [illegible], [illegible] (pl.), [illegible].
[illegible], the inventor of [illegible], [illegible].
[illegible], southern side of the Acropolis, [illegible].
[illegible], hallowed plain of, [illegible].
Cithaeron, Mount, [illegible], [illegible], [illegible].
——— ancient legends respecting, [illegible], [illegible]; natural features of, [illegible], [illegible].
Cities, ancient, in the vale of Peneus, [illegible]; in Thessaly, [illegible]; in Achaia, [illegible].
[illegible], first represented form by outline, [illegible].
Cleomenes, king of Sparta, [illegible].
Clepsydra, fountain of, at Athens, [illegible].
[illegible] hills, chain of the, [illegible].
[illegible] Venus, statue of the, [illegible].
[illegible], the ancient river, [illegible].
Coinage, when first introduced, [illegible]; of Athens, [illegible], [illegible], [illegible]; of the Peloponnesus, [illegible].
Coins, important guides in the different eras of art, [illegible]; those of Greece, [illegible]; of [illegible], Aegina, [illegible], and Corinth, [illegible]; of Athens, [illegible]; of the Alexandrian period, [illegible]; [illegible] upon them, [illegible], [illegible]; of Thessaly, [illegible]; of [illegible], [illegible]; of Epirus, [illegible]; of the Ionian islands, [illegible]; of Attica, [illegible]; of Corinth, [illegible].

Colonies of Athens, 148.

Columns of temples, origin and different styles of, 44, 56.

Cotytinus, a district of Attica, 211.

Constantine, degradation of art in the reign of, 82.

Chæropheron, ruins of the, 224.

Copaïc lake, 213, 223, 228; the implacidum of Homer, 369; its ringand streams, 210.

Corcyra, account of, 242 et seq.; its traditions and customs, 243 et seq.

Corinth, Doric temple at, 94; colonies of, 83; gulf of, 98, 213, 242, 311; coast of the, 311; view of the, 211; isthmus of, 210, 242, 433; mercantile advantages of, 113; destruction of, 361; her city and port described, 412 et seq.; Acrocorinthus of, 434, 437, 449; ruins of, 438; ancient remains of, 440; the Theatre, the Stadium, and the Amphitheatre, 442; local allusions to, by St. Paul and St. Clement, 441, 443.

Corinthian order, Callimachus its inventor, 94; of the temple of Jupiter Olympius, 62.

Cynon, bay of, 411.

Cnossus, coast of, 128.

Coronea, site of, 244, 250.

Cranana, early traditions of, 138.

Crania, ancient city of, 263.

Crannon, fertility of, 89; Thessalian plain of, 211.

Crisea, bay of, 213.

Critium, wealth and importance of, 74.

Cronium, Mount, 330, 382.

Citrallus, river, 241.

Cyclades, rocky group of the, 181, 185, 196, 300.

Cyclopean architecture, remains of, at Tiryns, 8, 430; at Mycenae, 17; at Larymna, 212; in Ithaca, 245, 262; in Cephallonia, 262.

Cyllene, mountains of, in Arcadia, 198, 330.

Cynætha, inhospitality of its inhabitants, 182.

Cynæ, lake of, 211.

Cynosarges, a district of Athens, 211.

Cynossema, sepulchral city of, 92, 326.

Cynthiad hill of Delos, 191.

Cynthus, the loftiest tower on which, 363.

Cypselus, bas-relief on the chest of, 11.

Cyrus, importance of his conquests, 21.

Cythera, island of, 134, 368.

D.

Dædalus, the early arts indebted to, 11.

Damasus, his invading of Greece, 138.

Daphnis, near Athens, view of, 131.

Daphnus, town of, 223.

Dædaleion, habit of, 264.

Dæmon, importance of, in ancient art, 7.

Deïalis, city of, 312, 330; its mythology, 232.

Dipoenus, fortress of, 182; fortified pass and Spartan camp, 379, 313.

Dejaneira, the wife of Hercules, 221.

Delium, its celebrity, 217.

Delos, central point of the Cyclades, 190, 363.

Delphi, temple of, 376, 384; oracle at, 377.

Delphos, source of the, 132.

Demades, the orator, his camp at Athens, 107.

Demetrius, remains of the ancient city of, 204.

Dibutades, of Corinth, the originator of modelling, 12.

Didascalia, compilation of the, 212.

Diazoma, early use of the, 56.

Diogenes, Plato's present of his to, 129; his residence at Corinth, 229.

Dionysia, a district of Athens, 211.

Dioscuri, represented on the coins of Locris, 124.

Dirce, fashioned in the hand, 43 (pl.)

Dodona, on the ancient site of, 124, 221, 223, 224.

Doric order, origin of the, 94; temple at Corinth, 93; characteristics of the, 85, 87.

Doris, the rugged district of, 220.

Drama of Athens, elements of the, 220, 221, 224; annals of, 220; writers, 219, 226.

Drymia ..., ruins of, 224, 229.

Drapery of early Greek sculpture, 26; of Phidias, 67; of the Alexandrian period, 78.

Drioka, hill of, 224.

Drymis, defile near, 133.

E.

Earth, ancient map of the, 20.

Echinades, islands of the, 216.

Education of Sparta, 417; of Athens, 410.

Euripus, port of, 164.

Egyptian sculpture, 18, 20.

Epaetus, the king of southern Greece, 138.

Eleusinian mysteries of Eleusis, 142, 143, 145.

Eleusis, situation of, 144; religious ceremonies and sacred Way, 142–144; bay of, 143; temple of Ceres at, 146, 147; view of, 147, 214.

Elgin marbles, group of, 161.

Elis, fruitful plains of, 194; innumerable symbols of, 114; the civilising influence of, 112; the Olympic games at, 113; territory of, 344; history and remains of, 380, 384; pacific character of, 293; coast of, 295.

Elæosinae, deities of at Athens, 295, 217.

Epetium, ancient power of the, 244.

Ephesus, ruins of, 173.

Epidaurus, temples of, 194; coast of, 194; view of, 201.

Epimetheus, port of, 302.

Epirus, general account of, 302—342; coins of, 248.

Epomeus, of Athens, statues of, 218.

Eraninus, a ruin of Argolis, 120, 121.

Erechtheum, ruins of the, 124; temple of the, 62 (pl.), 192, 198 et seq.

Erechthides, statue of, at Athens, 216.

Erechthonius, the ancient king of Attica, 142; early traditions of, 138.

Erigone, early legend of, 192.

Erotidia, games at Thespiæ, 243.

Erymanthus, the woody, 198.

Eubœa, coast of, 163, 170; its importance to Bœotia and Athens, 228.

Eumenides, temple of the, 212.

Euripides, a native of Salamis, 143; his tomb, 202.

Euripus, channel of the, 163; bridge of the, 224.

Eurotas, course of the, 399; valley and bridge of the, 129, 413.

Eurysthenes, rank of the army, 113.

Evans, Mount, view of, 428.

Eveuus, river, now called Fidaro, 216.

F.

Ferhat, Mount, colossal representations of, 224.

Fire, secret of the Corinthian Prytaneum, 22.

Flamininus, of Rome, traverses northern Greece, 22.

Foreshortening, early invention of, 26.

Form, represented by outline, 11.

Portrennor, near Jamaica, 324.

Forum of Rome, 144, 181.

Pheias lake, subterraneous works connected with the, 419.

Furies, temple of the, 217.

G.

Games, public, conducive to the arts, 62.

Gate of Lions, at Mycenae, 429, 432.

Geography, as applicable to astronomy, 221; with relation to Bœotia, 222; in Locris, 370.

Geology of Attica, 132.

Geraistian promontory in Eubœa, 163.

Gingenti, sacred fanes of, 101.

Glaucus, the inventor of conquering metals, 22.

Githeio, village of, 132.

Gold, early working of, 19; statue of Minos in, 21.

Gonophu, ancient city of, 211.

N.

its general boundaries, 181; its provinces never properly organised for national production, 188; visited by Strabo the Acropolis of Greece; 112; diminution of its various states, ib.; guided by Athenian Rome, 114; its subordinate history, ib.; absence of commerce and the arts there, ib.; its various empires and revolutions, its complicated political form, 126; general account of, 271 et seq.

Pittacus, the, a chart of the Pindus, 271; chains of, 24, 276, 273; its rise and course ib. 124, 126, 262; tributary affluents of, ib.; historical notices of, ib.; ancient cities in the vale of, ib.; bridge over, 224; its natural boundaries, 217.

Penteleus, a mountain chain of the Pindus, 161; its summit, ib.; its vegetable productions, ib.; its quarries of marble, 135, 136, 171, 172; its elevation, 126, 159; monastery of, ib.; the neighbouring country of, ib.

Pentheus attacked by Bacchantes, 262.

Pericles, period of his public life, 163; his works at Athens, 21 et seq.; his death, 81; and state of the arts from that period, ib.

Perennius, river of, 228.

Persians, some of the arts from their defeat, 48 et seq.; repulsed, 51; their defeat at the battle of Salamis, 140, 141; and at Marathon, 162; their monumental trophies to the battle of Plataea, 261; their vast numbers, ib.; their defeat and destruction, 266.

Phaeaces, of Homer, 117.

Phalerum, the harbour of Athens, 177, 178, 211.

Phalia, vale of, 291.

Pharsalia, battle of, 202; Pompey's defeat at, 202, 203; view of, ib.; the battle of, ib. noticed by Caesar and Lucan, 202, 204.

Pharsalus, the of the ancient Poet Bacchus, 164.

Phidippides, tradition respecting, 164.

Phigaleia, mountains near, ib.

Phocis, city of, 201; view of, ib.; its beauty and interest, 202.

Phidias, his statues at Athens, 48, 207; his drapery of his figures, 47.

Philadelphia, ruins of, 265; temple of Apollo Epicurius at, 262, 276, 276.

Phigalian marbles, 71.

Philip of Macedon, his march into Epirus, 258, 128.

Philip III. his campaigns into Lacedaemonia, 199.

Philopoemen, monument of, 52.

Philostratus, visited of, 113; a distinguished citizen of Athens, 113; their introduction of, 116.

Pandion, vale of, 270, 276; general account of, 272 et seq.; mountains of, 271, 272; picturesque view of, 276.

Phaeryx, battle of, 277.

Phyle, described place of, 149, 213; defended by Thrasybulus, 149; one of the principal passes over Mount Parnes, ib.

Pindus, the great mountain chain of Greece, 94, 271; the five rivers of, 21; view of, 94; different chains of mountains branching from the, 106; geographical territories formed by the, ib.; passes of Greece from, 272.

Pipe, invention of the, attributed to Pan, 120.

Piraeus, the harbour of Athens, 177, 178, 181; view of, from the Acropolis, 211; constructed by Themistocles, 181, 182; completed by Cimon and Pericles, 181, 182.

Pisidia, scenery of the, 261.

Pisistratus, Greek art under, 32, 271; his revision of the Homeric poems, 270.

Plataea, field of, 111; city of, 133; ruins of, 202; tomb at, ib.; topography of the battle fought with the Persians, 162; their preparations for the contest, 261 et seq.; military position of the Greeks, and their signal victory, 262—266.

Platanus, at the battle of Marathon, 163.

Plato, academy of, 162; his country seat, 112; his journal by Diogenes, ib.; his poetical verse at Mount Hymettus, 163.

Platanus, valley of the, 274.

Phaedrus, city of, in Attalia, 202.

Pnyx, the, of Athens, 178; the place of popular assembly, 211; stone forms of this, 211; view from the, ib.; the scheme of Athenian oratory, 213; interesting objects viewed from this, 211.

Poecile, the Stoa of Athens, 211; battle of Marathon painted in the, 211.

Docis, village of, 261.

Posture of Greece, the revival of national strength, 100—113.

Polybius, the historian, 201; birth-place of, 202.

Polycletus, the Greek sculptor, 66, 70.

Polygnotus, the most brilliant painter of antiquity, 71, 78; subjects painted by, 78, 142.

Pompey, his defeat at Pharsalia, 203, 204.

Poros, town and port of, 162, 240; ruins of, 262.

Portrait statues, early history of, 66.

Pottery, the mother of all arts, 6, 7.

Praxiteles, the Greek sculptor, 64; his statues of Love and of Venus, 241.

Prevesa, the modern town of, 201; its present appearance, 211; the Pasha of, ib.

Priam, death of, painted by Polygnotus, 42 (pl.)

Private, ancient Greek, 221.

Procne, mythological story of, 141.

Profile eye, representation of it, 11.

Proctl, fortress and ruins of, 262, 263.

Propylaea, of the Athenian Acropolis, 201, 207; its ruins, ib.

Prytaneia, refectory of the, 251.

Prytaneium of the Greeks, 251.

Psyttaleia, islet of, 141.

Provincial, modern village of, 261.

Pylos, harbour of, 261; the city of Nestor, 262; Homeric scenes at, 207, 208; history of Telemachus and Pisistratus from, 211.

Q.

QUARRIES of Pentelicus, 112.

R.

Raaba, vale of, 263, 264.

Rapids, Poet, the ancient bay of Phaedon, 113.

Religion of the ancient Greeks, its early introduction into Attica, 126; its total extinction, 126.

Rhamnus, city of, its temples, 164—167; remains of, 167; mountain pass from, 163.

Rhium, port of, 276.

Rhone, the subterranean channel of the, 111.

Rivers of Mount Pindus,—the Aous, the Arachthus, the Haliacmon, the Peneus, and the Achelous, 94; Virgil's poetical idea of, ib.; their communication with every part of Greece, 95; Mount Zygos, the central point of, 106; their advantage to Greece, 101; those of Attica, 181; of Boeotia, 269—271; of Thessaly, 271; of Aetolia, 271; of Epirus, 272.

Sparta, ruins at, 262; its ancient importance, ib.; identified with Chradiae, 229, 251.

Roman period of Greek art, 86, 87 (pl.) et seq.

Rome, Milton's description of, 21; her ancient origin from Arcadia, 101; the sacred Way of, compared with that of Athens, 118; military glory the aspiration of, ib.

Ruins of Athens, 170 et seq.; at Aegina and Eleusis, 138; near Jannina, 261; at Epidaurus, 213; of Greece, passim.

S.

Sacred institutions of Attica, 111, 187; and of other deities, 188.

Sacred Way, to Eleusis, 331; of Athens compared with that of Rome, 144; course of the, 313; near Delphi, 318.

St. Clement, his allusions to Corinth, 415.

St. Paul, his notices of Corinth, 411.

Salamis, battle of, 122; straits of, 111; bay of, 121; the village of Ambelakia, gulf and island of, 122, 123; the present site of, 136; battle of, 146, 181; commemorated by Æschylus, 123; view of, from the Acropolis, 314; and from the mountains of Eleusis and Phocis, 314.

Saïgenses, remains of, 211.

Salonica, the name of the ancient city of Thessalonica, ib.

Samê, ruins of, 353.

Samian terra-cotta figure found at, 31.

Sarcophagus, early bas-relief from, 31.

Santa Maura, island of, 354; the ancient Leucas, 353, 354.

Saphora, isle of, 414.

Sarcophagus, ancient, of a female, 342.

Sardis, ancient bronze figures found at, 8; Ionic temple at, 81.

Saw, early use of the, 15.

Scanian Rhodes, near Delphi, 311.

Scharnge, ancient part of, 353.

Sciagraphy, early origin of, 8; early specimen of, 34.

Scillus, village of, the retreat of Xenophon, 342.

Scio, isle of, 353, 354.

Sculpture, pieces of the, 34.

Scopas, the Parian sculptor, 65.

Scomenus, mythical tutor of, 70.

Sculpture of the age of Pericles, 56, 58; of the Phigaleian marbles, 71; Phidias, Praxiteles, &c., ib.

Sculpture, its primitive origin, 6; progress of, 56 et seq.

Sculpture, importance of Aulos in considering their execution, 4; at Thebes, 18; at Rhamnus, 18; at Selinus, 34; of Ægina, 46, 51; of the Theseion, 52, 56; of Greece, examined from the method of Pentelicus, 171, 172.

Scyllean promontory, now called Skyllo, 342.

Selinus, sculpture of, 34; temples of, 162.

Sheath, for drawing the scenery of Parnes, 314.

Shepherds, the life of, superstitious, 142.

Shield, number of, furnished by Athens and Thebes in the Trojan war, 145; Argos building the first one, 214.

Shrines, mercantile advantages of, 194; the modern Basilica, 219; view of, ib.; ornaments found at, 342.

Sigean Inscription, 84.

Silhouettes, a peculiar style of art, 3.

Silver coins of Athens, 188, 191.

Simonides, the Ceolian poet, 23.

Smilis, the early mythical artist, 15.

Socrates, anecdote of, 431.

Soil, of Arcadia, unpropitious to agriculture, 142.

Sophocles, a native of Colonus, 432.

Sparta, most serious when she had no walls, 134; valley of, described, ib.; general bulwarks of, ib.; boundaries of, the city of, ib.; ruins of, 134; vale of, the fertility, 135; compared with Athens, &c.; education at, 135; view of the plain of, ib.; road from, to Mycenæ, 138.

Spartans, their possession of Mount Parnes, 431; defeated by the Thebans, 335.

Sperchaius, the river, 229; the beautiful valley, ib.

Sphacteria, island of, 351; battles of, 262.

Sphacteria, city of, 262.

Sporades, rocky groups of the, 101.

Stadium, at Athens, 292; at Delphi, 324; of Olympia, 347; at Nemea, 354.

Statistics, for the geographical survey of Greece, …

… section, the ancient Laconia, 292; second, Mount Taygetus, 292; third, Mount Parnassus, ib.; fourth, Helicon, ib.

Statues, of wood, in the Homeric age, 15; of bronze, 15…

…; use of gold, 71; crude decoration of, 52; of Sunium, 52; architectural, ib.; of a Greek warrior, 12; of Athens, 58, 61 (pl.). See the illustration.

Stoa Basilicus, at Athens, 213.

Stone, scarcity of in Assyria, 22.

Sunocheme, trilithon from, 16.

Sunium, the Athenaeum capital, 345.

Stymphalus, in Arcadia, view of the lake of, 142.

Styx, view of the valley of, 229; current and valley of the, 227, 228.

Sun, and Cronos, 329; journey of, 331; mountains of, 212; its fortress, 330; its citadel, 331; historical notices of, 330.

Sunium promontory, views of the, 192, 202, 344; temple on its summit, 191; the Modern Cape Colonna, 344.

Sunium, temple of Minerva at, 192.

Syra, town and isle of, 460.

T.

Taenarian promontory, the most southern point of the Grecian peninsula, 168.

Tanagra, site of, 316, 331.

Tapestry of Crete, 342.

Tatoi, village of, ...

Taygetus, Mount, elevation of, 137; view of, 135; Row of modern from, 135; plains of, 137.

Telamachus and Pisistratus, their journey from Pylos, 434.

Temenos, the sacred inclosure of Athens, 161.

Temps, valley of, 229; egress of the sea through, 229; view of, 229, 229; hydrographical origin of, 229; military character of, 229; scenery of, ib.

Teisias of Corinth, his remarks, 31; of Eretria, 68, 69, 72 (pl.), 188, 190; at Thermodon, 23, 53, 54; temple of Victory at Athens, 77, 292; at Bassae, 71; at Apollo Epicurius, 71 (pl.); on the Sunium promontory, 191; of Ceres, at Eleusis, 346, 347; at Sunium, 191; at Pæstum, 191; the Parthenon, 72, 205; the Erechtheum, 52, 205; of the Furies at Athens, 52; of Apollo Epicurius at Athens, 344; of Delphi, 318; of the Winds, 205; of Jupiter Apollo, 205; at Bassae, 205; of Latona at Apollo Epicurius at Bassae, 205, 207; of Jupiter near Mycenæ, 335; of Apollo, at Delphi, 345.

Temples, structure of, 34, 36; their inner temple system of, 36, 37; their first erection at Athens, 36, 61; of the city of Rhamnus, 191, 192; in the street of Tripods, at Athens, 292.

Tenos, rocky cliffs of, 103.

Tapsiloi, town of, the ancient Antigonea, 326.

Teatro, fortress of, 231.

Theatre of Athens, 183.

Thebans, their victory over the Spartans, 334.

Thebes, architecture of, 18; athletic superiority of its inhabitants, 161; in Bœotia, city of, 314, 315; plains of, 314; natural and social advantages of, 171; view of the plains and city, &c.; remaining elements of—the institute, the Dirce, and the Cnopus, 316; elevation of, 314.

Thebais, temple at Rhamnus, 191, 192.

Themistocles, commander of the Greeks at the battle of Salamis, 146; compared at the battle of Marathon, 122; trophy of victory to, 134; beside the Piraeus, 122; fortifications of, 208; his tomb, 208.

Theriso, the modern name of the ancient Theseion, 161.

Thessaly, final view of the, 37.

Thornton, citadel of, 161.

Thermopylae, pass of, 111, 225; battle of, 361; view of, 225; the notice of various passes, 336; physical character of, 214.

Theseion, its finest elevation, 52; its sculptures, 53 (et pl.); genius associated in the, 41.

Theseus, bones of, discovered and brought to Athens, 61; statues of, 62; the reign of, an important epoch in Athenian history, 112 et seq.; temple of at Athens, 109, 111, 112; his oaths, 140; his character, ib.; with captivated to, 141; his labours compared with those of Hercules, 141, 213; superior to Hercules in intellectual qualities, 163; destroys the monster of Attica, 112.

Thespia, ancient city of, 241; historic interest connected with, 21, 242.

Thermionics, ancient city of, now changed to Salonichi, 21, 61; its fertility, ib.; its ancient military fame, ib.; its climate and soil, 131; general account of, 275—306; basin of, 276; legends of, 277. Plains of, ib.; its ruins, ib.; its topographical character, ib.; legends of, 271, 278; its numismatic history, 201; origin of the name, 202; the aborigines of, ib.; Julian Caesar's campaign in, 202; influence of the soil on the character of its inhabitants, 271; remains of cities in, 201.

Thisbi,—is it the Ithome of Homer? 212 et seq.

Thoricus, harbour of, 152; ruins of an ancient theatre at, ib.

Thrasybulus, his defence of Phyle, and expulsion of the Thirty Tyrants, 152.

Tilphosa, fount of, 211.

Tiryns, Cyclopean walls at, 6, 122.

Tiresias, the augur, 246.

Tolmides, death of, 214.

Tomb of Midas, in Phrygia, 24.

Tombs the depositories of ancient works of art, 1.

Topolias, lake of, 193.

Trachinia, province of, 101.

Trachis, rocky hill of, 221; province of consecrated to Hercules, 221, 222.

Traditions of Greece, 160.

Tripezza, ruins of, 201; view of, 201.

Treasury of Athens, 421; of Atreus, at Mycenae, 114.

Torina, defiles of the, 451.

Tricca, castle of, 221.

Trikeri, castle and town of, 506, 265.

Trieden, near Delphi, 217.

Triopium promontory in Cnidus, 101.

Tripods, street of, at Athens, 222.

Tripolitza, town of, the ancient Pallantium, 128, 129, 132.

Trœzen, in Argolis, early traditions of, 162; city and castle of, 141; bridge of, 422.

Trophonius, cave of, 243.

Tumulus, ancient, on the Æginetan coast, 18.

Turkish bravebard, representation of, 213.

Turks, slaughter of by the Greeks, 414.

Twelve Gods, altar of the, at Athens, 218.

Tymphrestus, Mount, the modern Belushi, 199, 211.

Tyrtæus, a native of Aphidnae, 144.

U.

Ulysses, his description of Ithaca, 333; reminds of his honour, 334.

Ulysses and Nausicaa, Homeric notices of, 360.

V.

Vase painting, ancient specimens of at Athens and in Italy, 8, 9; early history of, 21—36; various names and specimens of, 22 (pl.); the peculiarities of Arcadians, 40; Greek head from a 391 important changes in, 34; fight figures on a black ground introduced, 29, 30 (pl.).

Vases, early specimens of, 7; sepulchral ones from Athens, 208.

Tennis, sculptured figures of, 24 (pl.).

Victory, sculptures from the temple of, 72 (pl.); ruins of the temple of at Athens, 193, 208.

Virgil, his poetical idea of the rivers of Greece, 91; his pastoral muse inspired by Arcadian scenes, 122.

Volcanic appearances at Ægium, 190.

Volo, town of, 191, 201.

Voïci, bronze statues from, 11.

W.

Wheel, early use of the, 12.

Winds, temple of the, 208.

Winged hall, from Rhamnaход, 19.

Winter in Bœotia, 241.

Worship, early objects of, 10.

Writing, not generally practised at the time of the Trojan war, 11.

X.

Xenophon, his retreat at Lycorium, 287.

Xerxes, his defeat at the battle of Salamis, 191; his throne captured and preserved in the Acropolis, 192; his visit to the mouth of the Peneus, 276.

Xyle, Cape, 422.

Z.

Zacynthus, situation of, 356; the ancient city of, 861, 362; its derivation, 362.

Zakhouka, Mount, the ancient Lyceum, 189, 190.

Zante, town of, 361.

Zarvo, town of, 226.

Zygo, Mount, the modern name of the ancient Lacmon, 241; view of the heights of, ib.; the grand source of the rivers of Greece, 98, 190; ascent to, 222.

Zymeno, near Delphi, 213.

www.ingramcontent.com/pod-product-compliance
Lightning Source LLC
Chambersburg PA
CBHW022127020426
42334CB00015B/801